THE

WACKENTUTE

DIARY

MICHAEL MCINERNEY

Disclaimer: This is a work of fiction. Names, characters, places and incidents either are a product of the author's imagination, or are used fictitiously. Any resemblance to actual persons, living or dead, events, or locales is entirely coincidental. The opinions expressed belong to the characters, and should not be confused with the author's.

Cover art: AHILL Design

ISBN-13: 978-0-9905679-0-5

Green Mouse Press
P O Box 442
Belmar   New Jersey 07719

Acknowledgements

As usual with my titanic struggles and meager accomplishments, I could not have completed this project without the help of many others. This book is the result of the efforts of the people below. Whatever accolades may result we share, the errors are entirely mine. I want to thank William Tierney, who coached me on the ups & downs. 'Doctor Pete' Freundlich and the entire staff at Friendly Dental (the best in New Jersey), for their interest, information and support. Merry Brennan – a mentor & teacher (of galactic dimensions). Nancy Noe – a very smart and forgiving editor. Ashlee Hill – for a picture worth 136,000 words. The BAC Writers' Group – for the push. Paula – for the never ending enthusiasm, Bina & Bob – for the whimsical DNA. Bob, Tom & Jack – for setting the bar, and always being the safety net. Rob, Kate, James & Andrea – for the encouragement and faith. And Nancy – for the help on so many levels.

For Nancy

THE WACKENTUTE DIARY

PART ONE

If you can keep your head when all about you
Are losing theirs and blaming it on you,
If you can trust yourself when all men doubt you,
But make allowance for their doubting too.
. . . .
If you can dream—and not make dreams your master;
If you can think—and not make thoughts your aim;
If you can meet with Triumph and Disaster
And treat those two impostors just the same.
. . . .
Yours is the Earth and everything in it ....

Rudyard Kipling

"All over the world Chaos may roam;
But <u>THIS</u> is the place that it calls home."
Anonymous

Prologue

In a library somewhere, quite possibly even The Library of Congress, sits a book which contains the infamous "Recipe for Disaster". If you open that book to the page containing that recipe, and scan down four or five lines, you will see the instruction, "Now, <u>slowly</u>, add in Ray Hryila."

Despite his all-too-frequent courtship of chaos, you would be hard put to find anyone who knew him who genuinely didn't like him (except his ex-wife who didn't like anybody). He was laconic and friendly. He possessed a charming naiveté and a warm smile. He was hardworking yet laid-back. And although he lacked certain social graces, he was usually welcomed into most circles.

It wasn't that he was clumsy, but Hryila with a shovel, or Hryila with a power tool, or Hryila with anything that was hard and could be moved, usually resulted in something getting broken. It might be as inconsequential as a twig, or perhaps as vital as a bone, but something was going to snap. His current address was a testament to that rule of thumb.

Ray Hryila started his own landscaping and gardening business while in his midtwenties, roughly 10 years ago. Married to his high school sweetheart, they worked long hours trying to make the business grow. He and a small crew did the outside manual labor; his wife handled the books and sales in their small store/office. He was happy with his lot in life, because he was doing what he loved to do. He didn't own a tie, and wore jeans every day. It was outside manual labor that didn't require any technical skills or expensive equipment. He would mow lawns, trim shrubbery and trees, clean yards, and on occasion, lay down some sod. To his wife, it was hard work that was not producing satisfactory results. At some point she began telling her husband that they needed another employee. She said they needed someone who could do outside sales, and help around the office. So she hired her second cousin for the job. Although Hryila never remembered actually agreeing to this, Stevie showed up shortly thereafter. Hryila had never been able to argue with his wife.

He didn't wait long before casually mentioning to his wife the added help was apparently producing no results. And, initially, he was right, but only for a short time. Three months after struggling through the summer, his wife showed him a stack of twenty dollar bills she said was profit from the landscaping jobs the cousin had lined up, and that Hryila had completed. It had surprised him when he saw the cash.

"You can't argue with a pile of twenties!" Hryila thought out loud. He did wonder why these jobs, that weren't very different from any of the jobs he had done before, were now so profitable. And there hadn't been so many more of them either. But there was no arguing with that very impressive stack of cash!

Other things changed too. Over time the small office and store became a little fancier, and certainly more professional in its appearance. There was almost new office furniture, and new phone lines. The yard out back, which had once been sparse and shabby, became more orderly, and cluttered with new products, plants, and assorted greenery. Several new sheds and small prefabricated greenhouses appeared one day along the back fence. "What are we gonna do with those things?" he asked his wife when he first noticed them. "What did they cost? When they get here?"

When she didn't answer, he asked again. He was not going to let it drop. "Yesterday! The day before, if you must know! If you kept your eyes open you wouldn't ask such dumb questions." Not satisfied she had closed the book on this topic, she added, "Don't bother with them because they're none of your business. They're part of the store." That sounded odd to him, because he was part of the store! This was his business too. But her angry reaction clearly left no room for debate.

Over the next three years the business grew enormously. And while Hryila was pretty much in the dark about what Stevie was doing most of the time, there was no denying that the business was flourishing. And Stevie, who seemed to Hryila to be completely inept in everything else, somehow seemed able to line up more and larger jobs, which resulted in greater profits. A new green Ford F250 Super Duty pickup truck was purchased. And there was a rear seat in the cab that was large enough to carry the work crew to various job sites. The company logo was emblazoned on the side.

Hryila, unknown to his wife, was looking around at various homes for sale in the area with an eye for getting a bargain. He felt that getting their own home and moving out of the old apartment would offset the distance that had grown between them as their business grew. He thought that perhaps they might even start a family, even though she disagreed with that notion whenever he brought it up.

Although things certainly weren't perfect in Hryila's life, they had come a very long way in three years. The business was flourishing, and producing new and wondrous changes for both him and his wife. He couldn't help seeing some of those changes; at the same time he was oblivious to certain other signs. And then he failed to see a stop sign. Literally.

He had lent his truck to Stevie that morning, and Stevie had been late getting it back to him. As a result Ray Hryila was running late on his own daily chores, and his mind wasn't on his driving. He went through the stop sign going 25 MPH. That, in itself, was bad. But it got worse. The car he "T-boned" was a police car.

Now, on a positive note, no one was injured. He hadn't been speeding; the seat belts were fastened all around; the air bags deployed. As a matter of fact, both the policeman and Ray walked away from the accident unscathed. That, no one could deny, was a good thing. But as the policeman walked away from his smashed patrol car, he walked past Hryila's pickup truck, and that was, for Ray Hryila, a bad thing. Because as the officer walked past the rear of Hryila's truck, he glanced into the back and spied a small, somewhat vaguely familiar, five leaf twig lying there.

The rattled policeman, understandably already in a foul mood, now got really angry. "What the hell is that?" he growled at Hryila. With an admirable display of agility a man of his age and girth didn't often possess, the policeman bounded up into the bed of the truck and began inspecting every inch of space back there. And things, for Hryila, went from bad to "worst day of my life." In the space of what only seemed like a few minutes, his life was forever changed. In short order the police arrested him; cuffed him; then read him his rights; all "firsts" for him. After a short ride to the police station in the back of a patrol car, he remembered the sequence of events as mug shots, followed by fingerprinting. The ride, the posing and the fingerprinting were another three firsts.

He thought to himself how terribly wrong this day was going when finally permitted to make his one phone call. He didn't try to call a lawyer; he didn't know any. He tried to call his wife. There was no answer on her cell phone, nor the phone at the office. He didn't realize it at the time, but by then she couldn't take any calls. She was also under arrest.

It would not have been any use calling cousin Stevie either, had that thought occurred to Hryila. Stevie had been across the street getting a sandwich at the local deli when the four police cars roared up in front of the landscaping store. Stevie, with no great insight, correctly analyzed the meaning of the commotion, paid for his sandwich, walked out the front door of the deli, turned right, and kept going. He had been down this road before and decided immediately to put as much distance as possible between himself and that store. Yes, he thought to himself, I think I'll take the afternoon off.

Stevie, believing his complicity would not be divulged, returned later that day to his apartment to pick up some traveling necessities. His faith in his partner proved misguided when he was immediately grabbed by the waiting police

Once the police saw the twig in the back of the truck with the greenhouse sign on the door, their eyes lit up. In no time at all they had a search warrant, and descended on the store. The secluded, and locked, sheds and greenhouses out in the back couldn't have been more obvious if they had had neon signs on top of them. The final count of marijuana plants growing behind Hryila's store numbered in the hundreds.

It wasn't a great surprise to Ray Hryila that Stevie wasn't his wife's cousin. And, truth be told, it wasn't much of a surprise at all that his wife and Stevie were lovers. It did surprise him to learn that Stevie was a first-rate cultivator of marijuana. He not only was able to grow it pretty well, but was also quite capable in the areas of sales and distribution too. His talents with marijuana, coupled with Mrs. Hryila's business acumen and drive, had forged a very successful partnership, on several levels. The landscaping business had been a very good cover, and a wonderful way to launder the cash. This enterprise was thriving, and probably could have for many more years to come. But Ray Hryila got behind the wheel of his truck, and nature took its course. And that course had led him two years ago to his current address at Overbrook.

The Correctional Center at Overbrook was a prison in the New York State penal system. More specifically it was a minimum security facility where convicted felons of non-violent crimes were sent to serve out their terms. Most of the 1028 current residents (as they were called) were first offenders and/or white-collar criminals. And, as far as prisons went, it wasn't a bad place to be.

There weren't any high stone walls, or menacing strands of barbed wire strung from forbidding looking towers at Overbrook. There weren't any meandering searchlights at night. There were 14 different buildings of various sizes on the grounds. But size was the only variant. Each building was a square, sand-colored concrete block structure. The walls inside each one of these buildings were painted pale yellow. Every floor in the complex was painted institutional gray. There was a chain-link fence that looped around the wooded outside perimeter of the complex, but that was more to keep people out than in.

It did, of course, have the usual roll calls and bed checks that occur at any prison. And the drudgery and monotony of the every day routines weren't any better at Overbrook than at any of the other facilities in the system. But it was an accepted fact that anyone who tried to escape from here would probably succeed considering the lax physical restrictions on the residents, as well as the layout of the facility. It was just that escaping wasn't considered a good idea. Because when the escapee was re-captured, as almost all eventually are, he would not be sent back to Overbrook to finish his sentence (with extra time added on as a penalty for escaping), but to a medium, or worse, a maximum security prison which would be draconian compared to Overbrook. No, Overbrook's staff did not worry too much about residents trying to leave.

New residents at Overbrook were sent initially to a building called "The Tank." This was the reception area that new arrivals stayed in for up to a week, until they were assigned to their more permanent quarters and work assignments. The five buildings that made up the barracks complex were the tallest at three floors each. Each floor was divided into two sections of five pods each. Each pod, separated by lockers and partitions from the other pods, was designed to contain six residents. There was no privacy at Overbrook.

The four main work assignments at Overbrook were Administration, Dietary, Laundry, and Maintenance. Working a prison job was not mandatory at Overbrook, yet most residents had one. The jobs were not very interesting or challenging, and the compensation was paltry. But the alternative to working was confinement to your pod for the entire day. Most residents would spend up to 35 hours a week working for one of these departments during their stay at the facility. And because each one had its various pros and cons, there was a never-ending debate among the residents about which one was better than the other. Transfers from one department to another were not uncommon, but depended largely on who you knew, as well as luck and timing.

The Administration Department was, by and large, all the clerical jobs at the prison, and easily the most coveted. And, because so many of the residents here had committed a "white collar crime," there was no shortage of people capable of doing clerical work. The problem, of course, was that there were more people available than jobs. It was the smallest department by number and the waiting list for people trying to get into this department was quite long.

Those who worked in Dietary usually ate better than the rest of the population, but most often worked odd hours, and even odder shifts.

The Laundry Department was probably the least-desired assignment in the prison. While the laundry workers always seemed to have newer and nicer clothes, the monotonous nature of the work, as well as the physical aspects of working in the noise, the smell, and the heat generated by the huge washers and dryers, made it the last choice of almost everyone. Residents who were disciplined for one thing or another were frequently reassigned to the Laundry Department.

Maintenance was the largest department by numbers, and was the most diverse in type of work performed, and more often than not the most strenuous. People arriving at Overbrook with special skills, like an electrician, carpenter, or plumber, would be placed into this department. Most of the others in this department without those special skills wound up pushing brooms, waving paint brushes, or driving lawn mowers. A worker could be assigned one day to rake leaves, and the next day to repair a fence. The variety of the jobs, and the fact that many of those jobs were "outside work," made most of the people in this department prefer it over any other department.

Joseph David Hamilton arrived at Overbrook in the late summer, three years ago. He spent four days in the Tank before moving on to his assigned living quarters, and a job in the Laundry Department.

Disliking Laundry immediately, he began inquiring about reassignment. He understood, through some preparation he had gone through before coming here, that Administration was an unlikely destination for a "cherry" (new arrival), and Dietary was only slightly better than Laundry. Probably more by chance than anything else, he was reassigned to Maintenance a few weeks later.

The living quarters he was assigned to were designated "C3/E5". All that meant was that his bed and locker were in the "C" building, third floor, East wing, in pod #5. The other men already in that pod were named Crinci, Durante, Leigh, Flaherty, and Hryila. Crinci, Durante and Leigh were "short-timers," and as such had less than a year to go before their scheduled release. The tall lanky Hryila seemed the friendliest. His casual manner and easy smile seemed somehow out of place in a prison to the new arrival. But it didn't take long before Hamilton felt it was genuine. Yet he remained wary of his new surroundings and of Hryila too. He had been advised to be cautious. "Keep ya eyes open, and ya mouth shut! Don't trust nobody." He followed that advice, and kept mostly to himself. It would take some time to settle into this strange new world.

Pat Flaherty was the oldest of the group in age and seniority. He was serving 8 years for bookmaking, and various counts of fraud, and although small in stature, he was the undeniable leader of the pack. He was at the center of every discussion, and assumed himself to be the authority on every topic. He stood barely five and a half feet tall, and weighted less than 130 lbs. While his head was completely bald, his face was never clean-shaven. Both his grin and his nose were large and crooked. And he had charm to spare.

He had been a boxer in his younger years, and had enjoyed some amateur success; or so he said. He had turned professional before he was eighteen and found success at that level far more elusive. He admitted that he was never more than a so-so club fighter who had bounced around in small town venues, always on the under card. Although certain that he won more than he lost, he never put actual numbers to his record. And he was always quick to add that he really hit his stride after he stopped fighting and became a trainer and a manager. He also got involved in promoting fights too. That, he said, was where the real money in boxing was. He assured Hamilton, and anyone else who'd listen, that he was totally innocent of any wrongdoing on the outside, and it was his former partners who did all the misdeeds that ultimately put him here at Overbrook. He asserted that the bookmaking charges were trumped up. There were very few people who knew Pat Flaherty who bought into that story. But there was one aspect of him that made him very popular with his fellow residents. He was in charge of the Overbrook Recreation Center.

The Rec Center had historically been an underfunded, and sparsely equipped, gymnasium that was available to residents during certain times of the day. And like many of the less critical administrative posts at Overbrook it was staffed and operated by residents themselves. Its years of neglect and shabbiness ended when Flaherty was assigned as the new Resident Director three summers ago. How that assignment came about was the subject of wide speculation and debate. But no one could debate the improvements and general upgrading of the facilities since he had taken over the job. Officials at the prison wondered why two residents, who had been master plumbers prior to their convictions and who, incidentally, also happened to be huge horse racing fans, volunteered nearly fifty hours of their own free time to work on the rebuilding of the showers in the gym. Some of the supplies for this renovation were also mysteriously donated by some residents. In fact, since Flaherty's tenure as director began, the Rec Center had enjoyed a remarkable inflow of donated items, including much-needed new athletic and gym equipment. The very limited official budget of the Rec Center for these sorts of things was hardly taxed at all. And although there were occasional suspicions that there was a great deal of gambling going on at the Rec Center, nothing was ever proven.

But there was no doubt at all that there were a great many other things going on there. Various athletic contests, and organized team sports were open to all residents, and enthusiastic participation was commonplace. A touch football league in the fall had eight teams in it. And the summer softball league that had only eight teams three years ago now had 20! The playoffs at the end of each season generated intense interest, far beyond what the officials had thought possible. There were times the exaggerated reactions by certain residents at the outcome of some games astounded officials.

And in a somewhat less mysterious way, Hamilton's future took an incredibly fortunate turn for the better, one night after dinner. He had been working in maintenance, mostly mopping and cleaning floors. All he could say in favor of that was that it was better than the alternatives in the other departments. The conversation that night in the pod, just before lights out, had centered on the upcoming National Hockey League playoffs and a debate started between Leigh, who was from Boston, and Crinci, who was a fan of the Philadelphia Flyers. Flaherty sat amused as he watched the two argue some point about the upcoming series between those two teams. Hamilton, who usually said very little, suddenly interrupted and corrected Crinci on some finer point of playing wing on a hockey team. When Crinci argued back, it became very clear, very quickly, that Hamilton knew exactly what he was talking about.

The next morning Flaherty took Hamilton off to the side before breakfast. "You know something about hockey?" he asked.

Uncharacteristically, Hamilton boasted, "I know a lot about hockey."

"Yeah? How come you know so much?" Flaherty wanted to know. He sensed an opportunity. Hamilton explained his background in the sport, which included the fact he had gone to college on a hockey scholarship. Pat Flaherty's eyes lit up. As for Hamilton, it was really the first time he had had anything remotely like a personal conversation since he had come here to Overbrook. Flaherty looked at him for a moment, and then asked, "Does anyone else here know that you played ball?"

"Hockey," Hamilton corrected.

"Whatever," Flaherty shrugged.

Hamilton shook his head. Flaherty wasn't sure how he could use this, but he was sure that this was an opportunity. Knowing something that other people don't know is like money in the bank, he said to himself. Filing this piece of information away, he looked at Hamilton and said, "How'd you like to come work in the Rec Center?"

That invitation was immediately accepted by Hamilton. One of the good pieces of advice he had received before coming here had been to use the time he had to be here as productively as possible. "Don't be bitter," he was told. "Learn a trade. Take up some hobby you never had time for before. Read every book you were supposed to read in high school, but didn't." And the one other suggestion that now struck a chord here was, "Get back into the shape you were in back in high school." He thought that working at the gym would give him the chance to do that. And it did. Virtually every day he spent at Overbrook, for the rest of his stay here, he exercised. And that not only included using the free weights in the Rec Center, but also running around the inside perimeter of the facility time and time again.

The hours Hamilton worked at the gym were usually long, and frequently boring. But on the bright side it allowed him access to workout equipment, and the free time to use it. A never-ending supply of dirty towels needed to be washed and dried in the gym's own machines, and the floors and equipment needed to be cleaned every day, but there were also times when the gym was empty, and Hamilton took advantage.

Hryila told him, in one of the many quiet chats they had as they wiled away their hours in jail, that he had sometimes suspected that something was going on with the business that just wasn't right. He just couldn't believe that the jobs they were doing were as profitable as they seemed to be. But he didn't look at it very hard. Besides, that part of the business was handled by his wife and he was glad he didn't have to deal with it. He agreed that his indifference had contributed to allowing the illegal enterprise to flourish as long as it did, and grow as large as it was. And when it ultimately crashed and burned, he wasn't as remorseful as one would suppose. "Lost everything: to seizure; to fines; to the lawyers. But, hell, I hadn't earned it in the first place. It wasn't mine anyway!" It was "phony," he told his pod mate. "I never really was doin' good as a landscaper, like I thought. The pot was doin' good . . . but the landscapin' sucked! It was phony!" Hamilton asked him how things stood with Mrs. Hryila. "That's as dead as last Christmas's goose," he said. "As far as me and the Mrs. are concerned," he said, pausing for a moment, "it was over long before we got busted." Hryila looked at Hamilton, and smiled. "If I was lookin' for any bright side to this whole thing, I guess I could say I got off a lot easier than she and Stevie did. The judge really hammered them two at the sentencing." He shook his head and chuckled. He would always conclude, "Ya know, when I get out and start over, I'm gonna be a lot better at it than I was the first time I started out."

Hamilton was amazed at Hryila's acceptance of proportionate blame; his inability to see any benefits in harboring bitterness; his innate sense of optimism. He realized that Hryila's approach allowed him to close his eyes every night and sleep well. It also allowed him to wake up in the morning and greet the new day. These thoughts, as well as following through with some of the other advice he had received before coming here, would make Hamilton a very different man by the time he left Overbrook.

Chapter One

2 ½ Years Later

Wednesday October 30

Today was best described, Hamilton thought, as a *transition* day. It certainly wasn't a highlight day in his life, nor a milestone, as some might have called it. It wasn't a day marked by high achievement, like a graduation or the day his team won the state championship in hockey, or the conference titles in college. The happy days in his life that stood out like his wedding day, or, he thought sardonically, even the day his divorce became final would always be remembered. But this wasn't really a happy day; it was a "transition day." This was a day that would separate periods of his life that would be very different from each other. Today was a day of remembrance of the three years that had gone before, and of expectation for all the years ahead; and how incredibly different those two periods would be. Today he was being released from The Correctional Center at Overbrook.

He was ready to leave. He had been anticipating this day for three years now, he thought to himself. He shifted his weight in the slightly wobbly gray metal folding chair trying to get comfortable. It was a lost cause. He glanced up again at the three clerks on the other side of the room-wide counter. They showed no sign that they even knew he was sitting there. One, a tall man in short sleeve pastel shirt and loose tie, seemed genuinely busy. The other two chatted back and forth with each other or into their phones briefly when one would ring. Occasionally they poked the keyboard of their computer for a minute or two, and then went back to chatting. Two

1

other prisoners, Hamilton knew only faintly, sat a few feet away from him discussing something about heating ducts.

Like every other morning for the past few years he had been awakened at 6 AM, and marched off to breakfast at 6:30 with the rest of section. Back from the mess hall by 7:15 the other residents cleaned up their pods, and prepared for the day's work which started at 8 AM. But this morning Joseph David Hamilton cleaned up his pod for the last time. When the others marched off to the day's assignments, Hamilton, as instructed, just sat on his stripped-down bunk and waited for a Corrections Officer to come get him. While he waited he noticed how quiet the building was with most of the residents now gone on to their assignments. He would occasionally hear footsteps, or a cough from somewhere that broke the silence. He even wondered if maybe they had forgotten to come get him. He got up a few times to look out along the hall to see if anyone was there. He thought about trying to read something to pass the time, but knew he wouldn't be able to concentrate. It was almost an hour before a guard came and took him, with all his personal belongings to begin the process of "checking out."

It was now after 10 AM, and he had been sitting in the waiting room of the Administration Building for someone to finally get around to releasing him. He gazed out the window to his right and saw the bright October day. He would be out there soon . . . in the cool, fresh, *free* air! The Administration Building was the closest one to the main gate at Overbrook. It was tantalizingly close to what the residents called "the free world." When he was led into the building that morning he was brought into the main waiting room. It was a room with two rows of gray metal folding chairs facing a long counter than ran the width of the room. Behind the counter there were four metal desks, side by side facing it. Along the left side of the room were three cubicles, and along the right side were file cabinets. Behind the wall with the file cabinets were two small offices. Up on the second floor were two small offices, a small conference and a large file room, and the large office of the Superintendent of the Facility. In a regular prison he'd be called the Warden.

Out on the rows of the metal chairs in the waiting room sat three men. Two of them sat together in the second row talking about, and gesturing toward, a diagram one of them had on his lap. Hamilton sat alone at the end of the first row, staring at the floor, lost in thought. He wore a barn jacket over khaki pants. On his feet he wore black work boots: and next to his feet were a large canvas bag, a knapsack and a shopping bag. Acknowledging the line from an old Grateful Dead song, "What a long strange trip it's been" he thought to himself. How he had come to this point in time . . . this place.

He didn't really regret much. Oh, he would have done some things differently, but not much. He still, to this day, did not feel personally responsible for what had happened. He hadn't done anything wrong. He hadn't tried to cheat anyone. He had never had any reason to do what he had been charged with. He had made choices, and had delegated some responsibility. In hindsight some of those choices had been bad choices, and the responsibility should have been kept closer to home. He had, unconsciously, badly misjudged some people. "Failure to supervise" was the phrase that brought him down. He always believed, sincerely but perhaps a bit self-servingly, that the entire affair should have been handled in Civil Court, not Criminal. But that was all in the past, as unchangeable as yesterday's weather. He had let it go a long time ago. "It was as dead," Hryila would say, "as last Christmas's goose."

He looked down at his boots, and realized that they felt very comfortable. Five years ago he would not have been wearing comfortable boots, but more likely they would have been expensive imported shoes. In fact those shoes probably would have cost more by themselves, than the coat, shirt, pants etc. that he was wearing today. He thought about how life had changed so much for him over the past five years, and then how it had changed once again in the last two and half months. He thought about his lawyer, Bob Weller. And he thought about how Bob Weller was also his good friend. It had been a long and torturous road from the initial accusations of criminal activity, through discovery, on through the negotiations and final reluctant acceptance of the plea bargain. Weller, who initially was nothing more than a "hired legal gunslinger," became a pillar of strength and a good friend to him. When the legal battle was over, Weller had continued to stand by him, and continued to counsel him on the many problems he then had to face.

Not the least of which had been Desi! Weller didn't handle the divorce, but had recommended a good lawyer, and saw it through with him. It hadn't been a very contentious divorce, as many of them can be. In the Matter of Daniella Espinosa-Hamilton vs. J. David Hamilton, the case was resolved in a matter of weeks. It was a somewhat uneven distribution of assets, but Hamilton had a lot on his plate at that point in time. In need of liquid assets for legal fees, and having very little time, he was forced to acquiesce on most points of contention in the divorce settlement. Desi and her legal team, fully aware of his dilemma, were not shy. They were courteous, but not generous. Hamilton firmly believed that Desi didn't then, and probably hadn't since, lost a minute's sleep over the terms of the decree.

Over the next few years Bob Weller had maintained contact with notes, and phone calls, and even several visits after Joseph had been convicted. So a few month's shy of his third anniversary at Overbrook, Hamilton was only mildly surprised when he received a note from Bob that he was coming up to see him next Saturday. Hamilton didn't get many visitors.

On that following Saturday, they met in the Visitors Center and sat down at a table in the corner. It was noisy, as it always was on a Saturday, as they exchanged pleasantries and small bits of gossip about mutual friends for a few minutes. They followed that by discussing a few bits of personal business that needed some attention. Finally, Weller looked at him for a few moments in silence, and then said, "How would you like to get out of here?" Smiling, he waited to see how Hamilton reacted. Hamilton just stared back. "Technically, you're eligible for parole at the end of October. And under normal circumstances, you wouldn't get it on your first go around. But . . . " He trailed off, and smiled broadly. "But I was talking to my brother, Jim . . . You know, he's a doctor? . . . two weeks ago and he told me an interesting story. He has this friend who's a doctor too . . . and this doctor has a practice up near Lake Erie somewhere that is going to hell-in-a-hand basket. Complete shambles. He needs help. He needs somebody with administrative skills . . . with strong administrative skills. Who can organize . . . and streamline . . . and budget . . . and set office protocols . . . with financial discipline . . . you get the picture?" Hamilton continued staring back at him. "This doctor friend is, according to my brother, a very good doctor . . . but a very bad administrator. His practice is in trouble. He is knee-deep in paper work, and months behind in every day necessities. And this practice is primarily set up on the poorer side of town. This is no 'Park Avenue practice.' And that, my good friend, would be ideal for you." Hamilton squinted and tilted his head, slightly confused at what he was being told. Where is he going with this he wondered to himself? Is this about parole? He had not seriously entertained any thoughts about an early parole. He had convinced himself a long time ago that he was going to serve, at least, four years based on what prosecutors had told him when he took the plea bargain. He remained silent. "The ADA who prosecuted you is long gone. He headed out for greener pastures a year ago. Went into private practice defending the same corporate officers he used to prosecute . . . now he defends them for very large fees! He won't care. The colleagues he left behind in the prosecutor's office don't care about you. Your scalp was a pelt on his belt, not theirs. That makes the Parole Board the only obstacle. And once they hear that you've already got a job waiting for you; and that that job has . . . well, certain 'social redeeming values' to it . . . . I think they'll go for it." Weller repeated that he was certain that with Hamilton having this "'socially redeeming" job in a completely different line of work, and far away from where he had gotten into his legal mess, it would probably be viewed very positively. "You'll be starting over in a different place . . . with different people. I think they'll like the idea." Weller stayed silent for a few minutes to let in all sink in. "But . . . But . . . " Weller continued now in a low voice, "There's always a 'but.' You, of course, have to be willing to go there and do it. It is, as I said, in some godforsaken little burg way up near Lake Ontario. The pay will be . . . ."

Hamilton interrupted, "You said it was near Lake Erie a minute ago?"

Heller chuckled silently and then asked, "Does it make a difference? Lake Erie or Lake Ontario; it will be a long way from New York City." He put up his hand, and said, "Let me finish my thought. The pay will be miniscule. At least compared to what you were making back at OCS. But," Weller's face brightened up again, "At least, you'll be out of here! And if all goes well, maybe after a year or so, you can change jobs, something back in New York City perhaps? The key is that initially you'll be employed . . . in something socially redeeming . . . away from New York . . . away from Wall Street." He paused a moment, then said, almost triumphantly, "They're going to buy it!" Smiling, he went on, "Of course, you're going to have to have a chat with this doctor. He has initially bought into the idea, but he, of course, wants to talk to you. My brother, and I, have spoken to him and built you up. He's a good guy who needs help." Weller smiled broadly across at Hamilton. "So are you," he added after a moment. Weller sat back, and watched as Hamilton tried to understand what had just been said.

"He knows where I spent the last three years? He knows why I'm here? He's okay with this?" Hamilton finally asked.

"Yes, yes, and yes. He knows what he's getting. He wants to talk with you of course, but he is desperate for help. And someone with your managerial skills, at the price he can pay, is a godsend. He knows that." Bob was smiling. There wasn't really much to think about, but Hamilton wanted to think it over anyway. Weller gave him some additional information about the proposition, and the time frame he thought it would take to work it out. Hamilton took notes on a piece of paper Bob gave him. Hamilton studied the paper until it was memorized.

It was arranged that, at first, the doctor and Hamilton would talk over the phone. And if that went well, perhaps the doctor would drive down to Overbrook to have a face-to-face meeting with him. The phone call was set up for the following week with the doctor, whose name was John Gustafson.

A week later, after the call went reasonably well, as predicted by Weller, the personal interview was arranged for a few days after that. The Doctor came and talked with Hamilton in the Visitors Room at Overbrook. Hamilton calculated his age as somewhere closer to 60 than 50. And the doctor reminded Hamilton of the character Henry Fonda played in *Mr. Roberts*. He was lanky without being tall; his speech was measured, yet warm. He seemed to be able to smile easily. Hamilton liked him immediately.

The interview lasted less than an hour, and Hamilton was left with the impression that the Doctor was not impressed. He was disappointed by that because his hopes of getting out of Overbrook had been raised, and he thought he might like working with this man. He was truly surprised two days later Bob Weller called him to tell him the Appeal for Parole would be filed that afternoon! The interview had gone "wonderfully," Doctor Gustafson had told Weller, and Hamilton was exactly what he needed at the clinic. From that moment on, Time, while it never seemed to go by quickly at Overbrook, seemed to slow down to a crawl.

"Hamilton? Who's Hamilton?" asked the clerk suddenly appearing behind the counter. The man in the barn coat looked up.

"That's me," Hamilton said looking up. Motioned to the counter by the clerk, he approached.

"You're Hamilton, Joseph D.?" the clerk asked. When Hamilton nodded the clerk told him to collect his bags and come inside the barrier. He led him to one of the small offices there and showed him inside. Deputy Superintendent Piakas, sitting behind the desk, told him to sit down on one of the chairs facing his desk as he began leafing through the personnel folder in front of him.

"This is your last stop here at Overbrook," Piakas said without looking up. Hamilton had already passed through the General Services office to clear up any financial and personal matters...he had had his "Exit Physical" . . . he had packed most of his belongings into two cartons, and shipped them up to his new address upstate, arranged for him by Dr. Gustafson . . . he had made his goodbyes to other "residents," and some guards too. "I'll try to make this as brief as I can. I guess you're pretty anxious to get the hell out of here?" Piakas smiled. Turning pages and asking questions, Piakas kept the conversation going for ten more minutes. Several times he reminded Hamilton that he had a "maximum of 72 hours to contact the Department of Corrections up there in Wackentute County, and check in with your Parole Officer." He assured him, "You don't want to screw around with this, or you'll wind up right back here . . . or someplace much worse . . . before you know it!" Piakas flipped through more of Hamilton's file, and occasionally handed Hamilton pages that carried information, instructions, suggestions, and personal data of all kinds. After one more warning about checking in with the local parole office Hamilton was led out of the building and steered toward the front gate. He was free to go.

Thursday - October 31
Friday, Saturday, Sunday - November 1, 2, 3

The first four days in Newcomb, New York were a whirlwind of activity for the newly paroled Joseph David Hamilton. First, of course, was checking in at the county parole office. He located the apartment the doctor had arranged for him to rent. It was close to where he would work. He relocated an old savings and checking account into a nearby branch. He braved the lines at a Motor Vehicle Office to get a re-issued driver's license. And on Saturday he paid a visit to a local department store for household items he hadn't thought about in a very long time. The "to-do" list was very long. And before he was able to cut that list in half, Monday morning arrived, and it was time to go to work.

Chapter Two

It was cold and windy, but very sunny, on this early November morning. It was much like the late fall weather Hamilton had known as a boy in Michigan. It had been mentioned to him somewhere along the line that winter arrived early in the Wackentute Valley, and it stayed cold until May. He didn't doubt that this morning.

He arrived for work at the clinic just a few minutes after 8 AM and found it already humming with activity. Entering through the bright waiting room, he introduced himself to the young lady behind the counter, who introduced herself as Lindsay. He noticed immediately that she had a great smile, with huge dimples in her cheeks. She was probably in her early twenties, he thought to himself, and thought she was cute despite the nose ring and eyebrow piercing. She wore virtually no makeup, but compensated for that lack of adornment by having multiple earrings in each ear, and at least three rings on each hand. Her hair style reminded him of a football helmet, and the color was various shades of black and maroon. The lab coat she wore partially covered the hideously yellow tee shirt she had on underneath. It had some logo on it that had swords in it, and some words, but Joseph couldn't make out what it said. When he had first approached her she had looked very busy and distracted. But after she had flashed that smile he couldn't help but smile back. And if her appearance might have seemed, at first, odd to him, her smile made everything else disappear. He liked her immediately. Apparently expecting him, she asked him to wait a moment, and then turned and yelled over her shoulder for "Dr Gus."

After a few minutes the "Dr Gus" she had called for came out of an examining room in the corridor. Joseph recognized him immediately as the

8

same doctor who had come up to Overbrook to speak with him several weeks ago.

He collected Joseph, and led him into a small room he said was his office. They sat and spoke for only a short time. The doctor welcomed him to the clinic's staff, and said he hoped Joseph was ready for the hectic pace of the clinic's daily routine. The doctor reiterated what he had told him in previous conversations. It was a general practice that treated everything that came through the front door. They, of course, were not specialists, and on many occasions sent patients onto the county hospital over in Port Newhampton, or referred them to specialists throughout the county. He recited some statistics that Joseph wouldn't remember 10 minutes later, about patient load, gross billing, and average hours in a work week. This conversation was constantly being interrupted by various members of the staff, and as each one intruded, Gus was sure to introduce Joseph to them. Apologizing for the interruptions, the doctor explained the clinic was having a normal busy day.

When a nurse stuck her head in the door and said, "Gus, I'm sorry, but we need you in D right away!" the doctor rose and took Joseph to the front desk. Before hurrying off he assured Joseph that they would sit down and talk later.

At the front desk he instructed Lindsay to "Have Olney give him the grand tour so he knows where everything is."

Olney turned out to be a man roughly thirty years old. He was short and thin, with long black hair slicked straight back on his head. He had a large pointed nose and lively eyes, and an Adam's apple that stuck out almost as far as his chin. Joseph's first impression was that Olney probably didn't have to shave more than once a week. He told Joseph that he was in charge of maintenance, and assured him that it was he who kept the clinic running.

As Joseph followed Olney all through the building, the activity surrounding them seemed to be at a fever pitch everywhere. People in nurses' attire came and went. People in lab coats hurried in and out of doorways. When someone yelled "Spill" Olney excused himself and rushed away, leaving Joseph standing by the front desk.

"Hi" said a voice behind him, and Joseph turned around. "Who are you?" asked a pretty blonde woman wearing a lab coat, a stethoscope, and a great smile. Her head was tilted over to the side and her eyebrows were furrowed indicating she was waiting for an answer.

"I'm Joseph Hamilton," he said after a moment's hesitation, introducing himself for probably the tenth time that morning.

"What's wrong with you?" the lab coat pleasantly asked. There was no name tag, Joseph noticed.

"Nothing!" he answered shaking his head, surprised at the question.

"Then why are you here?" she smiled.

"I work here," he answered, now getting a little flustered.

"What do you do?" she said now, without a smile.

"Who are you," he managed to get out, trying to regain some composure.

"I'm Dr. Gustafson . . . now answer my question. What do you do?"

"Ana!" Dr Gus interrupted, coming out of his office behind her. "This is Joseph. I told you he'd be starting with us today. He's going to handle all the admin stuff." He turned to Joseph, and continued, "This is Dr *Ana* Gustafson. My daughter . . . " he paused a moment, then added, "and my colleague." Joseph extended his hand, about to say "hello" again.

She ignored his hand. "You said a 'Hamilton' would be starting today, not a 'Joseph'," responded an apparently annoyed Ana.

"I said I was 'Joseph Hamilton,'" Joseph corrected her.

She ignored Joseph altogether, and continued to her father, "You also said he was tall and …." She didn't finish her thought. "This guy is not tall," she continued after a moment. She turned and looked at Joseph again, then back at her father and said, "You need your eyes checked." Not waiting for agreement, or a comment, she whirled around and went back into Examining Room C.

"She's not always that cheerful," Dr. Gus smiled at Joseph, and then also returned to his patient.

Olney returned and retrieved Joseph a few minutes later. He continued the tour throughout the building, introducing Joseph to staff members whenever they crossed paths. That included Mena, who was the senior nurse and radiated authority, and Figgit Nuuf who was in charge of the lab and seemed as odd as his name. Joseph knew he would never remember all the names and their jobs. He made a mental note that after he got settled in he would suggest that all staff members wear name tags. He had no idea at this time how far down the list of priorities that suggestion would fall.

When the tour was completed the layout of the large building was completely jumbled in his head. It included the waiting room and administrative area inside the front door. From there a maze of corridors led to offices, examining rooms, labs and storage rooms around every corner. The largest room of all was the medical records file room. Joseph needed a map! Olney told him he still hadn't seen it all, but he was saved from further confusion when Dr. Gus grabbed him away from Olney so they could talk.

They sat down once again in his cramped office. Dr. Gus began by explaining that the former office manager had passed away a year ago, and that he had taken on that additional job while they looked for a replacement. That former office manager had been Olney's mother. She had taken over the job when Dr. Gus's wife had died five years earlier. Olney's mother had been a terrific housekeeper, but not such a terrific office manager. But that was okay with him, as he had been willing to overlook her shortcomings in that department. Olney's mother and father had worked for the Gustafson family in one way or another for over twenty-five years. After she had passed away he never got around to hiring the replacement they needed, and things had gone from bad to worse.

Ultimately he came to the obvious realization that the situation was out of control, and he hoped that Joseph would be able to get things straightened out. Joseph said he felt confident he would make things better, and was eager to get started. The doctor told him to use Olney, if he needed him, but gently suggested that he wasn't very good "in some things." Joseph understood, and said he felt he wouldn't need too much outside help. As for office space, and other odds and ends, Gus said that Olney would provide him with whatever he needed. Gus pointed to four cardboard cartons on the floor, and said that those were his "Administrator's Office." Joe could take them, and set up shop "wherever you can find the space." This was his first sign that the job ahead was going to be no walk in the park.

Joseph found Olney and asked him where the manager's office would be. Olney had no idea. He asked him if he knew where the office files were. Olney didn't know that either. Olney did know where his mother's office used to be, "but that was just used for storage now." When Olney led him to it, Joseph found out that Olney wasn't kidding. The small room was crammed with miscellaneous boxes, furniture, and trash.

By midafternoon he had found another storage room that looked like it hadn't been used in months. It was far from empty as cardboard boxes were stacked floor to ceiling nearly filling it. But it was near the front desk/waiting room, and more importantly it had a working ceiling light! That was something the first "available" room he had discovered did not have. Using some of the boxes already there as a makeshift desk and a straight-backed chair he had found in one of the dark storage rooms, Joseph started in by opening the four boxes from Gus's office and spreading their contents out. It took only thirty minutes before cold reality started settling in.

The clinic's checkbook had no recorded entries for the last two months. Checks were missing. There were many large gaps in the numbered checks sequence in the register. Several large envelopes, marked "Payroll," were filled with check stubs, uncashed checks, and multiple tax forms. A shoebox inside one of the cardboard cartons was marked "accounts payable." Inside were bills, envelopes and statements in no apparent order. In another folder were copies of Gus's personal tax returns from two and three years ago. Joseph hoped fervently that there was a box, or better yet several boxes, somewhere with a lot more accurate and current data in them He wouldn't realize it for a few days, but his hopes were in vain.

With Olney in tow, he went exploring again late that afternoon. Only after going into several rooms did he realize he needed a plan. At the very least he needed a *floor* plan! Unfortunately Olney wasn't very much help. As far as he knew there was no floor plan. Joseph went back to Gus and ambushed him between patients. Gus wasn't any help either. Joseph, in frustration, finally drew up a schematic of the building with Olney's help, and a lot of walking around pacing off distances.

Later, Dr. Gus found Joseph going through forgotten boxes of supplies... in a forgotten closet... in a forgotten storeroom. "Joseph," he said, "it's closing time. Time to go home. Come on, let's go have some dinner."

Joseph was surprised when he looked at his watch and saw it was nearly 8 o'clock. It had been a long hard day filled with some very hard physical work. He had been lifting and moving heavy boxes and files, as well as some furniture, and had sweated a lot more than he had thought an office administrator would be required to do. And all of that was compounded by the almost total confusion about what was going on around him. He wondered if he would fit in with these new colleagues. Gus and Lindsay were certainly nice enough, and Mena the nurse and lab tech Olney seemed to be too. But some of the others had come across as a bit *standoffish!* Gus's daughter had seemed outright hostile. Although he was tired, and the thought of going home and right to bed was appealing, he jumped at the chance to sit down with Gus. There was a lot they needed to talk about.

Tuesday - November 5

It didn't take long for the people at the clinic to begin deflecting to Joseph every matter that fell remotely into the business side of running the clinic. By midmorning, of this his second day here, he was fielding questions from the staff, patients, vendors and suppliers. And in most cases he had no answers. He tried to learn on the fly from Lindsay, whom, Joseph was beginning to think, always had a smile on her face that showed off those world-class dimples. She called him "Boss," and, to his surprise, he liked that. She liked it too, because it wasn't too formal, like "Mr. Hamilton" would have been. It wasn't too familiar, like "Joseph" or "Joe" would have been.

He also came to realize that she possessed that sunny disposition most of the time, despite being constantly bombarded by patient and staff demands. She was apparently the "clinic expert" on all matters pertaining to health insurance too. It wasn't that she was truly an expert on these matters, but only that she knew more than anyone else. The state insurance program was the most common coverage in the clinic (when there was coverage at all). It was, not surprisingly, very unwieldy. Private insurance plans were less common, but equally bewildering. Lindsay was helpful, but was so busy with her other responsibilities that getting her to focus solely on it was impossible.

Vendors and suppliers seemed, at first, relieved that the clinic had finally hired a business manager. Then they complained bitterly when they were told that – No! – they were not about to be paid in full for all the bills that were outstanding. Their appeals to be paid ran the gamut from friendly requests to threats to "cut the clinic off." Having no phone in his make shift office didn't help matters as Hamilton often had to field calls on an extension on someone else's desk. The account representative at the phone company refused any further services to the clinic, such as moving or installing new phone lines, 'until the past due charges at the clinic were eliminated'. In fact, the rep mentioned that cutting all phone services was under consideration, "by the supervisor."

At one point late this afternoon Joseph sat back in his chair and sighed deeply. He had just been threatened by an irate supplier, who had been yelling that he was "going to come over there and punch your lights out." Outside his office he could hear parts of several conversations. There was a baby crying somewhere. Names were being called out, and the phones seemed to ring nonstop. People dashed by the doorway of his office every few seconds. He had a list on his desk of phone calls he had to return. There were several people he had tried to reach, and who, he was sure, would not return his call. They would have to be called again. He had to get Olney to move some storage boxes from their present location to another location. And that location was yet to be determined. And he hadn't seen Olney in hours. He also needed Lindsay to explain some problems he was having in the insurance reimbursement procedures. He wasn't really sure she'd be able to help; but he didn't know who else to ask.

Amid all this cacophony and confusion, he suddenly had a memory jar loose. He thought back to the New York City heydays of his time at OCS Financial. More specifically he remembered those days when a financial deal would all come together and close. He pictured the large conference room in the executive suite at OCS's headquarters. It was on the fifteenth floor with the magnificent view overlooking the adjoining park, and the Hudson River beyond that. It was furnished beautifully with lush carpeting and fine prints along the walls, and with that enormous conference table of dark wood in the middle of the room. It served as ground zero for the culmination of the deals that OCS had orchestrated. He could picture the frenetic activity going on whenever the lawyers, accountants, advisers, consultants, owners and entrepreneurs, with their armies of assistants, would gather "to dot the i's, and cross the t's." Papers would be passed around, and signed. Copies would be made, and documents would be collated. Instructions to banks, ("What bank is that? Where? Do you have their number?") with myriad alterations and corrections (Did Doug see this? Did he agree to that?") would fly hither and yon. And the noise! ("I never said that!") Oh what a din would be raised by people talking over one another. ("No! No! No! We agreed to a 3.2% floor.") Talking, or even shouting, (ESCROW! Escrow, damnit!") to people standing nearby, or across the table, or even across the room. And Joseph could see, in his mind's eye, amid all this activity and commotion, his able and trusted administrative assistant, Margaret Mary Fitzgerald, moving around the room coaching, prodding, advising and correcting everyone until the deal was done.

Tall and pencil thin, with her rimless glasses perched on the end of her nose, always dressed in a dark-colored dress, she whirled around the room from cluster to cluster, always smiling, using her soft voice to get what needed to be done, done. It didn't matter how big or little the deal was, or how complex or straightforward the contracts were written, it always seemed that she knew what had to be done; and when it had to be done; and who had to do it. She appeared to be in total control of the entire process. Nothing ever fazed her. And then he remembered that sign, slightly larger than a postcard, hanging from a thumb tack in the wall next to her desk. It was a small brown wooden plaque with gold lettering on it. It said:

> All over the world Chaos may roam.
> But THIS is the place that it calls home.

He wished Margaret Mary Fitzgerald were with him now.

Wednesday November 6

The first two days at the Wackentute Walk-in Clinic had ended with Joseph completely dazed. In a way it reminded him of his first week in "the Tank" at Overbrook. Nothing . . . not the environment, the routine, nor the people he met were anything like anything he had ever experienced before. But at least when he had gone to jail he had been "prepped" by a man Bob Weller had hired.

The week before Joseph had to turn himself in to the authorities, he sat down in a conference room at Weller's law office with a man introduced as Mr. Anthony. His business card stated he was the president of "Incarceration Consultants, Incorporated." Mr Anthony was an imposing figure. He was taller than Joseph's six foot three frame, and probably weighed close to 300 pounds. And to Joseph, those 300 pounds looked very solid. His hands were large and his handshake was almost painful. He had a shaved head, and wore sunglasses despite being indoors.

His voice was more of a growl, and he spoke very fast. Joseph's initial impression was that this meeting with Mr Anthony was not going to be very pleasant. What this Mr Anthony did, for a fee, was prepare people for their time in jail. He was all business, and very professional. He immediately advised Joseph to take notes, and ask as many questions as he wanted. Mr Anthony, it turned out, was very well informed about Overbrook, its routine, and the people who ran it. He assured Joseph, "Ya could do a lot worse!" as he cocked an eyebrow and nodded.

Three hours later, Joseph was reeling from the information download. He had been given a long list of things to remember, and an equally long list of things to forget, when he "went inside." He was told about many new things to expect, and also about some very familiar things he would have to do without while he served his sentence.

"You know . . . doin' time is all about time," Mr Anthony instructed. "You can sit around . . . moanin' about how long you been in there; and about how long you got to go. Forget that! It don't change nothin'. Use the time you got for somethin', not nothin'."

That kind of comprehensive tutoring session would have been equally beneficial for him here. Somewhere in the middle of the afternoon of this his third day, he sat in his new makeshift office, amid stacks of paper in no discernible order, listening to the clamor of a very busy medical practice, and wondered what he had gotten himself into!

Thursday November 7

By mid-morning on another cold, windy Wackentute Valley morning, Joseph was still looking for a host of missing data. This time he was in the largest room in the building. This was the room where all the patient charts and histories were kept. Shelving units lined all the walls, and also made several long rows in the middle of the room. While Joseph wandered up and down the aisles looking for anything that looked like it wasn't "Medical Records," he noticed that the walls themselves were cinder block, and he asked Olney why this room hadn't been finished. He really didn't expect an answer, but Olney surprised him. Olney hadn't followed him all the way into the room, and but was standing in the doorway. "This wasn't always the Record Room," Olney said, "It used to be supply room. See?" he said, pointing to the shelves along the back wall. Joseph looked that way and was surprised to see a large door almost totally hidden behind a jam packed shelving unit.

"What's that door?" he asked. "Where's it go?"

"Outside," Olney said without interest. "Used to take in supplies from trucks through here when this was a supply room. Used to be filled with stuff in here. All the stuff they needed came in through here. Kept a lot of stuff they didn't need in here too. Lotsa junk. But that was a long time ago. They decided they needed this room for the records."

"Oh! So this was like . . . a loading dock? What did they do with all the stuff that was in here?" Joseph asked, just trying to make conversation.

"Moved it to other places . . . threw some stuff out. A lot of it went down the basement." Olney yawned.

"The basement? The basement! Are you kidding? There's a basement?" Joseph was stunned. "When were you going to tell me there was a basement?" Olney ignored Joseph's reaction and went on to explain that there wasn't anything down there "except some junk and stuff. There's some boxes and other stuff down there too. We don't use it anymore, since the elevator broke a while ago." Then added, after a moment's hesitation, "And there's maybe some child eating spiders down there too." Joseph just stared at him. Olney smiled and said he was just kidding. He explained that his mother used to tell him that just to keep him from playing with the freight elevator when he was young and used to hang around the clinic while his Mom worked. Olney said he liked going up and down on the elevator when he was little. Joseph ignored the remark about the spiders, but asked where the elevator was. Olney reminded him once again it didn't work anymore, and pointed to a nearly obscured door behind a file rack along the side wall.

A few minutes later, and with Olney now a very unwilling participant, the two men ventured down the back stairs into the basement. They spent the rest of the day taking inventory of a very large quantity of "some junk and stuff" in the dimly lit, dingy, dusty and cramped basement. They did not come across any "child eating spiders."

Friday November 8

By midday the basement inventory was almost complete, and Joseph had begun moving this newfound treasure trove of supplies up to the main floor. Hauling the cartons up the stairs one at a time was tiresome work. Olney, in all fairness, bore the brunt of it. Deciding where to put this all these newly discovered items required some nimble rearranging. Moving some of the furniture up those narrow stairs required a lot more than that. In the space of only a few hours, getting the freight elevator repaired and back into service had soared up the "priority to-do list" in Joseph's mind. Into one previously unused room - with a now- functioning ceiling light because Joseph simply replaced the burnt out bulb! - Joseph began moving

16

all medical supplies. He recruited Mena to pass on their usefulness. Office supplies he began putting near the front desk. Long forgotten stores of stationery, as well as insurance forms – some hopelessly out of date - were uncovered. He found eight cases of powdered baby formula underneath a tarp in the corner. No one could remember where they had come from, or how long they had been there. The expiration date on them had passed long ago.

Along with some dated financial data, including purchase orders and receipts, they found a hoard of long ago forgotten lab coats and supplies. In one back corner they uncovered two full pallets of copy paper for a machine that Olney said hadn't worked in over a year and seven rolls of fax paper that were hopelessly obsolete. They even came across some old office furniture, which Joseph appropriated for his new office.

Saturday November 9

By the early afternoon Joseph was sitting in his "new" chair, at his "new" desk, staring at the ceiling. His office now had a file cabinet (with one missing drawer) and, of course, no phone, but it was a start. Papers, file folders, and scribbled notes on small scraps of paper lay all over the desk. Some folders were piled on the floor. He couldn't look at them anymore, so he just stared at the ceiling. The previous five and a half workdays were a jumble of problems, confusion, discoveries, and demands. Random bits of data (some undoubtedly important, some meaningless- he didn't know which yet) came at him in a constant stream from the moment he walked in the door in the morning until he slipped out at night. Every attempt to organize anything was derailed almost immediately. The material needs of the clinic were still hopelessly obscure. And the financial structure was almost a complete blank. And he realized that, worst of all, *he didn't know what he didn't know!*

He sat and stared, and decided he would have to start over. He wouldn't attempt to solve anything. He wouldn't even attempt to identify problems. He would begin by finding out what he had. What he knew. He would organize. Categorize. He would create a Balance Sheet for the Wackentute Walk-In Clinic. And from that balance sheet he would create an income statement. The balance sheet would be the structure . . . the bones and organs and muscles and tissues of this "beast." And then he would learn how it worked. He would create an income statement that would show how this beast functioned. His entire professional career had been based on his ability to understand a company, and its problems and potential, based on what he could analyze from its financial statements, starting with its balance sheet. In the past, teams of accountants had created and cross-checked the data before presenting it to him. Not this time! This time he would create it too. He would start from scratch, and put it all together. "That's the job that needs to be done," he said out loud.

"What job?" Olney asked from somewhere in the hall.

The question brought Joseph back to reality. He stood up, noticed that the clinic was unusually quiet. He checked his watch and saw it was after 2 PM. He went out into the hall and found Olney sitting on metal folding chair. From the deserted hallway and from the lack of noise Joseph had assumed the clinic was closed and empty. "What are you still doing here?" he asked the forlorn-looking Olney.

"Doctor Ana said I should stay until after you left, then lock up. She didn't want you left alone in here." Joseph wasn't sure that was concern on her part . . . more likely a lack of trust. But he didn't think asking Olney could shed any light on it, so he let it go.

"Come on Olney, let's get out of here. I have to go to the mall to do some shopping, if you drive me there I'll buy you lunch." Joseph was still without a car, and considered it a fair trade-off to buy lunch for Olney in exchange for the ride home.

Olney's car was a beat-up Buick that was, at least, ten years old. It was rusted in spots, and made horrible noises. But to Olney it was freedom. It allowed him to travel around on his own. He was espousing on the joys of automobile ownership when they passed by a park, and something about it caught Joseph's eye immediately. He could see that it had a large open pond area where maybe fifty people were ice skating. Joseph stared through the car window at the people gliding along on the ice. Off in the distance on the other side, some children were playing hockey. He looked at some good skaters twirling around, and some bad skaters trying desperately to remain upright. He was mesmerized by this very ordinary scene. He hadn't been on skates in a very long time. And it was, he thought to himself, exactly what he needed! He asked Olney about the park, and was told that people skated there all the time. The lake, named in honor of General George Armstrong Custer, was almost a mile long and up to a half mile wide.

After lunch Olney had left, leaving Joseph to his shopping spree at the mall. Grabbing a taxi back to his apartment he packed away his purchases, did some household chores, and was finished by 6:30. He was hungry, and decided to treat himself to dinner in the only restaurant in Newcomb that he knew. The Fireside Inn was the place Gus had taken him that first night, and it wasn't too far to walk.

The interior of the Fireside Inn was divided into two rooms, each with its own door to the street. The first, and larger room, was the dining room and was square in shape. It was filled with 15 tables of varying sizes. The tables were topped by red-checkered tablecloths and surrounded by four to eight barrel chairs each. The walls were wood paneled, and the decor was rustic. Lights made to look like old oil lamps hung from the ceiling rafters, or were attached to the walls.

The second room was the bar. This room was smaller and more of a rectangle. The bar ran along one long side, and several small tables with chairs, a jukebox and a pool table were scattered around the rest of the room facing it.

After dinner, Joseph entered the barroom and picked out an empty stool and sat down. The smiling bartender approached, and introduced himself as Dudley. Walter "Dudley" McVeigh had been a bartender his entire adult life. Whether working the bar, or sitting on stool in front of it, Dudley had probably spent more time in a saloon than anyone else in the Wackentute Valley. A bit over 45 years old, he looked 65. Tall, frail, and almost totally bald, he was the picture of ill-health. He wore thick glasses, and had unsteady hands as a result of a nervous condition. He had ulcers due to an incredibly poor diet. He slept poorly, and drank far too much. He always wore a white dress shirt and tie when he worked, and tonight was no different.

Joseph, who hadn't been in a bar in a very long time, absentmindedly ordered the first beer he saw on tap, even though that wasn't what he really wanted. Sitting there, at the bar, began to feel surreal to him. It was only two weeks ago – to the hour- that he was folding towels, just out of the dryer, at the Recreation Center back at Overbrook. Now he was sitting in a bar, sipping a cold beer, watching a hockey game on TV, and could – if he wanted – get up and leave whenever he wanted. It was such a unique sensation he felt conspicuous. Everyone else in the bar was, of course, completely oblivious to these kinds of thoughts. It was the furthest thing from their minds. Not Joseph; he felt it intently. He hadn't experienced something like this sense of freedom since before he was arrested. It was probably the first time the recent transformation in his life had really sunk in. It felt great.

The reverie he was going through was interrupted when a goal was scored by one of the teams playing hockey on the TV. As the replay was shown in slow motion, Joseph was again reconnected with old feelings. Having played hockey throughout his younger years, he was able to see the finer points of the goal-scoring play before the announcer pointed them out. He wanted to tell someone about the intricacies of the goal. He wanted to tell someone about feeling free, and how absolutely great that feeling was. He felt as if he had been cold for a very long time, and was now starting to get warm.

When the bartender noticed his near-empty glass he asked if he wanted another, Joseph stopped him. "No, I think I'll switch to scotch. Do you have any Islay scotch?" He asked although he thought it highly unlikely that this local bar would have any of this rare brand in stock. The bartender's blank stare told him he was right. Joseph hadn't enjoyed his favorite drink in . . . in . . . ? He wasn't sure. He couldn't remember the last time! He asked the barman if he had any Balvenie or Macallan. The barman, after scouting around the bottles behind the bar, produced a Macallan 12, and showed him. "Straight up . . . . water on the side," said Joseph.

"That must be good stuff," said the man wearing a green baseball hat sitting a few empty stools away to Joseph's right. "You can tell because they don't sell much of that in here," he said, smiling. This somewhat obscure knock on the bar's clientele was picked up by the bartender, who immediately said that most of the patrons were higher class than some riff-raff, like he was. He called him "Roove."

The man called Roove got off his stool and extended a hand, and introduced himself. The first thing you noticed about Roove was his infectious smile. He was a good looking thirty-something, and although not quite as tall as Joseph he looked very solidly built. He looked like he hadn't shaved in several days, and his long, uncombed black hair probably hadn't seen a barber in quite a while either. He repeated his name to Joseph, and explained it was short for Reuven. Joseph smiled back, reached over and shook his hand, and introduced himself.

They chatted for a while, exchanging bits of vague personal information and commenting on the game. While Joseph had just recently moved into Newcomb from outside the valley (he didn't say from where), Roove said he had lived here his whole life. They both admitted they liked hockey. When Roove asked him why he had moved to the valley, Joseph told him about his job at the clinic.

"Oh, hell yeah! I know the Walk-In Clinic. I've known Gus since I was a little kid. Been goin' to him, and the clinic, for years. Fact is, I've even done some work for them on occasion. Couple of odd jobs, here and there. What do you do?"

"I am doing admin for them. Office manager and such."

"Yeah, I guess they could use some help with that. Mrs. . . . what's her name? Olney's Mom, used to do that for them. That was one tough old bird, that one. She's been dead over a year now, right?" He didn't wait for an answer. "They ever get that freight elevator fixed? Last time I was there we had to move some crates and stuff. Elevator was broke so we had to haul that shit up and down the stairs." He shook his head and made a face to indicate that it wasn't a good memory.

"Still broke," was all Joseph said. Joseph was going to mention that the fact that the clinic had a basement was recent news to him, but never got it out. Suddenly Roove reached into his flannel shirt pocket and took out his cell phone. He looked at the screen to identify the caller, and then opened it and said, "Hey!", as he walked away to a quieter spot to talk. A few minutes later he was back. He scooped some of his money off the bar, leaving some as a tip, said goodnight to his new friend and the bartender, and was out the door and gone.

A moment later the bartender explained to Joseph, "He has a 'sweetie' over near the mall somewhere." Joseph hadn't asked. "And every Saturday night, after she gets her little kids to bed, she gives him the 'all clear' and he scoots over with a six pack and a pizza, and they watch a movie.....*or somethin'*" he said with a wink. Dudley kept up the conversation. He told Joseph that Roove was quite a character. And although Joseph hadn't asked, he told him, "Plays guitar in here every so often when we have something going on. Not regular, of course, just every so often. He ain't bad," he said earnestly. After a pause, he added, "He's not Nicky Four Fingers Pasternak, mind you, but he ain't bad." Joseph had no idea who "Nicky Four Fingers Pasternak" was.

The confusing "Pasternak" reference, and with the scotch on top of the beer beginning to take its toll, Joseph decided to call it a night. He finished what was left of his scotch, refused another, and went home. He had an early rise planned for the morning, and he was really looking forward to it.

Sunday November 10

There is a certain exhilaration you feel when you are moving very fast. It's not hard to imagine that jet pilots feel it, especially those who fly the smaller, and more nimble, fighter jets. And although it is difficult to understand, Einstein was right, because as the air and scenery go whizzing by faster and faster, time does slow down. And although they aren't going quite that fast, drivers of race cars or motorcycles must feel it every bit as much. The only thing that could be more exhilarating is going at great speed under your own power. Skiing downhill under control, or ice skating at break neck speed, produces a rush that is very hard to beat. This was one of the reasons why Joseph had played hockey most of his life, and had missed it so much when he stopped. And this was why he was out on the frozen Lake Custer on this early Sunday morning in his new skates.

He had arrived early at the lake, and for the first twenty minutes or so he was virtually alone. The ice was smooth and unmarked. He only heard the familiar hissing sound his skates made as he wheeled around alone on the ice. He loved that sound, and with the bright sunshine and wind rippling his jacket as he moved easily around, he imagined himself back in the Michigan of his youth. He hadn't skated in many years and was just a little unsure of himself at first. His brand new skates felt odd on his feet, and he thought it would take some time getting used to them. But, surprisingly, it all came back to him before long, and the skates felt fine.

By the time the morning wore on and other people began arriving and joining him on the frozen pond, he was moving easily. He skated away from where others began skating, and kept a sharp eye out for any warning signs of thin ice. But the lake was large enough to afford him all the space he wanted, and before an hour was up he was moving around with much of the agility and speed he had possessed when he was much younger. The old feelings of exhilaration came back too. He had somehow forgotten that excitement of going fast …. going very fast.

He surprised himself when he glanced at his watch and realized he had been out on the ice for close to ninety minutes. The measured sprints and sharp turns had blended into each other seamlessly. He was tired, sweating, and very thirsty. The cold air was starting to give him chills when he slowed down. But he felt wonderful. The past hour and a half of hard skating had melted the mental and physical fatigue he had accumulated during his first week of work at the clinic. The exercise hadn't solved any problems, nor spurred any great insights into the mountains of work that awaited him on his desk back at the office tomorrow morning. But he was, undeniably, refreshed. He reluctantly called it a day, and skated back to the bench on the side to change back into his street shoes.

"You move very well out there, you know," said the man who skated up to where Joseph was sitting. "I had my kids watching you," he smiled, "They are very impressed." The man turned slightly and gestured to two little boys behind him. "Oh man! Where's Dennis?" he suddenly yelled. In unison the two little boys pointed off to the left. The man issued an order to the two boys that sounded something like "Stay" and zoomed off after his other wandering child.

When he returned moments later, with "Dennis" in tow he again complimented Joseph on his skating. They exchanged names, a few other pleasantries, but his three boys were chomping at the bit to get back to skating. In a moment they were off, in different directions, with their father in hot pursuit.

Monday November 11

The very first thing Joseph did upon arriving at the clinic this very cold morning was grab Dr. Gus for a five minute chat. Yesterday he had rehearsed his argument for getting his own key to the building. He would point out that his work schedule did not necessarily coincide with anyone else's on staff. The key would allow him access whenever he needed it, without burdening others on the staff. He had several other points he had mentally prepared, which he felt would clinch the argument. But Dr. Gus cut him short. "Oh sure, I thought you had one already," he said. He pulled a key off his own keychain, tossed it to Joseph and told him to have a copy made. That was too easy, thought Joseph.

Several hours later the conversation in Gus's office started getting loud. An exasperated Dr. Ana was trying to get her father to see the error of his ways. "Don't deny it...I know you gave him a key! He now has access to the building . . . whenever he wants! You can't think that's a good idea?"

She was standing in front of his cluttered desk. He was slumped down in his chair behind it, smiling up at her over the rims of his glasses that were perched on the end of his nose. "He works all hours. You've seen him. He's in here early .... he stays late. He's working longer hours than you or me. I think he'll work Sundays if we let him. What's the problem?"

"In here alone? Are you kidding me? Dad, This guy's a convict! How can you trust him?"

"He's an *ex-convict*," her father corrected her. "And he went to jail because people who worked for him stole money, not him. If we're going to let him run this place we have to trust him."

"Dad, try to remember he's a criminal. And I want you to also remember that we have some pretty valuable things in here. And I am referring to the Narcotics Closet!"

"Ana," he said smiling up at her, "I appreciate your concern, but the fact is he . . . " Dr. Gus hesitated a moment, then added "well, he went to jail because of math, not meth." He was pleased with his witticism, and smiled. She wasn't, and didn't smile back. Dr. Gus concluded by saying in a flat tone and straight face, "I just don't think we have to worry."

"Maybe you don't think so, but I don't feel so sure. I'm going to watch him like a hawk. If he so much as takes a pencil home, and I'm going to scream for the State Police!"

"If anyone's getting robbed here, it's us." Joseph had appeared suddenly in the doorway. "How are we supposed to operate if we don't charge people for the service we provide?"

Surprised at the sound of his voice, Ana turned around to face him. She wondered for a moment how much he had heard. Then, not caring, she dismissed herself and left, saying that she had patients waiting. Dr. Gus waited until she was out of the room before saying to Joseph, "That's a big problem. We like to think that we treat sick people here; and being able to pay for it is a secondary concern."

"That's all well and good, Gus, but we have to be responsible too. Those that can afford it should. And those that can't . . . well, that's what insurance is for. If people come in here, and don't have private insurance, we can help them apply for state aid." Joseph didn't think he was being unreasonable in the slightest.

"We do charge, of course, and most of the patients here . . . maybe three quarters of them . . . do depend on the state paying for their care. But the state is very slow reimbursing us. The other insurance companies we bill are almost as slow. But the state is the bulk of it." He paused for a moment as he thought about how bad it really was. "Poor Lindsay," he said as the thought suddenly occurred to him, "she has most of the billing dumped on her." Gus went on to explain that Lindsay not only did the billing, but was usually responsible for covering the front desk, as well as various nurse's aid duties that sprang up here and there. "She was taking classes to become an LPN; but I think she gave that up. I agree that we've piled quite a bit of work on her."

"Look, Gus, I'm going to need her focusing on our Accounts Receivable going forward. She has a better understanding of the process than anyone else here. And that's not saying much!" Joseph was waiting for Gus to disagree, and was surprised when he didn't. "I am going to need her to get better at it, and faster at it. I want her to spend more time on it. And that means she will have less time . . . no, make that she will have 'No Time' for anything else. She and I are going to become very good at getting our money back. And until we do, you and the rest of the medical staff will have to cover up for her. At least until we can get someone else to do it. And that," he said shaking his head, "considering our current payroll restrictions, is very unlikely to be anytime soon." Before he left Gus's office they agreed that Gus would advise the medical staff, that for the time being, Lindsay would be unavailable to them.

Joseph's tête-à-tête with Lindsay a few minutes later went far better than he anticipated. She listened, without objection, to the plan he laid out. He told her she would work the front desk screening patients. But she would not be screening them medically. She was to screen them financially, only. She was to get personal data generally, and insurance data specifically. And every spare minute she had was to be spent working on the backlog of unreimbursed claim forms that Joseph was beginning to uncover. Her only comment was a mysterious "Finally!" when he was through.

Tuesday November 12

Some parts of the accounting picture were starting to fill in, but large gaps still remained. The Accounts Payable part of the puzzle was the most complete, relatively speaking. Joseph felt sure that suppliers, in their own self-interest, would be very helpful filling in the blanks.

Accounts Receivable was a disaster. Joseph learned that while some patients had medical insurance which covered most of their bills, many other patients had no insurance at all. While New York State provided medical coverage for many people below certain income levels, no one at the clinic seemed to have a complete working knowledge on what those levels were. Assigning Lindsay to attack the problem yesterday, he felt, was a good first step.

In the past, pursuing overdue payments to the clinic did not seem to fall into anyone's job description. That was no longer true. An obvious problem had been identified, and a possible solution was now in place. However, getting people to fill out forms for payment *before* seeing a doctor seemed to almost everyone, patient and staff, an alien concept. But Joseph was adamant in making sure that Lindsay, at the front desk, began insisting on it despite some howls of protest from some walk-ins. He planted himself near that front desk and allowed no one to get past her without the proper paperwork completed. Insurance forms slowly became less mysterious to him, as he and Lindsay were constantly on the phone to insurers with question after question. Joseph felt that prompt and sure insurance reimbursement was the lifeblood of the clinic. And it wasn't peculiar to the clinic. Timely Accounts Receivable was essential to the welfare of any business. It would be a priority going forward. Missing payments were just part of the problem. There were records that were missing. Documents related to every aspect of the clinic's operation were not to be found. The only paperwork that seemed to be complete was the medical records of the patients. Everything else seemed to be sketchy and hopelessly incomplete. Joseph kept asking anyone who'd listen where the inventory records were kept. Anyone Joseph would ask would refer him to someone else. Tracking down long-,abandoned file cabinets, or file cabinets that had disappeared, produced very little.

The staff had finished their lunch and had gone when Joseph came in for a cup of coffee. Sitting by himself, he wondered how he was going to solve this. He couldn't control the administration of the clinic without a basic understanding of what had gone on in the past. He had no basic framework.

The thought came to him from he-didn't-know-where! His initial reaction to that revelation was embarrassment that it hadn't occurred to him sooner. He was a trained accountant, and he hadn't thought of it until now. He was up in a flash looking for Dr. Gus.

"Who's your accountant? Who does your books? Who does the tax returns for the clinic?" He could have asked another five questions without taking a breath, but Dr Gus saw where this was going.

"Of course! You ought to contact Carl. I'm sure he can help you figure out a lot of the stuff you're looking for. I probably have his number in my office." Joseph followed Dr. Gus back to his office, and helped him ferret out the phone number of Sufton & Snow CPA LLC.

Joseph wasted no time getting back to his own office and calling the accountants. The first number on the crumpled old business card that Dr. Gus had found was "no longer in service." This did not bode well to Joseph. He tried the second number, and a soft voice answered, "Hello?"

His first reaction to the voice was disapproval that a business phone was answered with a simple "Hello." Undeterred he said, "I'd like to speak to Carl Sufton, please."

The soft voice said, "He can't come to the phone. Who's calling?"

"This is Joseph Hamilton. I'm the administrator for the Wackentute Clinic . . . and I need to talk to him about our account. He's our accountant. When will he be available?"

"Well, he's napping right now. But I don't think he can help you very much anyhow. He doesn't do accounting anymore, you know?" said the voice. The information that Mr. Sufton "was napping" somehow annoyed Joseph, until he heard the part about him "not doing accounting anymore". When he heard that he stopped being annoyed and started being worried. He put aside his worry, and asked to speak to Mr Snow. He wasn't sure where this was going but he felt sure it wasn't going to be good. "Mr. Snow?" answered the voice, "You want to talk with Mr. Snow? Who's Mr. Snow?"

Joseph was now back at *annoyed*. He reminded the person he was talking to that he was calling Sufton and Snow ...Public Accountants. "Wasn't Mr. Snow Mr. Sufton's partner?" he asked. Joseph felt sure that if the firm was only a two-man partnership, either man would be familiar with the account.

"Dad never had a partner," answered the voice of the apparent daughter of the accountant. "He just used the two names to make the practice sound bigger. At least I think that's why he did it." Joseph's heart sank in his chest. "Dad stopped doing accounting a while back, anyhow. After he got sick last spring, it was," she went to explain. She and Joseph went on with their conversation now that the confusion had cleared up. She offered to let him come down to her father's old office and take whatever papers he might find and need.

Wednesday - November 13

The day started off with Joseph's alarm clock not going off when it should have. Amid snow flurries, he arrived late for work at the clinic, and was feeling guilty about it. And to make matters worse it seemed like all hell had broken loose at the clinic as he walked in the door. For some unknown reason every bleeding, contagious, moaning, psychotic person in Wackentute County converged on the clinic . . . before 10 AM! By 10:30 every examining room was occupied. Every staff member was doing two things at once, and someone was calling their name to do something else. Patients were howling, sneezing, coughing, or bleeding. There were no empty chairs in the waiting room, as several people stood at Lindsay's desk insisting that they had no time to fill out any forms, and needed to see a doctor RIGHT NOW! Several times Joseph went to the desk to yell right back at people that they would fill out those forms before they were seen by any doctor. Tempers were getting short.

An elevator repairman had just finished telling Joseph, after spending all of ten minutes examining the workings on top of the unit, that the motor was "burnt out". Gears had fused and had rusted over. The warranty had expired long ago. There wasn't going to be a quick fix, according to the repairman. A new one was his recommendation, and considering anything less "would be a joke." There was nothing humorous about the estimate of "somewhere in the $50,000 range" to get it running again. The fact that the elevator was not really essential to the operation of the clinic was the only positive Joseph could take away from this episode.

"I ain't got no goddamn insurance . . . so there's no goddamn reason I gotta fill out that goddamn form. I just came in here to get my goddamn pills," some guy yelled at Lindsay. Joseph had had enough. Out of his office he came like a man possessed, and got right up into the face of the shabby man in front of Lindsay.

"Fill it out . . . or get out! That's the only two choices you have. You got a problem with that?" Joseph said, leaning over the Lindsay's desk. The man stared back at him, clearly unaccustomed to being treated this way at the clinic.

"That's all right," said a voice behind Joseph. "He can come in and see me." Joseph whirled around to see who was undermining his authority. Ana stood there smiling.

"No, he can't!" said Joseph loudly and firmly. "He fills out the form first." Everyone in the waiting room watched. Ana wasn't smiling anymore. She started to say something, but Joseph cut her off. "No one...NO ONE .... sees medical staff before filling out the form."

"I give him some placebo every few weeks, he's . . . " she whispered. But he cut her off again.

"NO ONE....not anyone gets to see medical staff without registering here at the front desk. There are no exceptions. None!" Ana decided against confronting him here and now, and asked to see him immediately in her office. Joseph followed her there, but not before telling Lindsay again that everyone fills out the form first.

Once back in Ana's office she slammed the door. "How dare you disobey me in front of patients! Don't you ever contradict me again!" She was furious. So was he.

"Don't you ever contradict me – ON MATTERS OF OFFICE POLICY – in front of staff or patients again! You handle the medicine! I'll handle how we run things around here. GODDAMN IT! This place is like a frat house. Everyone does as they please. I've seen riots with more organization! If this clinic doesn't get its act together it is going to close down. If it doesn't . . . " Just then Gus opened the door, and peeked in.

"Getting a little noisy in here. You two want to calm down a little?"

"He wanted Alphonse to make out an insurance form," Ana said with a derisive laugh to her father, after he stepped into her office and closed the door behind him. What Ana and Gus knew, that Joseph didn't know, was that Alphonse was a homeless vagrant. He was well-known to many people in Newcomb, and especially to those at the clinic. Ana turned back to Joseph and spoke to him as if she was talking to a child. "He has been *treated*," she emphasized, "at the clinic for years with sugar pills. They make him feel better. That's all it is. You're getting carried away, you need a reality check."

"I want everyone . . . every single person who walks or crawls through that front door to be treated . . . to fill out this form. Regardless of what that treatment consists of! This place is going broke. That's the reality." Joseph paused for a moment to let that sink in. "Unless we somehow increase our revenues dramatically, and start paying some bills, we will be shut down by creditors. And if they don't do it, the IRS probably will. Have you filed tax returns in last two years? I can't find any records. Hell, I can't even find any filing cabinets. Oh, there are some downstairs in the basement. But, we can't bring them up here. You see, they're too big to fit up the stairs. And we can't bring them up on the elevator, because the elevator doesn't work. And right now it looks like it never will. And as long as I'm on the topic, you know what else I can't find?" His voice started to rise. "I can't find any audited statements at all. You know why? Your accountant . . . RETIRED . . . at least six months ago! You don't have an accountant." His eyes darted between the two doctors he was facing. "You don't have any current financial records. You don't have any tax records. There is nothing in the files. They cannot be retrieved from your computer system – IF they're in there - because you don't have a functioning computer system. And even if you did, we couldn't print them out because you don't have a working printer. Or a reliable copier! Or any of those normal standard items one would find in most business offices." Now he was shouting. "Like paper! . . . or staples! . . . which you don't need because I can't find a stapler . . . or paper clips . . . or rubber bands . . . or pens . . . or even pencils." Joseph finally ran out of breath.

For several seconds both doctors just stared at the winded Joseph. Then, suddenly, Ana pulled a pen from the top pocket of her lab coat, handed it to Joseph, and said, "Here's a pen . . . now go back to work." She walked out of the room and left the two men alone. Gus closed the door behind her, and asked Joseph if it was truly that bad. Ten minutes later both men came out of Ana's office and headed off in different directions. Gus had patients waiting. Joseph had Gus's support to make things right."

And Alphonse, helped by Lindsay, and fudging more than a few answers, completed a state insurance form before getting his sugar pills. Lindsay's approval of the "Boss" was growing by leaps and bounds.

Thursday - November 14

Shortly after 9AM Joseph and Olney borrowed Gus's truck and headed off to the former offices of Sufton & Snow to retrieve the boxes of the clinic's financial records that Carl Sufton still had remaining from his now-closed practice. The soft-spoken daughter of Carl Sufton was only too glad to let them in and sort through the records and take what they wanted. She watched as they collected files, ledgers, folders, etc., crammed with data going back eight years. After several hours of collecting, they hauled it all back to the clinic. And on the way back they made one short stop at an office supply store. They were back by noon, and several people at the clinic asked them what they had been up to all morning. "Finding buried treasure!" Joseph told them.

However, the boxes from the former accountant would have to wait for another day to be closely examined. Joseph had a one o'clock appointment with the vice president of the bank that had served the Wackentute Clinic for the past 20 years. And he planned to keep that vice president, and several of his clerks, very busy that afternoon.

Joseph was at the bank until late that afternoon, and then once more traveled back to the clinic loaded down with cartons of clinic data. And with these mountains of new data to be sorted and digested, Joseph settled in for a very long night.

Friday - November 15

The head nurse Mena, who was normally the first to arrive every morning, found Joseph already there. His disheveled appearance made it obvious he had been there all night. She didn't comment on it, and neither did he.

The new payroll system, which was generated by the bank, was put into operation today, and its flaws became instantly obvious. Many of the checks generated by the new system had errors in them. Omissions, miscalculations, and blatant clerical errors seemed to rule the day.

But one by one the errors were corrected in Joseph's office. Staff came in one at a time and the corrections were made. The spelling of the name on lab tech Figgit Nuuf's check was corrected. Mena's withholding amount was correctly reduced by several *hundred thousand* dollars! Both Gus's and Ana's checks were correctly changed to Direct Deposit at the bank. And several others on staff, now aware that this was possible, asked to be added on to the direct deposit list. Olney's payroll check was perfect. The payroll system was the main topic at the lunch hour. Everyone, but one, marveled at the new system.

Ana grabbed her father and pulled him into his office, and slowly closed the door behind them. She waited a minute to gather her thoughts, and then said in a hushed voice, "He's signing checks? You gave him permission to sign checks? Are you out of your mind? Geez, Dad, I think you ought to re-think this a little bit before he disappears into the night with our cash." She was in dead earnest. She shook her head slightly, and exhaled slowly.

After a moment, he quietly said back her, "We don't have any cash to disappear into the night with!"

Saturday - November 16

Every so often someone would say something, or something would happen, that would remind Joseph of the transition in his life. When he left the clinic after work Saturday afternoon he had a feeling that reminded him of the day he left Overbrook, although it wasn't nearly as intense. He hadn't really hated Overbrook. He certainly didn't like it, but he had come to terms with it. He could not, then or now or ever, adequately described how good he felt when he left. Leaving the clinic this Saturday he felt the same sense of relief he had felt then. When he left Overbrook he knew he would never be back. Here, of course, he knew it was only going to be a short respite, and he was actually looking forward to coming back to the ongoing challenge his new job presented. But the weekend presented a break, and he was looking forward to it.

The prior week had contained some small, very small, victories. And the promise of bigger ones could be seen in the future; perhaps the very distant future, but they were out there. On the plus side had been the long and informative afternoon he had spent at the bank on Thursday. And one of the results of that long afternoon had been the timely and somewhat accurate production of the paychecks.

On the negative side was Ana's surly response to them. And the source of her displeasure was still a mystery to him. The accountant – or *lack* of one – was a major problem that had only just reared its head. The unknown possibilities of how bad things were might turn out worse than even he thought. Although, reflecting on that on his way home, he didn't see how that was possible.

Arriving at the Fireside, again after dinner, he greeted the bartender and ordered his scotch. He soon recognized the fellow in the green baseball hat again, and the two men exchanged waves. Seated several stools away from each other, they only sporadically exchanged comments about the hockey game on the TV. Joseph, who had been out of touch with the real world for the past three years, unintentionally made a remark about not knowing the young star on the newly powerful Chicago team. When Joseph had left for prison several years ago, this current All-Star was in Junior Hockey, and Chicago was in last place. Not wanting to explain his unfamiliarity with current events, Joseph cut the conversation off. When Roove got into a conversation with several other men at the bar, Joseph was left to himself.

Again a thought occurred to Joseph suddenly, as he watched the TV camera pan the bench of one team after they had scored a goal. Several players were wiping the sweat from their faces with towels as they settled back on the bench. Those sweaty towels reminded him of where he had spent his Saturday nights not too long ago. Glancing at his watch to be sure of the time, he realized that at just about this time, three short weeks ago, he was probably folding towels that were just out of the dryer at the Rec Center. It had been one of his jobs to wash and fold the towels that the residents used when using the gym. Fresh clean towels at the gym had been another improvement brought in by Irish Pat. He thought about Irish Pat, and where he probably was at this very minute. Hamilton imagined him sitting in his little office at the Rec Center, and watching his own personal TV. He certainly wasn't folding towels! No, he had, quickly, recruited someone new to replace Joseph at the gym to do those menial tasks. Hryila, on the other hand was probably relaxing in the day room in C3, watching TV. Or, Joseph smiled, he was just as likely, picking up the broken pieces of a glass he had just dropped!

Joseph thought of some of the other residents of Overbrook he had known, and tried to picture what they might be doing at this moment. And as he did, he kept comparing that to what he was doing now, and to where he was right now. He thought about the dinner he had had at a fast food place a little while ago, the choices he had made about where and what to eat. He went when he wanted to go. He wore what he wanted to wear. And the shirt and chinos he wore were not identical to the clothes other men around him were wearing. Women and children, rarities at Overbrook, were commonplace. There were so many changes, large and small, in his life now from what his life had been just a month ago. The more he thought about it the more he saw the differences in his life then and now. And most remarkable of all was how these changes had occurred in such a short time.

He looked around the bar knowing that no one was having these same thoughts. He almost felt sorry for them all, because these thoughts were so wonderful. He remembered a line in an old Neil Diamond song that said, "Getting lost, is worth the coming home." He had gotten lost, and had lost among other things, three years; but this regaining of freedom, this "coming home", was glorious!

Sunday - November 17

After a week of overcast skies, cruising around the ice on a beautifully sunny morning was like a tonic to Joseph. With the temperature well below 30, the ice was perfect. There was hardly another skater in sight. Again he felt the exhilaration as he moved around the entire circumference of the lake.

As he returned to the bench on the shore where he had started, he saw the same father-son group that he had spoken to last week. The father was, again, chasing after the littlest of his three sons. With the father distracted, the two older boys were meandering away in the opposite direction. Joseph headed off after them to shepherd them back.

"Thanks," said the returning dad, acknowledging Joseph. "You guys have to stay together, or we're going home," he warned his kids. They, of course, first objected, and then agreed. They began skating off when Joseph suggested they circle the entire lake, as he had just done. Father and sons all immediately agreed that was a great idea, and invited Joseph to join them. Not quite ready to call it a day, he agreed.

After brief introductions, the three boys led the way with their father, and their new friend, close behind. The father was Phil Podalski, and his three sons were Karl, Anthony and Dennis. The boys, who frequently veered right and left, somehow managed to keep generally on course. Phil and Joseph kept a constant eye on them, especially the youngest boy, Dennis.

Joseph, in answer to Phil's question, said he was new to the valley. Phil volunteered that he too, in a sense, was new to the valley. He had been born in the valley, but had moved away when he was 12. He grew up near Albany, and had gone to school at Niagara University. While at school, he met a girl he had known in his youth here in Wackentute. With that as common ground, they renewed that childhood friendship, and it grew and grew. "Needless to say, I married her. Twelve years and three kids later we both decided we missed this place. So we moved back a few months ago. Haven't regretted it for a second," he smiled broadly. "Except on paydays!" he added, "Left a good-paying job, and it has been tough getting re-started here." He sighed slightly, and then asked Joseph, "How 'bout you? You married?"

"Divorced."

"Oh man, that's too bad," Phil said.

"Actually it isn't 'too bad,'" Joseph disagreed. But he really didn't want to talk about that so he asked Phil what he did for a living.

"I'm a CPA," he said, and then took off after Dennis, who had just scooted off to chase after some birds.

Chapter Three

"Three hundred and twenty thousand?" Joseph said, barely above a whisper. "That's not possible." He shook his head, and was slightly annoyed with himself for apparently miscounting. He began the tally again. Packing lists, delivery receipts, purchase orders, bills of lading, and invoices began to pile up. Cross-checking them while looking for duplicates eliminated nothing. Going very slowly and carefully, he tallied up the total number of examination gloves that had apparently been delivered to the clinic over the past half year. He then compared that number with what his unofficial inventory tally had been. Of course, the numbers didn't match! And the difference of over 33,000 did not fall within his definition of "relatively close." And what annoyed him most of all was that he was unsure whether either number was accurate.

This exercise had all begun when he discovered five cases of these gloves stacked between the refrigerator and the wall in the pantry. He thought at first that they had been part of the supply he had found in the basement, and that for some unknown reason Olney had brought them upstairs. When asked, Olney said he hadn't moved anything.

After punching a long line of numbers into his calculator he looked at the display. "No . . . can't be," he whispered to himself. He looked again at the number in the display of his calculator. "Three hundred, twenty one thousand, four hundred," he said very slowly to himself. He stared at the number. The number was probably right, in a sense. It was an accurate total of what these receipts said had been delivered. "White . . . blue . . . green," he sighed, "Small . . . medium . . . large . . . extra-large? What are we doing with that many gloves? Who ordered these things? Who uses all these things?"

34

He needed to talk with Mena, now. Finding Mena, and finding her momentarily unoccupied by any emergency, they sat down and had a cup of coffee in the pantry. As always, she was helpful. In the span of 10 minutes she explained to Joseph everything he needed to know, which wasn't really very much, about the use of examination gloves at the clinic. She also knew how, and from whom, they were ordered. There was a room she referred to as Surgical Supply, and in it she stored medical items that she used on a regular basis. Just supplies, she repeated, never medicines or perishable items.

Joseph knew about it, and had tried to inventory it. It was hopeless. Things went in and out of there like a whirlwind. Realistically, Inventory Control was a distant goal. But he knew without that control the clinic was bleeding money. Money it did not have.

Over the course of Joseph's first two weeks at the clinic very little of the daily goings on seemed to make sense. It wasn't surprising that the medical jargon, operations and procedures were alien to him, but the basic business practices were unlike anything he had ever experienced before. He didn't understand much of what went on, but he knew one thing for certain. The clinic's operations were irrational, completely disorganized, and would – without doubt – lead to the practice going out of business. He wasn't sure how long that would take, but the ultimate outcome was a certainty. It was a time bomb . . . and it was ticking.

He didn't even have the raw data he needed to prove his argument, but cornering Gus to lay out the facts he did have became his immediate priority. He was fairly certain that he could not delay delivering the bad news, so he pressed the doctor for a meeting that very afternoon. Several hours later the two men sat in Gus's office for what amounted to a "business facts-of-life" lecture by Joseph to Gus.

In order to make sure he had Gus's attention, he started out with a few dramatic points. "There are 250 tongue depressors in a box. Each box costs us $13. There are 12 boxes in a case; and that case costs us $156. I have located, in various locations, 20 full and two partially full cases of tongue depressors here at the clinic. That is . . . if you're keeping score . . . slightly more than $3000 worth of tongue depressors *sitting on our shelves*. That isn't good. But, that's hardly worth noting compared to another situation I discovered. We currently have roughly 300,000 examination gloves in the building. Unless you plan on giving everyone in the county a physical exam in the next 72 hours we are *overstocked*. A box of 100 gloves retails for $3.99. And for some reason which escapes me, we do not receive bulk discounts on anything we buy from anybody. I'm looking into that." He waited a moment, and then continued, "There are 20 boxes of these items in each case. There are 27 cases on each pallet. And we have, if my inventory is accurate . . . and I am not absolutely sure it is . . . five and a half pallets of surgical gloves at various locations throughout the building. The cost of that inventory is nearly $12,000. This is just one of 20 or so items that I have identified so far that we have poorly inventoried. Now I realize that these gloves won't spoil as they sit on our shelves, but we can't afford to tie up our cash on inventory we don't need. Case Pharmaceutical would not send us . . . Ampicillin?" He questioned if he were pronouncing that right. Gus nodded. "Case wouldn't," he continued, "send us the Ampicillin we ordered last week because we are so far behind on payments. We have gloves instead." Then he said it again, slowly to be absolutely clear. "We have 300,000 surgical gloves instead of Ampicillin." He paused here to let it sink in further. Gus opened his mouth to say something, but Joseph cut him off. He had the floor and wasn't going to yield. "We have an X-ray machine in the lab that is so old that parts can't be found for it to keep it working. And despite the magic that Figgit performs on it regularly, it could break down for good at any moment. Miller Diagnostics lent it to us when they took our newer one, which isn't exactly state-of-the-art either, for repair. They won't bring that one back until we pay our past due bills. We often have to send our patients out for X-rays now. I'm not a doctor, but I am sure that that is not an efficient way to treat a patient. I do know that that is a more *expensive* way to treat a patient. We are *paying* people to do what we should be doing ourselves. I have learned that most sales reps we deal with will accept orders from virtually anyone here at the clinic. Just to see how bad things were I had Olney call the printer to order copier paper. Yes, copier paper! The same printer who knows our copier is broke and won't repair it, took the order. He had the nerve to tell Olney it would be COD. The people who supply coffee for our pantry deliver nothing but decaf, and charge us for a full range of products. They deliver it once every week whether we order it or not. I was told we had canceled that service months ago. I told them to stop last Thursday . . . and they delivered a full order -- all decaf -- again today! Luckily I saw it coming in, and refused to let the delivery man bring it in the building. We almost had a fistfight."

The specifics of Joseph's discourse were beginning to spin out of control in Gus's head. Joseph could see him trying to corral them. "Let me simplify it for you, using the gloves. First, it is bad administrative practice to have no central procurement. You know, ordering. Secondly, it is very bad business practice to have excess inventory. We, incidentally, had to throw out baby formula that we got from God-knows-where because it had passed its expiration date months ago. And thirdly, strike three; it is bad financial practice to have this excess inventory because it ties up money we can use for other necessities. It's dead money sitting there." Gus nodded, Joseph continued. "Some of these problems probably don't seem very serious to you." Joseph didn't let Gus say a word. "And some . . . like the coffee, I guess, aren't. But the Ampicillin, for instance, is serious, and can lead other companies to start worrying, and consider cutting us off too. These people talk to one another, and word gets out. Some of these people have no mercy, and," he paused again, "some of these people are dishonest. I am fairly sure that at least one outfit has been double billing us. And a few others are shipping substandard or expired products." Joseph finally stopped talking, and Gus said nothing. He looked at Joseph for a moment, and then he looked away. "I'm not trying to be dramatic, Gus," Joseph finally said. "But you could lose this place."

Joseph spent the next few hours coming up with a list of changes that were absolutely necessary, he thought, for the clinic to survive. He told Gus, in their second meeting of the day, that he had no delusions that this list would guarantee survival. In all likelihood, he admitted, this list was incomplete. But it was a start. And they had to start right away. Joseph told him he had no idea how much time they had to turn it around. Uncharacteristically, Gus stopped seeing patients for the next 45 minutes as he and Joseph went down the list point by point. When they finished, Joseph had a mandate.

"Oh, one more thing," he said just before leaving the office, "You and Ana have computers in your offices. Is it absolutely essential that they be kept there?"

Gus thought for a moment, and then said, "No, not really. We've had them for quite a while." He paused again for a moment, thinking. "Use them on occasion for researching something on the Internet, or contacting other doctors for quick consults, and such. Why?"

"I'm going to move them. Yours, and Ana's too. I'm going to give one to Lindsay for her desk. She needs it desperately. We've learned that you can submit claims to the state electronically. It cuts the turnaround time by more than half. The other computer can be put on the nurse's station, where it can be used by everyone. If you have any personal data on yours, I suggest you download it on a disk as soon as you can. I am going to have Figgit scrub the hard drives clean as soon as possible." He paused a moment, then said, "I'll tell Ana." He wasn't looking forward to that.

"No, you're not," was her response a few minutes later when he caught up to her in the hallway and tried to explain his plan. "I need it. I use it all the time."

"For what?" he asked. She felt liked she had been punched in the stomach. She couldn't believe he had the nerve to question her. Before she caught her breath he went on, "It will be placed right at the nurses' station. It will be available whenever you need it." She started to say something, but he cut her off again. "It will make a big difference to our payment schedule if Lindsay has one on her desk. It's important," he added.

"It's important to me too. I need one. I do a lot of ordering . . . essential things we use here," and then added, "Online."

"Not anymore!" he said flatly, "And be sure to ask Figgit to download any personal things you have on it. It's about to become community property."

Tuesday - November 19

In the midst of the daily chaos and stress, Joseph found a "breath of fresh air" in the lunch room banter that occurred almost daily. Sometime after noon each day there seemed to be a lull in the activity, and many of the staff gathered in the pantry to take their lunch. While emergencies and workloads often played havoc with routines and schedules, most days found the lunchroom crowded as staff members grabbed a few minutes for lunch. And while conversations and debates could range far and wide, it was often Figgit Nuuf, the clinic's resident technician, who took center stage and led the group off on wild tangents.

Based on his unusual name and peculiar speech it was widely assumed that he was foreign born. But from where was anyone's guess. People wondered if his native culture ordinarily transposed first and last names which led him to call everyone by their last name, while insisting he be called by his first. No one knew! Lindsay said that she had once asked Figgit what nationality he was, and he had jokingly responded by saying he was "a man of the world!"

Figgit was small, very thin, and slightly pale. His hair was black, short and always neatly combed. It looked like he went to the barbers twice a week. He was always neatly dressed, both in his ever-present lab coat as well as the dress shirt and tie he wore every day beneath it. He spoke with a distinctive, yet unidentifiable accent. If English were indeed a second language, he spoke it very well. He spoke in very precise manner, and with a cadence that had a very slight pause after every few words. And he spoke this way about topics very few other people had ever even considered.

His opinions were very precise, and once brought out, seemed to have been well thought out. Many of the noontime discussions centered on topics that Figgit had introduced. Joseph, like virtually everyone else who met him, liked him immediately. Figgit's abilities in the lab, both in performing tests and procedures accurately and quickly, as well as in keeping the equipment operational, were almost legendary. The clinic was very lucky to have him. His lunchtime lectures were considered by all as an enormous bonus.

"No, you see . . . it is a commonly accepted rule of thumb . . . not only in fashion . . . but also in the related disciplines . . . cosmetics and personal grooming, and such . . . that the relative size . . . of the ear to the tie knot . . . must remain in the two-thirds to three-quarters parameter . . . if there is to be proper symmetry . . . anything outside that creates a disproportion . . . "

he shrugged, "that, simply, offends the eye." He said it with absolute certainty. "I am not surprised that you . . . whose fashion sense leans a little closer to Goth than high fashion . . . might be unaware of this." Without missing a beat or taking a breath he turned to a salesman joining the staff for lunch, and said, "You, Mr Fillmore, who, like most people in sales, depend on an amenable appearance . . . must, of course, be aware of this."

"What?" said the salesman in the suddenly quiet pantry. He had been discussing a pending order with Mena and had missed the beginning of the conversation. Joseph would come to learn that falling behind in a Figgit conversation was equivalent to missing your first three punches in a hockey fight. You might as well just go down and cover up.

Lindsay didn't yield the floor. She raised her hand, as if in a classroom, and asked Figgut, "You're telling me that the knot in the tie has to be three-quarters of the size of the guy's ear? And I should notice this on guys? This is important?" and then added, "Most guys I know don't even wear ties." She seemed slightly embarrassed by this admission. But she knew Figgut well and teasing was something he would never do. It was just that she found this concept more than a little odd. This shouldn't have surprised her.

"Take Mr. Hamilton here," said Figgit gesturing toward Joseph who was sitting across the table from him. "No, that won't do." There was a short pause as he looked at Joseph with a pained expression. "He, of course, is not wearing a tie." He nodded at Joseph. "Nor does he, apparently, ever." Figgit was so matter-of-fact in the way he said it that Joseph wasn't sure he was being criticized.

Figgit turned slightly to his left and pointed at the visiting salesman who still trying to figure out what was going on. "Please, take a look at Mr. Fillmore here." Now being the center of attention in the room, the salesman put down his sandwich quickly, and sat up straight. "Fasten your tie properly for a moment . . . if you will, Mr. Fillmore," Figgit said, and salesman instantly complied. Everyone looked at the now flustered salesman. "You see that the tie knot is far too big, and it is, as such, a complete distraction to the entire facial composition. It is . . . what? What would you say Mr. Hamilton? The knot is probably just as large as the ear? You agree?" He glanced over his shoulder at Joseph.

Joseph, now somewhat flustered himself, tried to gauge the relative size of the man's ear to the size of the knot in his tie. He looked at the tie, then back at Figgit to see if there was any trace of a smirk on his face. But Figgit was also staring at Mr. Fillmore. Not sure what he was really supposed to say, he turned to Figgit and said, "They look about the same size to me."

Figgit nodded twice, apparently in complete agreement with Joseph's assessment. "Had Mr. Fillmore tied his knot tighter . . . thereby making it smaller . . . or used a narrower tie in its place . . . he might have easily achieved that proper proportion. That would make his appearance far more acceptable.... in cosmetic terms, of course. You see, as the structure of the 'Y' line . . . is addressed each morning as he dresses . . . ."

"What's the 'Y Line'?" Mena interrupted.

He turned toward Mena, a look of surprise on his face. It would never have occurred to him that someone didn't know what this was. He would have to explain it. "The science of Human Physiology . . . has developed what is called the 'Y Line.' It is the guideline for what is considered . . . the attractiveness of the human face. It is all based . . . on proportions . . . on symmetry." Figgit explained in a measured voice. People in the room said nothing, and the undeterred, unfazed Figgit continued. "Sometimes referred to as the Wine Goblet Phenomena . . . it represents the shape of the human face . . . from the eyebrows down to the collarbones. The outline, of course, starts at the ears and goes down along the jaw line to the point of the chin . . . down the center of the neck . . . past the Adam's apple . . . pronounced or not . . . and then out to the sides along the collar bones. Best observed when not obscured by clothing. The actual 'goblet' is the face . . . and its rim is, of course, the eyebrows . . . it moves down past the eyes, nose, cheek bones and mouth. These are obviously the most essential components; but the Y Line . . . it must be in proper proportion in order to frame it all."

There wasn't a sound in the room when he stopped talking. People were frozen in mid chew. Mr Fillmore wasn't moving. Some held various liquids in their mouths, unable to swallow until he was finished. Figgit went on, peering studiously at the now frozen salesman, as was everyone else in the room. "You will see in Mr. Fillmore's case . . . the neck is certainly big enough to accommodate a larger knot in the tie. A very much wider knot, in fact," said Figgit, again without a trace of ridicule. "But, unfortunately, the ears are not adjustable . . . and cannot vary according to knot, or neck size. No, it is the knot that must adjust to the ears. In Mr. Fillmore's case . . . this is not being done." It sounded sad the way he said it.

The salesman was absolutely speechless. So was everyone else. Figgit looked around the room at everyone's faces, and taking the silence as proof that his point had not only been made, but had been unanimously accepted. He picked up his half-finished cup of tea and said, "I've work to do." He was out of the room before anyone moved.

At 2 o'clock that afternoon Joseph had scheduled a series of meetings with several of the clinic's largest and, probably, most-neglected suppliers. He wanted them each to realize that they were not alone, and that every effort was being made to bring their accounts up to date. He also wanted to meet a few of them face to face. He considered himself a very good judge of human nature and wanted to put a face with the often irate voices he had been dealing with on the phone.

Three hours later Joseph had run a gauntlet through four very hard-driving vendors. And there had been one vendor who hadn't even shown up! The four who did show up, however, left in a better frames of mind than the ones they had when they arrived.

Certainly not all the problems had been solved. That, of course, hadn't been expected. But with reinforcing documentation and paperwork provided by them, a good many problems were now clearly identified. Reluctantly, Joseph summoned a few staff members to come into the office to clarify certain points of contention. He was reluctant to do this because he wanted a wall between the people at the clinic and the vendors. It was important, of course, for the staff to choose what they needed for their job, but not from whom it was obtained.

By the day's end people on both sides had a much better feeling about the relationship. And Joseph had a much clearer feeling about the relationship with the vendor who had skipped his appointment. On his fourth try to get him on the phone, he succeeded. The conversation wasn't pleasant. Apparently used to treating the clinic with a condescending, often rude, manner, the vendor tried that with Joseph. And Joseph responded in kind. Threats soon began flying back and forth, and both parties raised the probability of lawsuits. The vendor denied all wrongdoing, and vacillated between being conciliatory and threats of both physical and legal action. Joseph, who just wanted to let him know "there was a new sheriff in town," allowed the argument to go on only as long as it needed to establish his credibility. As soon as he felt this was done, he shouted into the phone that they'd see each other in court, and slammed the phone down.

He noticed, as he looked up, several faces in his office doorway. The volume and tone of his voice on the phone had attracted the attention of several staff members. He looked at them, and smiled, "I think that went pretty well."

Before she left for the day, Joseph found Lindsay and asked how she was doing. He had begun doing this, and would do this every day going forward, because the process of reimbursement was so critical. Lindsay gave him an update about how many cases had been submitted, both current cases and those in the backlog. He always asked what she had learned that day, and what she could teach him. And he always inquired if there was anything he could do to help her. He encouraged her and complimented her. He would constantly assure her that what she was doing was as important a job as anyone's at the clinic.

She, on the other hand, was thrilled. She liked what she was doing. She was being told how good she was at it. She was nearly awestruck that Joseph had taken Dr. Ana's computer, and had given it to her to use. This was amazing to her, and in her eyes Joseph was a hero.

Tonight's discussion was pretty much like all the others. Lindsay gave him an idea about how many claims were submitted, as well as a few new twists in the procedure she had discovered. But tonight Joseph wanted to know about the delays in payments. "If we are sending in as many as we are, why aren't they paying them?" Lindsay said she didn't know. "We have to find that out, don't we?" he said. She agreed.

Wednesday - November 20

It had started snowing late last night, and by the time Joseph had made it into the clinic this morning there were six inches of new powder all over the Wackentute Valley. It was very cold, and a gusty wind was driving the snow into drifts. Driving was treacherous.

Whenever, in the past, there was a snow emergency, the health providers in the area got together to pool resources. The general hospital, at the west end of the valley by Lake Ontario, had already called to offer whatever help they could, and make sure that the clinic would be able to help the people at this end of the valley. Staff members arrived at irregular times, and all had a tale of woe concerning their trip to work.

A few minutes before 9 AM, Phillip Podalski arrived at the clinic for his 9 AM appointment with, as he said, "Mr. Hamilton". Lindsay sized him up from behind her desk. Podalski was perhaps five and a half feet tall and appeared slightly overweight. His ears and cheeks were rosy red from the cold weather outside. His head was uncovered, and showed a short haircut with thinning reddish hair on top. He wore a very heavy coat over a brown suit. His button-down dress shirt was a pale yellow, and the tie was brown. Black rubber galoshes hid whatever shoes he was wearing.

Lindsay brought him back to Joseph's office. They sat in Joseph's crowded office for an hour discussing the role Joseph wanted the clinic's accountant to play. In a matter of minutes they were "Phil" and "Joseph," and agreeing on many other topics as well. Joseph had learned many years ago that candor was absolutely essential in the relationship between principals and their professional help.

It was assumed (Joseph would check references, of course) that Phil was proficient in his work. But he would also have to be versatile. There was a wide ranges of problems at the clinic that would require his professional mending, and "more help is not on the way" Joseph assured him. Joseph reiterated that Phil was going to have to shoulder a very heavy load pretty much by himself. They discussed some areas of immediate concern. First Joseph ticked them off as Phil listened intently. Then Phil recounted his experience and expertise in those areas, but reserved any opinions about specific remedies "until I've had a chance to give them a closer look." And finally Joseph got around to compensation, which he secretly felt, was inadequate. Surprisingly, Phil assured him that that wouldn't be a problem.

What Phil knew, and Joseph didn't, was that Phil hadn't been able to get very much work since he had arrived back in the valley last May. He had waited until tax season was over before closing up his practice in Syracuse and moving here. He had done some small auditing jobs an old family friend had given him. And he had done some temporary work through an agency too, but it had been very sporadic. He was going through his savings faster than he had planned, and this job with the clinic was something he needed very badly. And although the compensation was far below what he should be earning, it was at least something. In addition to which, it would provide him with some needed exposure to the business community that might possibly lead to other clients. Besides, it would get him out of the house where his wife and children were driving him crazy!

What Joseph knew, and Phil didn't, was that Joseph planned to work Phil hard. Very hard. And if things turned out right . . . if the clinic regained its footing down the line, and its finances got healthy again, then he would somehow make it up to the accountant. But he didn't tell him that. He didn't want to make promises he couldn't keep.

For the rest of the morning the two men went over what financial records were available. It slowly became clearer to Phil what the enormity and complexity of the problems were. The solutions to these problems were not apparent then, nor would they be any time soon. But they were, at last, being faced by someone with the ability to do something about them.

Arrangements were made for Phil to take some space in a partially used storage room. Joseph promised to upgrade the creature comforts as soon as he could find alternate space. Phil, thinking of the mayhem at home, was grateful for any office space at all.

Thursday - November 21

Planning a staff meeting at the clinic was absolutely futile. There wasn't any time during the day that would allow for any large percentage of the staff to congregate for a meeting. And trying to schedule a meeting before the clinic opened in the morning, or after it closed at night, was met by disbelief, revulsion, or outright rebellion. No, unfortunately, for Joseph laying down the "new rules of the road" would require that he do many, many one-on-one meetings.

He prepared for these meetings by creating a script that he would adhere to religiously. He understood that he had to have everyone at the clinic working in unison. No exceptions. The actual policies and procedures could change over time, and as needed. But everyone's adherence to them needed to be absolute. He came to call this script his "Broken Bones Speech."

He stood across the table from Figgit and a part-time lab assistant. He had cornered them in their lab, and had closed the door behind him. They were his captive audience for the next 10 minutes. His spiel was short and sweet. "I am not going to set any broken bones for as long as I am at this clinic. I am not, ever, going to prescribe one pill. I will never take anyone's blood pressure, and I certainly will never take a urine sample from anyone!" He smiled, hoping to set the listeners at ease. "You, on the other hand, will never write a check for the clinic. You will never have to deal with vendors, insurance providers, or anyone else on the business side. And when you want some supplies . . . some equipment . . . something that needs to be purchased, you'll come to me. Tell me what you need . . . and I'll order it. No exceptions." He cautioned, "You don't have to fill out any paperwork, any forms or requisitions. I'll do that. You just have to tell me. You will never have to order anything. You will never have to accept delivery on anything. Ever." He stopped for a moment here to let that sink in. Then he went on talking in a voice that almost sounded as if he were conspiring with them. "If you have ordered something in the past few days, and it hasn't been delivered, you better tell me, now. Because I'm telling our suppliers that all open orders are canceled, as of today. I'm also telling them that from today on . . . if I don't order it . . . from now on . . . with our order number on it, it will be considered a *personal* purchase on your part, and you'll be responsible for paying for it out of your own pocket!" A pause here by Joseph again allowed his audience to grasp what he was saying. He wanted them to understand and, by some physical movement or statement, acknowledge what he had just said. "I will not accept delivery, nor will the clinic pay for it. I am not going to pass judgment on what you buy. That will remain your responsibility. But how we go about getting it will be mine. And mine alone." He stopped here to let his listeners take it all in. He expected some to object, but very few did. He assured them that the new process would be kept simple. He also assured them that this new process was absolutely essential. And in an attempt to establish his own authority on these kinds of matters, he did not tell anyone that Gus was in total agreement.

Friday - November 22

Ana, with a deep sigh of exasperation, turned to Joseph and asked, "What are you staring at?" She couldn't help notice him across the pantry maneuvering himself around behind her as she prepared her customary lunch of salad and yogurt at the counter near the sink.

"Your hairdo," he said, gesturing with his hands around his head. Her hair was pulled back over her head just like every ponytail you've ever seen. But then came the difference. At the back of the head where it was invariably bunched into a ribbon, or scrunchy, or.... whatever, hers was different. Hers went into her wide ribbon, and never came out! At the far edge of the binding the hair was cut. In essence, it was a "stub ponytail." "I've never ... " he trailed off for a moment, then spoke up again, "It's very unusual, that's all. I don't think I've ever seen it worn like that before." It was almost apologetic the way he said it.

She didn't take it that way. Not at all. "Considering your recent history, I wouldn't think you've seen very many women's hairstyles of any kind lately!" she said flatly. Staring at him, she continued, "You can't possibly consider yourself qualified to judge ... "

"No. No. No," he interrupted her, trying to defuse the situation that she had turned hostile in a heartbeat. "I'm not judging it at all. It's very nice. I'm sure you love it that way. And I wouldn't suggest changing it for a million dollars ...."

Lindsay, who was sitting there, jumped in trying to be a peacemaker. "Really, Dr. Ana, I've always meant to ask you ... I like that style a lot ... and I've never seen it anywhere else either ... where did you come up with it?"

Ana, momentarily surprised by Lindsay's comment, turned to her, and smiled. "It's called a "Belgian Bob." And, you're right. It's one of the reasons I wear it like this. It is unique." She waited a moment, and then added almost sheepishly, "It's also very low maintenance. Takes almost no time to fix up in the morning." She turned slowly back around to face Joseph.

She started to say something. It started with, "Hamilton, you're a ... " and the last word could have been either "fool" or "tool". But she suddenly changed her mind about continuing this conversation, and abruptly left the room. Neither he, nor Lindsay, nor anyone else in the room heard exactly what she said. Joseph had wanted to give his "Broken Bones Speech" to the people who were in the pantry now, but that little confrontation took the air out of his balloon, and he went back to his office.

Although by now most staff at the clinic had heard the speech, he had not been looking forward to giving it to Ana Gustafson. It was she, he suspected, who was the most egregious in wantonly spending the clinic's sparse resources. He had hoped to give Ana the "Broken Bones Speech" under more ideal conditions, but he realized that he was simply stalling. He resolved not to sugarcoat the speech to Ana. She would get the same speech everyone else at the clinic had got. He gritted his teeth, and got up and went to her office.

He found her finishing her lunch. He asked for a few minutes. She refused. He sat down. "It's important, and will only take a minute." It's now or never, he told himself. Not allowing her to interrupt, he launched into the speech. Worried he would rush it, he intentionally slowed it down a little bit. It was over in two minutes, and she never said a word. They sat facing each other in awkward silence for a moment. Joseph had expected her to disagree with it. To argue some point, more likely to argue with the entire policy. He was keeping Gus's full agreement and support at the ready. It wasn't needed.

"Is that all? Are you finished?" she asked. Then, without waiting for an answer, she got up to leave and said, "I've got patients waiting," and was gone.

Saturday - November 23

Roove Hagedorn slipped out of the blustery cold dark evening into the Fireside Inn shortly after 7 PM. He hung his well-worn barn jacket on a hook near the door, but kept his green baseball hat on his head. The hat, with its locally famous, forward-leaning white block letter "B" logo on the front, was as worn and faded as his jacket.

He greeted the three men grouped together at the center of the bar like the old friends that they were. Exchanging some caustic and sarcastic, yet good-hearted, comments with each of the other men there, he settled onto a barstool to watch the hockey game on the large TV at the end of the bar. Catching the bartender's eye and nodding was all that was necessary for Roove to be served his customary long-necked bottle of beer.

Fifteen minutes later Joseph came in alone, and sat down on a barstool a few feet further down the bar from Roove. He ordered his scotch, and settled down to also watch the game. "Hey, you becomin' a regular?" someone asked him. He turned to see Roove's wide grin looking back at him.

Roove introduced him to the other men standing there. Whitey, Magoo and Tully said their hellos and returned to their conversation, which centered on the relative merits of two famous movie policemen – John McClain versus Harry Callahan. Joseph was not as well- versed on the topic as these men were, and paid more attention to the hockey game.

Roove and Joseph talked intermittently, mostly about the hockey game. Joseph found himself, at one point, talking about what one team was doing wrong on its power play. The look on Roove's face told Joseph that he was being too technical, and he shut up. Roove asked him if he had played much hockey, and Joseph had simply said, "Yeah."

As the score of the game on TV became more lopsided, the two men became less interested. Their conversation wandered from the game to other things. Roove jokingly mocked the other three men at the bar, wondering out loud, how late their wives were going to let them stay out tonight. One of them, Joseph thought he was the one called Magoo, came right back at Roove saying "those people in glass houses shouldn't throw stones." As if right on cue, Roove's cell phone buzzed, and a few minutes later Roove bid everyone goodnight, and was gone.

The three other men soon followed, and left Joseph at the bar alone with only the bartender. The now familiar Dudley was kept busy by a large party gathered around two tables, and Joseph sat by himself. Not quite ready to call it a night, Joseph stayed for one more drink. Enjoying it slowly, and not really paying attention to the sports highlight show on TV, he let his mind wander. He remembered Roove's remark earlier about him now being "a regular."

Saturday nights at the Fireside . . . tomorrow morning he would skate again at Lake Custer . . . probably see Podalski, and his kids, again too. There would be some household chores he'd have to do with the rest of his day; and maybe sneak in a couple of hours at the office again while it was so quiet. Then Monday would dawn and the long days at the clinic would follow. That job was anything but routine. But the challenges it presented made every day unique. It was probably too early in the process to really call it a "set routine," but he did like the way it was setting up.

He still had no car, and getting around was a growing problem He realized he would have to solve that sooner rather than later. He had recently discovered a local gym, and had joined up earlier today. He had developed the habit of regular exercise while in prison. While the very long shifts and menial tasks were a drawback to working at the Rec Center at Overbrook, the ready access to the exercise equipment was a definite plus. To get back to that schedule of regular exercise was on his "need-to-do" list.

He acknowledged to himself that he hadn't read a book or magazine in the month since he had left jail, and that was something he had managed to do regularly when he was in prison. There is a lot of "down time" for people in prison, Overbrook and everywhere else. Even his job at the Rec Center presented frequent blocks of time when there was nothing to do. He fortunately rediscovered the enjoyment of reading good books. When he had left school his reading had transitioned into mostly business-related material. When he arrived at Overbrook he brought with him a list of "The One Hundred Greatest Novels." And while he had already read some, he was determined to complete the list while in jail. That hadn't happened, even though he had made tremendous progress. Most of the books weren't available in the skimpy prison library, so he was dependent on receiving them through mail order. That was not an easy project from a jail, where access to catalogs and the Internet was very limited, but he had made the effort, and reaped the reward.

He sipped the last of his scotch and got up to leave while mentally committing to do three things. He was going to get back to work on that novel list, and he was going to resume regular exercising. Where he was going to find the time for these he did not know; his days were pretty full now. But the third thing was not going to be denied. He was going to appreciate every minute of his life more.

Sunday - November 24

Skating with Podalski this morning was, for the first time, more business than pleasure. The Podalski boys were unusually cooperative. They stayed relatively close to the two men as they all skated around the lake at a leisurely pace.

"I'm still lost," Podalski admitted. "Lot of pieces of the puzzle still missing."

"We'll get there," Joseph said with false assurance. "This isn't really a very complex situation. We are basically a service provider that has to tighten up its procedures." They talked about things that could be done, and should be done. They talked about where they saw problems, and in a few instances, where they saw a quick fix. Joseph felt that now that he was there, and in charge, and with Podalski focusing on getting the financial picture organized, the clinic could, if given time, solve its problems and continue providing health care to the community as it had done for years. "The real question is . . . do we have the time?"

Neither man spoke for a long time, with the exception of Podalski occasionally telling his boys not to wander off. After a while he turned to Joseph and said, "I don't think we do. I don't think we have enough time. I can't make an accurate forecast – I don't have enough data – but I think we 'hit the wall' by January 1st.... February 1st, at the latest. If the projections I have made are accurate.... and they shouldn't be; the data they're based on is very incomplete.....the clinic will be absolutely, totally insolvent by March! Checks will be bouncing all over the place. The vendors will know it; they're going to shut us down. And I may as well tell you now: the IRS has to be looking at us. We are tripping financial warning flares all over the place." They were again silent for a time.

"We need some magic, Phil. What can we do? "

"We don't need magic, Joseph, we need money. Again, I'm working with incomplete data, but I think the overriding problem is lack of cash. Simply, it is 'negative cash flow.' And it seems to have been 'negative cash flow' for quite a while. Too long! I don't know how much you can cut expenses, but I think the real problem may lie on the other side of the ledger. It's just that we don't have nearly enough income coming in to stay afloat. The insurance providers are really slow in reimbursement payments. I know the reimbursement formula is pretty much a fixed rate, so we can't hike that. But is there something that can be done to speed up the payments? I can't really help with that, but I think Lindsay is buried by a backlog of payments going back a very long time.

"I'll look into it," was all Joseph said.

Monday - November 25

"We're broke here!" Joseph said to the two Dr. Gustafsons over an early cup of coffee. "We simply don't have enough money coming in to cover the bills." He moved in his chair, and then added, "I don't know how much time we've got to correct the problem."

Ana answered first. "We have more patients now than we ever did. And with your . . . " she hesitated for a moment, choosing her words carefully, "your insistence on getting *everyone* to make out the proper paperwork . . . why aren't we rolling in cash?" Visions of Hamilton waltzing out the door late at night with bundles of the clinic's cash tucked under his arm floated through her mind. She thought that she might share this picture with her father.

"The reimbursement process is time-consuming. The turnaround is always slow . . . and for us it is worse, for a lot of different reasons. We have to find a way to speed it up, and contain expenses, or we're going to have a real problem, probably by year end."

Gus spoke up suddenly. "What do you suggest we do? We can't lay off anybody; we are running this clinic with a skeleton staff now. We have cut expenses everywhere we can. We don't pay most of these people competitive salaries now. Most of these people could make more money someplace else. They stay here out of loyalty. If it goes bankrupt, it will break their hearts." Gus wasn't arguing the point; he was heartsick.

"W. T. Ashton went bankrupt, and didn't close for another 15, or something, years!" Ana said cheerfully.

"Who?" said Joseph.

"W. T. Ashton," answered Gus, "'Cane King of the Union, and Walking Sticks for the World.' That was their slogan. Biggest employer this county ever had. At one time they had about a thousand people working in their plant. Everyone knew their slogan, "Cane King of the Union & Walking Sticks for the World", and it was plastered all over the county for a hundred years. Started out making canes and crutches for Civil War veterans, and there was a big market for that at the time. Used wood from Canada to make their cane . . . of all kinds. Maple, oak, whatever you wanted. Standard or custom-made. They became the largest manufacturer of canes in the US. In the late eighteen hundreds walking sticks became quite the rage, and W. T. Ashton was all over it. Made a fortune for old Willard T. Ashton Sr . . . Willard T. Ashton Jr . . . and Willard T. Ashton III. Unfortunately, for Willard T. Ashton IV, the walking stick fad ran out of gas sometime before the First World War, and by World War II aluminum was replacing wood in canes and crutches. It was a long, slow, spiral down for Old Willard the 4th, his company, and the economy of the entire valley." On that dismal note the meeting broke up with no resolution to their problem in sight.

Tuesday - November 26

An early morning meeting with Lindsay started his day. This was beginning to be an everyday affair. He would gently question her about the number of claims submitted the day before. How much money did these claims represent for the clinic when they were subsequently reimbursed? How many were currently pending? He wanted to know if any private insurance company had paid off claims. Were any companies being particularly stubborn about these claims? And always . . . always . . . he asked if he could help her. The last thing he wanted to happen was for her to feel overwhelmed. Working down the backlog of insurance claims was probably the single most important job facing him.

Her demeanor in these morning meetings seemed, at first, a little like she was overwhelmed. She answered his questions shyly, and asked none herself. She bit her lower lip as she listened to Joseph, and was clearly embarrassed when she couldn't answer one of his questions. His constant assurances and encouragement didn't seem to ease her discomfort. He would have preferred hiring more clerks to help her wage this war against the backlog, but budget restraints made that impossible. The one glimmer of light was that with Podalski now on board working the financials full-time, Joseph had more time to spend on special problems with the backlog.

Joseph's second meeting every day was with Phillip Podalski. The two men would meet in Joseph's office as soon as Podalski arrived each day. It was more often than not quite brief, as Podalski would update Joseph about what had been done yesterday, and what would be done today.

The financial agreement Joseph had made with Podalski was, fortunately, not based on the number of hours spent working. Outside accountants, much like lawyers, frequently work on an hourly fee schedule. Because Podalski had virtually no other clients, it just seemed like he worked at the clinic full-time. The clinic couldn't possibly afford Podalski based on the number of hours he was putting in. Joseph had secured the services of the accountant with a flat fee "for straightening out the books, and completing an internal audit."

Joseph had come to like the CPA from the start, both personally and professionally. As a matter of fact, he felt a little guilty for getting him so cheaply. But the well-being of the clinic was the single most important priority, and Joseph fully realized that clinic couldn't afford to pay him what he was worth.

Joseph would spend the rest of the day watching over everything else. There were always past due bills to pay, phone calls to take, or make. He would check with Olney every day to be sure that the deliveries were handled properly. Supplies needed to be obtained and distributed. The building and all the machines and equipment in it had to be kept in working order. And that required something just short of magic, because so much of it was old and overused. Work schedules for the full- and part-time staff were constantly being juggled. And based on those schedules, payroll had to be created. And without fail, he delivered his "Broken Bones Speech' again and again to anyone who would stand still long enough to hear it. It soon became popular for whomever was getting the "speech" to respond quickly, "Yeah, I know . . . I know! If I order it, I have to pay for it!"

Wednesday - November 27

"If it were for us it would have an Order Number. What's the Order Number?" Joseph asked the deliveryman.

The man looked at Joseph as if he had asked him to explain quantum physics. "I don't know about any 'Order Number'," he finally said. "My boss says to bring this stuff over to the Wackentute Clinic . . . give 'em the yellow copy . . . have 'em sign the green copy, and bring it back. That's what I know. I don't know nothin' about no 'Order Number'." The man stood in the doorway to the delivery area. Olney stood behind Joseph, quietly proud that he had followed Joseph's instructions perfectly. "Come and get me if anybody tries to deliver anything to the clinic," Joseph had told him....and he did. If the "Broken Bones Speech" was to have any meaning, Joseph decided, he would have to take the responsibility – and time – to personally sign in every package delivered to the clinic, at least for the time being.

Not quite a half hour after the driver had been turned away, Joseph got the call he knew was coming. "Who the hell are you, and why you sendin' the order back?" said a very gruff voice. Joseph managed to get the introductions done between him and the irate voice on the phone before it continued, "I sent over the stuff you asked for . . . and now you send it back? What the hell's goin' on?"

"I didn't order it. If I had, it would have an Order Number on it. It has no number, so I didn't order it." Joseph repeated. "I didn't take it in because, I guess, someone else did order it. I don't know who that is. But it wasn't this clinic."

"Bullshit," was what the voice said. "It was your clinic, all right. Somebody there called up and ordered this stuff, and I sent it over. Now sign the damn delivery sheet, and send back my driver."

This was going nowhere, and Joseph had better things to do, so he said, "The Clinic didn't order this. It has no Order Number . . . it isn't ours. Deliver it to whomever ordered it," and hung up. Before returning to his work he found Olney and complimented him on how well he had done his job. Olney beamed.

Two hours later, a very angry Dr. Ana cornered Joseph in the hallway. "You sent back the antiseptic I ordered? Are you out of your mind? You think I just casually wanted to get some? We use that every day! We need it....EVERY DAY! If we don't have any, we can't treat patients! We would have to . . . " she paused for a moment to catch her breath.

Joseph grabbed his chance to talk. "We have plenty on hand. Mena said we may use as much as five gallons a week. We have ten gallons in the supply room now. I can have another twenty gallons here in two hours." She stood in front of him with her mouth wide open. He didn't want her to start talking again so he went on, "You know, you really shouldn't worry about things like this. You have much more important things to worry about. We have this covered." He relented, and stopped talking.

She started to say something, and then stopped. She then started again, but never said a word. She gestured with a wave of her hand, paused, and then her eyes brightened, "Sure, that's just antiseptic, but what if it was something you don't know anything about? Medicines or surgical supplies? You think we can depend on you to know what we need, and when we need it? This might be just an ordinary business to you, but the well-being of out-patients is a lot more important than your little requisitions and accounting pads." She shivered, she was so sure she had made her point.

"You are so right," he said. She flinched. "The well-being of the patients this clinic treats today is the most important thing that happens here." He let that hang in the air for a moment, then continued, "And, also, the well-being of the patients that will be in here tomorrow. And next week . . . and next month! And if we don't take care to do this right we are jeopardizing that care. And no one, least of all you, would want that. And if we all do what we do best, we can guarantee that care." He nodded with certainty to her.

She suddenly noticed that several people were standing around listening to the conversation. She looked back at Joseph, and said in a much quieter voice, "Harry wants me to come pick it up! Says I have to take it." She tilted her head to one side.

"Tell him 'No,' if you want to call him. And tell him I said you are not allowed to accept delivery. If he has a problem, or starts to give you an argument, tell him to call me. He knows the number." Joseph turned around and started to smile as he walked away.

Thursday - November 28 (Thanksgiving)

The clinic was closed today. Joseph didn't arrive until 8:30 AM. He made coffee, sharpened some pencils, stacked some files on his desk, and downloaded some programs onto his new laptop. After he logged onto several shared sites he began to work in earnest. It's amazing what can be accomplished when there are no interruptions, no ringing phones. The first and only break he took that day was at 1:30. Noticing the time, he called a local pizza shop and had a sandwich delivered. They weren't very busy.

He could have had a holiday dinner with the Podalski family. And several other people had asked over the preceding week if he had "Thanksgiving plans," but Joseph had politely declined, saying vaguely he "had other plans." These "plans" kept him at the clinic until 10:30 that night. He could have stayed later but he wanted to eat some dinner and then go home to bed. He wanted to be fresh tomorrow morning when he would be back at the clinic by 7 AM.

One of the day's accomplishments was a balanced Clinic checkbook, now going back three months. He had also spent several hours poring over medical insurance reimbursement policy and procedures, both private and New York State. He was determined that the clinic would get its money.

Friday November 29

Historically the day after Thanksgiving was a light day for the clinic. Mena said she thought that people were too busy thinking about the onset of the holidays, and shopping, to get sick. In any case, the walk-in traffic proved to be light. The number of patients that came through the doors turned out to be less than half the normal day's count. The medical staff spent a good portion of the day standing around chatting. That was not the case for Lindsay, Podalski, and Joseph.

While Podalski basically worked alone, dissecting data that Joseph had loaded on his laptop, and refining it, Joseph and Lindsay huddled over the stacks of unreimbursed claim forms that needed to be cleared. Mostly individually, but occasionally jointly, they attacked one folder after another.

Completing forms, solving problems, teaching each other what they didn't know, they worked the piles down.

The office of the New York State Insurance Office also considered this day a "half holiday", and had a skeleton crew working. Joseph and Lindsay lobbed calls into them from early morning until shortly after three in the afternoon. That's when the calls stopped getting picked up, and they assumed the state workers had sneaked out early for the day.

It would have been better, of course, if they had stayed for the full day but a great deal had been accomplished anyway. Shortcuts had been taught, questions answered, explanations offered, and most of all, a relationship among several staffers and Lindsay had been established. She would use that relationship to the clinic's great advantage.

Saturday - November 30

Joseph arrived at the Fireside Inn well past 10 o'clock. It was late, and he was tired. He had had a very long day. The medical staff had had another light day, and Joseph had insisted Lindsay and Podalski leave at noon. He had told them he would be leaving himself shortly thereafter. He had half-believed it when he said it too. But when he started to "finish up," one thing popped up after another, and before he realized it it was past dinnertime. Giving himself a deadline, he worked another couple of hours before he almost fell asleep at his desk. He packed up, and left.

He was so tired it even occurred to him to skip his usual Saturday night diversion but, after thinking it over, he believed he had really earned it this week. When he arrived, he was surprised that it was so empty. He thought that because it was a holiday weekend that it would draw an even larger crowd. But, it wasn't, and it really didn't matter; he just wanted to have a drink before going home to bed.

Roove wasn't there, but Joseph thought it was later than usual, and Roove had probably left earlier to head over to his girlfriend's house. Dudley corrected him when he mentioned that, and said, "No, he wasn't in tonight. Maybe later, but he had a gig tonight over at the Raccoon Lodge."

"A gig?" asked Joseph.

"Yeah, he's playing for some party that rented the hall out tonight."

Joseph asked, "That's what he does for a living?" For no reason Joseph could think of, that just seemed very odd.

"No, not a full-time musician," corrected Dudley, "He just plays every so often when someone needs a guitar player." Dudley thought for a minute and then added, "You know, he ain't all that bad . . . "

Joseph jumped in and added, "But he's no Nicky Pasternak, right?" He said it, but he had no idea what in the world that meant.

Dudley agreed immediately, "Got that right! Four Fingers could do it all. And with just four fingers too!" He went on to say, "But he ain't bad. Plays Simon and Garfunkel stuff. Plays some Jimmy Buffet, RPM, Willie Nelson. . . you know, classic stuff."

"What does he do for a living?" Joseph asked.

"Nothin," Dudley said, "He's retired, kinda. On disability from the state. Total, 100% disability. Just cashes his check every first of every month. But don't tell him I told you; he don't like to discuss it."

"Why not?"

"Seems he got the disability under questionable circumstances, if you know what I mean. He ain't allowed to discuss it. Part of the agreement."

Joseph gave him a puzzled look. "What do you mean?" Joseph wanted to know. Things like gossip, and "telling tales out of school" had never been something Joseph had ever been interested in, but there was something intriguing about this fellow Roove.

"Well, like I said, don't tell him I told you, but he got this sweet deal from the state."

Dudley went on to tell Joseph that Roove hadn't done much after high school. He had bounced around from one job to another without really latching on to anything. Oh sure, he continued to play his guitar here and there, but nothing that would pay the bills on a regular basis. "But then, somewhere along the line," Dudley said, "he put in an application to be a NYS Park Ranger. It wasn't exactly the kind of job most of his friends thought he would want, but that was just like him. He's a tough one to figure out. Yeah," Dudley paused for a minute, "He always said he felt better working outdoors, and he figured that being a Park Ranger would have a lot more to do with animals than people; and that suited him just fine. It didn't exactly work out that way, though."

"He stuck it out for awhile, which kinda surprised everyone," explained Dudley. "But then, a few years ago, he was assigned to be part of the security detachment at the Annual Peace and Love Concert Festival at Garfield State Park." At this point Dudley leaned over the bar, and spoke in a hushed tone, "Right in the middle of 'Mellow Yellow' - you know that song, by Donovan, I think – right in the middle of it, this brawl breaks out right near where Roove is standing. There's these two women wailing the hell out of each other! Roove tried to ignore it, I'll bet, but they were causing quite a commotion. Now, he told me once he couldn't see who was winning, but in a situation like that, he thought it best to separate them by getting the bigger woman under control." Dudley took a breath, and shook his head. "Said he got them apart, and was trying to get the big woman turned in the other direction. Well, in hindsight, the big one was not the one he should have been concerned about. Said all he could hear her saying was 'Watch it! Watch it!' He wondered 'Watch what'? Seems the other woman, the little one, had gone and got herself a metal folding chair, and just then proceeded to whack Roove, who was facing the other way, with it." Dudley grimaced for a moment at the thought, and then he continued. "Sent Roove over a bench, and down a bunch of cement steps. Spent two weeks in the hospital in traction. Said he could hear a phone ringing for three days after she hit him."

Joseph started to smile, but caught himself. That's not funny, he told himself. "Sounds like he took quite a shot!"

"Oh, he was hurt all right. He wanted to press charges, of course. And sue, too! You better believe he wanted to sue. But then these guys come into his room a day later, and say they're lawyers for the woman 'who accidentally pushed him'. Roove told them to go to hell. He was suing. It turns out these guys not only want Roove to not press charges; but to forget about the lawsuit too. Now get this," Dudley winked, "This chair-swinging wild woman is the wife of some big shot politician. Not only that, it seems the fight starts because Mrs. Politician here– whoever she was, Roove ain't allowed to say – was high as a kite on who-knows-what? This banshee was ballistic, according to Roove. It's not normal to be that hostile when you're high on some *Jamaican joy-stick*, you know. That lady was on jet fuel." Dudley nodded knowingly. "And get this . . . her date for the evening turned out not to be her husband . . . and not 21 years old, either. The arrest report had it all down." Dudley was telling the story with delighted enthusiasm now. "Seems that Mr. and Mrs. Politician just don't want this to go to court, or get into the newspapers, or anywhere else. They are determined this little episode don't ever see the light of day." Dudley stepped back from the edge of the bar, and smiling broadly said, "So they came up with a deal." He nodded his head twice, and finished the story by saying, "And that's why Roove was retired on 100% disability."

"That's amazing," was all Joseph could say.

"So," Dudley said smiling, "The only thing he has to do now is cash his check on the first of the month ... every month ... for the rest of his life. Oh, he has coupla things going on the side. He's got that guitar thing going. He tends bar every now and again. And if you ever need to get a bet down, I think he can handle that for you, too. He keeps himself occupied, I guess, but not real busy. It just isn't his way."

Dudley added one more thing before turning around to take care of some customers at the other end of the bar. "Remember, don't tell him I told you all this. It's supposed to be a secret."

Sunday - December 1

The regular Sunday morning skate with Podalski was short. The weather had turned cold again.... very cold, and the sky was an ominous, dark gray.

And with a very strong wind blowing across the wide open lake it was difficult for skaters to even maintain their balance. This was especially true for Podalski's youngest child. He kept trying to skate, and the wind kept trying to knock him over. The wind was winning.

Between rescue attempts by Podalski to keep his son upright, he reiterated what he had been saying all along. "I don't know if the checks we wrote last week will clear. I'll go to the bank first thing tomorrow morning, and see what I can do," he said sadly to Joseph.

Joseph was well aware how thin their margin for error was. "I can't ask anyone not to cash their paycheck." Shaking his head, he took a few more strides, and Podalski easily kept up alongside. "I think we are going to be okay for the next few days. I think we're good until Friday."

"How do you figure that? I'm pretty sure . . . I'm damn sure we're overdrawn."

"No," Joseph said, a small smile appearing on his face. "The check we made out to Lucci Medical? The one for thirty plus thousand dollars?" Podalski nodded. "I never signed it. And I had Lindsay drop it in a mail box in Port Newhampton Saturday night. They won't get it until Tuesday, at the earliest. If they don't notice it, and deposit it; it'll be a few days before the bank shoots it back to them. If I can duck them for a day or two, we're good till Friday . . . maybe the whole weekend."

"That's dishonest," the CPA said nodding, "But, damn, it does buy us a few days." On that very dubious cheerful note, Podalski collected his frozen children, and headed home. He dropped Joseph off at the Fireside Inn "to take care of some personal business." From there, an hour later, Joseph went back to the clinic to work on the backlog of claim forms.

Monday - December 2

One would expect that people coming back to work from a long holiday weekend would be calm, cool, and collected. At least at first they should be, anyhow. The first few people back to work at the clinic were just starting to get themselves back into the swing of things when Dr. Ana came through the back door like a cold blast of Arctic wind. The slammed door behind her put everyone on notice she was on the warpath. Storming into the pantry, she demanded to know "who-in-hell" was parked in her space out back. Joseph, who was making up the first pot of coffee on the machine, glanced in her direction, and quietly asked, "Are the spots out there reserved?" He thought she might be kidding, until he saw the look on her face. "There are no signs," he said, as if apologizing.

That answer, was to her, so preposterous that she couldn't come up with a response, and was momentarily speechless. Mena, who was absolutely immune to the venom that Ana possessed in unlimited supply, jumped in and said, "There are no reserved spots out there that I know of . . . it's first come – first served."

Ana totally ignored what Mena said, and spoke directly to Joseph. "The spots closest to the back door are reserved for Physicians. Always have been!" she declared. "Whose red minivan is that?" she wanted to know.

Mena again spoke up, "Good Lord! Is that right? I've been parking in the closest spot to the door for years. Why didn't you ever say anything?" Mena hid a smile as she walked out of the pantry. Joseph took his coffee, and followed her out the door. He had no intention of identifying his new car. Ana stood there, staring at the back wall, and seethed.

On the first Monday of every month, for the past several years, Joseph received a phone call from two old friends back in Brooklyn, New York. They had been, at first, been business partners; then tenants; then finally, friends. He had looked forward to their call every month, especially when he was in Overbrook. They had been one of his few links to the outside world while he served his sentence. They had been his friends before he went to jail and, and unlike all too many others, had remained his friends afterward. And there weren't many of those around after his legal troubles started.

These monthly calls would last anywhere from 10 to 30 minutes, and always lifted his spirits. They shared small daily triumphs, and also some tales of woe. He always looked forward to them. The call he had received last month had come during his first week at the clinic. It had come during those first few hectic days, and had been cut short due to the chaos. This one lasted a little longer and, as always, made him feel better.

After that call, Joseph checked with Lindsay to see if she had heard anything from the State Insurance Department. It had only been a few days since he and Lindsay had begun cutting into the backlog of claims, and he didn't really think they would begin getting their money so soon. But he wanted to be optimistic because he knew that this revenue was so badly needed.

Several hours later Joseph walked out of his office to get a cup of coffee. He was thinking about how to consolidate the many vendors the clinic dealt with into a more manageable number. Some of them had been supplying the clinic for many years. And some had been very generous in matters of terms and late payments. But it just made sense to reduce the number. And he fully realized that doing that would ruffle some feathers. It was probable that many of them had long and warm personal relationships with Gus, as well as with Ana and Mena. This would require some delicate diplomacy.

In the middle of his reverie he noticed that the noise level around him was unusually loud. Turning his attention to the room he saw several of the staff talking excitedly over one another. Mena was gesturing to a patient with her hands waving in the air. The patient, with bloodshot eyes, red nose, and hacking cough, was trying to catch his breath. Lindsay was flushed, and had her hands curled into fists, and up at her mouth. He thought she was about to shout. She glanced over at Joseph and said something he couldn't hear.

For a moment, Joseph couldn't tell what the excitement was about. He couldn't tell if it was good or bad news. Movement to the side caught his eye, and he turned to see Gus and Ana coming out of his office with a big man in a business suit.

"Is it true, Mayor?" Mena said to the large man with Gus. "After all these years, is it true?" she said, now stepping in front of Gus.

It was Gus who answered. "According to the Mayor here, they have a pretty good case."

"Oh my God," said Mena, "If we have to give that trophy to Port Newhampton it would break my heart. It would break everyone's heart. I couldn't bear to look at that park again if it wasn't there." Joseph thought she was going to cry. Then she made a face and asked, "What in God's name will happen to the plaque if we give up the trophy? We'll have to throw it away!"

"Goddamn them," rasped the man standing there in a hospital gown. Suddenly everyone in the room began talking again, except Joseph. A part-time nurse was speaking to a salesman. Olney seemed to be arguing with Ana. The man referred to as "Mayor" was trying to tell Gus something, but he couldn't get Gus's attention. The sound level rose until people in the waiting room were all lined up at Lindsay's desk, and others were pushing through the door into the treatment area.

It took 10 minutes to get some order restored. The staff went back to work, as patients returned to the treatment rooms they had wandered out of when the ruckus began. People in the waiting room returned to their seats, but not to the magazines they had been reading before. They spoke with one another in excited voices. Lindsay sat at her desk staring at her screen. Joseph grabbed a now refocused Mena by the arm, and asked what that had been all about.

She shook her head sadly, and said, "The Blades want us to forfeit the Geetha Trophy."

PART TWO

"The credit belongs to the man who is actually in the arena, whose face is marred by dust and sweat and blood; who strives valiantly; who knows the great enthusiasms, the great devotions, and spends himself in a worthy cause; and who, knows in the end the triumph of high achievement; and who, at the worst, if he fails, at least fails while daring greatly."

Theodore Roosevelt

"But need we risk our precious purckles!"

A. Ronald (Superfly) Jardine DDS

Chapter Four

Inclement weather was rarely a factor in the volume of traffic through the front door of the Wackentute Clinic. Today's weather, much like yesterday's, was cold, windy and overcast, yet the climate in the clinic was balmy compared to yesterday's storm clouds. Upon arrival this morning Joseph had made sure not to park in any of the spots nearest the back door. Saving a few extra steps hardly seemed worth the grief that Ana so freely dispensed. And with the reclamation of her parking place restored, Ana breezed into the clinic this morning with a nice word and a smile for everyone. Joseph quietly felt everyone there owed him a word of thanks for his gesture!

It would not be her pleasant demeanor, however, that would be the central topic of discussion for the staff today. Most of the buzz around the office among the staff, and patients as well, centered on the proposed forfeiture of something called "the Geetha trophy."

It did not, however, consume Joseph. Joseph was again splitting his time between handling calls from irate suppliers and making irate calls himself to the slow paying insurance companies. He asked Lindsay several times about the status of the claims they both had worked on and submitted over the long weekend. The total represented only a small portion of what was actually owed to the clinic, but it would be a welcome respite to the cash flow problem they were dealing with. Lindsay told him that the reimbursements in the past were never returned within days. She went on to tell him that it usually took several weeks before they would be paid. That answer, which he really already knew, just wasn't acceptable. He worried about this all morning as he worked on other problems.

Moving into the staff pantry at lunchtime he was not surprised to find the staff members there discussing . . . again . . . "Geetha." Preoccupied with problems of his own, he hardly listened to the lively conversation going on about their prized "trophy."

"My Dad used to take me to games when I was little," said Lindsay. "Those were better memories than the Christmases, or the birthday parties, or anything."

"I met my husband because of Geetha," Mena suddenly said. Most people in the room expressed some surprise, and someone asked her to explain. She went on, "Yes, I was working in the ER at County right out of Nursing School. I was doing weekends, and one Sunday he comes in with a fractured arm! He was moaning and groaning. Seems he had this awful collision, and wound up going over the boards. He played for the Blue Canes, a long, long time ago. Still has his sweater though," she smiled brightly. "Doesn't fit him anymore," she assured everyone, "Not by 50 pounds, I bet!" she laughed.

The conversation went all over the place as various people recounted various tales about this "Geetha." People who were "players" were referred to, and after each comment some people laughed, while others just shook their heads. Names and references meant nothing to Joseph, but the enthusiasm that these people had for their topic intrigued him. Someone would mention a name, and others would respond with laughs or derision. After Mena said, "Pastor Pittou," several people in unison said, "The Club!" A technician, who happened to be working at the clinic that day on some broken equipment for Figgit, told everyone, "And don't forget 'The Lump on the Stump'!"

Everyone laughed at that. Other names were thrown around which brought up just as much laughter. None of these apparent nicknames, again, meant anything to Joseph.

Then the technician said, "Hey, how about Superfly? Can't leave out that mouth!" The people in the room tried not to laugh, but couldn't help it. They took quick peeks in Ana's direction, and tried to hide their smiles.

"Oh, be nice," she said, waving at them. "He can't help it. And besides, he hardly does it at all. You're all being so mean." She had a very small smile on her face, and shook her head disapprovingly at them all.

"He did it all the time," Olney said. "Every time he was on the ice, he'd be yelling all that mumbo-jumbo all over the place."

"Olney!" Ana cautioned him, "Don't exaggerate." People all around the room looked up at Ana, and then turned away, not wanting to risk eye contact. "You make it sound much worse than it was," she continued, but a little more seriously now.

"He did too," Olney argued, "Used to say that weird stuff all the time. Didn't matter if he was winning or losing. Even during time-outs, I heard him. We all did." Olney looked around at all the other faces looking for confirmation. But no one said a word. Ana focused solely on Olney.

"No, he didn't," she insisted, "Only when he is highly agitated . . . " she paused, "highly stressed . . . highly emotional . . . " she added, and then paused, searching for the right words, " . . . you know . . . highly . . . physical . . . *intense* . . . moments." She shook her head trying to say it right, "Only then . . . does he . . . sometimes . . . " her voice suddenly trailed off. Without Ana's moving her head, her eyes scanned the room. Everyone was looking at her, smirking. She tried to say something about getting back to her patients, but her voice cracked. She was gone in an instant. Two seconds after she left the room, it erupted in laughter.

As Mena left the room she stopped next to Joseph, and said, "She and Superfly used to be quite an item." She winked, laughed again, and went back to work.

Wednesday - December 4

There was no word from the State again today, and Joseph continued hounding Lindsay with questions she couldn't possibly answer about where their reimbursement was. Podalski advised him that he didn't know where the money was either, and perhaps Joseph should stop asking him. Joseph asked him again late in the afternoon. It got to the point where some staff at the clinic started purposely avoiding Joseph.

As fixated on the reimbursements as Joseph was, it seemed that the rest of the staff was fixated on the town meeting scheduled that night concerning Geetha. A few of the staff volunteered to close up the clinic that night which allowed Gus, Ana and Olney to leave a little early to attend that meeting. Aware, as was everyone in the clinic, of Joseph's fixation on "reimbursements," Gus suggested he join them to get his mind off that problem for a while. "It'll do you good to go and see a little bit about what makes this valley tick."

When they arrived at the town hall there was already a crowd of people sitting around. Mayor Mooney soon called the meeting to order. "I guess I'll run this meeting," he said smiling, "Not as the mayor, but as you all might remember, as the last captain of the Bombers." He had been the captain of the Newcomb Bombers Geetha team during the last season they had played, eight years ago. "As many of you already know, Port Newhampton wants us to give up the Geetha . . . wants us to forfeit the trophy . . . or more exactly give *them* the Geetha." There was an immediate, and very vocal, reaction by almost everyone in the hall.

"It's ours!"

"Tell 'em to go screw themselves"

"What the hell for?"

"B.S.! We won it!"

"All right, everyone calm down a minute and let me explain." After a minute or two, the mayor continued. "There seems to be some question about whether we won it fair and square." There were some voices raised again, but Mooney talked over them and regained the room's attention. "They say we used a *ringer*." And once again there were objections raised, and questions asked, but Mayor Mooney plowed on. "The rules of the league were always clear that you had to be a resident of the town you played for. And it seems we had a guy who wasn't a resident....a *legal* resident, anyway. Folks from Port Newhampton came to my office today, and showed me some proof that kinda makes me think they're right." That set off a commotion that Mooney didn't even try to stop. He let it run its course for a minute or two as many people wanted to know who it was they were talking about. Who was the "ringer"? Mooney held up his hands for silence, and then simply said, "Pistol." Disbelief and defiance were shouted from everywhere.

A loud voice in the back said that that was impossible, and that he had gone through school with "Pistol." He stood up and said, "Hey, I've known Pistol since the third grade. We lived a half a block away from each other growing up." Joseph, and several others, turned around to look at the man who was speaking. Joseph recognized him immediately. It was the guy he had met at the bar, Roove.

Moonie raised his hands again to silence the crowd and continued, "He moved to Newcomb when he was seven or eight . . . and had come from Maine, his mother told people. But the truth was he wasn't born in Maine either. He and his Mom were illegal aliens."

"Goddamn," whispered Olney. "Pistol's Mexican?" he asked in disbelief.

"Pistol and his Mom, were from somewhere in Canada," Moonie said, "Snuck into the country apparently . . . I don't know why. She had some relatives in Little Sittlerville. Stayed there for a year or so, and then moved here, with little Pistol." The room was quiet for a minute as people pondered this revelation, and then someone asked how they had found this out. "Think Bilge told them," said Moonie flatly. That set off another round of shouted questions and objections.

"It figures she'd rat him out," said Roove from the back of the room again. Joseph and many others turned around to look at him. The scruffy man in the well-worn jacket and green hat was leaning against the wall. He took a drink out of something he held inside a brown paper bag. "I shudda seen that coming," he said, almost sadly.

"Are you drinking beer?" asked the mayor. "Christ almighty, Roove, this is the Municipal Building! You can't have an open container of alcohol in here. Get rid of that!" said the clearly exasperated Mayor Mooney.

Roove looked around and saw Deputy Sheriff McGuire stand up and begin to take notice of him. Roove raised the bag to his mouth and finished whatever was in there. "It's empty. Okay?" he said tossing the bag and its contents into a trash can. Moonie asked him what he had meant by "that figures." "Well, I talked with Pistol on the phone a couple a months ago, and he told me things hadn't gone too smooth on that trip he took with Bilge. Said they never made it to California. Matter of fact, he said they split up before they even reached the Mississippi River."

The back story Joseph would learn later was that Pistol and Bilge had dated off and on for most of last year, and had then decided to head off to California right after the New Year.

"You spoke to Pistol? On the phone? How is he?" several people asked.

"Where is he?" someone added.

"Yeah, well, he called me from California one night last May....or maybe it was June?"

"Where in California?" asked Mayor Mooney.

"Said he was calling from Santa . . . *somewhere* . . . maybe Santa Rosita? I don't remember." Roove shrugged, paused for a moment, and then continued, "In fact, he said he was calling from the Santa . . . *somewhere?* . . . Police Station! He didn't say what he was doing there; but he wasn't under arrest. Just answering some questions. He was down there at that station 'cause they wanted to talk to him about some stuff. And this cop that was talking to him got all pissed off about somethin', and just got up and left him sitting at this desk . . . all by himself. So Pistol got bored just sitting there, and decided to pass the time making some calls on the phone that was on the desk there. He said he remembered my number, so he called me. We passed some time telling some old stories, and then I asked about 'Bilge." That's when he told me the trip with Bilge was downhill from the very start. They weren't out of Wackentute an hour and she was bitchin' and moanin' about being thirsty . . . and hungry . . . And bugs hittin' her in the face and hair and blah, blah, blah. So he says to her, 'With all yer yappin', its amazin' yer don't have none in yer mouth.' Well, not surprisin' that don't sit well with her; as she ain't one for CON-structive criticism. So she gets real testy, and starts givin' Pistol all kinds of attitude. She was goin' on and on, Pistol says, and then wantin' to stop every half hour for a burger . . . or more exactly for a cheeseburger . . . actually what he said she wanted was a double cheeseburger, and some fries, and a milkshake, and on, and on, and on . . . and he, well, he starts *reconsidering* this whole idea of the trip out west with her. By the time they reach Indiana, Pistol says he knew it wasn't going to work. Besides, he thinks with both of them and all their gear tied up on the back of the bike, he's sorta worryin' about bendin' the frame!" A few people around the room laughed at that, but Roove continued. "He knew somethin's gotta go. And he says he knows she ain't gonna go easy. So he pulls off the highway, and he tells her he's got to re-tie their gear on the back; which is loose he says. He gets off, but leaves the bike runnin'. She gets off. He unties her bag and puts it down. Then he spins around and lets go with a right hand that oughta settle things quick."

There wasn't another sound as most people in the room suddenly sat up straight, and leaned toward Roove. He had their attention. "Thought he was gonna nail her good," Roove continued, "Dead square on the jaw. But, damn, you all know her," he said to his hushed audience, "she's as quick as a cat. He gets a piece, but it was a glancing shot Pistol said. Knocks her off balance, and she staggers, but she don't go down." Joseph stared at Roove in the back of the room. Had he just heard that right, he wondered?

Roove went on, "He knows he's only got a second or two before she gets her feet underneath her, and comes on back at him, so he jumps on the bike and heads off down the street heading back toward the entrance ramp of the highway. Now if you know Pistol's big-ass bike you know that thing can move once it gets goin'. But it does take some time to get up some speed." Joseph took quick glances to his left and right, trying to confirm what he thought he had just heard. Had this "Pistol" guy just punched his girlfriend? People around him sat listening intently to Roove's tale.

"By the time Pistol reaches the corner he's gainin' speed, but he can hear her footsteps and growling comin' up behind him at a pretty good clip." Roove paused here for a second as the people in the room stared at him. They may have been looking at him, but their mind's eye could only see Bilge at a full gallop catching up to Pistol's dash for survival. "He told me that he could tell just from the sounds she was making that she was bent on mayhem. And he figures she probably woulda caught him . . . if he'd a stopped for that traffic light. Which, considerin' the circumstances he, of course, did not. When he had gone on through he heard screechin' brakes behind him and figures she didn't stop for the light either. He didn't turn around to look though. Hell, he didn't turn around to look, he said, till he was in Missouri. Didn't stop the bike until he was in Kansas."

The room remained quiet when Roove stopped talking. Everyone in the room, with the exception of Joseph, knew Pistol. And they all knew Bilge, too. Joseph wondered what kind of man Pistol was, that he would hit and then abandon this woman, his supposed "girlfriend?" Everyone else in the room knew Pistol as a bit of a rebel, a man who played by his own rules, and who liked to live on the edge. But he wasn't a fool.

Bilge, on the other hand, wouldn't have expected or wanted their sympathy. Her strong sense of self-reliance and independence would not allow her a moment of self-pity for her dilemma of being assaulted by her boyfriend and deserted hundreds of miles from home. She had only wanted two things at that particular moment as she watched Pistol roar off down the highway. She wanted to get her hands around Pistol's neck. And she would have liked a cold beer too. Other than that, she was perfectly willing to get on with her life.

There is an old saw that states, "To a person with only a hammer, every problem is a nail." Bilge lived her life with a hammer in both hands. Anyone who crossed Bilge would suffer inevitable consequences. She did not suffer fools, or their transgressions, kindly. Anyone who confronted her had better be prepared for the onslaught that would surely come. She was headstrong. She was tough. And she did not tolerate disagreement easily. In her athletic past she was known to be the roughest, toughest, fiercest competitor in Wackentute High School history. Male or female! Most people in the room didn't think Pistol hitting her with his fist wasn't ungentlemanly; they thought it just plain foolish. Hitting her with anything smaller than a Chevrolet was just inviting retaliation. The people in the room, knowing Bilge, just sat shaking their head in silence.

After a moment Moonie spoke up. "Let's get back to business. Okay? Now we know how they found out . . . Pistol musta told Bilge about it when they were together, and I guess Bilge told the Blades when she got back. 'Hell hath no fury like a woman scorned.' And that would go double where Bilge is concerned" People all around the room nodded silently in agreement.

"Now that she's hooked up with Caveman, you had to figure that information would get passed on sooner or later," said Roove.

"What do you mean 'hooked up with Caveman'? Is she back here in the valley? With Caveman?" someone asked.

"Yeah, she's tending bar down in Port Newhampton. At Caveman's place, The Cozy Cockfight. It's that biker bar down on Water Street," said Roove.

"Biker Bar! Bullshit! That's a topless bar!" objected Evelyn Harding, sitting in the second row. Her background as a grammar school teacher and wife of an insurance salesman shouldn't have qualified her as an arbiter of what constitutes the difference between the two types of bar. But no one brought that up. No one said anything. The picture of Bilge working in a topless bar was in everyone's mind. And it wasn't a pretty picture. The look on many people's faces was similar to the one you would have when you see somebody sneeze on someone else's eyeglasses.

"It's a biker bar," reasserted Roove, "place is always filled with those guys. And besides, Bilge ain't dancin' topless . . . she's workin' the bar . . . fully dressed." There was a moment's hesitation, then, "Well, mostly dressed." A sigh of relief went around the room.

"Place is always filled with topless dancers too," argued Harding. "It's a topless bar!"

"Place only got two . . . maybe three dancers at any one time," argued back Roove.

"Okay, okay," said Moonie, "let's get back to Geetha. What are we going to do about the trophy?" Several voices offered several ideas. Conversations sprang up all around the room. It seemed everyone had an idea.

"Give it back to them. The thing is a public eyesore," whispered Ana. Joseph looked around in amazement and wondered what a "Geetha" was. And what was a "Geetha trophy"?

After an hour of discussion, arguments, interruptions, shouting and the complete abandonment of Robert's Rules of Order, Gus suddenly had the floor and called for order. People settled down to hear him out. "I think, and that's depends on Mayor Mooney here being convinced their evidence is valid, I think that we have to . . . ' he raised his hands to keep the crowd at bay, "give it up. BUT . . . " he shouted, "but they don't get it either! Here's what I propose we do." The room grew quiet. "We have another – one time only – tournament. Winner takes the trophy!" The room was silent as people around the room considered the possibility. "We invite all the teams from the league to play in one final round robin tournament. AND," he shouted, and then repeated, "And only players who played back then; the *ones that stepped over the boards then* [using a phrase familiar to Geetha fans to describe players] can play in this tourney. We don't want a bunch of young studs from The Cozy Cockfight elbowing their way into the tourney, ruining the tradition, and stealing the trophy." There was some murmuring in the room, and then it got louder.

Among the many voices that began to fly around within Joseph's hearing, Ana's voice was the loudest. She was shouting at her father. "You are NOT playing that damn game again. You've got arthritic knees, your back isn't right. Hell, you've had a hip replacement!" Her father was clearly amused.

"I know, I know," he said to her softly. She settled back into her seat. Conversations continued around the room. People turned this way and that way, making comments to people close by, and to people across the room. Once again Mayor Mooney took the floor and called for order.

"I like the idea, but I don't think we have enough Bombers to field a team. We've all gotten a little older since we last played. Some of us might not be in shape to play again. And not only that, we lost Pistol . . . we won't have either of the Olzycki brothers . . . " Moonie was thinking out loud. Suddenly peering over his glasses, he looked down at Gus. "Gus, can you play?" he asked.

Ana answered the question for him. "No! He cannot. I'm his physician and I refuse to allow him." She wasn't kidding.

"That's four players gone, at least" said the Mayor, "Who have we got left?" Names were thrown around, and the only ones Joseph recognized were the Mayor's and Roove's. The Mayor scrambled to write them down, and finally looked up from his paper and said, "We have at most, eight players left from the old team, and that isn't going to be enough even if they all can still play."

"Go to the other teams and float the idea. See what they think," said Gus. The meeting broke up after the Mayor said he would check in with the other teams and let them all know what happened.

"Let's go get something to eat. I'm starved," said Gus.

Ana, Gus, Olney and Joseph settled in, ten minutes later, at the Fireside Inn. Orders were placed and drinks were served. Joseph asked no one in particular, about "Geetha" and the "Geetha trophy."

Olney jumped at the opportunity. "It's the national game of Wackentute County," he said with certainty. Joseph could see Ana shaking her head. Joseph had no idea what that meant, and Gus chimed in.

"It's a game peculiar to this valley. I don't think it's played anywhere else. But around here it was a big thing for as long as anyone can remember."

"It goes back to Revolutionary War," said Olney.

"No, it doesn't! Where did you get that?" asked Ana almost painfully.

"Does so! Mr. Davis, down at the high school, said he saw it in a book about the colonies. Said it was in a book in the library when he went to college in Boston. Heard him say it myself," asserted Olney. Ana chose not to argue the point, despite believing that Olney had stopped listening to teachers by the third grade, at the latest.

Gus took up the lesson and said, "Anyway, it has been played around here maybe as far back as the Civil War. And certainly since the early 1900's. That's when the local paper began reporting the scores of local games. We can trace it back that far. Being surrounded on three sides by the mountains and with the lake on the other side, we're sort of isolated here. And, insulated too, I guess," he added. "For a long time we didn't have much contact with most of the outside world. Wasn't until the late1940's that we had a clear radio signal in the valley; and it was approximately 20 years ago, when cable TV came into the valley, that people could get reliable service. The mountains kind of blocked out the signals before that. We didn't get most sport broadcasts and couldn't follow most teams, so we made our own fun. And Geetha was a big part of that."

"But what is it?" asked Joseph.

"Well," Gus said, "It's a little like hockey . . . it's played on ice . . . but unlike the hockey puck the thing that has to be pushed around is bigger, heavier, . . . more like curling." He voice trailed off.

"It's a little like hockey, but slower," added Ana, "But it is far more brutal than curling!" Olney and Gus said nothing, which indicated to Joseph that they didn't disagree. Ana wasn't through. "It is uncontrolled violence . . . it's madness . . . it's some sort of testosterone fueled male excuse for beating one another senseless."

"No it isn't," protested Olney, "it's a great game."

"Ana isn't a fan of the game," Gus said needlessly. "Maybe I better explain it," Gus went on. "Its origins are unclear."

"No, they aren't. It comes from the original settlers of the valley. The Wackentute Indians." Olney was on a roll. "Way back in the 1600's...." he started.

"Oh God," moaned Ana, in exasperation.

"Way back in the 1600's" Olney repeated, "These two bands of Wackentutes were living on opposite sides of Lake Custer. Only it wasn't called Lake Custer back then. Then it was called something else; not Lake Custer, but I don't know what. No one does. Some Indian name. Anyways, the band on one side woke up one morning, during the winter when the lake was frozen over – like it is every year – and saw the Geetha lying there on the edge of the lake...on their side of the lake. Well, they..."

"What is a 'Geetha'?" Joseph interrupted. Out of the corner of his eye he could see Ana shaking her head again. Gus was smiling.

Olney took up the challenge. "'Geetha' is a Wackentute Indian word for . . . er . . . it means . . . er, dead moose'." Everyone was silent for a moment.

"Dead moose?" asked Joseph, wondering if he had heard correctly.

"Yeah . . . more like dead moose carcass . . . a moose carcass, really," Gus said seriously, as he nodded his head. Joseph looked at the three people with him one at a time. He really expected someone to start smiling. No one did.

"Moose carcass? Really? There's a Wackentute word for that?" He really thought he was being teased, but Olney nodded. Gus just looked back at him. Ana had her head down. She wanted no part of this.

"People . . . hunters . . . woodsmen say that when it's time for a moose to die, they will just go off into the woods, lie down and curl up into a ball . . . and die. I guess it's something like the 'old elephant's graveyard legends' in Africa. I don't know if it's true or not, but it makes for a good story," Gus explained, and then shrugged. Joseph again looked at his three companions one at a time, expecting to see some sign that he was being flimflammed. But their faces were blank. Gus continued, "Yeah, well legend has it that this band of Wackentute Indians wake up one winter morning, and find this geetha on the edge of the lake. Their edge. Now no one in the band knows where this thing came from . . . no one saw it the night before, so they figure it probably died on the other side of the lake and that that band of Wackentutes, over there, pushed it over here to their side in the middle of the night just to get rid it. So, they waited until that night, and then they push it back to the other side! Now the next morning that side wakes up and finds the geetha on their side! They, of course, come up with the same explanation for it. So then they wait till nightfall, and push it right back over. Now this goes on for a few days until both sides stop botherin' to wait until nightfall, and start shoving the thing across the ice in broad daylight. Before long the two bands are out on the ice at the same time pushing it this way and that. Hence the game begins."

"Wait a minute . . . that's what the game is? Pushing a moose car . . . a *geetha* around on the ice?" asked Joseph.

"It's a lot more complicated than that. It has developed rules and traditions over the years," Gus said quickly.

"No it isn't," Ana said, "That's exactly what it is. A bunch of grown men . . . pushing a large lump of something . . . around on a frozen pond, while trying to beat each other senseless . . . ."

"As I said, Ana is not a big fan of the game," said Gus, cutting her off. "There's a lot more to it. First, we don't use a *real* geetha. We haven't used one in a very long time. For one thing there just aren't any around – real moose – anymore. Hasn't been one seen in the valley in over fifty years, I guess. What we have used since has been anything we could find that would be about the right size and weight. I remember our last season, we used this big sack of sand; must have weighed 150 lbs. That wore me out."

Olney jumped in, "Yeah, the home team in any game has to supply the geetha. That's the rules. And teams take a lot of pride in getting a good geetha in the game. The Bombers used that sack of sand. Blades used those stuffed duffel bags with all that duct tape around them. Remember?"

"How do you play?" asked Joseph.

Gus was going to speak, but let Olney take the lead. "You need four guys on a side. There's a center, two wings and a titman . . . " he got out before being interrupted.

"Excuse me?" said Joseph.

"Oh Lord," moaned Ana.

"A 'titman' is," interrupted Gus, "actually a 'titulaire.' It's a French word meaning 'bearer.' The titman is the guy pushing, or just handling, the geetha for his team. And only one guy on the team can be touching the geetha at any one time. If two, or more, touch it, intentionally or not, it's a foul. And that means the other team gets a 'free start.' A 'free start' means the other team gets sole possession of the geetha on its own 'start spot.'" Joseph was starting to get lost, and Gus could see it. "Let me start at the beginning."

The dinner was finally brought out and the four began eating. All through dinner Gus explained the game to Joseph, with Olney adding comments constantly. Ana occasionally said something disparaging about the game, or a rule, or a player. After a while it all began to make sense to Joseph.

Sometime during the early fall, people from around the valley would show up at Corrigan's Pond, an inlet off to the side of Lake Custer, and place a barrier all around the edge of the pond. These 'sideboards" would be three 2X4's nailed to posts; and then these posts would be driven into the shallowest water all around the edge of the cove before the water froze for

71

the winter. They'd be driven deep into the mud so just the 2X4's would be above the water level when it froze. Corrigan's Pond was roughly oval and about 150 yards long and 100 yards wide. At both ends, where a hockey goal net might normally be placed in a rink, a spot on the ice was painted red. On this spot, in a game, a "pezzle" (neither Gus nor Olney had any idea of the origin of the word) would be placed. An ordinary bowling pin could be used as a pezzle. Or sometimes a plastic two liter soda bottle filled with sand was used. Anything that could stand upright could be used. And a few yards in front of each team's pezzle spot was its 'start spot,' which was painted black.

The object of the game was to knock the other team's pezzle off its spot by hitting it with the geetha. Each team, of course, tried to prevent that by pushing the geetha away from its own pezzle. Each team would send out four skaters at a time, the titman, two wings and a center. The center and wingmen would act as blockers for the titman. The opposing titmen would push and shove the geetha, or push and shove each other – as long as they were in contact with the geetha. One of the few rules was that only one man on each team could be in contact with the geetha at any one time. And only a player in contact with the geetha could be in contact with the other man in contact with the geetha.

Players could switch positions while on the ice, and often did. A violation of any rule resulted in a "free start" for the offended team. That meant the offended team could take the geetha down to their "free start spot," and after devising some plan amongst themselves, they would start back up the ice toward their opponents' pezzle in sole possession of the geetha. The defending team would have to wait on the advancing team until they had crossed the line at the center of the pond. The advancing team had the advantage of the momentum its unopposed running head start afforded them.

They talked about the game all through dinner. Olney jumped from one aspect of the game to another with dazzling speed, leaving Gus, and even Ana sometimes, to fill in the blanks. They explained that players were usually good skaters, and diagrammed plays and coded words and signals were common during a game. And that the many towns from the surrounding valley had fielded teams for many years. Teams had uniforms and team colors, and they had remained fairly consistent over the years. Newcomb, for instance, had been The Bombers for as long as anyone could remember. Their colors had always been dark green and white, and their logo — portrayed prominently on their uniform sweater — was a forward-leaning capital "B" on top of a skate blade. Olney drew it on a napkin, after borrowing a pen from Gus. Joseph recognized it as the logo on Roove's old, green baseball cap.

And Gus, explained Olney, had been the best player the Bombers ever had. Gus tried to object, but Olney wouldn't hear of it. Even Ana nodded approvingly. Gus finally dismissed it by saying that his prime playing days were long gone! Joseph tried to imagine Gus on the ice in what he had been told was a fairly brutal contest. He couldn't picture it.

The "Geetha Trophy" was a three foot high bronze statue of a moose that was given at the end of each season to the town of the championship team. At the end of that last season the trophy had been "permanently" awarded to the last winning team . . . The Newcomb Bombers. The town had proudly placed the trophy on a six foot high stone pedestal in the middle of the small village green at the center of town. Joseph had seen the statue several times when passing through town, but had never read the plaque on its base.

The conversation touched on other teams, and their uniforms and colors. Names were mentioned, and reputations were discussed, but little of it made sense to Joseph. Outside of the clinic and a few people he had met, Joseph knew very few people in the valley. It seemed to him that quite a few of the names mentioned seemed to be nicknames, and he mentioned that. He was told that that was common in Geetha. Many, or even most, of the players went by nicknames. Olney assured him it was not only traditional, but "very cool too."

Although it was traditional for the team names and colors to remain the same, some things in the league did evolve. Players long ago would wrap themselves in layers of sweaters and sweatshirts for cushioning, and wear two or three watch caps for head protection. By the time the league had died out, pads designed for other sports became popular with players; and everyone now wore a hockey, or lacrosse, helmet for protection. Some towns in the valley had fielded a team for as long as people could remember. Other towns joined, or some dropped out of the league, from time to time. The league itself had its last season eight years ago when interest had finally petered out. Gus explained that as fewer towns fielded teams, the proud tradition of Geetha dwindled in popularity. Kids who were now getting a steady diet of broadcast sports were losing interest, and simply stopped playing Geetha.

"Oh yeah?" objected Olney, "what about 'The Lump on the Stump!' He never lost interest. He never missed a game right up till the end. Can't have a game unless the Lump on the Stump is there, right? I bet he'll be right there up front if we play again."

"Oh now, let's be nice" Gus said, but he was smiling. Ana shook her head, and smirked.

"Who's the 'Lump on the Stump'?" Joseph asked.

Gus explained that a local schoolteacher named Byram Lomb was probably the biggest fan of Geetha in the valley. "He hasn't missed a game down on Corrigan Pond since he was old enough to walk. Never played....but loved to watch the game. No one was more disappointed when the league stopped playing than Byram Lomb." Joseph looked around the table, and they were all smiling. Gus continued, "He'd always arrived early for every game, and found his "perfect spot" . . . down close at pond side . . . perched on some tree stump . . . with his picnic hamper at his side. To some of the people in the valley he was Geetha's biggest fan. But to some of the less charitable people around he was known as 'The Lump on the Stump'." Gus smiled, and then added, "He's quite a local legend."

"And who is 'Bilge'?" Joseph asked, remembering the name from the story Roove had told.

"Actually," Ana said, "It's Ruth Mary Bilger. But she doesn't like being called Ruth . . . or Ruth Mary . . . or Ms. Bilger even! So she's been "Bilge" ever since she was a 'little girl.' Ana considered what she said for a moment, and then continued. "Actually she never even was a 'little girl'. She was big even when she was little . . . if you know what I mean? But being big never stopped her from being good. She might be the best female athlete this valley's ever seen." Olney and Gus immediately objected, but Ana hushed them. "She's a few years younger than me, and we never played against each other. But she owns most of the records for female athletes in the valley." Gus recited a few instances where that wasn't the case, but Ana disregarded him. "I may have been a little faster than she was, but she was a lot stronger. And definitely tougher! She was big, fast and mean. And absolutely fearless! I bet most of the men in that league were glad she never played Geetha." Olney and Gus smiled in agreement. Ana continued, "Bilge, on many levels, is a force to be reckoned with. If she had caught up to Pistol that day he hit her.... Pistol would still be in traction."

"She sounds pretty fearsome," Joseph concluded. "Doesn't sound like someone you'd like to run off with."

"Oh, don't get the wrong idea. She's not some old hag. I bet even most people would have to admit she's kind of good looking."

"What!" Olney sputtered.

"Now be fair, Olney!" Ana shot right back. Gus said something about agreeing with his daughter. "Okay, she is a little bigger than most women. And she's pretty solidly built." Ana added quickly here, "BUT she is not fat! Not by a long shot. She may not be a beauty queen in the classical sense, but she stands out in a crowd. That's for sure."

"You know how to describe her?" Gus broke in. "She is as tough as nails. Life hasn't been exactly kind to her, but she never whined about it. She doesn't ask for sympathy, nor does she give any. You know what she is?" asked Gus. "She's a warrior and a fierce competitor." He added. "I've seen her play. She's got an intense will to win. It's almost frightening. She just doesn't allow anything to stand in her way."

They all sat silent for a moment, and then Olney said, "If Pistol ever comes back to Wackentute, he better watch out! She'll cripple him." Ana and Gus silently agreed. Then, after another momentary pause, Gus added, "Remember when O-G crossed her? He paid for that misjudgment."

"He deserved what he got. He asked for it," said Ana. Joseph asked her what she meant. She waved him off saying, "That's a story for another night. Let's go home, I'm bushed."

Thursday - December 5

For some unknown reason this day turned into one of those days when nothing seemed to go right. The weather was wet and nasty, and so were most of the patients who walked through the door at the clinic. And they came through the door, non-stop, all morning. Crying babies, tubercular coughs, and sneezes of typhoon proportions went on all day from the time the front door opened at 8 AM.

Joseph remembered that he heard the phone ringing when he came into the building 45 minutes earlier. It hadn't stopped, that he could recall, anytime since. The entire morning was a blur. And there were no messages, nor money, from the State Insurance Department.

Checking in with Lindsay, apparently too many times that morning on issues related to insurance, even caused her to sneer at him. Badgered by irritable patients and an irritable Joseph too, she suddenly yelled at him that she needed a break, and was going outside for some air. It wasn't a request that he cover the front desk for her. It was more like an ultimatum. He had been badgered all morning too, and wasn't feeling any more chipper than she was, but an instant after she yelled . . . she was gone.

He sat down at the front desk, and was promptly sneezed at by a teenage boy with red watery eyes, a stuffed nose, and "no fucking idea who my insurance coverage is." The phone on Lindsay's desk continued to ring, with the other two lines blinking on hold. It was at this moment Lindsay's computer crashed.

The chaos and mayhem reigned supreme for the next hour or so. Lindsay had come back, and after helping her out for a time until things calmed down a little, Joseph excused himself and made his way back to his office. His phone was ringing as he entered, but he ignored it. He looked down at the phone and saw that he had 14 messages on voicemail. He correctly assumed none of them were casual calls by someone just looking to chat. Deciding that he would need another cup of coffee before plunging into his day's work, he headed off to the pantry.

The trip to the pantry, and back, surprised him. With all that was going on around him; with the overflow patient load creating havoc with the overburdened staff; with people rushing this way and that, the only topic being discussed by anyone was "Geetha." Two of the 14 calls on his voicemail had to do with Geetha! Someone named the vaguely familiar name of "Magoo," left a message saying he couldn't reach "Gus," and wanted to know if he was going to play? "You work with Gus, so would you mind asking him and getting back to me?" He left a number!

As Joseph began returning business-related calls it became obvious that the miserable weather was making people miserable too. At least the ones he had to deal with were miserable. The suppliers he called were less than cordial. Just when he started thinking that there wasn't a nice person in the entire valley, Figgit Nuuf walked into his office carrying a large machine. He put it down on the center of Joseph's desk, and said, "It is dead." There was a pause. "I cannot resurrect it." he said sadly. "I have done what I can. It has been teetering . . . " He suddenly glanced around the walls of the office, noticing the bits of paper Joseph had tacked all over. For a moment he studied them, and then, just as quickly, dismissing them said to Joseph, " . . . on the brink of final breakdown. There's nothing more I can do, we must have another." He paused again, and then added, "Today."

"What is it?" Joseph asked. He was more interested in giving himself a moment to think than actually knowing what it was.

Figgit thought for a moment, trying to answer the question in words that he thought Joseph would understand. He began to say, "It's a T C Colorado K60 S . . . " his voice trailed off for moment, then re-started. "It's a micro-hematocrit centrifuge," he added without any enthusiasm. Figgit thought to himself that Joseph would probably know what a centrifuge was. He may have even heard of the manufacturer, TC Colorado. He felt it was safe to assume that Joseph would think that a "micro hematocrit" was a very small hematocrit. But there was very little chance that he would know what a hematocrit was! And the fact that this machine could rotate 20 standard 75mm capillary tubes at better than 14,000 RPM's was so far outside Joseph's area of expertise that Figgit could do nothing but smile.

"What will a new one cost us?" Joseph asked in dead earnest. They were immediately back in his area of expertise.

Friday - December 6

The first thing Lindsay did this morning was print, in large block letters on a piece of cardboard, a sign saying, "I HAVE NOT HEARD FROM THE STATE . . . I DO NOT KNOW ANYTHING MORE THAN I DID YESTERDAY." She kept it on her desk, and held it up every time Joseph came near her. Joseph, despite an incredible urge to ask her anyway, left her alone. No matter what he tried to do that morning, the question "What can I do that I'm not already doing?" kept circling through his head.

Mayor Mooney's timing was perfect. He walked into the clinic at the same moment that the pizza, which the staff had ordered for lunch, was being delivered. Although he had only stopped by to update Gus on his meeting with the Blades, his being a politician meant he wasn't shy about joining them for a slice, or two.

In between mouthfuls he told Gus, and the eavesdropping rest of the staff, that the Blades were willing to play, again, for the trophy. They had agreed to set up a full meeting for all interested teams, and would hold it next week in the Presbyterian Church in Little Sittlerville. When Mooney had brought up the fact that the Bombers were missing four former players, the Blades had reluctantly agreed that a couple of substitutions would be allowed. Their roster of eight years ago was intact. But they insisted that the newcomers would have to be over 30 years old, which would make them the same age as the original players were now. It seemed that they were wary of the other teams sneaking "young studs" onto their roster. They also insisted that all players that were going to be substitutes had to be at the meeting next week to be approved in person, and be able to prove their age, and that they were legal residents of the town that the team represented. They didn't want any more "ringers" to screw things up.

"Where are we going to come up with the four extra players?" Gus asked. Moonie just shook his head. Gus turned his head, and scanned the people in the room. "We need some help." he said. "Know any good skaters?" he said to no one in particular.

No one said anything for a moment, but then, unexpectedly, Joseph said, "You have two good skaters right under your nose here." The lunchtime crowd in the room all turned and looked at him. Gus cocked his head and furrowed his eyebrows. Doubt was all over his face. Joseph smiled and said, "Our accountant is a terrific skater. None of you know that? I skated with him, and I can tell you that he can really move around on skates."

Several people expressed a little surprise and doubt at what he said. "And what makes you an expert on skating?" Ana asked him, a little louder than everyone else's comments.

"Because I can skate too," he said quickly. "I can skate very well, if I have to say so myself." A few people in the room tossed some doubtful comments at him, but he held his ground. Olney and Ana seemed very skeptical of both Joseph's and Podalski's ice skating ability. They both lobbed questions at him while the conversation in the room moved on without them.

Moonie and Gus continued their discussion about getting the four replacements for their team. They bandied names around that meant nothing to Joseph, and others chimed in frequently. And it seemed no matter who was mentioned, there were serious objections to their current fitness, or abilities, or even availability for the new tournament.

Joseph, who was put off by the lack of faith in his skating ability, had turned his attention back to more pressing problems. He was washing off a plate he had used for lunch in the sink when he heard Gus, again, remark that they needed help. "Yes, we do," he answered absentmindedly, but he wasn't thinking about the Newcomb Geetha team. Unlike almost everyone else in the office . . . unlike almost everyone else in town, he was thinking about the Wackentute Walk-In Clinic.

Gus, who didn't realize they were talking about two different things, smilingly said, "Christmas is coming. Maybe we can ask Santa for some help?"

"Does he carry any cash on that sled of his?" Joseph deadpanned. Gus suddenly realized that Joseph was talking about something totally different, and said nothing. "Why don't you and I have a little talk?" Joseph said.

Once back in Gus's office Joseph updated the doctor on the financial status that was becoming more critical every day. He explained that the clinic needed a cash infusion quickly. He had hoped that some of the money owed to the clinic by the state would have come in already. That, unfortunately, hadn't been the case, and Joseph wasn't sure when that would happen. Gus, of course, wasn't able to shed any light on that situation either. He wanted to help, but he really didn't know very much about this whole process. He was sorry. "I wish I could do something," he said softly.

"So do I," Joseph said. He thought for a minute, and then asked the doctor, "Do you know anyone up in the State Insurance Department? A director . . . or a commissioner . . . or anybody?" The doctor shook his head.

Suddenly Joseph had an idea. "How about at County Hospital? You know any doctors, or even better, anyone over there who does liaison work for them with the State Insurance Department? Anyone over there who can help us with this?"

Gus let out a sigh, and shook his head "no." But, he smiled, "I can make a few calls to people I do know over there who might be able to help." It wasn't the answer Joseph had wanted, but it was something.

Two hours later Joseph was working with Olney as they processed in a large delivery. It was from a supplier who had been on the phone earlier that day saying this would be their last shipment until they received payment for supplies they had already delivered, and were long overdue for payment. Some of those things being delivered were critical to the operation of the clinic. Discontinuing their delivery was not an option. Joseph was trying to figure out how they were going to be able to satisfy the suppliers' demands. In the middle of his reverie, Joseph heard Olney say something about how he appreciated the help he was getting. Joseph brushed it off, saying that he was glad to be able to help. That phrase, 'being glad he was able to help', struck a chord.

Bob Weller had said that to him! On many occasions! "Jesus Christ! Bob must know people in Albany. His firm is 'connected' to those people up there. Hell, they're all Democrats. Damn! I bet someone in his firm knows the governor." That, of course, was wishful thinking, but it was an avenue that ought to be explored. He looked up at Olney, who was staring right back at him. "I gotta go," he said apologetically to him, "I gotta make a phone call. I'll be back as quick as I can."

He called Bob Weller, but couldn't reach him. He left an "URGENT-PLEASE CALL ME BACK ASAP" message with an unimpressed secretary.

By half past seven that night the clinic had closed, and Joseph was about to lock the door behind him when his cell phone rang. Fumbling with it in the cold and dark rear parking lot, he finally got it to his ear. The familiar voice of his lawyer was on the other end. Joseph let himself back into the building, and went back to his office. Their conversation lasted over an hour.

Saturday - December 7

For the first time, in a long time, Joseph did not pester Lindsay with any questions about insurance reimbursement after they both arrived at the clinic this morning. Instead he went straight to his desk and went over the notes he had taken during his phone conversation last night. He had an agenda that he had to follow. There were facts to be checked and other calls to make. And there were a few incoming calls that he expected, which he was excitedly looking forward to.

By noon he was reminded of the fact that not everyone works on Saturday. He had been unable to reach most of the people he wanted; and one incoming call in particular never came. He was somewhat disappointed, but optimistic on the whole that he once more had a plan. And despite the fact that Lindsay regarded him warily every time they crossed paths this morning, he never once asked her about insurance. He asked her about her weekend plans.... about a sore elbow she had mentioned.... and about a TV show she had said she had wanted to watch. But nothing about insurance; she was flabbergasted!

He didn't leave the clinic until after 2 PM, in a vain hope that a missing caller would surface. None did, and although slightly disappointed with that, he left the clinic with a slight bounce in his step. He felt he just may have turned a corner.

Walking into the Fireside Inn later that night Joseph's step still had that bounce in it. It had been a good day, and a few drinks to top it off were just what he wanted. The few faces that were becoming familiar to him, including Roove's, and Dudley's, along with some that were not so familiar, sat clustered at the far end of the bar. He had briefly met three of them two weeks ago here in the Fireside. An exchange of greetings and a few introductions later, Joseph settled in for what he thought would be a relaxing evening.

One of the people that he had met before was "Magoo," and Joseph remembered him from the phone message too. It turned out that Magoo was not only Deputy Sheriff McGuire, but was also one of the players that had been part of the last team of Geetha players for Newcomb a number of years ago. As a matter of fact, all the men standing there had been on that team. There was Magoo, who was well over six feet tall, and weighed at least 250 lbs. Two other guys about that same height but weighing somewhat less were called Jeepers and Whitey. Two smaller men, both sitting on bar stools, like Roove, were introduced as Tully and Smoke. Magoo and Whitey, Joseph noticed, were both wearing identical green jerseys with the word "BOMBERS" stenciled across the front. It seems Joseph had walked in on what was an unofficial "Geetha Championship Team Reunion." And like almost any reunion, there were stories to rehash. And some of those stories were not so complimentary!

Jabs and zingers flew in all directions. It didn't seem to Joseph that anyone was escaping, and everyone seemed to be enjoying it all immensely. Only when they referred to "Gus" was any reverence shown. With explanatory side comments to Joseph, Roove explained that "Gus" was indeed the very same Dr. John Gustafson of the Wackentute Walk-In Clinic. Although some other players could be mentioned in the same breath with Gus, most people in the discussion felt he was the best Geetha player they ever saw.

"Man, it's a shame he can't play again. Even at his age, I bet he could still play," Smoke said.

"He was awesome," confirmed Jeepers.

"Oh, we'll miss him all right. But Roove here will pick up the slack," Magoo said.

"We're gonna miss Pistol too," Roove nodded. Everyone added a comment of agreement to that.

"Should be able to replace the Olzycki brothers, though." A few of them laughed.

"Hey," said a guy named Tully, "Jimmy could play okay. He was pretty good."

"Yeah, but Eddie was a train wreck. Used to scare me just watching him," Magoo added.

"Why aren't those two playing? They move away?" Joseph asked, innocently enough.

There was an awkward silence for a moment, then Roove said flatly, "Neither one can make it." He paused again, then continued, "Jimmy's doing . . . what?" he looked around at the others. No one said anything. "He's doing 3 to 8? . . . 4 to 10? . . . up in Easthaven. Been running tax free cigarettes out of the Carolinas up here to the valley for years. They asked him, nicely if I remember correctly, to quit doing it the second time they caught him. But that boy don't listen too good," he said finally.

Joseph looked around, and saw them all just shaking their heads. "What about the brother? Eddie, wasn't it? He get caught up in it too?"

No one said anything, at first. Then Roove spoke up again. "No, Eddie wasn't involved with that. Eddie, unfortunately, is . . . well . . . well . . . Eddie's doing eternity at West Glen Memorial Park."

"That's a little cold, Roove. Don't you think?" asked Smoke, shaking his head.

Someone else said that indeed Roove was being too hard on the "dear departed Eddie Olzycki." Roove immediately disagreed. "Hey, I liked the guy more than any of you guys did. I admired the son of a bitch. The man died trying to prove a point. I admire that!"

"What the hell are you talking about?" The group talked over each over as each man disagreed in turn. "Man, are you crazy? What point?"

"He was trying to prove that you can drink and drive, and...." Roove said, and was going to say more, but he was drowned out by the others' hoots, and cries of disbelief that he could say such a terrible thing.

"Whoa, man, how can you say shit like that?" Magoo said, but he was smiling.

"Jeez, Roove, that's just plain mean. Okay, Eddie was an idiot, but you shouldn't say bad things about the dead. It's bad luck."

The conversation got away from the Olzycki Brothers and after another round of drinks wandered off into a realm of inside jokes they all seemed to enjoy. Most of them, however, were lost on Joseph. His attention drifted off to the hockey game on TV. It was a good game, and after a while he was focused on it. That focus was soon shattered when the conversation around him suddenly grew very loud.

"No, wait a second! I forget," Tully was saying to Jeepers, "which Lee sister did you take to the prom?" There was a slight pause of expectation, and then he added, "Was it Ug-ly, or Beast-ly." It was an old joke, but still funny to them all.

Jeepers began objecting strenuously, "No, no, no," he was insisting. "I wouldn't be criticizing anyone else's prom date if I were you," he said to Roove. The others were laughing. By the comments being passed around it became obvious that Roove's date had been the girl named "Bilge." Joseph had heard her talked about before.

"That wasn't a 'double date', Roove," said Whitey. There was a pause, and then he added, "That was more like a 'one-and-a-half date.'" The group howled in laughter. Roove spun his bar stool around to face the TV. He had heard this joke for years. The old teammates continued to laugh, and the man named Jeepers explained to Joseph that both Roove AND Pistol had taken Bilge to the prom.

Roove turned back around, and completely ignoring the others said to Joseph, "We both wanted to go. He wanted to take his motorcycle . . . and of course, you can't take a date to the prom on a motorcycle. So I picked her up at her house, and drove her there in a car I borrowed. She arrived in style! I drove her to the after party too. So that worked out great." Stopping to take a quick breadth, he went on, "Pistol loved to dance. I don't. So she and him danced all night. Perfect! Everybody was a winner." Roove turned back to the hockey game.

There were some hoots and objections to that last remark. After a moment or two, Jeepers added casually, "Would have loved to seen her get on that bike in that dress she was wearing!"

"That was a dress? Holy shit, all this time I thought it was painted on," said Smoke.

The laughing continued. Again Roove turned back around, and speaking directly only to Joseph said, "Ignore these lowlifes. You have to understand that Bilge wasn't about to wear some frilly pink chiffon ball gown piece of shit. No, that was never gonna happen. She wore a little something different." He started to turn back around, then reversed back to Joseph once again, and said, "I thought she looked kinda good. A little different than the rest of the ladies, maybe. But good."

"Jesus Christ, Roove," said Magoo, "She looked like a geisha on steroids!" Tully spun away trying to swallow a mouthful of beer, while the others were laughing very hard.

Again Roove turned around, and ignoring the others, spoke only to Joseph. "She ain't fat. She is kinda big boned, though. She wore one of those long oriental dresses. You know, made of satin, or silk? High neck collar, long sleeves, and straight down all the way to the feet. Musta had 50 buttons all the way down the side?"

"I think they are called Mandarin dresses," Joseph offered, after a minute.

"Yeah well, I don't know what they call them, but she wore one." Roove could remember it as clearly as if he had seen it yesterday. "I'll admit it was kinda tight. She . . . "

He was immediately interrupted. "'Kinda tight'! Jesus Christ, Roove . . . you fuckin' kiddin' me?" Whitey asked in disbelief. The other guys were slapping each other on their shoulders they were laughing so hard. Finally

Tully regained his composure and said, "Tight? You could see her tattoos through it." That set them all laughing uncontrollably again. A few wandered off, laughing hysterically.

While they were all lost in their merriment Roove leaned over and whispered to Joseph that the dress had been really tight. "How she got it buttoned up is a mystery to this very day." There wasn't a hint of a smile of his face. "If she had sneezed, they'd still be diggin' buttons out of that gym's walls."

Sunday - December 8

As Podalski and Hamilton skated together this morning, their conversation centered solely on where they could find any additional income. The money from medical insurance providers was dribbling in at a very slow pace. They were optimistic that they could speed up the process as they worked on it, but in reality, that was going to take time. And time was something that was in shorter supply than cash!

Joseph brought up the possibility of outside "help." He couldn't be specific, and wasn't sure in all honesty that it would happen, but it was a possibility. Podalski, who understood all too well that any source of income would be welcome, pressed him for details. "We are a 'non-profit'; at least I think we are," Joseph said. "That has to be confirmed. You and I, and a lawyer I have roped into this, have to get that nailed down. Make sure what our legal status is. And if we aren't, we are going to get there fast." Podalski just stared at him. "Do you know anything about 'grants'?" Joseph asked. Podalski admitted he didn't. "You may have to know a lot very soon. Or everything an accountant needs to know about them, anyhow. And learn it very quickly. Still have any old textbooks around the house?" Podalski nodded. "Get them out. Look up everything you can about grants. I have a conference call scheduled for 9:30 tomorrow morning; I think you should be in on it. Sorry to spring this on you, but I didn't want to waste any time."

The accountant began peppering him with questions, but Joseph was unable, or unwilling, to answer most of them. After a short time Podalski realized he would get no more information from him on the "grants" topic, so he asked about Medicaid, and other insurance money. And although Hamilton was far more willing to answer these questions, he didn't have much more information about them either. Yes, there was still an enormous amount of reimbursements due to the clinic. And although the backlog of submissions had been reduced significantly, the actual reimbursements were still "stuck in processing" at the respective insurance providers.

The two men continued their skate as they discussed various ways that the logjam could be broken. Joseph mentioned that "he had a very good friend, who just may have some very good friends in Albany, who can help us," but it was only a possibility. They admitted to each other that every possibility had to be examined.

Late in their skate Podalski sped up suddenly, and quite rapidly, to retrieve a son from the edge of some older boys' impromptu hockey game. Once he got the boy out of harm's way he returned to Joseph's side. "By the way," Joseph said, "You're from this valley originally, aren't you?" Podalski confirmed that he was. He had lived here until his twelfth birthday, before moving away. "Did you ever play Geetha?" asked Joseph.

"Only choose-up games. The organized leagues didn't accept kids under 13. Played a lot, but never got into the Youth League. Why?"

Chapter Five

The scheduled conference call included Bob Weller, one of his partners, as well as Joseph and Podalski. And the newest face at the table belonged to Mayor Mooney. He was not there in his official capacity as Mayor of Newcomb, but simply as a local lawyer who would act as The Wackentute Walk-In Clinic's counsel. A very unsettled agenda had been planned, and they were soon going off in all directions. Joseph, to his credit, tried to keep everyone on track. Various people chimed in with suggestions and instructions; there were tasks and points that needed researching. Joseph tried to keep the workload as light as possible on the three *pro bono* participants on the call. In the chaos of multiple conversations going on at once, it occurred to Joseph how valuable Margaret Mary Fitzgerald had been back at OCS in what seemed like so many years ago.

When the call finally came to a close, Joseph was surprised to see that only an hour and a half has passed. It had seemed so much longer to him. Mayor Mooney left to go perform some official municipal business, but promised to return for lunch. Phil Podalski was gone moments after the call ended. He had a mountain of tasks in front of him. Joseph sat for another fifteen minutes alone in his office mapping out a 'To Do" list that he hoped would keep everyone on track, and on schedule. There were tasks to be performed, documents located, and very little time for it.

In what seemed like no time at all, Joseph spotted Mayor Mooney, wearing a broad smile, reenter the building and head for the staff pantry. Checking his watch, he saw it was half past twelve, and time for lunch. And he was curious to know the cause for the mayor's broad smile, so he quickly followed him into the pantry. He didn't think the mayor could have done very much for the clinic in the short time since the conference call had ended. He would soon find out that the mayor's smile had nothing at all to do with the business of the clinic.

It must have been a slow day because shortly after the mayor arrived, Gus and Ana, as well as several other members of the staff, came in to join him. After a few assorted lunch preparations, everyone sat down and waited for the good news that the mayor's smile promised. "I think I have some pretty good news" he said. "We have our first replacement! Paulie called me last night to say that he'd ask his brother-in-law, B-Ball, to play." The mayor was beaming.

"B-Ball? Is that Ronnie Rowe? Can he even skate?" asked Gus, who looked dubious.

"Yes, he can," the mayor pronounced emphatically, "I didn't think he could either, but Paulie says he can skate okay. And he lives on Pipp Street. West of Earhart; and that makes him a resident of Newcomb." He paused for a moment, and then added, "He can't turn too good, but he can stay up. And, God," the Mayor said, "he is a beast. We can use him if the going gets tough. Remember, we haven't got the Olzycki brothers anymore."

This wasn't remotely the news Joseph had hoped to hear, but even he got caught up a little in the mayor's enthusiasm. "B-ball? Sounds like an athlete to me. Was he a basketball player?"

Ana cut in, "No," she said flatly, "Not even remotely. 'B-Ball' stands for 'bowling ball.' He resembles a bowling ball. He's round . . . close to the ground . . . and as hard as a rock." Looking around the room for confirmation, she asked, "What is he?" she asked no one in particular. "Five and a half feet tall? Probably weighs 250 lbs."

"More," someone said.

She went on to say to Joseph that B-Ball was the youngest son of Russell Rowe, The Refuse King of the Wackentute Valley. The Rowe family had a large share of the trash collection business in the valley, and was involved in all kinds of various trucking businesses. And to the amazement of all their former teachers, they were very prosperous. "Why is he getting involved in this?" She asked no one in particular. "He never played when he was younger."

"It gives him a chance to get back at the some of the Blades, maybe" said the Mayor, "Maybe he wants to settle some old scores that go back to Paulie and Dee-Dee's wedding."

"That could be," said Gus, "*That* was some wedding." Several people around the group nodded knowingly.

"What happened?" Joseph finally broke the silence and asked. No one said anything for a moment.

"Mixing up the Rowes, and some of those biker friends of Paulie, was just a bad idea. Add in a bunch of the truck drivers from Rowe Trucking, and it's a wonder it stayed as peaceful as it did, for as long as it did."

"Fight started before the cocktail hour was over."

"You could tell there was going to be trouble when the first keg ran dry before the wedding party even got there."

"There was a thirsty bunch at that wedding, all right!"

"Between the truck drivers, and the bikers, and Pistol, Roove, and Paulie and the Rowe brothers ..... it was a bad mix."

"How many people were at that reception, anyway?" Mena asked.

"Counting the State Police?" asked the mayor.

"Why not? They stayed for cake," said Ana, shaking her head.

The conversation got back to the upcoming tournament, and the team that Newcomb would have to field. Most of the people in the room nodded agreement when Gus lamented that they would need more help. Joseph, who was currently trying to unwrap his lunch, and only half listening said absentmindedly, "Man....do we ever!" He was thinking of the clinic, not the Geetha team. Several of the people turned and looked at him. They were surprised at his interest in their Geetha dilemma. He noticed the looks immediately, and decided to camouflage his reference to the clinic. After a moment's hesitation he suggested that they should ask Phil Podalski if he wanted to play.

"Who?" said Olney, "Podalski? He's a shrimp!" Several others were shaking their heads, but Joseph persisted.

"Hey! I've said it before, I've seen him on skates. If your team needs skaters, this guy can skate like the wind. He can fly!" he insisted.

Mooney was interested, but wondered about his size. "What is he? Five foot eight? A hundred and fifty pounds? That isn't big enough." Shaking his head, he waved off the suggestion.

"He's taller than that," argued Joseph.

Gus objected too. "This is a pretty physical game. I think he may be a little *overmatched.*"

"Wait, you said that guy, B-Ball, is only five foot six, and no one's objecting to him."

"B-ball's all muscle. Even between his ears he's all muscle. He can take care of himself," said Mooney.

Joseph wouldn't relent. "Maybe Podalski isn't as heavy as this guy, B-Ball, but I'll bet he can skate rings around him. He is a really good skater. I've seen him. And isn't there some expression that goes, 'It isn't the size of the dog in the fight . . . it's the size of the fight in the dog'?" He looked around at the group. "I've gotten to know this guy recently and I think he's pretty tough. And I've seen him on skates. I think you ought to ask him, anyway."

Gus looked across the table at Joseph, and said, "Being tough may not be enough. And more importantly, what do you know about skating? Can you skate?" Gus had been preoccupied with Moonie last Friday when Joseph had answered this question before.

"To tell you the truth, I can skate very well." He answered directly back at Gus.

Olney jumped in, "This ain't 'Ice Capades' skating, Joseph. This is a lot meaner than that ice dancing."

"It's a very strenuous game, Joseph," Gus said gravely, "you will definitely break a sweat playing it."

Ana added in a sweet voice, "You'll *break* more than a sweat."

Moonie took over, "Look, this is a tough game. And someone better know how to skate real good if they're going to step over the boards. It's no fooling around," he warned.

Joseph was a little insulted by the way they seemed to be dismissing him. He, of course, would let Podalski make up his own mind, but he was going to volunteer. "I'm in …if you want me?" he said.

"No!" said Ana, "You'll get murdered." Gus ignored Ana's objection, and again asked Joseph again if he could really skate.

Joe smiled at them, and explained that he had been born and raised in Michigan . . . "*Northern* Michigan," he said for emphasis. That didn't seem to impress them. He told them he had learned to skate before he was five. He had played hockey almost all of his life, including college hockey. "My college team played in the 'Frozen Four' my junior year. I was a center, but I also played a lot at winger too. I can skate," he said with certainty. He looked around the table, feeling that he had made his point. Mayor Mooney explained to anyone who didn't know, that the "Frozen Four" was the premier collegiate championship tournament for hockey. That produced small gestures of acknowledgment that maybe, just maybe, he had a point.

"Why don't you come down to a practice, and watch them play a little before you sign up? Okay?" said Gus.

"I'll ask Podalski if he wants to come too," said Joseph. "Like I said, I've seen him skate and he can move." They decided that it was okay if Joseph brought Podalski along, if he wanted to give it a try too.

"You're gonna get killed," said Olney, smiling.

Suddenly Ana asked a very important question. "Are you both eligible?" She asked it with a straight face.

"Oh yeah, let's not get into that mess again. You're both currently legal residents of Newcomb, and over thirty? Right?" the mayor asked.

Joseph answered again, smiling, "No problem. We're both over thirty, and are definitely legal residents of the state."

"Did you say 'legal', or '*mandatory*'?" Ana asked smirking.

Just then the phone rang in the pantry, and Lindsay answered it. She listened for a moment, said "Okay," and then pressed the button to put the call on the speakerphone.

"Hey!" said a voice that sounded like it was coming from a deep cave, "You there, Moonie? I got some good news." The caller was Paulie, although it was difficult to make out the voice because of the background echo.

"Yeah, I'm here" replied the Mayor, "Gus is here too. Where are you calling from? You sound like you're in a hole."

"I'm down at your office . . . at Town Hall. Your secretary told me where you were."

"You're in my office? My secretary . . . let you in my office? You're on my phone? You're in my office . . . Is she in there with you? Is someone in there with you?" The mayor was clearly not comfortable with that thought.

"No, no, no," Paulie assured him, "I not really *in* your office. I'm on my own cell phone. I came down here to Town Hall to find you, and Miss Fierce told me where you were." he said.

"It's 'Pierce', Paulie, Mrs. Pierce; and tell her I said that you are not allowed in my office," and added, "No offense."

"No problem, Mayor. Look, I just wanted to tell you that I got a call this morning. Guess what? B-Ball is going to . . . Aaarrrgggg . . . " he suddenly groaned. But then quickly continued, " . . . play with us. His dad gave him weekends off as long as the tourney lasts. Isn't that great? Now we only need . . . oooooo," he sighed heavily into the phone and then said, " . . . a couple more guys." Paulie's voice came out of the speakerphone and sounded very, very resonant.

Mayor Mooney was looking at the speaker as if he could see Paulie in it. "We're going to have some practices before any game gets played, you know? Make sure he understands he's going to have to go to them." And after pausing for just a moment, he added, "And, where are you calling from? You sound like you're in a tunnel."

"Oh he wants to play . . . he'll show up for practice." And then suddenly he added a long, soft "Whew!"

"Where are you calling from, Paulie? Where are you right now?" the mayor wanted to know.

"From Town Hall, I told you."

"Why are you making those noises? Where in Town Hall exactly?" Mayor Mooney asked suspiciously.

"I'm in the crapper, takin' a dump. Why?"

Gus, with a sour look on his face, reached over and clicked the "Off" button. The mayor was up in a flash, leaving the remnants of his lunch on the table, and out the door, muttering, "I gotta go." Everyone understood.

Tuesday - December 10

Getting a call from the IRS was only, in the rarest of instances, a piece of good news. The call Gus received, and that was passed along to Joseph, was not one of those rare good news calls. They wanted to see the principals of the clinic. They wanted to see the financials of the clinic. They wanted to ask a lot of questions. And they were not open, in the least, for negotiation on any of these points.

Mooney had only recently become counsel for the clinic. But even if he had been on retainer for years, he would not have qualified as the kind of tax attorney Joseph knew they were going to need. Again he leaned on his friend, Bob Weller. But this time Joseph knew that getting the kind of help he was going to need was going to cost him. He asked if Bob, through his network of associates, could suggest someone in the area who could provide that kind of help. Bob said he would call him back, and hung up.

Joseph sat for a long time wondering how, in God's name, he would be able to pay the legal fees that he felt sure were coming. He called Podalski, and briefed him on the call. They agreed that they had a lot of preparation work to do. He spoke jointly with Gus and Ana to tell them what they could expect to happen. He didn't try to sugarcoat anything. If he skewed it at all, he was overly pessimistic. There was plenty of gloom to go around.

By mid-afternoon the news had spread throughout the clinic. It seemed that everyone on the staff was aware of the impending descent of the dreaded IRS. Various staff members came up to Joseph with words of encouragement, and votes of confidence that he would steer them through the trouble. "I am sure we have nothing to worry about with them," he lied to every well-wisher.

Late in the day, Lindsay peeked into Joseph's office and said, "Boss, there's a call for you on the main line."

"Who is it?" he moaned.

"Mr. *Someone* ... from *somewhere*," she said innocently, and disappeared before he could say a word.

He shook his head, and picked up the call. "Hello, this is Hamilton."

"Mr. Joseph Hamilton?" said a voice.

"Yes, this is Joseph Hamilton ..... Who is this?"

"My name is Sadim . . . "

And before this "Mr. Sadim" could say another word, Joseph interrupted, "How can I help you, Mr. Sadim?"

"How can I help *you*?" the caller asked back.

Joseph was busy and he didn't want to be playing silly phone games, so he said, rather bluntly, "Who are you, and what do you want?"

"I told you," the caller said, "My name is Sadim, and I'm the Regional Coordinator of the New York State Medicaid Department. I was asked by Deputy Director Bryant to call you. You seem to be having some difficulties with reimbursements?"

After a few more minutes of give-and-take between the two men, Joseph learned that Sadim was responsible for every facility in a three county (including Wackentute) area that used the Medicaid system His job was to visit the various health care providers updating them on new policies and procedures in the system. He provided instructions and tutorials to new providers and refresher courses to the ones already using the system. He also made emergency trips to facilities that were having serious problems. When he added this at the end of another sentence, Joseph jumped on it!

"We need you here right away. We are having enormous problems in processing the claims, and as such, have a huge backlog," Joseph assured him.

"You are?" Sadim said, sounding surprised. "I keep a pretty good watch on the Monthly S & R Report; frankly, I don't remember seeing The Wackentute Clinic numbers standing out." Joseph had no idea what the "Monthly S & R Report" was, and said so. Sadim explained that that report was produced by the Central Office in Albany, and showed the statistics of submissions and reimbursements by every provider in the state that had been processed that month. "Your numbers, admittedly, have declined quite a bit over the past year, but, otherwise, are not very noteworthy. I assure you; I checked them very carefully before I made this call."

"We've sent hundreds! Hundreds and hundreds! And while many are returned to us with obscure notations on them . . . many more seem to have just disappeared in the mail!"

It was Sadim's turn to interrupt. "In the mail? You mail them in?" he asked slowly.

"Yes," Joseph shrugged. "Of course."

"Why aren't you submitting them electronically? Who mails them in anymore?" Suddenly Joseph could hear laughing on the other end of the line. Before he could say in no uncertain terms that it wasn't funny, Sadim said, "I'm sorry. That isn't funny. It is, however, ridiculous! Medicaid went to, primarily, electronic submissions over a year ago. While there may be some stragglers still around, almost 98% of the submissions are now electronic. Good God! Where have you been?" There was silence at both ends of the line for a moment. "And where in hell are your submissions going? This isn't funny."

Joseph agreed with him immediately. It wasn't funny. They continued talking about what Joseph and the clinic had to begin doing immediately. First of all, send no more claims through the mail. Sadim would investigate in Albany to find out where all the clinic's claims were piling up. And he promised to do what he could to have some staff there begin working on them immediately. He promised to send some updated instructions on expediting the claims procedures and, especially, electronic submissions.

"You said you make regular on-site visits to the providers in your area. Can you come see us?"

"I'll put you on the schedule right away. I rotate through my territory visiting the larger providers every four months. I make side trips to the smaller clients that call for some help while I'm in their area at that time." Anticipating Joseph's next question, he went on to say, "I am currently in Lumburg. Do you know where that is?" He didn't wait for an answer. "I'd estimate 80 miles north of Newcomb. I'm scheduled to be down at Wackentute County Hospital next in . . . ' there was a momentary pause as Joseph could hear him flipping some paper on the other end, ". . . I will be down seeing the County Hospital in Wackentute in early February and . . ."

"NO!!!" Joseph unintentionally yelled into the phone. He couldn't see him, of course, but Sadim nearly dropped his phone. "We need you now. Tomorrow. Can you come tomorrow? We are in desperate shape." Joseph paused, while Sadim collected himself. "We might not be here if we have to wait until February."

Sadim thought he was being dramatic, and realized that others were just as needy, and probably as impatient as he was. They had to wait their turn too. He started to tell him this when Joseph interrupted.

"When were you last here?" he asked, but didn't wait for an answer. "You haven't been here in a very long time I'll bet." Joseph was guessing, but he was right. "You've been to County....probably 3 times? Four times in the last year? Probably more than that since you've last been here. You have probably been to every single facility on your schedule at least once since you've last been here. In all fairness, we wouldn't mind waiting our turn....but you are way overdue for a visit here. And, believe me, no one . . . no one on your agenda is more desperate than we are."

There was absolute silence on both ends of the line. Joseph thought for an instant to continue pressing his case, but didn't. Finally Sadim said, "I can be there Friday. That's the absolute soonest. And for Chrissakes, don't say anything to Mr. Bryant."

Wednesday - December 11

Joseph had left a message for Gus to see him as early as possible this morning. Gus thought it was going to be about budget cuts or, even more distasteful, personnel cuts. He wasn't looking forward to the conversation, but went to see Joseph before he saw his first patient. Joseph surprised him when he recounted his call with Sadim yesterday. To Joseph it meant that help was on the way with the Medicaid reimbursement. He did not say it may be "too little – too late." Gus, somewhat relieved by the news, asked several who, what, and where questions that Joseph could not answer confidently.

Phil Podalski and Lindsay had also been left messages to see Joseph about this very same thing. And when both were told that help was on the way, they were equally skeptical. Podalski really didn't think that whatever assistance this Sadim fellow was going to bring would be enough to stem the tide. No one in the building had a better quantitative grasp of the problems the clinic faced than this accountant. Lindsay, on the other hand, dealt with the frustrations and tribulations that this colossal quagmire presented daily. She saw no "light at the end of the tunnel." She wasn't going to quit, but she no longer felt that things were going to work out. One couldn't help admire her tenacity in the face of what she thought was certain doom.

"The minute the guy walks in the door Friday I want him going through our backlogged claims," said Joseph. "We have to be ready to bury him in work. I don't want him getting coffee. Going to lunch. Talking to his wife on the phone. Nothing!" Joseph discussed with Lindsay how to best utilize this Sadim from the moment he showed up. "And we don't let him leave! I want to handcuff him to the desk. Keep him here all weekend; if we can manage it. He has to teach us how to do the easy ones. He has to do the ones that keep getting kicked back to us." Joseph was talking fast. He was excited. "Lindsay, we have to be teed up for this guy the minute he shows his face. Phil, you have to be available the entire time he's here. Maybe even pull up a chair, and stay in the room he's working in. He shouldn't be left alone for a minute." Phil was nodding in agreement. "Lindsay, let's get a desk all set up for him." He paused for a minute, and then said, "The little alcove right by your front desk! Where the copier is. That can go somewhere else for the time being. Yeah, we'll move a table in there. We can move your computer in there too. The cord is long enough, right?"

"He'll have to have access to the computer if he's going to show us how to send claims in that way!" Lindsay was getting caught up in the excitement. "I can listen to everything he says from there, without leaving the front desk."

"You're going to be the 'leg man', Phil. If we need anything, you are going to get it." Again Joseph paused, thinking things through. Then he added, "I am going to sit on his lap. He won't be able to get up; and if he burps, I'll know it!" They sat for another thirty minutes planning exactly how they were going to "ride this Sadim until he dropped."

Mena covered for Lindsay at the front desk while they brainstormed. Various members of the medical staff noticed their long and animated meeting. A few of them thought that the conversation was about proposed staff cuts. Sidelong glances toward Joseph's boisterous meeting became more common as it continued. Gus, noticing the distraction, went in to find out what was going on.

"You've got everyone on the staff worried to death about what's going on in here," Gus said, as he walked in with a pained smile on his face. "What is going on?"

"We are making plans for when this guy from the state shows up. The Boss doesn't think he plans on staying very long, and we are plotting ways to shanghai the sucker," Lindsay said. "Can we borrow some chloroform from the supply cabinet?" she suddenly asked, laughing. Joseph smiled, and Podalski even grinned. Gus wasn't absolutely sure she was kidding.

The meeting broke up, and Lindsay and Podalski went off to their jobs. Gus lingered behind. When they were out of earshot he asked Joseph earnestly, "Will there be cuts? Are we going to have to let some people go?" He gestured toward the door and said, "There are some pretty worried people out there."

"Can we afford to let anyone go? I thought we were pretty much bare bones now."

"I can't think of anyone out there right now who we can do without."

"No, I don't think we have any fat on the payroll either. No," he repeated, "I don't think we can trim anybody right now. As for the money . . . well, I won't lie to you, Gus, it's tight. Very tight! We are just barely hanging on. I hope no one is expecting a raise anytime soon."

The conversation lagged for a minute, and Gus showed no signs of leaving. Unsure why, and to break the silence, Joseph asked him about the references that had been made a few days ago concerning Paulie and Dee-Dee's wedding. Gus laughed a little bit, and said it had been a very nice affair, if you disregarded the fight. He explained that there had been some hard feelings dating back several years to an episode between Paulie, Roove and Pistol and a few of the other guests at the wedding. They were truck drivers and part-time bikers who worked for Dee-Dee's father at Rowe Trucking. Gus leaned back and launched into the story.

Several years prior to the wedding, a group of bikers took over a building that was located right next to the interstate highway that ran through Port Newhampton. The building was nothing more than an old concrete block truck garage whose owners had gone bankrupt, and was then subsequently abandoned by them. It had been fenced off and padlocked by the County, and then forgotten. This particular group of bikers, who had easily dispensed with the County's padlock on the chain linked fence surrounding the building, claimed the derelict structure and affixed a padlock of their own. And now that they had a clubhouse, they decided that they should go all the way and give their little group a name and a logo. Lacking any certifiable creative geniuses on the naming committee, the name they finally agreed on was "Satan's Sherpas." And the logo, after much debate and furious negotiations, emerged as a devil's face placed on V shaped handlebars, and crossed pitchforks beneath. And, as anyone knows, any good gang name requires a slogan to go along with it. Fittingly, that slogan turned out to be, "bearin' his EVIL to the world." They thought that that was very cool. So cool in fact that they decided to proclaim it to the world. Their name and logo appeared as patches on all their jackets in no time at all. And soon thereafter it was perched on top of their broken down clubhouse too.

The derelict building just so happened to have one redeeming aspect. On the roof was a large billboard. And it could be seen by everyone who traveled along that adjoining interstate highway. In fact it was so well positioned that anyone traveling along that interstate, in either direction, had to see it. And that amounted to thousands of people every day. One day it suddenly dawned on them like a religious epiphany that their name, their logo, and their slogan should be painted up on that billboard for the entire world to see. So shortly thereafter, on that billboard, artfully inscribed in bold black lettering, "SATAN'S SHERPAS" appeared above their logo, with their slogan beneath "Bearin' His EVIL to the World." They were deliriously giddy with how well it turned out.

In less than a year of illegal occupation they had made several improvements to their clubhouse. There were numerous strings of lights strung along the walls and overhead; a stolen stereo system with multiple speakers blasted out heavy metal rock-n-roll nonstop; and a number of dilapidated refrigerators housed their hoard of cheap beer and cheaper vodka. And to power it all they had illegally tapped into a municipal power line. As for furnishings, they had collected a variety of dirty, torn, and stained furniture, with threadbare rugs for the concrete floor. They thought they had the best hangout of any gang – motorcycle or not – in the valley. They thought they had the best name and logo too. And the billboard was, literally and figuratively, over the top.

That was why it came as a stunning blow to them when they invited Pistol to join their club, and he refused. Of course, Pistol loved his motorcycle. And he loved the outlaw nomadic lifestyle that motorcycles have always suggested. But Pistol just wasn't much of a "joiner."

Not willing to accept the perceived snub, a few of Satan's Sherpas waited until Pistol was somehow otherwise occupied, and then proceeded to locate, and beat the hell out of his motorcycle with aluminum baseball bats.

This, not surprisingly, did not sit well with Pistol. He was furious, and it didn't take him two minutes to figure out who the culprits were. He had to be restrained by his lifelong friends, Roove and Paulie, when he first discovered the damage. And just to be cautious, these two best friends babysat him for the next several days worrying that if they didn't he would have gone off after the entire gang by himself. He loved his bike.

Finally, after a few days of talking it over, he agreed with them that a frontal assault wouldn't exact enough revenge. And besides, Roove was starting to hatch a scheme that was beginning to make a lot of sense.

Several days, or more accurately nights, of reconnoitering gave the three friends the information they needed. Armed with a hacksaw, pliers, some electrical wiring, and two cans of spray paint – one white and one black – they descended on the Sherpas' clubhouse on a Tuesday morning at 3 AM. Peeking in a window, they saw several motorcycles parked inside. After making sure that the building was unoccupied (they threw a brick through the window which brought no response from inside), they each scurried off to complete their specific assignments.

The County Fire Department arrived too late to save anything that was inside the building. The "electrical fire," the official report said, had been started due to faulty and illegal wiring; it had spread quickly throughout the building because of old, dried out chairs, sofas and carpeting. The five motorcycles parked inside had ignited, and their fuel tanks had only added to the blaze. The nearly windowless concrete structure had allowed very little heat to escape, and the inside of the building, and all its contents, were incinerated. The outside did remarkably well, however. Neither the walls nor the ceiling had collapsed. And other than some very minor smoke damage, the billboard on top was unscathed.

Well, not exactly "unscathed." Sometime prior to the fire someone had apparently climbed up the long access ladder on the tall billboard, and altered it slightly. Someone had used one can of spray paint to alter the gang's name, and the other can of spray paint to add a letter to the slogan. The gang's name had been altered to read "SATAN'S HERPES". Not surprisingly the gang did not find any of this the least bit funny. The letter "T" was inserted into their slogan, so it now read "bearin' *T*his EVIL to the world". This too did not amuse them. Their logo, on the other hand, was left perfectly intact, for all to see.

Adding frustration to the embarrassment was the fact that whoever had done this had also sawed away the access ladder to the billboard after they had finished their handiwork. Now there was no way for anyone to reach it. The supporting struts were made of steel, and as such were nonflammable. Burning it down was out of the question. No, they soon came to the conclusion that the billboard would remain as is. Boldly showing their cherished logo, but with their new name and slogan, to thousands of passing cars every day for years to come.

Thursday - December 12

The first call of the day to Joseph was from a lawyer in Syracuse. He introduced himself, and said that he was calling because Robert Weller had asked him to do so. He said he was a senior partner in his law firm, and that he specialized in tax matters. "I understand you have a problem. If this is a good time for you, why don't you tell me about it?"

There are times in everyone's life when it appears that doom is inevitable. When there doesn't appear to be any escape from encircling circumstances that you are sure will finish you off. And, usually it happens. But then, on very rare occasions, something totally unexpected happens. Or better yet, *someone happens*. An old friend shows up willing to lend you the car you desperately need for the date you have that night. Or a close friend offers to lend you the money you need . . . for whatever it is that you need. And sometimes this manna from heaven doesn't have to be tangible, either. Maybe it is something as simple as an arm around your shoulders, or words of encouragement as you face what you thought were insurmountable odds.

Today, for Joseph, it was a very confident and competent-sounding lawyer. Before it went too far, Joseph had to be honest with the man. "I don't know how we're going to pay you. You probably can tell by the nature of the problem that we are not too well off, financially."

"These things always seem to work themselves out. Now, why don't you tell me what the problem is?" Joseph, holding his hand over the mouthpiece, called to Lindsay to find Podalski, and "get him in here quick." The call lasted over an hour.

The rest of the day was spent not only with the day to day routine, but with preparing for the visit tomorrow by "The Medicaid Man," as Lindsay called him. An unusually light load of walk-in patients allowed the staff to relax a little bit. They were also breathing a little easier because Gus had relayed to them that the rumor concerning lay-offs was not true.

The lunchtime gathering was a bit more crowded, with more lingering than was usually normal. Not even Joseph, who normally grabbed his lunch and went back to work, skipped out quickly today. He walked in to the pantry just in time to hear Figgit say, "I think there is more than just Plate Tectonics . . . at work here . . . although, undoubtedly . . . it plays a very important role." No one said a word. "It is obviously . . . as one would suspect in all the physical sciences . . . simply not possible to say it is random." Figgit nodded, and looked around at his listeners. Everyone he looked directly at nodded right back to him. Without a hint of disagreement in the air, Figgit went on, "Now, as you know . . . the earth has approximately 198 million square miles of surface area." There was a pause, and then, almost apologetically, he added, "Slightly less actually . . . but the exact number escapes me now." No one else in the pantry offered an exact number. "Of that surface, less than 30% is land . . . or 57 million plus square miles . . . and the water surface comprises the rest . . . more than 140 million plus square miles." No one was disagreeing. "Now what is amazing is the disparity . . . between land distribution in the Northern Hemisphere . . versus the land distribution in the Southern Hemisphere!" Without waiting for anyone to add, or object, he went on. "In the Northern Hemisphere there is a land to water surface ratio of 60 to 40 percent." Then he shrugged, and said, "Approximately, of course." He went on in a voice that could only be described as full of wonder, "And in the Southern Hemisphere? That same ratio of land to water is a paltry 20% to 80%!" He looked wide eyed around the room. The lack of amazement he saw in his listeners' faces puzzled him. "I find that astonishing." he finally said. "How can that be explained?" he wanted to know. "Geophysicists are wrestling with that problem, even as we speak . . . And, no doubt, Plate Tectonics and gravity are part of the answer . . . I'm sure we all agree with that . . . " No one said a word. "But the disparity between the two hemispheres . . . is, indeed, perplexing."

"How does he know this stuff?" whispered Ana, suddenly standing right next Joseph.

"I have no idea," shrugged Joseph. "But I don't doubt what he is saying. I would never bet against him."

"I wouldn't either." she said, and left. It occurred to Joseph that that might have been the first conversation he had had with Ana since his arrival which contained no rancor.

Later in his office as he was preparing the instructions for tomorrow's payroll, Joseph was pleasantly surprised to find out that the checks would all clear. Not by a very comfortable margin, he sighed, but they would clear, and that was good. It had been a very good day.

Friday - December 13

The minute he walked in, Lindsay knew who he was, and just stared at him. There wasn't really anything remarkable about the way he looked, but Lindsay stared anyway. He was a little taller than average, and about average weight. A plain raincoat covered a sports jacket and tie. His short, black hair gleamed, but Lindsay thought that that was probably due to the rain outside. He was carrying a large briefcase, and had a laptop bag hung over his shoulder. For reasons she could never explain she knew who he was the instant he came through the door. When he approached her desk he never got a word out. "You're Mr. Sadim. Wait right here," she blurted out. She started to turn around to get Joseph, but stopped short and turned to look at Sadim again. "I will be right back!" she assured him. This time she left.

Sadim's arrival was met with smiling faces by the entire staff. Lindsay's loud pronouncement of his name when he came in identified him to them all. Everyone on staff knew he was expected, and they all knew what his visit could mean for the clinic. It came as a bit of a surprise to him, however. He was unaccustomed to such warm receptions, and he thought it was very unusual. But this turned out to be only the first of many unusual aspects he discovered about this clinic.

He had only a minute to think about it because the receptionist was right back – as promised – with another man. All three introduced themselves, and then they brought the visitor back to Joseph's office. Lindsay disappeared, ostensibly to get his workplace ready. Joseph and Sadim got down to business.

In less than 15 minutes Joseph laid it all out for Sadim. It was nearly a monologue, because Joseph didn't stop talking. If Podalski hadn't come in and introduced himself, mid-meeting, Joseph would have been the only one who said anything. When he finally had finished his summation of the clinic's massive problems with insurance reimbursement, Sadim sat eerily silent. Joseph felt a panic attack coming on. Sadim sat there silently staring across the desk as if he had heard nothing. He eyes appeared to Joseph to be half closed. "I'd like you to start going over our requests, to see what we're doing wrong. We need these long overdue reimbursements, badly." Joseph was almost pleading.

Sadim finally said something. "Let's begin." It wasn't the rousing response he had hoped for, but at least he said something, Joseph thought to himself. He led him out to the alcove next to Lindsay's desk. Joseph noticed she never took her eyes off him. Looking for some positive note to all this so far, Joseph saw how she was watching him, and thought that if he tried to leave she looked like she would pounce on him.

The table where the computer had been set up for Sadim was also piled high with folders containing overdue reimbursement requests. Sadim insisted Joseph sit down in front of the computer, and he would sit on his right. Lindsay leaned back from her front desk to watch. The first few cases were complicated, and Sadim realized how poorly versed these two people were in processing these forms. He started to assert himself. This was his territory. He abruptly told them both that it was pointless working on these difficult ones until they had acquired some skills on the more mundane. He picked up several files and quickly went through them. And in even less time he had them both working on separate files.

The first thing that had to be mastered was quickly extracting the pertinent information from the medical charts of the patients. And he assured them that it was far easier to do than they had been doing up until now. As with any process, anywhere, there were safe shortcuts to take. And as with any government process, anywhere, there were acronyms and abbreviations that, when understood, made the process a far simpler matter. The people on the other end, i.e. the government clerks, were handling hundreds of these claims a day. They look for certain things. Keep it simple for them, and they will breeze through your claims. Sadim was speaking faster now. Joseph and Lindsay said nothing.

The second thing that was important was getting both Joseph and Lindsay comfortable with the electronic filing system. This turned out to be easier than either one of them suspected it would be. Access to the State's system opened up a new world to them both. Forms they needed for every claim were, of course, in limitless supply online. There was less data to input when the system already recognized the sender. Time after time, line after line, Sadim provided them with ways to process these claims in a fraction of the time they had spent previously. Piles of claim forms shrank. At one point Joseph picked up a file, and saw the table top underneath! He had whittled one stack down to nothing. Absentmindedly he checked his watch. It was after 1 PM. He was hungry, and had to presume both Sadim and Lindsay were too. Pleased with the progress they had made he relented a little and suggested a "short" break for lunch. Joseph had no intention of letting him out of the building for a lunch break, and offered to buy him lunch. But Sadim politely refused, saying he had brought his lunch with him. The three went to the pantry and sat down. Figgit wasn't there, and Joseph was glad. Figgit might prove a bit unnerving to a stranger.

Ana was there with Mena, and they were discussing a concert that neither one of them wanted to attend. "I might have to go," Mena said reluctantly. "My middle one is in the band at school, and they'll play, of course, for the choir."

"No offense," replied Ana, "but I would have to be tortured before I go."

"I know what you mean," nodded Mena.

Joseph introduced the doctor and nurse to Sadim, and then asked, "What concert?"

"The one kicking off the King Wenceslas Festival . . . over in Lower Wenwenee. It starts next Friday, you know?" Mena answered offhandedly. The answer made no sense to either Joseph or Sadim. Their faces showed it. "Oh," Mena noticed, "You've never been here for the King Wenceslas Weekend Winter Wonderland Festival over in Lower Wenwenee. They have it every year. It's huge. Everyone in the valley goes."

After a momentary silence, Ana added, "Everyone but Roove Hagedorn goes, you mean." Mena smiled.

Joseph didn't get the joke, and asked, "Why doesn't Roove go?"

"Ask him sometime," was all that Ana said, and left. Mena just shook her head as she cleaned up her lunch things and then left too. Sadim finished his small lunch first, and as soon as he did the other two stopped eating too. He was going to be shadowed as long as he was in the building. Joseph was thinking about how he would deny Sadim the opportunity to go outside for a smoke break, or to get some fresh air, or whatever. He was mildly surprised when Sadim, himself, suggested they get back to work.

The afternoon went by as quickly as the morning had. Both Joseph and Lindsay had gained a fresh new competence at the art of requesting medical reimbursement. But as the afternoon wore on, Joseph began thinking that the luxury of having Sadim sit with them was fast coming to a close. They had, indeed, become more adept at the process, but he was right there with them at their elbow and correcting their missteps instantly. Tomorrow he would be gone.

Trying to learn how to process claims correctly while thinking of ways to keep Sadim at the clinic for a longer period of time was taxing Joseph. The best he could come up with was a weak inquiry about whether Sadim did 'consulting work."

"'Consulting Work'? On medical claims? I doubt there's a very big call for that," he answered.

"I don't know," Joseph disagreed, "Places like ours have a tremendous need for that kind of help." The thought of finding the money to pay for this "consultant" never crossed Joseph's mind. But in the world of business Sadim would be classified as a "rainmaker"': someone who directly generated revenue. One could always find the money to pay for them!

"This place is a bit unusual. Not many places I've ever been at are this backed up. Besides, who'd pay for it when the state does it for free?"

"I bet there's a call for it. You said that your schedule is full for months going forward. And I'm not saying you should quit your job, but you could probably earn a few extra bucks doing it nights and weekends."

Sadim thought about that for a moment, then disagreed. "Wrong," he said. "If Mr. Bryant found out I was charging people for this he'd fire me. The truth is that this isn't brain surgery. I can be replaced. Or even much worse, he'd bring me back into the office in Albany. I'd have to deal with that jerk every day. I don't think I could do that. And I need this job."

The conversation went back to the claims still stacked on the table, and the tutoring went on. Joseph offered to buy him dinner when 6 o'clock came and went. Sadim again refused and explained that he still had a two hour drive in front of him. He stayed later than Joseph had even hoped for, and only left when the clinic closed for the day at 8 PM.

Politicking right up until the moment, Sadim put his car in gear and drove away; Joseph only got Sadim to vaguely promise he would be back soon. Standing in the dark and cold parking lot watching him drive away, he suddenly realized Lindsay was standing next to him. "I hoped you learned a lot more than I did today, Lindsay. I have a feeling, with him gone, a lot of what I learned today left with him."

As Sadim pulled away Lindsay said something. When she said it, the very first impression Joseph had was the certainty in her voice. And the second thing he noticed was that she had hardly said a word all day. That wasn't like her at all. And all she had said was, "He'll be back, Boss."

Saturday - December 14

If there had been a vague reference to the King Wenceslas Weekend Winter Wonderland Festival in the pantry yesterday, today it was the talk of the town. Every conversation, all morning, around the clinic dealt with "K4W," as the locals referred to it. Joseph stared in wonder at the excitement that had grabbed all the staff members, as well as patients, who beamed as the topic was discussed. Stories and jokes were passed around about the history of K4W, which apparently went back generations. He never had any doubt what the prime topic of conversation was going to be in the lunchroom today; and Mena didn't let him down.

She was telling Lindsay and Gus about the time she had let her oldest child try the "Slide for Life." "Marianne was a freshman in high school, and was badgering me to let her do it," Mena said laughing. "I knew she was scared to death, but her friends were all going to try, and I didn't have the heart to tell her she couldn't."

"I did it the first time when I was a freshman too!" Lindsay laughed. "I did it every year after that until I nearly broke my neck in Collar Bone Corner in my sophomore year at college." Everyone in the room laughed a little, and nodded knowingly.

"What did you do?" asked Joseph. Several people started talking to him, but then they relented, and let Mena take the lead.

"K4W has several contests every year, for teams and individuals, besides the food and flea market extravaganza. Oh and there's the concert too . . . along with the general carnival atmosphere." Several people jumped into the conversation at this point naming their own favorite parts of the festival. Mena waited a moment, and then continued, "The contests are run by the County Volunteer Fire & Rescue Squad as a fundraiser. There are usually four or five, different contests open for competition. They change over time, but the Slide for Life is the granddaddy of them all." She explained that competitors come from all over the county, made up of co-workers, or classmates, neighbors, families, clubs, etc. to compete as teams. "But," she went on to say, "although some of the teams and the contests change from year to year, the Slide for Life has been around for a long, long time."

"The 'Snake Race' has been going on for a long time too," Ana added. Several people contributed to the explanation of this contest to Joseph. It required teams of 10 people – 5 female and 5 male – that must have a combined weight of over 1500 lbs. Each team had to go through an obstacle course (arranged deviously by the volunteer firemen) while holding hands. The fastest team to complete the course was the winner. The obstacle course differed from year to year, but invariably involved a stretch of ice, a series of inclines, and an ambush of snowballs thrown by the other teams. If the chain of contact between members was broken - even for an instant- the team was disqualified.

"The Tub Roll too, don't forget," said Olney. "But that's not just for fun." He added, "People take that kinda serious." In the "Tub Roll," teams of three players pay a $25 fee to enter. Then two of them – the "pushers" -- push their tub, with the third member in it, toward a marker fifty yards out on the ice. The team that comes the closest to the marker wins a cash prize.

"Figgit took it very seriously two years ago. Didn't you?" Mena asked him.

"I admit, I felt success in that event could be achieved by simply reducing the basic factors to a mathematical formula." He turned to Joseph, and said, "I calculated my weight, and that of the tub, the temperature at the pond, all the variables; but I'm afraid my teammates did not follow my instructions on propulsion to the letter. My own fault. I'm afraid I opted to use brawn as a teammate, as opposed to brains. They got carried away and used far too much force." He looked at Joseph, raised his eyebrows as if revealing a dark secret, and said, "I think they did it on purpose."

"Went a good 100 yards past it, didn't you?" someone asked.

Took you a half hour to walk back with the tub, right?" said Olney. Figgit waved him off.

"Used to use a metal garbage can in the old days," said Gus. "Since they started using plastic tubs it has become a lot more scientific."

Figgit started to explain the calculations that were necessary for the accuracy needed to place the tub nearest the marker, but he was quickly interrupted.

"The "Slingshot" is somewhat like the Tub Roll, but in that contest you are trying for distance instead of accuracy." Ana explained that the same threesome would again place their lightest member inside the tub; pull it by ropes behind them as they raced as fast as they could to a line on the ice, and 'slingshot' it as far as they could. Traction, direction, and balance were factors that often led to mishaps for the "jockey."

"Why didn't you enter The Slingshot contest?" someone asked Figgut. "You showed you could travel pretty far in the Tub Roll."

"I didn't trust those morons," he answered.

There were several other contests recalled, as well as the seemingly mandatory tug of war on ice between teams. But the prime event seemed to be The Slide for Life. That was described as simply a sled race along a route prepared by the county's volunteer firemen. It had had the same route for the past 25 years. The successful completion of the run was a coveted right of passage by the people of Wackentute County. And more than just finishing the course was the attempt to be the fastest to do it. Every year, at the top of Armada Street, people lined up for their turn at the treacherous course. The fastest finisher each year was a local celebrity. Joseph overheard someone mention "Superfly's record," and thought he noticed a moment of reverence at its mention.

The conversation continued around the room. Some were talking about various strategies, both famous failures and historical successes, in the various events. Names were thrown around that brought praise, or derision, of past performances.

"No," Olney was insisting, "Superfly's record will never be broken. That's the best that there'll ever be. No one will ever beat that." He said it with absolute certainty.

"No, there's only one event at the festival that everyone will always remember," Ana said. Everyone in the room turned around to look at her. Several asked her which one she was thinking about. "When Roove did that new twist on the old favorite!"

Olney raised his eyebrows, and let out a sigh. Gus shook his head. Lindsay said to herself, "Wish I had been there. Wish I'd a seen it!" No one else said anything after that, and the room cleared out quickly.

Several hours later Joseph joined the usual group at the Fireside. For whatever reason there seemed to be a larger crowd here tonight and it included Mayor Mooney. The kidding and ribbing went on as usual, however.

To Joseph, a lot of the banter went over his head as it related to so much of their history that had occurred long before he arrived. At one point several members of the group were tormenting Magoo about some dating fiasco of long ago. It apparently had occurred at the King Wenceslas Festival. The mention of the festival reminded Joseph of the conversations he had heard in the pantry recently. Roove was standing right beside him at that moment, on the outskirts of the group.

"Oh, by the way, why don't you ever go to the King Wenceslas Festival over in Lower Wenwenee?" He asked quietly. "Someone told me to ask you that." Joseph smiled as he said it.

"Who said to ask me," he asked? Then, quickly, changing his mind he continued, "Never mind, forget it."

"'Forget it,'" laughed Magoo, who had obviously overhead. "Did you say 'forget it'? Christ, Roove, it's your crowning moment! The high point of your life! And you want to 'Forget it'?" Roove just shook his head and turned to the TV. "Okay, be that way! I'll tell him." Magoo turned to Joseph, and began the story. Every time he paused to take a breath, one of the others picked it up.

A local legend, by the name of Mrs. Rauss, had been the head of the Wackentute Valley School District Music Department for as long as anyone could remember. She ran her department with an iron fist, and tolerated no meddling by anyone. Nobody got in her way and survived. So when she retired, a lot of people breathed a little easier. And because she had worked very hard over the years she was looking forward to her retirement. But she hadn't fully realized that with retirement she would also have to give up all the extras that had come with her job. And that included Choirmaster of the Wackentute Schools Combined Choir, whose premier performance every year was at the K4W Festival Concert. When advised bluntly by her replacement — Mrs. MerriLuAnn Lomb — that her role as Choirmaster for the district was over, she fumed. And Mrs. Lomb had no intention of allowing Mrs. Rauss to interfere with one of the plums of the job, as she saw it.

Mrs. Rauss raged and fussed, and called in every old favor she felt she had, but all to no avail. Mrs. Lomb, as the new head of the Wackentute Valley School District Music Department, would call the shots with the school choir's performance. Finally, as a token of magnanimous goodwill (as Mrs. Lomb saw it), or because the Superintendent of Schools for the entire Wackentute Valley twisted her arm, she condescended to allow Mrs. Rauss to head up the *elementary* schools' combined choir. She could shepherd the grades K through 8 at the concert. That choir would be allowed to perform a maximum of four songs, not to exceed 20 minutes in total, on stage.

Mrs. Rauss smiled when she got the "good news". Inside she was volcanic. Mrs. Lomb nearly had her take an oath that she would abide by the instructions before she finally signed off on the compromise.

Over the next few days Mrs. Rauss came up with a plan which, she felt, would humiliate her successor, and clearly show to everyone who the better choirmaster was. The first thing she had to do was eliminate the children from the lowest grades - K through 3rd Grade - who would want to sing in the choir. They wouldn't have the "musical chops" to handle the performance she was going to produce. She was certain they would have neither the voices, nor the discipline, to handle what she had in mind. And she did not want their angelic little faces distracting from the performance and sound her group would deliver. She couldn't just forbid them from participating, and of course she wanted to mask the virtuoso performance she had planned with the older children. No, she thought, she would just segregate them into a separate choir. She'd have them sing one quick song, in under two-and-a- half minutes, and whisk them off the stage. She didn't even want to be bothered by the few rehearsals that would be necessary. She decided to assign some underling the job of leading this junior chorus. As she was no longer a department head, it suddenly occurred to her she no longer had any "underlings." She needed someone with at least a small familiarity with music. And that someone would have to work, if not for nothing, than maybe 20 bucks at most. After all, it was going to come out of her pocket. She didn't have to think about it for long because the name "Roove" came immediately to mind.

Yes, Roove Hagedorn. He had done some work for her in the past. Normally she would accompany her choirs and other school musical productions on the piano herself. But on those rare occasions when a piano was unavailable due to a remote location, or whatever, she had enlisted Roove, and his guitar to provide whatever subdued musical accompaniment she might require. His frequent spells of unemployment made him an ideal candidate for the occasional gigs. He was very inexpensive; he could play his guitar unobtrusively; and she felt she could browbeat him into doing anything she wanted him to do.

So she called him out of the blue one day, and told him what she wanted him to do. He politely declined, saying he really wasn't that interested in doing it. She dismissed his objections out of hand. She told him he would do it. She told him that she would tell him exactly what she wanted done. And then she went that one step too far . . . she told him that if he ever wanted to work for the Wackentute Valley Board of Education again he would do exactly as he was told. "You will handle those little shits. Get them together for a couple of rehearsals. Give them something simple to sing. Something they all already know, like 'Frosty' or something. Something sweet. Something SHORT! Get them to dress alike. Have them wear red and green. Or red and black. I don't care. Just get them ready by the Wednesday before the concert. I'll listen to them then. Don't screw this up, or I'll see you never get another dollar from the County. And Roove, the song better be short, or you'll be very sorry."

It really made no sense to threaten Roove. It only annoyed him. His frequent bouts of unemployment often came about because he felt it was his call to decide when an employer/employee relationship should end. If he was never going to work for Wackentute again, he felt it ought to be his decision to make.

And so he did.

In a flash of inspiration Roove accepted the assignment. Mrs. Rauss proceeded in shipping out the younger members of the Elementary School Choir to Roove, while she worked her fourth through eighth graders unmercifully. The program she had planned for them would have been no easy task for a college choir. And the way she thought she could make it work was through long, daily rehearsals. In a short time she had weeded out many of the kids who had initially wanted to sing. Some of the kids who stayed through sheer persistence, but who lacked a "superior voice" in Mrs.

Rauss' opinion, were criticized severely and openly. She was relentless in trying to weed out the lesser talents, as she saw them.

Meanwhile Roove's rehearsals with the younger choir were infrequent and kept very private. Not even the parents were allowed to sit in and watch. Because he did not intend to have many rehearsals, he told the parents he needed his choir's full attention, and parental presence would be a distraction. The parents were glad for the reprieve at this busy time of the year. There were no complaints. The parents would drop off their children for the occasional rehearsals, and then zoom off on other holiday errands, returning two hours later to retrieve their children.

The kids were told, on the other hand, not to reveal anything about the rehearsals. It had to be kept a secret, so their performance at the concert would be a "big surprise." Some of the children did reveal to their parents that they were learning the "grown up version" of a song that had different words, and they were a little worried because they didn't understand some of them. But with all the hustle and bustle of the season, the parents just told them not to worry, and try their best.

The Wednesday before the concert Mrs. Rauss had planned to watch a dress rehearsal of Roove's little choir. But Roove never scheduled that rehearsal, and called Mrs. Rauss that afternoon to tell her there was a measles scare going around, and he had called off the rehearsal as a precaution. Mrs. Rauss hadn't heard anything about any scare, but as she was no longer working at the school on a daily basis she accepted that she was probably a little out of the loop. For a moment she was uneasy with not seeing this junior choir before show time, but in a way she was actually glad, because now she could schedule another rehearsal for her beleaguered senior group. Before hanging up with Roove, however, she felt compelled to warn him again that his song had better be short. "What is it, anyway?" she wanted to know.

"Jingle Bells."

"Keep it short," she barked, and hung up.

"Count on it." he responded, to the dial tone.

When the King Wenceslas Weekend Winter Wonderland Festival finally arrived, Little Wenwenee was electric with excitement on that opening Friday night. The concert was always the kick-off event for the entire festival weekend. The concert was planned, as always, for the Arnold Theater at 7 PM. The Arnold, the largest theater in the Valley, could hold up to 800 people. And, as usual, it was filled to capacity with parents, grandparents, siblings, and friends of the performers scheduled to appear on the stage that night.

The first performance on the bill was traditionally the Valley's Volunteer Fire Department's "Singing Smokeys." These men were all firemen, and in their finest dress uniforms. They sang in the style of a traditional barbershop quartet, except that there were ten of them. And some were drunk.

They opened with their traditional version of "Good King Wenceslas," and followed it with "We Wish You a Merry Christmas." In hindsight it perhaps would have been better doing something a little easier to pronounce, and with fewer "S's". But when none of them passed out, nor got sick on stage, it was considered a modest success.

Next on the bill was the "Wackentute Valley Elementary School Junior (K-3) Choir." It was noted in the Concert Program that the choir would be accompanied by Mr. Reuven Hagedorn, on the guitar. It listed "Mrs. Rauss — Choirmaster." This little-noticed piece of information would haunt the woman for the rest of her life.

When the curtain swung open revealing the 21 children in the choir, the audience "oohed" and "aahed" at their indisputable cuteness. They stood seven abreast in three rows deep. The boys were all in black pants, white shirts, and red ties. The girls all wore black skirts and white blouses and had red bows in their hair. Roove sat on a stool to the side facing them; his back was to the audience. Mrs. Rauss glanced out from the wings where she was standing with her charges ready to go on next, and noticed this. She thought it mildly improper for him to have his back to the audience, but dismissed it. She was moments away from what she was certain would be her choir's triumphant performance.

The children stared at Roove in anticipation of the cue that would launch them on to the *"grownup version"* of the song they had been practicing for weeks. The audience that had burst into applause at first sight now quieted down. Roove waited for that silence. Smiling at his choir, he slowly lifted the arm of his guitar, and then brought it down.

The children began singing on that cue. But rather, it was more like talking. He had told them to speak clearly, and stay together. It was much more important to let the audience clearly hear the words of the *grownup version* than anything else. Stay together, and don't rush, he had repeated over, and over, and over again. They practically spoke the words to the hushed audience.

> "Dash up to the bar,
> Drink ten pints of beer,
> Grab a hold of Rudolph,
> Poke him in the rear,
> Don't forget to tip the stripper,
> Run naked through the snow,
> Set fire to your Christmas tree,
> And score an ounce of blow,

OOOOOOOOOH!
Jingle Bells,
Santa smells,
So does Mrs. Claus.
What fun it is,
To take a whizz,
When you don't have any sores."

OOOOOOH,
Jingle Bells,
Santa smells,
So does Mrs. Claus.
What fun it is,
To take a whizz,
When – you – don't – have – any –sores!!!

MERRY CHRISTMAS, EVERYBODY!"

The kids finished singing, and stood there wide-eyed, with beaming smiles. And that was rightfully so, for they had been told to expect thunderous applause.

There wasn't any.

In fact there wasn't a sound in the entire auditorium. You could have heard a pin drop! Not a foot shuffled. There wasn't a murmur, or a cough. And certainly not a word was spoken. Oh, it wasn't because everyone's mouth was clamped shut. If you had looked around the audience at this moment you would have seen a great many mouths wide open. There just wasn't any noise. Anywhere! After a few seconds of absolutely no response, the choir's wide smiles began to fade with uncertainty.

No one was moving. The young choir that had, at first, expected the roar of approval, grew more apprehensive at the silence. This massive pregnant pause lasted for 19 seconds. It certainly seemed in hindsight to many people there that it went on longer than that. But the recordings on many camcorders would show it only lasted for roughly 19 seconds. Because at that precise moment Pistol Graham, who was sitting in Row 20, stood up and shouted, "ONE . . . MORE . . . TIME!"

That broke the spell. Mrs. Rauss came roaring out onto the stage at a full gallop from behind the curtains on the right. She was a large woman, and she was wearing those laced up, thick, half high-heeled shoes, so the sound she made as she raced across the stage in the silent theater reverberated off the walls. CLOMP . . . CLOMP . . . CLOMP . . . CLOMP . . . .

She went flying across the stage past the choir (faster than anyone would have thought possible), and grabbed Roove by the hair, and without breaking stride kept moving right toward the curtains on the left. The sight of the nearly apoplectic Mrs. Rauss racing across the stage, with Roove in tow, apparently unleashed some of the onlookers in the audience. Many of them now began charging the stage. They came down the aisles like a Mongol horde. One can only assume it was to gather up their children. And as they were raging down the aisles toward the stage, screaming, pushing, and probably cursing, they came at the choir out of the darkened audience into the light around the stage. The sight of the enraged Mrs. Rauss, roaring across the stage and hauling Roove off the stool, only added to the chaos of the onrushing audience, and all this must have unnerved those little singers something awful, because they all took off screaming. And just at that moment there was an enormous crash from backstage.

Mrs. Rauss, still with a death grip on Roove's hair, had flown off into the wings of the stage on the left and run into a table with some old leftover stage props on it . . . pots and pans and things. She hit it hard, and the table, the props, and Mrs. Rauss and Roove went crashing to the floor. Roove remembered they were both lying on the floor trying to collect themselves when they both spotted a 10 inch frying pan lying a few feet away. Mrs. Rauss let go of Roove's hair to grab it, and he correctly assumed that once she got her hands on it, he was going to catch a beating. One-on-one he might have liked his chances, but if she has the pot . . . well, "Advantage, Rauss."

Released from the Rauss death grip, with his guitar still strapped across his shoulder, he decided to take this opportunity to head out the side door, up the alley, and into the night, leaving his coat somewhere backstage. Because of all the fuss going on, he had properly come to the conclusion that this was not the best time to retrieve it.

That was why he went back the next day; to reclaim his coat. To avoid attracting any attention he drove very cautiously when he got back to Lower Wenwenee. And because the festival was still on, some streets were blocked off and closed, so Roove wound up having to drive right past the Town Hall to get back to the theater. And who do you suppose was walking out of Town Hall just as Roove cruised by? None other than George Neidermeyer, the Mayor of Lower Wenwenee, and according to tradition, also the Grand Marshall of the entire Festival! He had, as you might have guessed, been present at last night's concert. He took one look at Roove as he cruised by and couldn't believe that he had the unmitigated gall to show his face back in town. He bolted between two parked cars into the street. Roove, not surprisingly already on high alert, saw him in his rear view mirror, and sped up. But because he didn't want to attract any more attention than necessary by speeding, he accelerated just enough to avoid getting caught by the frantic mayor, who was in hot pursuit on foot. The mayor interpreted this as "taunting," and it made him even more furious (if that was possible). And the mayor quickly came to the realization that he wasn't going to catch the car. Spotting some pieces of broken sidewalk at his feet, he scooped them up and began heaving them at Roove's retreating Corolla.

Roove had only been back in Lower Wenwenee a few times since that day, and always at night. He never got his coat back.

"The mayor threw rocks at your car?" asked a stunned Joseph.

"Technically, it was concrete. But, hell, I think he woulda thrown hand grenades if he had 'em! He was pretty mad," Roove assured Hamilton nonchalantly.

"Where'd you get those lyrics? How'd you get those kids to sing them?" asked the wide-eyed Joseph.

"Made them up myself," sighed the man in the green baseball hat.

"You got a real gift there, Roove."

Sunday - December 15

There were two topics Joseph wanted to talk to Podalski about this morning. He was going to have to talk fast, because it was very cold and the wind was gusting. Joseph was not planning on any long and leisurely skate today. It had even surprised him that Podalski had shown up with his children. "Oh, we're hardy stock . . . we Podalskis! Right, kids?" All three children responded back in the affirmative.

"First, let me ask you if you were able to nail down the tax status the clinic has?"

"Yes," he answered right away. "We are a Not-For-Profit organization."

"You're sure? We're not an LLC or anything like that? You're sure?" Joseph wanted to be absolutely certain. Podalski went on to list the steps he had taken to assure himself that he had it right.

After listening to the accountant make his case, he went on to the second topic. "Look, in the lunch room last week I told Gus and Mayor Moonie what a great skater you were." Skating easily alongside Joseph, Podalski murmured a "thanks," and nodded in agreement. He thought he was a good skater too. "They were talking about needing 'good skaters' for their Geetha team, and," Joseph hesitated for a moment, and then said, "I sort of volunteered you." Joseph peeked sideways at the shorter man to see his reaction. His face remained blank for a moment, and Joseph instantly regretted what he had done. He started to apologize, but Podalski suddenly let out a whoop!

"Are you kidding? OH MAN!" he yelled. His children turned around to look at him. He let out another yell, and then exclaimed to his now approaching, wary, children. "GUESS WHAT?" he shouted. They had half-smiles on their faces. Their Dad didn't get this animated very often. "I'm going to be on the Newcomb Geetha team!" He paused for a moment to let in sink in. More for his benefit, than for his children's, he suddenly began to run along the ice. He took four, or five steps, then stopped and whirled around to face his companions. "OH MAN . . . OH MAN . . . OH MAN!"

It took a while for Podalski to finally calm down enough for Joseph to talk to him. He apologized for not telling him sooner. He apologized for taking the liberty of volunteering him in the first place. He apologized for presuming he'd even want to play. And he told him he would be responsible for getting him out of this if that's what he wanted. Podalski heard very little of what was said to him. His head was swimming. He did hear Joseph talk about rescinding the invite, if that's what he wanted. He nearly jumped on the taller man, telling him to not even think about that. They discussed what they knew about the game, and the upcoming renewal of the league. The accountant was ecstatic.

Joseph thought about this later in the day. He had never seen anyone win the lottery, but this had to be close.

Chapter Six

"Hey, did you see all the signs they put up for this year's K4W?" Mena said to Gus the minute he arrived this morning. "This year's version of the King Wenceslas Weekend Winter Wonderland Festival is going to be the best ever," she declared. Everyone in the clinic seemed to agree. It was today's prime topic among the staff at the clinic. As a matter of fact, Joseph didn't even hear the word "Geetha" until nearly lunch. It amazed him about how fascinated the staff was with the "K4W." He looked forward to the lunchroom conversation.

There were eight people in the pantry by the time Joseph arrived to eat his lunch. Tales were being told of festival highlights of the past, and everyone was joining in. Joseph waited to see if anyone would talk about the Roove choir episode. But no one did, to Joseph's disappointment. They each spoke about their own personal favorite memories. No one could agree on what was the best thing at the festival. Everyone had their own favorite event; their own favorite memory; their own favorite thing to eat, or do. But they all seemed to agree on one thing. It was the best event in the entire year. And everyone seemed to agree that missing it was a serious mistake.

What happened next has been debated, by those present, ever since. The excitement and tale telling was going on full tilt. People were speaking over, around, and through everyone else. And Joseph, who was standing across the table from Ana, caught her eye, and said . . . something.

"Of course I do!" she said back to him. The rest of the people in the room stopped what they were saying in mid-syllable. Every eye in the room flashed between Ana and Joseph. There wasn't a sound. "What?" She said looking around, suddenly aware of the stillness. She was instantly on guard. Suspicious. She wondered . . . what just happened? She finally looked at Joseph, "What did you just say?"

Joseph, realizing something was amiss, thought back all of 10 seconds ago, and repeated what he had asked her. "'Would you like to go to the festival?'"

She was immediately shaking her head, "No. You asked 'Do you like to go to the festival?' That's what you said. You didn't say 'Would you.' You said, 'Do you.'" she paused for a minute. Her eyes scanned the room, and then back at Joseph. "Didn't you?" she said, almost pleading.

Perhaps a real gentleman would have understood her dilemma, and let her exit the situation gracefully. He could see in front of him a woman who was normally strong-willed, independent, and in control. But at this very moment she appeared as vulnerable and as fragile as a grape.

And he squashed her.

"Nope. I said "Do you.' And I believe you said, 'Of course I do.' So, let's say I'll pick you up at five? We can have an early dinner, and then take in the festival."

She stood there staring at him. Inside she was trying to remember if she was in the process of inhaling, or exhaling. She was too flummoxed to be angry. She nodded, and left.

The other people in the room couldn't remember the last time they had seen her speechless. One by one they cleaned up their lunch things, and went back to work, smiling. As Lindsay walked out of the room she patted Joseph on the shoulder, and said, "Way to go, Boss!"

The delight he got from that exchange was with him all afternoon. Not even phone calls from irate and rude sales managers could bring him down. He answered, immediately, every call that came in. He was cheerful and enthusiastic, no matter how dour the caller was. And in the middle of the afternoon he got one call which made his day even better.

The call certified the tax status of the clinic; and it was exactly as Podalski said it was. They were set up as a Not-for-Profit. We are, indeed, needy. We are certifiably needy. And we can, now, accept charity. He began re-working the plan he had devised with Podalski as they had skated around the pond a few Sundays ago. The certification had also removed any tiny doubt that he may have had concerning what motivated Gus and Ana to work as hard, and as unselfishly as they did. He would not let them down.

The meeting to organize the proposed tournament was scheduled to be held at 8 o'clock that night in Little Sittlerville, at the Third Presbyterian Church on Wepner Street. Holding the meeting in a church seemed appropriate to those who held the game in such high esteem. It seemed a sacrilege to those who considered the game nothing more than a fistfight held on ice.

The team representing Newcomb included Gus, the honorary captain, Moonie, the captain, Roove and Paulie, and the three "new" substitute players, Hamilton, Podalski and Rowe. They arrived a little early and joined the South Reddington Angels contingent that was already there. A few greetings were passed back and forth between the players on the two teams. Podalski and Joseph just sat and watched as a couple of quiet conversations were struck up. A few minutes later the representatives of the Braxtburg Town Blue Canes came in. Again, some greetings were passed around from group to group.

At exactly 8 o'clock the door in the rear of the church swung open, and in walked the entire team, or so it seemed, of the Port Newhampton Blades. They walked in two abreast, almost as if they were marching. They were dressed in various types of clothing; some were even wearing sunglasses. But every one, every single one of them, was dressed entirely in black. They sat down in unison, bunched together in the last two rows. A long silence followed as everyone already there twisted around in their seats to look in the low light at the Blades. Moonie started to stand and address the group, but was quickly interrupted.

A tall man rose from the Port Newhampton group and said, "It's eight o'clock. I don't think we ought to wait for anyone else to show up. If they're late, that's too damn bad." He smiled around the room, and then continued, "I'm 'Cobra,' but most of you know that already." He smiled again. "We know why we're here. We all know that the Newcomb Bombers got possession of the Geetha Trophy illegally. This meeting is to correct that injustice, and set the rules for a 'legal' tournament to decide who is to get the *permanent* possession of the Geetha Trophy." He paused for minute as all the Blades and a few other people around the room nodded in agreement. "I see we have the Angels from South Reddington here," he said looking at the men seated in the front row. "Always good to see the 'Torpedo,' and the 'Pastor.'" Cobra turned toward the group from Braxtburg Town, "Some faces I don't recognize over there among the Blue Canes . . . Hope Mr. Quarf hasn't retired?" he asked, again smiling.

"No, he ain't retired. He'll be steppin' over the boards when the game starts. You can count on it," said a very large man who spoke for that group. The seven other players in that group thought what the large man had said was humorous, and laughed among themselves.

"Okay, back to business. I see, also, that the Bombers are present. Hope to hang on the trophy, do you?" he said without a smile. He turned his attention back to the room in general. "It seems that East Blessing and Lower Wenwenee have decided to accept defeat gracefully, and not show up! Let's get started. What we've got to do tonight is set up the ground rules. Just so there'll be no fooling around with the rules . . . *this time.*"

The meeting went on for another hour as they discussed the frame work of the tourney. They discussed and debated the schedule, and it was eventually decided that each team would play each other team one time.

The team with the best record after three games would be declared the champion… ONCE AND FOR ALL! If two teams had identical records after the three games, then goal differential would be the tiebreaker. This rule would encourage running up the score, which seemed to appeal to the Port Newhampton Blades.

The schedule was drawn up quickly, and because all games would be played on Corrigan's Pond, a coin toss decided which team would be the "home team." This was important because the "home team" was responsible for providing the geetha that would be used in the game. Historically, teams took pride in their selection of what the geetha would be. The rules concerning this were loosely defined, but basically stated that the geetha should be a certain size and weight approximating that of the "historic geetha," i.e. a moose carcass. What exactly that amounted to, no one seemed to be certain. There was, of course, some leeway but, as always, the referee would be the final judge. Although not mandatory, it was not uncommon to show the referee a few days beforehand what the team was going to use. But it was never revealed to the "visiting team" until just before game time. This supposedly gave the home team a slight psychological advantage. The coin toss did not go well for the Bombers; they lost all three flips for their three games.

The selection of who would referee would be easy. The referee, or "White" as he was invariably called, would be Billy Shackleton of Lower Wenwenee. The Wackentute Geetha League had a member of the Shackleton family refereeing its games for as long as anyone could remember. They were truly the First Family of Geetha refereeing. He had already been contacted, and had welcomed the invitation.

A more difficult topic was discussed next. The sore point of who would be eligible to play was raised. Although several alternatives were discussed, the teams finally arrived at an agreement that if this was truly a "replay" of that last tournament, only the original roster of players should be allowed. Not mentioned was the reason most of the players wanted it this way. Because several years had gone by since that tournament, and since most of them were not the *young studs* they had been back then, they did not want to be replaced in this tourney by younger, newer players. But they agreed that because intervening time had scattered some of the original players to the wind, some replacements would be necessary, and allowed. But replacement players would be limited to no more than four per team. And these "new" players had to be the same age level that the old players were, i.e. 30 or older. They had to be legal residents of the town they played for. ("No more ringers," said Cobra, jabbing the Bombers again.)

These substitute players were now presented by their respective teams. Each proposed player had to show a valid driver's license, which was examined by the representatives of the other teams. And after a bit of useless debate, the three replacement Bombers, two for the Angels and two for the Blue Canes, were accepted. The Blades proudly proclaimed that their team was totally intact.

There was suddenly a lull in the room, and Cobra again took the floor. "I think that pretty much covers it. Right?" he asked no one in particular. "If there's anything else, bring it up with White. He can rule on it." Some people began to stand up and put on their jackets. "Wait a minute, everyone. Just settle down. There's one more piece of business," Cobra called out. He looked around the room while people hesitated a moment, a few mumbled something or other, but then resettled in their seats. Waiting until there was silence in the room, Cobra turned very slowly to the Blades seated behind him, and said, "You have the floor."

Joseph looked, as did everyone else, at a man seated in the rear pew who stood up very slowly. He moved around to the front of the room, and very, very slowly turned to face the other three teams. He was a tall, broad-shouldered man, and dressed like all the other Blades, totally in black. But, he was different. He had highly polished black boots coming out from underneath his black leather pants. His black leather vest, with silver studs, was worn over a black tight-fitting turtle neck sweater. His long thin face was squared off by a pencil thin goatee formed with geometric precision. It ran from above his upper lip, around the corners of his mouth down to his jaw lines, and coming back together at the point of his chin. A small spot of a "soul patch" was just under his lower lip. An eyebrow ran across the top of both of his deep inset eyes. He wore a small gold loop earring in one ear, and a diamond earring in the other. He had what appeared to be a large expensive gold watch on his left wrist. He was wearing a large pinkie ring, apparently a diamond, which glittered in the low light of the room. On his head was a black silk do-rag, which concealed whatever hair he had on top and only the long sideburns and six inch ponytail that crept out the back down his neck were visible. Joseph was, as was everyone in the room, completely captivated by the presence of the man.

"This is going to be good," whispered Gus, leaning over very close to Joseph, "That's Jardine." Joseph turned to look back at Gus and ask why it was "going to be good," but then the Blade began to speak. And when he started to speak, because he spoke so softly, everyone in the room seemed to lean forward to hear him.

"We play a very dangerous game . . . you and I." he said. In a voice only slightly louder than a whisper, "We step over that sideboard into the abyss . . . where our pride . . . our self-respect . . . our manhood . . . can be gone . . . . GONE!" he suddenly shouted, startling everyone, and then added in a whisper again, "in a moment." After a moment's pause he started, again whispering, "We don't know what the next moment will bring. It may be glory. It may be disgrace." He nodded knowingly. "We risk so much . . . so much," he repeated, " . . . for what?" He looked around the room as if he expected someone to answer. He paused briefly before beginning again, "We risk our pride . . . our reputations . . . we risk our well-being." He took two steps to his right, and then whirled around at the people watching him. There was a very short pause. "WE MAY VERY WELL LOSE OUR LIVES OUT THERE ONE DAY!" he shouted. Joseph thought the man in black was getting a little bit overly dramatic, but he said nothing. He glanced over at Gus, and saw he was smiling at the speaker. The speaker remained absolutely silent and motionless for a few seconds. No one else in the room moved a muscle.

"You've all been out there . . . over the boards. You've seen people get hurt. Each of us has dished out a little pain in our time, haven't we?" he smiled. People continued to sit motionless in the room. "We've given out a little pain . . . and felt a little pain too. Some more than others, right? Torpedo? . . . Baboo? . . . Caveman? . . . Sandman?" he asked, as he let his gaze scan around the room. Then he stood motionless again, his dark eyes peering into the crowd. "We risk our souls," he hissed after a moment of silence. There was another pause, "But need we risk our precious *purckles*?"

"Purckles?" whispered Joseph.

"Here it comes," whispered Gus.

"Battered and bruised," the man in black continued, his shoulders hunched over and his arms stiff by his sides, "We step back over the boards. Exhausted . . . spent . . . hurting, and perhaps even facing certain defeat, yet . . . yet," he said pausing between words, "We can still smile! We can still . . . What is that expression they use? Oh yes, we can still *grin and bear it*." He nodded, for emphasis and scanned his audience left and right. "In your heart you know you have fought the good fight. You know you have given your all. The cause may have been lost. And defeat may be the only thing you take from the frozen field of battle; but you can still laugh in its face. Smile at the enemy without shame; and grit your teeth for the trials yet to come . . . IF . . . If you had the foresight . . . If you had taken the precaution . . . the simple precaution of getting, and using," he said slowly, "the Jardine Vault," his arms shot up above his head triumphantly, "all will be well in the end."

"What did he just say?" asked the suddenly confused Joseph.

"Sssshhh," insisted Roove, sitting next to him, "He's on a roll." Joseph looked back and forth to Gus and Roove, unsure of what he had just heard. Both of them were staring at Jardine.

"The Jardine Vault .... Model T32 ... Series K300 .... researched .... invented .... developed and perfected..... and patented as the surest way to protect your irreplaceable smile," he said to the group, again nodding knowingly. "It allows you to play at your best! It allows you to play with the confidence that's so essential to playing at that highest level." Suddenly he was standing bolt upright, with his hands on his hips, and flashing the widest, open-mouthed smile Joseph had ever seen. His chest was heaving, he seemed nearly out of breath, but thundered on. "Made from space-age polymer plastic; it is strong, yet lightweight . . . with the patented air-flow ventilation system which allows maximum respiratory capacity."

"What the hell is he talking about?" Joseph asked Roove. Roove again motioned him to be quiet.

"I've always used it. Not because I invented it. No! I use it because it works!" He said with absolute certainty. "My teammates here – the Port Newhampton Blades – all use it. And not just because I insist that they do. But because it is the best protection you can get. A fitting can take as little as a half hour in my office . . . the procedure is absolutely painless. No injections . . . no drilling . . . no scraping . . . and if it's stolen . . . ."

"Is this a mouthpiece? Are we talking about a mouthpiece? Who'd steal someone's mouthpiece?" Joseph was astonished. Gus and Roove were smiling.

" . . . or if it's lost, it's replaceable in three days by re-using the mold I made when it is first custom fitted to your own mouth. I save all the molds in my own high security storeroom for just such an emergency."

"He has a 'high security storeroom' for mouth molds?"

"And how much does all this protection cost? What is the cost you ask? What's the value of that sense of security you'll have when you step over the boards?" By the look on his face he was absolutely mystified by the question. "'But it's only one short tournament we're playing,' you may say. Why get a Jardine Vault Model T32 Series K300 if we're only going to play a few games? you may wonder." With his left hand on his hip, and his right hand extended and pointing to his audience he declared in no uncertain terms, "I will tell you right now that if you only step over the boards for five minutes, and it saves you the agony and the expense that a shot to the mouth can cause . . . *intentional or otherwise.*" He let the question hang in the air for a moment, then winked knowingly to his audience, then went on, "How much does all this peace of mind cost? It's insignificant compared to the expense of having dental reconstruction done." He was so earnest it was painful. He stopped for a moment to nod again to his audience, "The Jardine Vault, Model T32 Series K300 *saves you money,*" he assured his listeners, "For the protection it is going to provide those wise, prudent players who take advantage of my special offer, it might very well save them many hundreds of dollars. Maybe a thousand? Maybe more!" He nodded knowingly for a moment, and then stood motionless. He then raised his hand, and his pointed finger swept the room, "It could easily save you thousands." He placed his hands on hips, his legs spread wide apart, moving only his head to scan his entire audience, he finished his spiel by saying, "And I do this as a public service to my Geetha-playing brethren. I do this because I am one of you. I do this because I care!" Joseph sat in disbelief of what he had just seen and heard. Before he could say a word Jardine again spoke, but this in a fast, flat tone of voice. "Ten percent discount to the first ten customers . . . all major credit cards accepted . . . call my office for an appointment. I'm in the White Pages."

Once back in Newcomb after the meeting, Roove suggested they stop off and have a few beers. Gus and Podalski begged off, but the rest of them went to the Fireside. Seated around a table, with beers served around, Joseph couldn't wait to ask about the Jardine Vault. "What's his story?" he asked, "And what is a 'purckle'?"

"You mean Superfly?" Roove grinned. "Yeah, he weirds me out too. Even if you've caught his act before."

"He speaks *in tongues*, Joseph," Paulie answered. Then by way of explanation he added, "But not in any tongue anyone else on this fuckin' planet uses."

"Superfly?" Joseph made a face.

"That's his nickname," Moonie explained. "Likes to think he's super cool."

"Cool or strange? Take your pick, but I'll tell you one thing. The dude can play Geetha," conceded Paulie. "He can play!' he repeated. "He's about as good as anyone in the league, I think." He looked around the table to see if anyone was about to disagree, and seeing no objections he added, "But man, he is strange!"

"Can't believe Ana was going to marry that shithead," Moonie said, almost as an aside.

"What!" Joseph blurted out. The others paid no attention to him.

B-Ball stared at his bottle of beer, and asked it, "What's a purckle?"

"Still doin' that mumbly shit," said Paulie shaking his head, ignoring B-Ball.

"'You heard that too? Thought it was me for a second. What was it? 'Your purckles'?" Moonie asked between sips of beer.

"Where does he come up with that shit?" asked Roove.

"What the fuck are purckles?" B-ball wanted to know.

"I was waiting for something. Even thought for a minute he was going to make it all the way through his spiel tonight without a hitch."

"Nah," Roove laughed, "Once he started getting into it I knew he'd derail somewhere."

"Hell, he's given that speech so many times, he could probably do it in his sleep. I thought he'd make it."

They all remained quiet for a minute, thinking it over. "Yeah, but when we start playing again," Roove chimed in. "I bet he goes right back to saying all kinds of weird shit again once he gets back over the boards."

Roove paused for a moment, and then added, "Makes you kinda wonder what's goin' on inside that fuckin' head of his."

"Fact is . . . he can play though. Don't forget that for a minute. He got game!" assured Moonie once again.

Joseph grabbed the floor, "Wait a minute . . . You said he almost married Ana? You're kidding, right?" He was staring right at Moonie.

Moonie shook his head and smiled, then answered, "I don't know if it really went that far. But she did date him for a while. It was just after she had moved back here, and he was the young stud doctor with the black Corvette. I guess to a lot of women he might look like quite a catch."

"He's a doctor?" Joseph asked.

"He's a dentist," explained the Mayor. "That's where "the vault" comes in. He makes them. Makes good money doing it! He's been doing it for years. I guess this is his last shot."

The conversation meandered from "Superfly Jardine" to his "vault", to his occasional lapses into nonsense words. Joseph didn't hear most of it. He sat there trying to picture A. Ronald Jardine, D.D.S. and Ana Gustafson, M.D. as a couple.

"No, really! What's a purckle?" B-Ball asked quietly, looking around the table.

Tuesday - December 17

The talk around the clinic today remained centered around the upcoming K4W. A few people did ask about the Geetha meeting that had been held last night, however. But neither topic was Joseph's primary concern this morning. He sat at his desk going over overdue bills, and trying to decide which ones would be paid. He wondered where the reimbursement payments from the state were. He asked Lindsay if she had heard anything from the Medicaid office. She hadn't, of course. They would have contacted Joseph, as the Office Manager. He called Sadim, and only reached his voice mail. He called four different private insurers who also owed the clinic payments. Each one was polite and helpful, but none would promise that he would be providing any significant amount of reimbursements any time soon. He reminded each one of them in turn that every little bit helps. Their responses were not enthusiastic.

The exercise with the private insurers took up what was left of the morning. When he finally went to pantry for his lunch, only Gus and Figgit were sitting there. They were discussing a medical test that had given off the wrong results. They did not know why, but suspected a faulty machine in the lab. "We can buy a new one for . . . " Figgit thought out loud, "less than

$10,000." He waited a moment, and then nodded. "Or, I believe, they can be leased."

"How much does that cost?" Gus asked.

"I think we can lease one for 300 dollars a month," Figgit said, and then added, "perhaps a little less?"

"Can we get a used one?" Joseph asked. Both men turned and looked at him. "We don't have a lot of money lying around right now for new equipment."

Gus looked at him, and shook his head, "I'm afraid with this kind of equipment, that's not really an option."

With nothing resolved, Joseph went back to his office. He passed by Lindsay and asked her if she had heard from either the state or Sadim. A bit exasperated at hearing that question again, she shook her head, and said, "Boss, I will tell you the minute I hear from Albany. Okay?"

Once back in his office, he sat and wondered where he would come up with the funds they so desperately needed. His gloom lifted slightly when he took an unexpected call from his two friends in Brooklyn. "Hey," they both shouted into the speakerphone on their end. He couldn't help smiling when he heard their voices. "Hey!" he replied back, although in a somewhat lower tone of voice than they had. "What's up?" he wondered out loud. They had never called him in the middle of the month before. They proceeded to tell him about some recent developments at their fledgling company, 2BIC. They were excited, and didn't want to wait for their next regular call in January. It was good news, and they wanted to share it. Joseph was pleased and excited right along with them. It was, indeed, good news for them, for 2BIC, and for part-owner, Joseph Hamilton.

Although there was no concrete timetable for what was going on, they had absolutely turned the corner. The call lasted another 15 minutes as they went over what sketchy details they did have. And when he hung up he wished he felt as good about the clinic as he did about the way things were going for Barry and Bernie, and 2BIC, and by extension Joseph Hamilton. He thought about ways he could include the clinic in their good fortune, but indefinite plans made very bad cornerstones for solutions to real problems.

He spent the rest of his day trying to source money for the clinic. "Where can I get money?" was a question he asked himself a hundred times. The famous quote by legendary bank robber Willie Sutton came to mind. Asked why he robbed banks, he had responded, "Because that's where the money is!" Joseph asked himself time and time again, "Where's the money?" It annoyed him that the only answer he came up with was that the state had their money, and wouldn't give it to them. He was frustrated and angry.

Wednesday - December 18

He asked Lindsay before she had her coat off whether she had heard from the state. She replied with "The Death Stare." He took it as a "no." He sat staring at the clock on the wall for almost an hour. It made no sense to process any bills; there was virtually no money in the clinic's checking account. He had called the bank at 9:03 to confirm the balance. He wanted to know from them if any overnight transfers, from any source, had made their way into the clinic's accounts. And without the ability to pay bills, taking calls from irate sales people made no sense either. It wasn't something he normally liked to do, but he refused to take any calls.

He called Sadim at 9:15. He called again at 9:40. Continually getting his voicemail was infuriating. "Where the hell is he?" he wondered. "Why the hell doesn't he return a phone call?" he asked anyone who wandered by his office. He went and got himself a cup of coffee, after trying to reach Sadim again, at 10:15. He ran across Lindsay in the pantry making herself a cup of tea. He complained to her about Sadim, and how he had seemed so nice when he had been at their clinic. "But now," he said angrily, "That creep has gone into hiding."

"No, he hasn't!" she said. "I just spoke to him." She was clearly annoyed.

"You just spoke to him? I've been trying to reach him all week! What did he say?" Joseph was incredulous. He wanted to ask more questions, but she interrupted.

"We just talked. He didn't say anything about you." Joseph nearly snapped. And Lindsay kept defending Sadim. This conversation teetered on the edge of civility for several minutes.

When the smoke cleared the explanation was that Joseph had been calling the office phone number, the one on his business card. And that office was rarely visited by Sadim, who spent 98% of his time on the road. He could retrieve his voicemails electronically, but did not do so more than once a day. The line was shared by other traveling coordinators and was notoriously unreliable. He had given them his cell number, but only Lindsay had held onto it! Embarrassed that the inability to connect with Sadim was mostly his own fault, Joseph got the cell number from Lindsay and raced back to his office.

The call to Sadim was answered immediately. After an amiable starting question of, "Hello, how are you doing,?" Joseph bombarded him with several more in rapid succession.

The only question Sadim answered with any degree of certainty was that first one. "I'm fine. How are you?" He, much to Joseph's dismay, was unable to provide any solid information that Joseph wanted to hear. He couldn't inform him of the status of the backlogged claims and therefore any subsequent timetable for reimbursements. But Sadim told him he was going to be in Albany tomorrow for meetings and would personally try to find the physical submissions they had been sending in, and that had apparently disappeared. He also said he would check on the recent electronic submissions that Lindsay had been incessantly sending since his visit here. "It's the state, remember. Nothing moves quickly, or smoothly. But I'll be there....and I'll see what I can find out. I'll see what I can do." It was a small consolation, but it was something.

After another call to the bank, which still had no good news for him, he continued to sit at his desk and wonder where he could source some funds. Asking yourself the same question over and over again unfortunately provides the same unsatisfying answer every time. He acknowledged regretfully, he was no fund-raiser. He had known some of them back in his heydays at OCS Financial. They had paraded around the executive suite about once a year in an effort to raise funds for various charities supported by OCS. Every executive in the organization was expected to contribute. And these fund-raisers were not shy in advising one and all that the CEO and Founder of OCS, Henry Kryder, himself would SEE the roster of donors and their contributions! There was no attempt at subtlety; they had a job to do, and felt that this direct and blunt approach was the best way to do it. And it surprised Joseph how successful they were year in and year out. He could have used them here at the clinic now.

"Jesus Christ!" he suddenly said in a hushed voice. "The Kryder Foundation! They make grants to all kinds of organizations!" He thought for moment, and then shouted, "WE'RE A CHARITABLE ORGANIZATION!" And added a more subdued, "Or close to it, God damn it!"

Getting up the nerve to call Henry Kryder after all this time, and all that had gone on, wasn't going to be easy. But the importance of making the call in an attempt to get some grant money from them was undeniable. He would just have to swallow some pride and do it.

After some sleuthing he came up with the new number for the executive suite at OCS Financial. It took him another ten minutes to work up the courage to dial the phone. He didn't recognize the voice of the woman who answered the phone. He wondered for an instant where Margaret Mary Fitzgerald was. He wondered if she even still worked there. He thought about perhaps asking for her, but then quickly decided to do what he had planned to do. He asked to speak to Henry Kryder, and gave his own name. The voice immediately told him Mr. Kryder was currently unavailable, and that she would take a message. Joseph left his name and number, and then suddenly decided to ask if Mr. Montoya was still Executive Director of the Kryder Foundation.

Calling Montoya was really not going to produce any tangible results. Joseph knew that for a fact. Henry made all the decisions concerning to whom, and how much the Kryder Foundation sent. The Board of Directors, as well as the Executive Director himself, merely rubber-stamped the recommendations Henry Kryder made. After all, it was mostly his money.

He called Montoya anyway, and Montoya, surprisingly, took the call. After an exchange of pleasantries and a very brief catch-up on each other's lives, Joseph told him why he was calling. He had expected Montoya to be completely noncommittal. He was surprised when he wasn't. Montoya told him that there wasn't any chance that the Kryder Foundation would, or could, do anything. The fiscal year of the Foundation was over, and they had closed their books already. He added, with patently false optimism, "that perhaps somewhere down the line something might be possible." He was plainly very uncomfortable on the phone, and ended the conversation at the first opportunity.

Joseph sat in his office without moving after hanging up. He had had no right to expect any grand resolution to money problems based on this one call, but he had hoped to find, at least, a glimmer of hope somewhere in it. He realized glumly that the future of this clinic was probably tied to his ability as a fund raiser. And, right now, that future was bleak.

Thursday - December 19

A long, sleepless night had turned into a gray, wet morning. He made his way to the clinic, driving through the sleet and rain, asking himself where he could find money. He toyed with the idea of finding someone else who was good at it. But he quickly came to the realization that the clinic didn't have that much time.

He trudged into the clinic and went immediately to his office. Other responsibilities he had were piling up as he focused almost all his energy recently on fundraising. Podalski appeared in his doorway. "We got some money," was all he said. Joseph leaned back in his chair. He didn't smile.

"How much?" He didn't ask who sent it. That was of secondary importance..

"Twenty-six thousand . . . four hundred and twenty-two dollars . . . and eighty-six cents." the accountant said. "And it's better than a check. It's much better. It's a bank transfer. It's in our account now. We could spend it today." He was trying hard not to smile, but it was obvious he was pleased.

Now Joseph asked, "From where?"

"An overnight wire transfer.," answered the accountant, misunderstanding what Joseph had asked.

"No, from *whom*?" he corrected himself.

"Albany. Medicaid," was the short response.

Joseph was pleased and disappointed at the same time. The payment was at least something. And it was certainly needed. But he knew it was only a fraction of what they had in the pipeline. He decided he would wait for Sadim's phone call from Albany. He was in that office today and Joseph would find out if – just maybe – the gates were opening up for them.

Instead, he called the four largest private insurers. They, of course, could care less how the clinic was being treated by the state. But it was something he could talk to them about. He could try to encourage them to outperform the state. It was something.

Like starving people at a table carving up a sandwich, Gus, Podalski, and Joseph sat for a half hour during the afternoon deciding how to piece out that $26,422.86. December 31st paychecks never entered the conversation.

Friday - December 20

Sadim had not called yesterday. Joseph was tempted to call him, but felt that if there was a fine line between persistence and pestering, he was probably already well over it. And he absolutely needed to stay in Sadim's good graces. He was their ace-in-the-hole at NY Medicaid.

Most of the morning was spent by Joseph writing checks. None of them were very large, and in that way there was more to go around. Making small payments to more suppliers hopefully would keep them mildly satisfied. Hopefully it would be enough to keep them from canceling current orders. After two hours of writing and rewriting checks to over 30 vendors Joseph had them in envelopes, sealed and stamped, and in Olney's hands on the way to the Post Office.

Feeling better than he had in several days, he celebrated by buying pizza for lunch for the clinic staff. Everyone made a point of stopping by his office to thank him. Everyone but Ana; she was a no-show. When the pies were delivered at 12:30 Joseph went and paid the delivery man. Gus asked him if that money had come out of the "recent windfall," and Joseph misunderstood he was kidding. He assured him, seriously, that he had paid for it out of his own pocket. Before he could join in the feast, however, he was summoned back to his office for a phone call. It was Sadim.

"Hello. I'm calling you from the parking lot," he said, trying to explain the background noise. "I'm out on my lunch break." Having trouble hearing what he was saying, and realizing he was also missing the pizza in the pantry, Joseph suggested that Sadim call him back when he got back inside the building after lunch. "No, I don't think that's a good idea. I don't want them to know what I've been doing for you. I don't think they'd like it that I was doing extra things for you."

This seemed odd to Joseph. "They would object to your helping a provider? A provider in dire need of help? Are you kidding?" he asked.

Sadim was embarrassed to admit that that's exactly what they would think. "They want us to stick to the strict guidelines of the job description. It's just the way they think." he said. "They would be pretty mad if they knew I was going through the bins in the back of the mail room looking for those physical submissions. I would probably get into a lot of trouble." Joseph couldn't see him, but Sadim was shaking his head at what sort of hell that would cause him from his supervisors. "But I found them."

Joseph said nothing, unsure of what he thought he had just heard. Background noises of traffic and static were the only sounds. "Say that again," was all Joseph could say.

"I said I found them. They were in the . . . " he voice trailed off when he suddenly realized Joseph wouldn't remotely care where he found them. He continued, "There are two full mail carts of them. They may be more, but I haven't come across them yet." Joseph was speechless. "I would guess there are over 1000 claims in those bundles. But I can't be sure. They are still in the boxes you sent them in. They were just sitting in the back there. No one knew who put them there, or what they were supposed to do with them. They could have sat there forever!"

Joseph was dazed. He didn't know what to say, or even ask. "What happens now?" he finally got out.

"I got a friend in the Special Unit. They handle anything out of the ordinary. Usually very big or complex claims. He's going to call me back this afternoon. They might handle something like this. But I don't know."

Joseph and Sadim talked for another ten minutes. Joseph told him that the clinic had important friends in Albany, and if he ran into a roadblock, to let him know. Sadim remembered all too well how Mr. Bryant had obviously been firmly instructed by his superiors to take care of the problem that the Wackentute Clinic was having. Sadim also told Joseph that he would continue trying to track down any other claims that were lying around the building collecting dust.

When Joseph got back to the pantry the pizza boxes were all opened, and people were enjoying their free lunch. It is a commonly accepted fact that one of life's finest pleasures is an unexpected free lunch.

"What did you say?" asked Olney.

"You had asked me if I had ever had peanut butter on a slice of pizza," Figgit calmly said to him. "And I said I had not."

"No, you didn't. You said something else. You said . . . something else." Olney said trying to remember exactly what he had heard.

Figgit sighed deeply, and said with his normal exactitude, "You asked, 'Figgit, have ya ever eatin' a pizza wit peana butter on it?' And I responded, 'Not nonce, nor ever."

"There! That's what ya said! You said . . . what? . . . 'nunce'? What's 'nunce'?" Olney was triumphant. Everyone else in the room watched quietly at the developing argument.

Figgit looked at Olney with sadness, and shook his head. "It's pronounced 'Nonce.' Not 'nunce.'" Figgit turned around the room looking for some sign of support. Except for eyes darting between the two, there wasn't a movement, or a sound for that matter, in the room.

"'Nonce'? What does that mean? That ain't even a word!" Olney declared. "Dr. Ana....is that, 'nonce,' is that even a word?" Everyone, including Figgit, turned to Ana.

Horrified by the possibility that she was being drawn into this discussion between Olney and Figgit, Ana's mind raced for an exit strategy. The only thought that came to her was the decision that she had to stop coming into the pantry at lunch time. Lately it had been one disaster after another. She was rescued, by of all people, Joseph.

"What does 'nonce' mean, Figgit? I am unfamiliar with the word," he said. For an instant . . . just an instant, Ana was grateful.

"I am surprised at you Mr. Hamilton. You are an educated man, if I am not mistaken. Ivy League? Isn't that so?" Figgit said, furrowing his brow.

"Graduate school, Figgit. Only graduate school and that was a business school, not liberal arts. We did not have any language arts courses in the business school."

"Pity, Mr Hamilton. You would hope they would provide a broader curriculum than that." Figgit unnecessarily adjusted his tie, and continued, "Nonce is a word . .a bit archaic I will allow . . . that simply means 'at the present time' or more simply, 'now'. Some scholars believe it was once used as part of the sequence of frequency of 'nonce – once – twice – thrice, and so on. Dating back, perhaps a thousand years . . . " People knew where this was going and began, at this point, cleaning up their lunches and heading back to work.

Saturday - December 21

Joseph stopped off on his way to work this morning to run some errands. As such, by the time he arrived the Saturday overflow crowd was already there. That did not surprise him. That fact that Sadim was there did.

Remembering that it was unwise "to look a gift horse in the mouth," he didn't ask why or how he was there. He stood behind him and watched. He found Sadim working on a stack of old claims, and was amazed at how quickly he worked through them, entering them electronically into the computer. He was sitting at the small cubicle desk that had been set up for him the first time he had come. Lindsay was just a foot to his left at her usual place on the front desk. She was busy getting the crowd of walk-ins to fill out forms, both personal and insurance. Every few minutes Sadim would tap Lindsay on the shoulder and point out some aspect of the claim he was working on. She would smile, but never say a word. She would only nod, and then look at him for a moment, and then go back to the work she had.

Joseph hated to interrupt him, but finally asked Sadim to join him in his office. Once there, Sadim updated Joseph on what he had done in Albany. His friend in the Special Unit was handling the carts of claims. A third cart had been found. ""Did you keep a record of everything you've submitted?" Sadim asked. Joseph told him the recent electronic submissions were easily recoverable. But the prior physical submissions that had covered the earlier part of a year would be very difficult. It would be a nightmare to gather it all back together if the originals claims were lost. "I will tell my friend to handle them with care, then. I'm not sure his group will process them. We can only hope," he added wistfully. "But their discovery caused quite a commotion. Somebody . . . I'm not sure who . . . but, somebody is in a lot of trouble. Whoever winds up responsible for processing them is going to be under a lot of pressure to do them quickly." Sadim was smiling broadly. "I'll tell you the truth. I thought you were exaggerating . . . wildly exaggerating . . . about how big your backlog was." And then in a low voice he added, "I am sorry."

Joseph waved off the apology, and thanked him for championing their cause. He also acknowledged that he knew Sadim took some professional risk taking on the challenge, in spite of how unfair that was. "But let's change the subject for a minute," Joseph said, leaning across the desk. "What about that payment we got, out of the blue, on Thursday? I don't know what it's for. What does it covers? Shouldn't there be some supporting documents, or something along with it?"

"The document explaining that payment is in the mail. If you didn't receive it yesterday, it should arrive today. I had the payment expedited, and that means sometimes the money arrives before the documentation.

"*You* had the payment expedited?" Joseph had picked up on Sadim's indication of his involvement. "You did it?" he asked. "And why 26,400-and-something dollars, and whatever cents? How did you come up with that number?"

"Well, yes, it was me," he admitted. He really didn't want to take undue credit for it. "When a Regional Coordinator realizes there is some backlog in claims payment, he can authorize what is called an AP405. That's simply an advanced payment. I had to fill out some forms justifying the amount.

And, then of course, some supervisor somewhere has to authorize it. Usually they just reduce the amount asked for, and send it through. I had requested $50,000 for you. That's a higher number than they usually get asked for. I knew that was never going to be authorized, but I didn't think they would cut it down by almost half. But the amount did raise some eyebrows, and brought it to the attention of some senior people there. That really got some people hopping down there."

Joseph sat there amazed, staring at their "hero." Sadim sat across from him not feeling anything like a "hero." He honestly felt that had he been doing his job conscientiously, the situation at the Wackentute Clinic would never have gotten as bad as it was. He felt it was his responsibility to monitor the providers in his district, and he should have noted the complete drop-off of claim requests from these people. No, he didn't feel like a hero.

"When can we expect the rest? How soon will we start seeing more of the backlog money?" Joseph wanted to hear words like "tomorrow," or "next week." He wanted to hear words like that.

Sadim shook his head, sadly. "It will take some time. Those bundles were a shock to the people in Albany. An amount that large is going to make them nervous. Even cautious! Depending on who is assigned to process them, it could take several weeks; maybe more. And it's the holidays; lots of folks there will be taking vacation time." He made a face, and then added, "It could take a couple of months." That option was completely unacceptable to Joseph. Without an inflow of money, the Wackentute Walk-In Clinic would be permanently closed down by February 1st.

"There are options," he said absentmindedly to Sadim, who had no idea what he was talking about. "There are always options."

He had no idea what the proper attire was for attending the King Wenceslas Festival, so he had worn a light gray turtlenecked sweater with dark gray pants, underneath a black blazer. He wore a heavy black topcoat with a red scarf over it all. On his feet were the very expensive imported loafers he had from his past glory days. He thought he looked very good.

"Slightly early" was a credo to Joseph. All of his life he had valued his time, and presumed others valued theirs too. He did not like to be kept waiting, and didn't do it to other people either. At 4:57 PM he rang the doorbell at the Gustafson home. Gus answered the door and let him in. Ana, of course, kept him waiting for a few minutes, and then came down the stairs with her coat and hat already on. She was wearing a snow white goose down parka on top of long black wool skirt, with tall black boots. And Joseph, as he had expected, thought she looked great.

Once outside they walked to the curb where he had parked his car. He opened the passenger side door for Ana to get in. She stopped, and gave the car a complete, slow visual appraisal. "THIS is really your car?" she asked.

"Yes it is. You knew that. Practically brand new. You like it?" he said smiling.

"It's a minivan! I really didn't take you as a minivan person," she said flatly.

"What kind of person did you take me for?" he asked back. She ignored his question and got in. After he got in and started driving, he broke the silence by saying, "It's four years old, but only has 25,000 miles on it." Ana knew vaguely what that meant, and was unimpressed. Her lack of response prodded him to continue. "I bought it from a friend and former classmate of yours."

"Who?" she asked suspiciously.

"Roove Hagedorn," he said, relieved that she had said something.

"Roove Hagedorn! Reuven?" she asked quietly, but in a tone of disbelief. It was almost as if he had said he could fly.

Joseph noticed the skepticism right away and asked, "What's wrong with that? We're teammates on the Bombers. And he said that you and he are friends and former classmates." Joseph was serious. These sorts of things meant something to him.

"First of all, Roove and I were only in a couple of classes together in high school....and he didn't show up for them very often. And as for 'friends' . . . my father and I have been his physicians in the past, but I don't think we've ever socialized. Drinking beer in the back of a pick-up truck out in some field is not my idea of a night out. And, as for being 'teammates' . . . and I can't believe you got roped into this moronic tournament."

When she paused for a breath, Joseph jumped in. "Ah, you're being too hard on him. He said the only reason he was selling it was because he already had a car. He hardly ever drove it. Like I said, it only has 25,000 miles on it."

"Did you have this car checked out by a mechanic before you paid him for it?" she asked.

He hadn't, but now felt that maybe that would have been a good idea. "Of course," he lied. This was followed with a discourse by Ana discussing how foolish it was to blindly trust people in general and Roove in particular.

Roove, she had known since high school where he was "one third of the infamous 'Los Trios.'" Los Trios, Ana explained, was composed of Roove Hagedorn, Pistol Graham and Paulie Moore. And then she told him the story of "Los Trios."

The three of them had become close friends when they were very young, and had stayed close throughout their school years. Roove's history with Pistol (then known by his first name, "Pearson") Graham went back to the second grade when Mrs. Arbastus from the Principal's Office brought the young Mr. Graham into the second grade class of Miss Sullivan right around Christmas. Miss Sullivan introduced him to the class, and sat him next in the only open seat in the classroom, and that was right next to Roove. Roove called him "Mr. Christmas" because he was wearing green corduroy pants and a red shirt. It wasn't meant to be an insult, but rather a simple observation. Pearson, uncomfortable to be starting his fourth school in two years, didn't see the difference, and told Roove to "shut up." It was a bumpy start to a very long friendship.

Despite that start the two boys became fast friends. It didn't hurt that they happened to live close by one another, and before long their mothers became acquainted as they walked the two boys back and forth from school. They were soon alternating the delivery and pickup of their young sons. Besides having somewhat unusual first names, both boys were only children of single moms. As they walked to and from school for the rest of the year they discovered they had a lot in common.

Roove (born Reuven) Hagedorn was the only child of Joan Hagedorn. She had fallen in love with Reuven Childress when she was 20 years old. She said "Yes" immediately when he asked her to marry him almost nine years ago. In their euphoria they had made love that night for the first time, and she got pregnant. He was gone within two days of learning about it. With an inner resolve most of her friends and family didn't know she had, she went on with her life. After Roove was born she went back to her job at North Valley Hospital, where she ultimately became an LPN.

Pearson Graham's early history had always been unclear, until it was explained fully at the meeting in Town Hall several weeks ago. He and his Mom arrived in Newcomb when he was eight years old. He had enrolled in the local grammar school and his mother found work at Dean's Lumberyard as a bookkeeper. Young Pearson hooked up right away with Roove, and seemed to settle in pretty well.

In the summer between their second and third year of school, young Paulie Moore moved nearby with his Mom, Dad and older sister. Paulie's Mom worked at a local beauty salon (and would one day own it herself). His Dad worked sporadically as a truck driver, but was fast becoming a full time alcoholic. He would disappear for days at a time, and finally disappeared completely when Paulie was in the seventh grade. Paulie's Mom didn't look for him, and no one in the family missed him very much. When the three young boys were coincidentally invited to the same birthday party that first summer, their moms' coordinated their rides back and forth, and Roove, Pearson and Paulie became acquainted. At the party both Roove and Pearson displayed a little shyness common to boys at that age when attending a party at a stranger's home. Paulie, on the other hand, moved around the room like he owned it. He wasn't shy about getting cake or any candy that was offered. He drank soda like a man dying of thirst. And whenever he got something, he got three; one for him, and two for "his friends'. The two other boys were dazzled by his brazenness and saw immediately that this new kid was worth having around. He wasn't aggressive; he wasn't rude; but he was a boy on a mission.

The three boys became inseparable, and a very independent group. They were reluctant to join any group or team, inside or outside of school. They played some sports, but none of them excelled. In the classroom they were slightly below average. But this lack of achievement in both academics and athletics didn't seem to bother them one bit. They shared everything. Lunches, treats, and toys were common property. Homework and answers on tests were also shared whenever the opportunity presented itself.

Around the time they entered the Middle School the three boys were playing some game one afternoon at the woods bordering Alamo Park. Pearson chased a ball that had gotten past him, into the heavy underbrush behind him. Instead of finding the ball, he found a gun. It was rusted over, and the grip on one side was completely gone. He called the others over and they excitedly examined it. It had obviously been there a very long time, and despite their best efforts, and mild safety concerns, they could not pull the trigger, nor cock the hammer back. It was rusted stiff. Over the next several days, after *obtaining* some lubricating oil and sandpaper from Gene's Hardware Store, they worked on the gun. But it was a lost cause; the gun was not salvageable. It didn't really matter that much to them. Other than its 'cool value" they had no use for it anyway. Deciding that holding onto a non-working gun was stupid, Pearson took it back into the woods and buried it again. They hadn't shown it to anyone, or even told anyone about it so the episode quickly came and went. The only residual effect was the fact that Paulie and Roove would forever call Pearson Graham, "Pistol." He liked that, and it became the name almost everyone called him.

Somewhere along the line they decided that they were a gang. And like any gang worth its salt they needed a gang name, a gang sign, and a gang handshake. The name they eventually decided to use was "Los Trios." Although none of them were Spanish, or spoke Spanish, or even took Spanish in school, they felt it sounded very impressive. The secret handshake was nothing more than a three fingertips slapped together three times followed by a "high five." That too, was very impressive they thought. The sign they adopted was a backward three, inside a triangle.

And this symbol ultimately gained certain notoriety in the Newcomb area over the years. It began appearing in places it shouldn't be when the three boys were in the eighth grade. Chalkboards, bulletin boards, the walls in and around the school building became the canvas of Los Trios. And, although at first, it was just a silly prank, it became a matter of pride and ingenuity by them to place it in very distinctive spots. It appeared, over the years, spray painted at different times on both the high school football and baseball fields. It was soaped onto the windshield of Principal Neubel's Cadillac, which had been parked in the fenced off "Teachers' Only" parking lot. To the amazement of just about everyone, it appeared on the wall of the showers in the girls' locker room one Monday morning. And as a final stroke of retaliation for years of "unwarranted" persecution of them (and many of their friends) by the Vice Principal for Student Affairs, Mr. DiVincenzo, they painted the sign on the roof of his house in the middle of the night. Although suspicions had run high as to who "Los Trios" was, they had never been caught, and, of course, never admitted to being the culprits.

After high school, as is often the case, Los Trios began going their separate ways. They still saw each other regularly, but not as often as in high school. They all rode motorcycles and they all played Geetha for the Bombers. But some changes started taking place.

Paulie had taken Dee Dee Rowe to the Senior Prom and never looked at another woman in his life. She was the younger sister of Ronnie Rowe, a classmate and "co-author" of many homework assignments and tests with Paulie. She was only a sophomore at the time, but she was more than enough woman for him. The youngest daughter of Russell Rowe had her eye on Paulie ever since he picked up her brother one day riding his motorcycle. She thought he was the coolest guy she had ever seen. Mr. Rowe had his doubts, and tried to persuade his little girl to set her sights a little higher. But she was not to be deterred, and held onto to her dream of one day marrying Paulie Moore. Her father, realizing after a long and protracted battle that he wasn't going to win, decided to accept the inevitable. But he also thought that he had better keep his prospective son-in-law under his close watchful eye and offered him a job working in the trucking company. Paulie slid into a comfortable life after graduation, dating Dee Dee, driving a truck and riding his motorcycle. Life was good.

Pistol had been working part time in a gas station during high school, and by his senior year, was putting in over 20 hours a week there. He spent less and less time at school. He had a penchant for working with his hands, and began learning automobile repair. While he didn't fall in love after high school (nor for many years after that) he did enjoy himself. He had an income, very few expenses, and he loved his motorcycle. The job he had, however, turned out to be not too steady. The owner of the gas station simply didn't need him on a fulltime basis. Pistol got occasional jobs at another repair shop, and just as frequently would disappear for a few days to go cruising across state lines on his motorcycle, especially during the warmer months. He had very few complaints.

Roove graduated with the best grades of the three, and considered college, briefly. But it was never really a serious option. He knew he was finished with school, but he didn't know what he wanted to do. He played some guitar, but not often enough, nor well enough to make a living from it. He wound up working a series of menial jobs, wrapped around long periods of unemployment. Painting, construction, roofing and siding jobs came and went. His sole goal on the job seemed to be to last long enough to qualify for unemployment insurance, and then arrange somehow to get on it. He refused offers of help in getting a job from Paulie and Pistol, seemingly content to let the world go by. While Pistol's life was centered on his motorcycle, and Paulie's was centered on Dee Dee, Roove seemed to wander from one thing to another. But this didn't bother him in the least. For Roove, there was a quiet contentment.

The decade following high school brought about some changes for Los Trios. Paulie, after a long delay, had finally married Dee Dee, and that union had produced two little girls. Pistol had, until this past winter been working as a mechanic for the largest motorcycle dealer in the Wackentute Valley. Roove's life had followed a more meandering path. It had been a series of short term jobs alternating with longer term periods of unemployment. And it had all led, somehow, to a position as a NY State Park Ranger. "He had some kind of accident while a Park Ranger," Ana said, "And he wound up on permanent disability." Out of the corner of his eye, Joseph could see her shake her head when she said, "He really shouldn't be playing in that stupid Geetha tournament either. He has serious back problems." Then she added, "I know. I've seen his x-rays." Joseph was going to ask her about those problems, but the town of Lower Wenwenee appeared just ahead.

County Road 141 had virtually no lighting of its own. Occasional street lamps at corners and neon signs on businesses passed along the road provided some of the light. The head lights of the minivan and the few cars passing in the opposite direction provided the rest. In was because of this lack of light that the glow from Lower Wenwenee could be seen from several miles away. As they approached it became very apparent that the little town was full of life. As they got close, Ana directed Joseph to a parking spot on a side street that was close to the restaurant where they were going to eat.

After he had parked his new car under the streetlamp, they started to walk the short distance to the restaurant. He suddenly stopped, and turned around. She noticed him out of the corner of her eye, and turned and followed his gaze back toward his car. "What's the matter?" she asked.

"I can't decide," he answered. "What color do you think it is?"

"What color *what* is?"

"My car. In sunlight it looks cherry apple, but in artificial light it looks like a metallic maroon," he said seriously.

Ana let out a long sigh. "Get a grip, Hamilton," she said shaking her head. "It's red."

Marie's Italian Restaurant was just off the main street of Lower Wenwenee. And much to Joseph's surprise, it turned out to be just as good as Ana had said it was going to be. Joseph, who had frequented many of the finer restaurants in New York City in his heydays, and had traveled to Italy several times, really enjoyed Italian cuisine. He was even surprised to find a bottle of wine on the wine list that he knew very well, and liked very much.

Leaving the restaurant after dinner, Joseph thought that although the evening had started a little rough, it was going quite well now. The conversation in the car had been a little strained, but over dinner they discussed Italian cooking, and Italian wine, and finally Italy itself. Ana had never been there, and Joseph knew it well. She had asked many questions, and he handled them all. They skipped desert at Ana's suggestion that "they leave a little room for Main Street." He didn't quite understand, but went along anyhow. They left Marie's and walked up to the main drag of Lower Wenwenee and the hub of activity for the King Wenceslas Weekend Winter Wonderland Festival. Turning from the little side street on to Main Street, he stopped abruptly.

It was as bright as daylight along Main Street. Loudspeakers set up on light poles relayed band music from somewhere out onto the crowd. Holiday lights and garland were strung from lamppost to lamppost. Every store, along both sides of the street, was lit up not only with its normal neon signage, but with additional holiday lighting of every kind. There were lit up secular displays of Santa Claus and reindeer and Frosty the Snow Man, of Nativity scenes, and Chanukah candles, and Kwanzaa colors!

The ice-covered street, totally devoid of both traffic and even parked cars, was lined down the middle with two parallel rows of baled hay approximately 30 feet apart. And between the lines of hay and the curb were rows of carts and booths, also lit up, selling everything from candy apples to stuffed zebras. The sidewalks were packed with people.

It took several minutes for Joseph to take it all in. Ana looked at him, enjoying his amazement. Part flea market, part food court, the din of the vendors' cries mixed with the music and general crowd noise helped to create an atmosphere he had never experienced before. He remembered that back in New York City how the city sidewalks seemed to pulse in December every year. This, he thought, exceeded that.

As Joseph and Ana began walking down the bustling sidewalk he came to see why she had suggested they skip desert at Marie's. Vendors along the way were offering food from all corners of the earth. There was funnel cake, roasted nuts, sausage and peppers, hot dogs, pretzels, hot chocolate, pierogies . . . every booth and cart seemed to offer something different. Hand-crafted, home-sewn, homemade items for every purpose under heaven were available. And all around him people were smiling and yelling and laughing.

And then an air horn sounded. One long blast. It startled Joseph, but most people seemed to ignore it. He did notice a few people moving into the street. Ana took him by the arm and led him between two carts into the street just behind the nearest row of hay bales. Again the siren sounded; this time two blasts. He looked at Ana, as someone said, "Here comes another one."

"What's going on?" he said to her.

"You'll see," she assured him. The line along the hay bales on both sides of the street began filling up with people. And no one was in the ice-covered street between the hay bales. People, in general, were looking off to the north end of the street, a gradual incline up past the police station, a few hundred yards away. "Remember we told you about "The Slide for Life?' she said, looking past Joseph in that same direction. "Well, here comes another idiot."

Suddenly there were several short blasts of the siren. The crowd suddenly grew quiet. But a moment later Joseph could hear a low roar rising up from the crowd in the street. It grew into a full roar as suddenly something flew out from the side street onto Main Street, sliding on the ice. He couldn't see what it was, but it was coming fast. Careening wildly, it came down Main Street at very high speed. He could see the shower of ice it threw off onto the crowd as it tried to straighten its course as it came down the incline that was Main Street.

Now under the street's bright lights Joseph could make it out. It was someone on a sled . . . traveling very fast. The crowd was now roaring as the sled came down the street. "Too fast" Joseph barely heard Ana say as the sled flew by. She was right. After another 50 feet from where they stood, these sledders were supposed to turn sharply left into Pipp Park, and over the finish line.

So many sledders over the years had overestimated their ability, or underestimated their speed, and failed to negotiate that final turn. That miscalculation came with a price, and led to that corner being known to one and all as "Collar Bone Corner." In an effort to make it less lethal, the firemen had softened it with bales of hay five high and three deep.

Some people must have agreed with Ana's dire prediction and turned away as this contestant approached that final turn. The noise reached a crescendo as the sledder realized his miscalculation and tried to avoid imminent catastrophe by yanking back with all his might on the left handle of his sled. But he was going much too fast, and the sled ignored him. The instant he crashed into the hay bales the crowd went instantly silent. Joseph saw the sledder's inverted legs form a perfect "V" as he sailed up into the air, and finally crashed back down into the loose straw and snow beyond the restraining wall. There was a momentary sympathetic "oooooooo" from the crowd, and then an appreciative burst of applause for the sledder. Then everyone went back to the booths and carts.

Joseph turned to look up the street again. When the sledder had come zooming down the street moments ago, something had caught his eye across the way. He thought he had seen a familiar face in the crowd across the street, and tried to find it again. But it was gone. He didn't say anything, but he thought he had seen Lindsay standing next to Sadim.

"I knew you were right, Ana, about him goin' too fast. He never had a chance," said Olney, who was suddenly standing next to them.

Greetings were passed back and forth among the three of them. "That's The Slide for Life? Joseph then asked.

"Yup," Olney answered quickly, "You do it yet?" he asked him. "Everyone's got to do it at least once. Right, Ana?" Ana said nothing.

"Why?" Joseph said, "Why, *at least once,*" he asked, repeating Olney's emphasis.

"Everyone does . . . It's a "rite of passage" here in the valley, and it's for charity. You have to do it. You aren't afraid, are you?" Ana asked him.

He was about to answer when Olney said, "How can you be afraid? Even little kids do it. They go really slow, but they do it. You afraid?"

Joseph looked to Ana for help, but the smirk on her face told him no help was coming. "Why can't I just donate the ten dollars, and not do the sled?" That made sense to him, and maybe Ana would agree if she said anything. But she didn't. The very faint smile on her face told Joseph that she was enjoying Olney putting him on the spot.

"Cause that would be chicken.... shit," Olney said sheepishly in front of Ana. "And if you don't go down you can't get a time.... so you can't win the first place prize. And that's also why ya gotta try it." It made perfect sense to Olney.

Joseph looked back and forth at Olney and Anna. He realized he was being manipulated by Olney. And he, who liked to think he had some negotiating skills, leapt to the offensive. "Have you done it?"

"I did it last year." Olney shot right back. "Right, Ana? She saw me."

"He nearly killed himself." Ana said jumping to his defense. "Lost control on the first mogul and went into the hay at the bottom of the hill." She shook her head in disgust. "But Gus and I are his physicians, and we forbid him doing it again . . . for medical reasons," she added. Olney nodded in agreement.

"And what about you?" Joseph asked Ana, "I presume you've done it?"

"When I was young . . . and stupid. In high school . . . twice!" she answered quickly.

"But you're not forbidding him, are you Ana?" Olney asked. "He can go, can't he?"

"I'm not his doctor, Olney. If he has the nerve, I can't stop him," she said smiling.

"A little help here," he pleaded, looking for a way out.

"You are on your own." She smiled at him. Secretly she agreed with him. She thought The Slide for Life was a reckless way to hurt yourself. But she was enjoying watching Olney make him squirm.

A sudden offer, by Joseph, to buy the three of them a hot chocolate didn't work to change the subject. If he didn't do this, he'd never hear the end of it. If he did go down and break his . . . collarbone, or something, he would never hear the end of it. His only option, he thought, was to do it very, very slowly . . . not get hurt . . . and never, ever do it again. He caved in, and agreed.

The three of them walked up Main Street in the direction of the starting line over on Armada Street. Olney talked all the way up there explaining strategy and technique for Joseph's run, although he himself had only made it to the bottom of the first hill. Ana told him only that controlling his speed was the best way to "survive" it. "You have to control your speed to get through those turns. And," she added reluctantly, "the more you weigh the faster you go. So," she hesitated for a moment, "I would strongly recommend you lose 50 pounds by the time we get to the top of this hill." She thought she was being quite witty, but Olney did not get the joke and looked at her strangely. Joseph just looked at her and shook his head. Feeling guilty, she offered a piece of good advice. "You're going to have a problem. The best way to slow yourself down is to dig your toes into the ice behind the sled. Drag your feet." She looked right into his eyes, and then said quietly, "Maybe this isn't such a good idea."

Ignoring the very small opening she just gave him, he looked right back and said, "These are very expensive shoes! I'm not digging them into the ice."

"Suit yourself . . . " She said after a brief pause, letting the moment go, "I'm just suggesting ways you can avoid something very painful happening. You should have worn cowboy boots. Those work very well. Do you have a pair?" She was now having trouble not laughing.

"Not with me." He replied sarcastically, not seeing any humor in this at all.

She went on to say that last year she and her father had brought Olney, but they had gotten separated in the crowd. Some "former" friends of hers, who knew Olney, had coaxed him – like idiots — into doing the Slide. They thought it was funny. She was evidently still very annoyed.

By the time the three had reached the top of Main Street and had gone one block over to the top of Armada Street, Joseph was having major reservations about what he was about to do. Even Ana was starting to have serious reservations, but said nothing. But Olney had enough enthusiasm for the both of them. He had already explained that you pay the volunteer firemen at the starting line the ten dollars first. Then they let you pick out a sled, or a saucer if you want to go down sitting up (which no one recommended). Joseph immediately passed on that idea. The fireman would give you a number, and call you in your turn. When it was your turn, you went to the starting line right at the crest of the hill, and lay down on your sled. That's when the firemen up there would blast the siren on their truck to warn everyone down below to clear the track. A few moments later, to signal everyone one last time to clear the track they would sound the siren again . . . this time two blasts. Then the firemen would get down next to you, and count down with the siren sounding off behind you . . . FIVE – FOUR – THREE – TWO – ONE - GO! . . . and then they would push you off down the hill. Ana joined in with some instructions. She told him there was a mogul on that first hill that was called "The Launching Pad." "It's a 'bump' that's halfway down that first hill." She warned him to take it slow. Olney said to steer toward the left side after the bump, and then cut hard to the right to get through the "S" curve at the bottom of the hill where Armada Street ran into Main Street. That section of the course was called "Death's Door," but he said he didn't know why. After that is Main Street . . . stay on the right . . . then cut hard to the left to get through "Collar Bone Corner" . . . and then there's the finish line. It all seemed so simple. Joseph had his doubts.

Two voices raged inside his head. One said he was insane to do this . . . he was too old . . . he'd break his neck. The other voice told him that it was just a sleigh ride . . . kids have been doing this for a thousand years . . . how bad can it be . . . he didn't want to look like a wimp to Ana and Olney.

"If it all goes well, and you don't kill yourself, it will take about a minute to finish the course!" said Ana, smirking again. "The record is 43 seconds, set quite a few years ago by Dr. Ron Jardine. I think you met him at the Geetha meeting?"

"Not formally," he replied, "But I have heard his *commercial*." Ana didn't get the joke.

The Fire Chief was pointed out, and Joseph went up to him and paid the ten dollars. The chief gave him a number, told him he was fifth in line and suggested he pick out a sled from a pile there. Olney and Ana started to give him their final words of advice, because they were going to head off down the hill to see him as he went by.

"Don't go too fast, and stay away from the hay bales," suggested Olney.

"You know," added Ana, "Maybe you shouldn't do this?" It surprised him when she said that. She was thinking that he probably hadn't been on a sled in many years. He was a big man and his weight meant that he would probably gain speed very quickly, and he would also probably have trouble controlling both his speed and direction. "I really hope you don't crash," said Ana. She then realized she sounded too concerned, so she added, "I do need a ride home."

I'll give ya a ride home, honey!" said a loud voice behind them. Others started to laugh. Ana spun around, hoping she hadn't recognized the voice. Joseph followed her gaze. A very large man in a sleeveless black leather jacket stood right behind her. On either side of him stood another ten people, in similar looking jackets, all laughing. Joseph's first reaction was that he looked vaguely familiar.

"William!" Ana said after a moment. "How are you?" she asked in a voice indicating no interest in the answer.

"William?" he yelled to the others. "It used to be Billy . . . or even Caveman . . . now it's fuckin' 'William'. What the fucks up wit dat?" he asked his friends. The black jackets repeated "William" and "what the fucks up with dat" to each other several times, and they all thought it hilarious. Several yelled "Hi!" at Olney, but he said nothing.

"Introduce me to your friend," Joseph suddenly said; trying to take the spotlight off Ana.

"Yeah," yelled William, "Introduce me to your friend, Ana." He again thought what he said was very funny, and laughed out loud. Most of his friends thought so too, and laughed along with him. Ana's silence and blank face weren't hard to read. She looked up and down the line of faces in front of her. She didn't nod, or say anything to anyone.

William broke the silence by saying, "Ana and me used to be very good friends. And it just so happens we had a very, very close mutual friend." This, apparently, was uproarious to the group who laughed and slapped each other on the back. Joseph, who had been looking up and down the line of faces since he first turned around, suddenly became aware that one of the faces in the line wasn't laughing.

That face wasn't even smiling. That face wasn't looking back and forth at the others, or shouting nonsense. The mouth on that face was closed and the thin lips were pressed together. But the most riveting feature was the eyes. Beneath dark full eyebrows they were close together and very big. And because they were so big he could see clearly that they were black. There wasn't a trace of color in them. Those piercing black eyes were focused, without blinking, and staring right at Ana. She was leaning slightly forward, and appeared to Joseph as if she was ready to lurch at Ana.

"Hello, Ruth Mary," said Ana to "the eyes."

"Hey," she said back very quietly.

"I'm Bill Cavanaugh," said the big man interrupting, "I'm a good friend of . . . the former *very good* friend of Ana's." The emphasis wasn't lost on Joseph. "He couldn't make it tonight. Shit! Is he gonna be sorry he wasn't here to see you . . . and your new friend too!" he laughed. Joseph watched as they all laughed again, except Ruth Mary. At the mention of his name

Joseph remembered the man from the Geetha meeting in Lower Wenwenee. This "Cavanaugh" was one of the Blades, the captain if he remembered correctly.

This felt uncomfortable and needed to be broken up; and right now Joseph thought. He turned to face Ana and Olney, with his back to the intruding group. "Hey! You two have to get going. Go on, right now. They're going to call me in a minute, and you have to be down the hill." Over his shoulder he said to the black jackets, "See you guys later," and took Ana and Olney's arms and ushered them to the sidewalk. ""Go. Start walking, right now. Go on!" he ordered. He gave them a slight push and whirled back around to face the group who were starting to edge over toward them. "Hey," he shouted, "Who's going down the hill with me? Don't tell me none of you guys are going to do it?" Distracted by his shouts, they lost interest in the departing Ana and Olney. For the next five minutes the "black jackets" made fun of him, and made dire predictions about his slide. Finally his number was called, and he gratefully broke away.

He went up to the starting line, where a volunteer fireman greeted him. "This your first time?" he asked. His nervousness was undoubtedly showing. Joseph nodded. "No problem, buddy. This is easy. Let me walk you through it." The fireman had him lie down on the sled, and then he pushed him to the starting line. Another fireman crouched down on the other side of Joseph. "Now listen," one of them said. "We're gonna blast the air horn one time. That's gonna tell everyone to get off the track down through town. You get nice and comfortable, and then we're gonna blast that air horn again . . . this time twice. That's the final warning to everyone down on Main Street to get behind the hay bales down there." The fireman was starting to talk faster, or that was the impression Joseph was getting. That was in line with his own heartbeat that was now also picking up the pace. His mind wasn't any slouch either. It began racing. "Can that downhill be steepening?" he wondered to himself.

The fireman continued, "That's also the signal for the timer down at the finish line to get ready. Then we're gonna count down with the air horn going off five times. Each time our guy in the truck there hits it, me and my partner here will be countin' down for you. We'll go 'five',' 'four,' 'three,' 'two,' 'one,' and 'go' . . . and we'll push you off the top here . . . and away you go. You'll head down the hill here . . . "

"Yeah, gravity will have its way," Joseph's thought to himself. The walk up to the top of Armada Street a few minutes ago had seemed like a slight incline. But now his eyes began lying to him as the descending angle of his route seemed to be, at least, 45 degrees.

"About half way down there's a bump . . . so hold onto your sled . . . hold on tight!"

"What? I'm going to let it go?" Joseph almost scoffed out loud.

"Past the bump, just aim your way through the 'S' curve . . . that'll put you on Main Street . . . yank this handle . . . you know how to steer a sled, right?

Sorely tempted to advise this young man that he was "born and bred in Northern Michigan," where steering a sled was learned before walking . . . he let it go.

"Yank the left handle to go left, the right handle to go right . . . pull hard on the left handle to get through that last turn – that's a mean one, that turn . . . and then straight on through to the finish line. It's a piece a cake, all right?

I won't dignify that with an answer he thought.

"Just like you done it when you was a kid." Joseph thought the fireman incredibly optimistic; incredibly simplistic, and how unfortunate it was that this would be the last person on earth he would ever speak with.

"Okay, you ready?"

"Why am I here?" Joseph whispered.

The fireman turned around, and shouted to someone, "FIRST WARNING." The air horn on the truck sounded loudly one time behind him. "Relax," the fireman said a few inches from Joseph's ear.

Joseph thought the fireman must be insane to think that that suggestion was appropriate at this time. After what seemed like an hour the fireman said softly, "Ready for warning two?" and shouted again to someone to blast away. The air horn screeched out two ear splitting blasts. The fireman let twenty seconds go by, and signaled the truck again to begin the countdown.

The air horn sounded . . . the firemen on both sides yelled at Joseph,

"FIVE!"

Again, another blast . . . and the firemen yelled,

"FOUR!"

The next time it sounded, it seemed to be lower than before. Probably because all Joseph could really hear now was his heart pounding.

"THREE!"

Suddenly he felt himself thrusting forward. He was off down the hill. "What the hell happened to "two" and "one?" he thought. "Christ Almighty," he said out loud. But before he had these thoughts out of his head he realized his face was being bombarded by . . . by what? He didn't know. He couldn't open his eyes to see. Into his forehead . . . up his nose . . into his mouth . . . in his ears . . . down his neck . . . hundreds, it seemed, of little missiles were pelting him. He turned his face to the left to protect his left side and peeked out of his left eye. He was traveling very fast down the hill, turned at a 45 degree angle. Water and ice and snow were flying up into his face off the runners of his sled as he skidded down the ice on Armada Street. No one had mentioned anything about wearing goggles. No one!

"Who said anything about goggles?" He heard himself yelling. "Did anyone say anything about goggles? No one said shit about goggles!"

No one along Armada Street heard him say anything. And the few people who actually saw his lips moving presumed he was just screaming. Many of the sliders did. He pulled hard on the right handle, trying to straighten himself out. At first he felt the resistance to the correction, but then he felt nothing at all. It took a moment for him to realize why. He was airborne.

"Ahhhhh shit . . . ." he heard himself moan, remembering now about "The Launching Pad." Before he could finish his thought he hit back down on the ice, jarring him badly. He lost his grip on the right handle. Now pulling only on the left handle, if just for a moment, he started to veer to the left. Fighting a new onslaught of ice chips, and struggling to find and re-grip the right handle, he bounced slightly off the left restraining wall bruising his left elbow. "SONUVABITCH!" he yelled . . . or thought he yelled. He wasn't sure which. Of course no one heard him.

By the time he found the right handle again, and looked up, he saw that "Death's Door" was fast approaching, as he was heading for the wall at the bottom of Armada Street. If nothing else he wanted to get further than Olney had, so he pulled the right handle, and pushed the left handle as hard as he could, and dug the toes of his shoes into the ice behind him to act as a rudder. The sled started to steer to the right. Again the ice chips and water from the runners bombarded his face. He moved his head all over trying to avoid the assault on his face, yet never lessening the force he was putting on the handles. The sled over-corrected as he was being blinded by the ice chips. When he next got a glimpse of where he was, he saw he was heading toward the bale of hay marking the right boundary of the "S" curve. He tried to steer to the left, but was too late.

On the bright side, he didn't crash directly into it, but rather it was a glancing blow to his right leg. That stung like hell. It also slowed him down slightly. But it also caused him to ricochet across the narrow lane in the "S" curve so he hit the left barrier as he exited, and he hit that hard! This particular collision involved his left foot. The force of this last collision had him rotating counterclockwise as he crossed out onto Main Street. The collisions, as well as his doing the slow rotation around, only added to his complete disorientation as to where he was and where he was going.

When he hit the right restraining wall of hay on Main Street he was facing north, and yet, was sliding south. He was going backwards! "I AM GOING BACKWARDS, FOR CHRISSAKES" he either thought, said, or yelled. This most recent collision had one positive effect. It caused him to begin revolving back around in a clockwise motion just as he began going down Main Street. The rotation, if nothing else, had him heading face first again. He wasn't sure, as he opened his eyes again, whether the pains in his body or the ice chips were causing his eyes to water, but his vision was seriously blurred. The collision with the restraining walls and sled rotation had slowed him down a little, but now the downhill slant of Main Street had him gaining speed once more. He attempted to dig his toes in again, but the pain in his left foot wouldn't allow it.

With whatever resolve he had left, he looked up and saw instantly that he was accelerating down the right side of Main Street, and "Collar Bone Corner" was fast approaching. Digging his right toe into the ice behind him, and yanking the left handle back so violently he nearly snapped it, the sled began crossing Main Street diagonally. Ice chips, again, were flying everywhere. Joseph squinted hard to see where he was going. After a moment of indecision and fear, he judged he'd make it past the inside corner of the turn and not plow headlong into the far wall of the dreaded Collar Bone Corner. It was a relief to him when he cleared the corner, but he immediately realized he was going to hit the far right wall of the final straightaway. "It will, at least, slow me down," he thought.

It happened, to Joseph, almost in slow motion. The snow bank approached . . . he hit it . . . and the sled and he went separate ways. When he landed, on his back, he continued sliding along the ice. He finally stopped when he hit something that offered no give. It was hard enough for him to jam his shoulder but, at least, he came to a halt. Although not a religious man, he thanked God.

Lying flat on his back, he opened his eyes and looked straight up and saw holiday lights on strings, and then heard noise. It was music, and people talking. Some were even shouting. A familiar face appeared above him, which he couldn't quite place initially. "You okay?" the familiar face said, "Oh man! That was some crash!" It was the CPA.

"Phil?" questioned Joseph, when the name suddenly came to him. He felt that his eyes were still rotating. Two other faces he didn't know suddenly appeared above him and smiled. A moment later these two men reached down and helped him to his feet. He leaned on them as they guided him to a nearby bench. They explained that they were EMT's, and just wanted to make sure he was all right.

"I never saw anyone finish without a sled before," said the EMT draping a blanket across Joseph's shoulders.

The other EMT knelt in front of him and asked some simple questions. Phil left to get him a hot chocolate. He recognized Phil's kids standing a few feet away staring at him. "Wow! That was some crash. Are you okay?" the EMT began. He was able to field a series of questions without thinking too hard. He absentmindedly answered the questions as he took stock of his physical condition. He saw immediately why his right hand was more battered, more raw, and colder than his left. The glove that had been on his right hand at the top of the hill was now gone. The whole right side of his body was more banged up than the left. He could feel his right shoulder starting to stiffen up. His right elbow and knee were bruised. But it was his left ankle that really ached, and his left foot was cold and wet. He looked down and saw why. His left shoe was gone.

Phil came back with the hot chocolate, and the EMT's moved away. Joseph was starting to recover as the ice that had accumulated in his hair, eyebrows, ears, etc. on his way down the hill now began melting and sliding down his face and neck. Droplets of cold water worked their way through the scarf that hung loosely around his neck. He felt it as each one worked its way down inside his shirt, giving him shivers as they slid down his back and chest.

"A bit sloppy, but you'll improve on your next few tries." a voice behind him said. He turned slowly. Ana stood there, smirking, dangling his missing shoe off one of her fingers.

"Thanks for retrieving the shoe. Where was it?" he asked, ignoring her comment.

Olney walked up just then, and said, "That was some crash. Told you to stay away from the walls. Why'd you let go of the sled? What was your time?" Joseph just stared at Olney, and didn't answer any of his questions.

After a moment a fireman approached and began to apologize. He explained that as they were doing the countdown up at the starting line, "Your friends came up behind us and pushed you down before we were ready." Joe still wasn't exactly clear-headed at this point, but he knew who they were talking about. "I'm really sorry, but I don't think we have an official time for you." Joseph assured him that that was okay, that it wasn't important. They wanted him to know it wasn't their fault. Again, he told him it was okay. The fireman persisted. "You won't have to pay the ten dollars . . . it's okay . . . if you want to do it again."

For the next several hours Ana and Joseph, with Olney occasionally in tow, wandered around the streets of Lower Wenweenie enjoying the sights and sounds of the King Wenceslas Weekend Winter Wonderland Festival. It was everything Joseph had heard it would be. He would have enjoyed it even more if he weren't hurting so much. Sore muscles and bruises, aching joints, wet socks, and a never-ending supply of ice trickling down his neck and back reduced the fun and frolic for him, substantially. And he, of course, had to suffer these hardships in silence. There wasn't any way he could mention them and still maintain his dignity and weather the shower of sympathy, however false, his companions would offer. A dry towel, a pair of warm socks, and a glass of scotch seemed to be the only three things that could not be purchased along that stretch of Main Street that night. It was after ten o'clock when Ana suggested they call it a night, saying that the festival would begin shutting down for the evening soon anyway. A bruised and battered Joseph Hamilton didn't argue, and declared himself recovered enough to drive them home, even though Ana and Olney expressed doubts.

In another half hour, he had dropped Olney off at his house, and was surprised when Ana accepted his invitation to stop somewhere for a "nightcap." And although he would have greatly preferred a double shot of scotch, he didn't argue too much when she suggested "coffee and pie" at the diner back in Newcomb.

A little while later they were sitting in the end booth at that diner. It was like every other diner he had ever been in his entire life. The glare of fluorescent lights against the white tiled floor almost hurt his eyes. Black formica tables were surrounded by dark red cushioned booths. An apparently very tired, or bored, or both, waitress took their order, and soon returned with their coffee, tea, and slices of cherry pie. The coffee was good (scotch would have been better), and the pie was fresh. Ana, who had touted the diner earlier, was right.

So as they both enjoyed this "nightcap," they began a tentative exchange of life stories. Ana was, by far, the less open of the two. He told her about his upbringing in Northern Michigan. He lost his parents when he was still quite young, and was raised by his grandmother. He had done well in high school, both academically and athletically. And he went away to the university on a scholarship. His grandmother had passed away while he was away at school, and he admitted that since then, he had not gone back to Michigan very often. He had only a few scattered relatives back in the Midwest.

"And your penchant for Italian wines? That comes from your travels over there?" she asked. Ana peppered him with questions, yet was very reluctant to say anything about herself. Ultimately she confessed too that she had "done well" at school. When he asked her about her athletic prowess that he had heard about, she almost denied it totally. Only after several pointed questions did she admit to doing "pretty well" in soccer, basketball and softball. She had finished college "in Boston" and had gone on to follow her father's footsteps by going to medical school. After she received her degree, she interned in New York, and had done her residency in Baltimore. She made a vague reference to working in Miami for a time, but because she "just got home sick" she came back to the Wackentute Valley to work with her father. She went on to say that after her Mom got sick and passed away, leaving her father and the practice just seemed to be out of the question.

For the most part she deflected his questions pretty well, but asked pointed ones of her own. "No Mrs. Hamilton?" she suddenly asked.

"No," he answered. "There was once, but not anymore." Thinking that she might interpret that as he was a widower, he added quickly, "Divorced. Just one of those things." She didn't say anything. And after a long moment of silence passed, he decided to explain further. "She bailed out when I got in trouble with the law." He made a half smile, and raised his eyebrows,

"She vowed for better or worse . . . but not for jail." Ana still said nothing. "She just wasn't built for that. She was pretty, and smart, and stylish, and a lot of other good things. But she just didn't have a 'struggle gene' in her entire body. She just wasn't made for it. She filed for divorce after I was arrested, and it was settled before I even went to jail."

"Do you still resent her for it?" Ana asked softly.

"Resent? No, not at all," he answered quickly. "Well, not anymore, anyhow," he admitted. Hryila had cured him of that. "Like I said, she wasn't cut out for what was ahead." He shook his head slightly, and continued, "She didn't have a 'struggle' gene, or a 'loyalty' gene, either," he added. "But I don't think she ever pretended to. She had me over a barrel. I was in no position to negotiate at that time. She took the beach house, all the jewelry, and most of the portfolio." Her turn, he thought to himself. "How about you? No Knight in Shining Armor?"

She looked across the table at him, thinking. Then she said, "An entire Round Table of them. But none of them turned out to be Lancelot."

Omitting the fact that he had also heard it elsewhere, Joseph said, "And if I understood Mr. Cavanaugh correctly, didn't the infamous Superfly Jardine also have a seat at that table?" That was a mistake, and he knew it the instant it was out of his mouth. The eerie silence that followed it wasn't necessary to make the point. How could he be so stupid?

When she finally reacted, she looked up at him, and smiled. "An error in judgment, perhaps. But it didn't last long . . . or cost me a beach house and my net worth."

No one likes to be reminded of their romantic blunders, even though they are something we all share. Some are more catastrophic than others, and then there are those who do it more frequently than others. But, then again, some people are able to look back and laugh. Some can't.

He smiled; they weren't alike. "We all make mistakes. Some cost a little more than others." He was willing to accept the criticism.

"Some cost more than money." She wasn't finished. "Didn't an 'error in judgment' get you in trouble with the law? Cost you . . . what? Three years?"

Ouch! He thought to himself. "We all make mistakes." he repeated. "Personal and professional. And both can be costly."

The mood at the table was getting darker, and he wanted to brighten it up, so he recited an old saw he had heard years ago. "Remember what old Ben Franklin (he was guessing) once said." He paused here for a moment. "Success is never final, and failure is never fatal." She said nothing, so he added, "I know I've learned from my mistakes." He was about to add to that by saying something about personal persistence, but she stopped him.

"It could be fatal in my line of work. I can't make mistakes."

His initial thought when she said that was to respond "Yes, but not fatal to *you*!" He thought it witty, at first. Then some common sense shouted at him to "shut up." "We all make mistakes," he softly insisted.

"I don't."

He looked across the table, and smiled. "You've got a string of ex-boyfriends, including Superfly, and carry very expensive medical malpractice insurance!" he said under his breath. He decided not to argue the point.

"Where is she now?" Ana suddenly asked.

The question somehow lightened the mood. Desi was no longer a painful memory to him, and if pressed he could honestly say he wished her well. "I understand she re-married. Snared herself a somewhat older, but very well-to-do, real estate developer out west. She, at last report, is living the 'good life' in sunny Southern California, and drinking copious amounts of chardonnay."

"Bitch," Ana said softly.

Chapter Seven

Sunday - December 22

No alarm went off on the table besides Joseph's bed this morning. He hadn't set it last night when he went to bed. And unlike many other Sunday mornings recently, no alarm went off inside Joseph's head either. He woke up by opening one eye ever so slightly, and realized it was later than usual when the mid-morning light almost blinded him. He re-shut his eye and tried to go back to sleep. He couldn't; it was too uncomfortable. Or rather, it was too painful. The bumps and bruises from his Slide For Life would be with him for the next several days.

His body ached all over, as he mentally took inventory of his physical condition while attempting to remain perfectly still under the blankets. It almost hurt to breathe. Even the slight adjustment of position to straighten out a sheet underneath him made him grimace. Remembering it was Sunday, he immediately dismissed any thoughts about going out for his regular skate. He realized that getting out of bed, taking a shower, and getting himself some coffee would be exertion enough considering the way he felt.

By moving slowly, and grunting a lot, he got through those tribulations. He found himself sitting at his kitchen table, half dressed, sipping a cup of instant coffee a half hour after waking up. He was exhausted by the effort. He was also angry. He was angry at himself for being manipulated into doing something so stupid last night.

But he was also somewhat pleased, in retrospect that the evening with Ana had, on balance, gone fairly well. Yes, he thought, it went fairly well.

Monday - December 23

There were eight more working days in the year. That wasn't nearly enough time to solve the problems they faced. Sadim was back on the road somewhere. Where, Joseph didn't know. But he wasn't at the clinic, or even more beneficial for the clinic, he wasn't back in Albany. Sadim had told him that there was virtually no chance that any more money would be coming from the state until January, at the earliest. He was sorry, but he was sure.

Joseph's Slide For Life adventure on Saturday night was apparently known by everyone at the clinic this morning. Everyone asked him about it. He had assumed that only Ana and Olney had been eyewitnesses to the fiasco and that Podalski had seen the ignominious end. But one person after another had told him they had heard about it, or some had even seen him "nearly kill himself." More than one person expressed surprise that he hadn't broken anything. "I feel fine. Never felt better," he lied to each and every one of them..

Podalski, thankfully, changed the subject to reiterate that he was thrilled to death to be part of the upcoming Geetha team. But he was equally morose that not another nickel was hidden anywhere on the balance sheet that could be used to sustain the clinic. He had explored, and exhausted any chance of further loans from any bank in the valley.

Lindsay (after asking, "Can you even walk?") threatened physical violence if he asked her about the state or private insurance reimbursements again.

He was sitting in his office doodling on a pad. "There are always other options," he said to himself, over and over again.

"Boss," Lindsay said from the doorway. Joseph looked up at her. Her face showed nothing. "There are some guys here to see you." The letters "IRS" came and went through his mind. He didn't need this.

"Who are they? What do they want?"

"I don't know; they didn't say. They want to talk with you." She said, and disappeared. But an instant later she reappeared, "One has blue hair," she said.

She didn't see him, but he broke into a wide smile. He was up in an instant, and went out front. There, standing out in the patient reception area, stood two men in their 30's. That was the only physical thing these two had in common.

Barry was totally bald and tall and thin and dressed completely in white. He was all smiles, and had brilliant white teeth. He talked loudly as he greeted Joseph with an animated bear hug.

Bernie stood by nonchalantly, as if he didn't know either one of them. He was short, and had an enormous head of hair. It was blue. Most of his clothes were various shades of blue also. He wore a long raincoat of navy blue over blue jeans. His sneakers were royal blue. The lenses of the sunglasses he had on were blue, as were the frames.

The patients in the waiting room couldn't take their eyes off the three men as they greeted each other warmly. They followed them with their eyes as they left the room. People in the Wackentute Valley did not see people like Barry and Bernie every day.

The three men settled down in Joseph's office, after he had closed the door. "What are you two doing up here?" Joseph started off the conversation. He looked expectantly at them. Bernie, of course, said nothing. His eyes, shaded by the sunglasses, scoured the walls to look at each and every thing that Joseph had pinned to them. Barry smiled and said, "We wanted to tell you the good news in person."

They only stayed for one hour because they had to return to New York immediately. When they left he began immediately to work the phones. He had very little time, and a lot of ground to cover.

In between phone calls he saw Gus and Ana talking in the hallway. "Something good may have just happened. I have to talk to the bank, and try something new. I'll need to talk to you both later." Unfortunately that "talk" slipped through the cracks until it was almost too late.

Tuesday - December 24

The clinic would close early on Christmas Eve. And although almost everyone had some place to go or some last minute errand to run, most stayed around for some champagne and crackers. An anonymous present exchange, with a very strict price limit on the value of the gifts, was done. Joseph had given a pen and pencil set to Figgit, and had received a bottle of Italian wine in return. This constituted their official Office Christmas Party. It wasn't very elaborate, but there was good cheer throughout the room. And that was what these things were supposed to be about.

Olney had cornered Joseph and was pelting him with questions about "that guy with blue hair." He, as well as so many others who had been there, had never seen someone with blue hair before. Joseph said, "You should have seen him when he had it colored green."

"Get outta here! Green?"

"I am not kidding you. He had it colored green for about six months once," Joseph was saying. Then he added, "And I mean kelly green. Not just some shade of dark green." Olney was shaking his head in disbelief. He couldn't get over it.

"How long have you known him?" Gus asked.

Before he could answer, Ana asked how he had met him. She said she found it hard to believe that they traveled in the same circles. Joseph didn't think she was complimenting him. "He and Barry had come to see me several years ago, with a business proposition." No one said anything, so Joseph continued, "They were looking for funding for some research they were doing." He shook his head, "What they were looking for was what is called 'seed money', or more properly "Venture Capital'. That's not what we did at OCS. We couldn't really help them."

"But you've stayed in touch?" asked Gus.

"Well, we did finally connect....in a manner of speaking. Later on." Joseph shook his head. "I'll admit they are a bit strange looking....but those are two very smart guys."

"Smart about what?" Figgit asked.

Joseph looked at him, and thought that Figgit, with his scientific background, would best understand what Barry and Bernie were all about. "Those two guys are the brains behind a small private company called 2BIC. And they have been working on something called 'voice activation electronics'."

Figgit said immediately, "That's already being done. That isn't very innovative."

"Now I won't pretend to understand what it is they have almost solved; but I have been told that it is more than innovative." He paused for a minute, and then said, "It is revolutionary!"

"And how are you involved?" Ana asked skeptically. "Or are you just friends?"

"It started out as what was going to be a short term, and small, investment. It has turned into a long term friendship." He decided against saying anything more. Besides, he had to make some calls to some bankers this afternoon, and he had better get started before they all went home.

Wednesday - December 25

· The clinic was as quiet as the proverbial tomb today. He was alone in the building. He had paperwork to fill out that had been emailed from New York late yesterday. The printer worked perfectly. He considered that the best gift he could have gotten on this Christmas morning.

He also thought it would be a perfect day to review the financial status of the clinic. It was a totally "dead" day as far as financial transactions went. Nobody would be moving money around on Christmas Day. With virtually everyone home with family and friends, he could access accounts and websites with ease. The phone wouldn't ring from one end of the day to the other. But if it did, he wasn't going to answer it.

And the year end was fast approaching. He had to be absolutely sure where they stood. "Anticipated problems can be solved." he whispered to himself. He wondered if that was actually some famous person's quote, or if he had just made that up.

The time went by faster than he had thought it would. He actually didn't finish all the small projects he had planned to do. But as organized as ever, he had his "to-do" list ready for the morning when he let himself out of the building at 7 PM.

Thursday - December 26

Apparently people who got sick on Christmas Day put it on "hold" until the 26th before going to see the doctor. The clinic was an absolute madhouse all morning. Lindsay was overrun by people in the waiting room. Joseph heard her yelling at one point, and went out to help her.

The medical staff had patients lined up along the walls outside examining rooms. They had literally run out of room to put them. Figgit and another lab technician were acting as nurse's aides trying to keep order in the treatment areas.

Lindsay stuck her head in Joseph's office. "Boss, some guy here to see you."

"Who is it? A supplier?"

"I doubt it," she said, "He looks like he's from the FBI." Joseph wondered what would make someone look like they're from the FBI to Lindsay.

"Jeez, I hope it's not the IRS. I don't need them here today." he muttered to himself as he got up to meet his guest.

He was stunned when he turned the corner into the reception area and saw the tall, impeccably dressed Bradley Taylor standing in front on Lindsay's desk. He was glancing around the room like he expected to catch something nasty any minute. Bradley Taylor had been a Vice President at OCS when Joseph had been there. He had been an assistant to Henry Kryder.

"Bradley!" (No one ever called him Brad), "What are you doing here?" was all Joseph could think to say.

Bradley heard him, turned and stepped toward him immediately. He extended a hand, and true to his nature, said without a trace of a smile, "Hello, David." When Hamilton was young he had been called "J.D." because his father was always known as "Joe." He had been JD throughout his school years, but upon embarking on his business career he somehow morphed into the more impressive sounding "J. David Hamilton." Bradley gripped his hand too tightly, and shook it. Then he added, "Henry is outside. He wants to see you."

Joseph told Lindsay he would be back shortly, and followed Bradley out the front door. Several people coming to or leaving the clinic stood in the parking lot looking at the large black stretch limousine idling in the driveway. He spotted Carl behind the wheel instantly. Carl was Henry Kryder's driver, and had been for years. But Joseph had always presumed

Carl was more than that. Carl was big, and Joseph knew that Carl was licensed to carry a gun. Carl didn't smile, ever. He was as serious as an unexpected call from your doctor.

Before he could walk over to the car, it started moving and settled into a parking space at the far end of the lot. Carl was out of the car the instant it stopped. He moved to the rear door and opened it. Tilting his head toward it he said, "Mr Kryder wants to talk with you."

Joseph got in and the door closed behind him. He was alone in the car facing his former boss at OCS, Henry Kryder. He hadn't changed at all, Joseph noticed. His neatly trimmed silver hair was exactly as he remembered it. He hadn't lost or gained a pound, it seemed to him. He was wearing a gray suit and blue tie. No doubt they were both very expensive. The two men looked at each for a minute in silence. Joseph secretly wished he had worn a suit today.

"Why didn't you call me when you got out?" Henry finally said.

"Why didn't you call me when I went in?" Joseph answered right back.

Henry allowed himself a small smile. "I think any direct contact between us at that time would have been . . . " he paused a moment, " . . . awkward." He was inwardly pleased at his choice of words. Then he quickly added, "For both of us."

Joseph didn't remember "awkward" being a concern of his at the time. But it was all water under the bridge now. "Let it go," he told himself. "Appreciate your coming all the way up here just to say 'hello.' It's a long way from Wall Street." Before Henry could respond Joseph added, "It's good to see you again. You look fit. Prosperous. Business must be good."

"We had to charter a helicopter to get us here. Did you know there isn't an airfield in this valley that can handle something . . . ?" He struggled to find the right word. "Modern?" Henry Kryder and other senior executives at OCS flew in private jets when travel was necessary. The only airport in the Wackentute Valley was a private field, only able to accommodate small single engine planes. He did not like being inconvenienced. He shook his head and returned to Joseph's remark. "Business is good. It's very good," he added. "Surprisingly so. We have bounced back from that 'Southampton Mess.'" That had been the phrase they had all used to describe it back then. "And now we have branched out into a number of other projects." Joseph recognized the small glint of excitement that Henry got in his eyes whenever he talked about business. Joseph remained quiet, so Henry went on. "We took OCS private. We call it HEK & Company now. That was the first thing I thought necessary. When you're a public company there are just too many people in bed with you. Now we can move onto projects…we can take necessary steps, and quickly, that we weren't able to take in the past. I think you'd approve of what we've done." Joseph smiled, but again said nothing. Henry began to warm up to telling the story. "We made

Parker an independent subsidiary ....” and he went on for the next 10 minutes, uninterrupted, speaking quickly and with animation.

When he was finished, or paused to take a break, Joseph broke in and said, “Sounds like you’ve bounced back. That's good. I'm glad.” Joseph was surprised at how he felt. There wasn’t any resentment at all. None. He was genuinely glad that Henry and his former colleagues at OCS had apparently rebounded from that “Southampton Mess.” Henry went on to explain in more detail the reorganization that his old company had gone through. How some personnel that Joseph had known had left, but that many had stayed and had somehow weathered the storm, and had grown and shared in the company’s newfound success. The growth over the past three years had been enormous.

“There’s room for more growth,” said Henry. “David, there’s room for you.” He added. Joseph started to stop him there, but Henry spoke louder. “We have a subsidiary . . . Falcon Associates . . . actually it’s a sister company . . . off-balance sheet . . . that is designed to spearhead our strategic moves. I spend half my time there. I should be spending more than that.” Henry leaned forward. “I can’t. Want to know why?” He didn’t wait for Joseph to answer. “Because someone has to run HEK .... day-to-day. Hands on. A full-time COO .... CEO .... whatever. Until I am certain that that is being taken care of, I can’t spend the time that needs to be spent at Falcon.” He paused just a moment, and then said, “You can do that. You can do that standing on your head, for Chrissakes.” He slapped his thigh, leaned back and smiled. He waited for Joseph to react, but he didn't. “David, we’re private now. We don’t have to worry about all kinds of regulators peaking in our windows, and beating down our doors anymore. We don’t have to answer to anyone. Or *hardly* anyone,” he corrected himself. “We do things now . . . *legally*, of course . . . that we didn’t dream of a few years ago. I’d like you to be part of it.”

To give himself a minute to think, Joseph threw out, “I'm on parole, you know.” Of course he knows that, you idiot! Joseph was thinking. He probably knows what I had for breakfast this morning. “I am not free to come and go as I please.”

Henry was waving his hand. “Nonsense, I believe you can accept a job anywhere in the state. I can have my people double-check that, but I think I am right.”

Of course he's right, Joseph was thinking. He's probably had a lawyer working on this for days already. “I've got a job here,” he said. “And, quite frankly, it's a challenging one. I've got my hands full right here.” Joseph glanced out the window and saw Olney standing on the steps to the clinic. He was gawking at the car. He turned his attention back to his former boss and continued, “And those challenges are the reason I called you, and Rich Montoya at the Foundation, recently. The clinic here could use some help.”

Henry Kryder had not taken this long trip up to this isolated valley to discuss the problems of the clinic. He ignored the comment. And another of Henry Kryder's less admirable traits was a tendency to be a bit smug at times. He reminded Joseph how smug he could be when he said, "I think I can be somewhat more generous, compensation-wise, than . . . " he bent over and looked out the window of the car to where the clinic's sign was and said, "The Wackentute Walk-In Clinic." The clinic's problems were not a primary concern to him, and he did not want the conversation to dwell on that.

"Can't explain it," Joseph said looking right into his eyes, "But I like it here."

Henry Kryder remained silent for a moment, and then said as honestly as he was capable, "I may owe you something. I'm not sure." Joseph doubted that. He felt that as well as he knew Henry Kryder, that the man didn't broach topics he wasn't absolutely sure about. He never left things to chance. "I heard a story from someone on the prosecution side of this whole Southampton Mess. It might be true." He cleared his throat, collected his thoughts, and then proceeded. "I was told that you were offered a deal." Henry stopped for a moment and pursed his lips. He looked at Joseph, tilting his head slightly. "They offered you a deal that would reduce . . . not eliminate . . . but reduce your sentence . . . if you would indicate that I was somehow involved." They looked at one another, saying nothing. Henry then continued, "I, as you well know, was not involved in that in any way, shape or form. Any statement to that effect would have been easily proven to be perjury. On that I have no doubt." Henry was covering his bases rather well, thought Joseph. Here, in the privacy of his own car he was making sure that if anyone were listening he was admitting to nothing. The old phrase "Deny till you Die" occurred to Joseph. "But having said that, even though charges against me would have been ultimately proven false, well, they would have been . . . let's say, unpleasant. And would have cost me a great deal of time, effort and money. Your refusal to take that 'dirty deal' is a tribute to your character." He nodded and leaned back in his seat, almost as if there was a burst of applause.

"Let me set the record straight. They never offered me a deal to turn on you. You don't owe me. There were many conversations about who did what, and when. I told the truth, as I knew it. I didn't say you were guilty of anything . . . because I didn't think I was guilty of anything. And you were a further step removed than I was. You don't owe me anything." They sat silently for a moment, each with his own thoughts. Henry Kryder had come up here to retrieve an asset. J. David Hamilton was a very valuable asset once. And Henry Kryder was absolutely sure he could be one again. Henry Kryder had built an enormous and highly profitable organization using his talent, his wits, and his insight. He did not accept "No" as an answer. What brings this young man back? It needn't be this weekend; he thought to himself, I have time.

"You called Montoya, at the Foundation? What's that all about?" He smiled.

The entire visit with Henry Kryder lasted nearly an hour in the back of that limousine. And when it was over the New York executive had not gotten what he had traveled all the way up here to get. Joseph Hamilton was staying in the Wackentute Valley. At least until he had secured the future of this little clinic. To Joseph's disappointment, the Kryder Foundation could not give the clinic an immediate grant. Its books were closed for the year. Henry was more than willing to renew the conversation after January 1. In the meantime, Henry promised to make a few calls to bankers he knew concerning an upcoming initial public offering of a privately held stock.

Friday - December 27

Time was very tight. He had no margin for error. He called the bank to make absolutely certain that they would call him when they received the packet he would send them overnight. He also wanted to actually hear the loan officer say that everything was set, and that he would call him when the money would be transferred.

The overnight envelope from the bank arrived at the clinic at 10:30. Lindsay had been coached to look out for it, and tell Joseph the minute it arrived. He had it in his hands before 10:33. He took it to his office and read the documents inside, carefully.

The information packets for Gus and Ana were laid on top of their desks. In bold letters, notes were attached to the documents advising them of their importance and the time constraints involved. He thought it best not to hunt those two down and hound them for their signatures. There was no sense in adding any more drama to the situation than there already was.

There was time to kill while the two doctors read through the documents. He went to the pantry to calm down. His timing was perfect. Figgit was standing at the sink with a look of total disbelief on his face. A salesman that Joseph didn't know sat at the table, and was in the middle of an explanation to Figgit Nuuf. "It's a coincidence," he said, "Nothing more than that."

"Coincidence?" Figgit repeated. "A coincidence is something . . . of insignificant occurrence." There was another pause. "A haphazard fleeting juxtaposition of two factoids . . . which mean nothing in the grand design. These, on the other hand, are THE TWO . . . ," Figgit exaggerated the words, and let them hang in the air for a moment, " . . . most important figures of their era. For a thousand years . . . before or after." There was another pause. "At the Dawn of the Christian Era . . . and you see no significance . . . beyond . . . 'coincidence'?" The salesman shrugged indifference. He obviously didn't know Figgit, and he didn't realize this was far from over. "I don't think one can overemphasize the importance these two people have contributed to our culture." He glanced left and right. "Easily the most important people of their era . . . and arguably of all time!" Figgit was standing as tall as he could. His legs were spread apart, and his arms were crossed over his chest. He looked, almost, as if he were ready to fight. "And they have the same initials!" he whispered, wide eyed. "The Latin alphabet has 26 letters . . . which results in . . . " he thought for a moment, and then continued, "676 possible two letter combinations." He looked at the salesman with an amused grin on his face and said, "And at no other time . . . in the entire recorded history of time . . . are the two central figures of the era linked with common initials." He frowned at the salesman now, and then said, "Coincidence?"

Preoccupied with his own problems, Joseph asked, without really thinking, "Who has the same initials?"

"Jesus Christ and Julius Caesar," someone said.

"What?" he said reflexively. He was suddenly aware he was in the conversation, and experience told him he shouldn't be.

"Mr. Rugen here sees no other forces at work, other than simplistic ….'co-in-ci-dence,'" Figgit said the word syllable by syllable, "That the two most influential personages . . . of the entire era . . . have the same initials. He sees nothing more than that!" Figgit was shaking his head in dismay.

Mr. Rugen began to say that the initials probably weren't even the same if you take into account the spelling of their names in ancient Hebrew and Latin. Figgit seemed ready to explode when Ana burst into the room.

"Gus's office. Now!!!" she commanded Joseph, and left.

A few minutes later the two doctors and a confused Joseph met in Gus's office. "What is this?" she asked. Ana handed Joseph a few sheets of paper as he sat on the small metal folding chair in front of Gus's desk. She seemed very upset. Gus sat behind his desk as Ana stood next to him.

Joseph looked at the papers, and recognized them instantly. He looked up at the two blank faces opposite him. "It's the loan application. I need you two to sign it, so I can get it back to the bank today." He waited a moment, and then added, "I told you both about this last Monday." He looked back and forth at the two doctors staring at him across the desk. Ana disagreed, saying she knew nothing about it. Gus remembered something being said, but admitted he hadn't really focused on it. Joseph decided not to argue.

"I can see it's a loan application. It says so, in bold letters, at the top. Why are you asking Dad and me to sign it?"

"You're the principals of this practice; you have to sign it."

"Why are we getting this loan? What's it for?" Ana asked quickly.

Joseph tried to be patient with her, despite her combative tone. "We are going to do two things with this money. First, we are going to upgrade our computer systems. Hardware and software! And secondly, we are going to pay off everything we owe to Seward Supply. All past due bills and invoices. Everything." He was about to go on, but Ana interrupted him.

"Why? Why are they getting preferential treatment? I'm sure there are others who have waited longer for past due payments than Seward. And new computers? We have computers! And, finally, why are we doing all this with borrowed money? Aren't we in enough debt? You keep saying we're nearly bankrupt. Why borrow more? And, oh by the way, if we're so deep in debt, why would the bank lend us more? And who the hell is this bank? I never heard of them!" She scanned the loan application looking for the bank's name. It kept her quiet for a moment, and Joseph welcomed the break. Her questions were harsh, and more like accusations. Her demeanor revived in him unpleasant memories of prosecuting attorneys. He slowly turned his gaze to Gus. Gus was looking right back at him, with a slight smile on his face. Joseph wasn't sure what that smile meant. Did Gus agree with what his daughter was insinuating, or was he sympathetic to Joseph's plight?

"We are paying off Seward because they're our biggest supplier. They are one of the largest medical suppliers in the country, providing the largest array of supplies to practices like us. They offer not only a full spectrum of medical and surgical supplies, but also office supplies. They are very competitive on price, and they also turn around orders extremely fast. They have an automated ordering system that is the best in the business. Which, by the way, we will have full access to as soon as I get our new computers up and running. We don't need excess inventory. We need them. And we need them happy. And they have a deal that any client that has a zero balance on their account at year end automatically qualifies for a 2% discount on ALL orders for the next year. That's an extra 2%, on top of their many other discounts. Did I mention they are cheaper than almost everybody else to begin with? That's why I'm paying them in full!" He paused a moment to catch his breath, but wasn't about to be interrupted either. "Now, let's get back to the computers. Not only are they necessary for our supply and inventory problems, they are desperately needed to process our insurance claims. It isn't possible to do it manually anymore. Lindsay, who is working like mad, simply can't handle the workload. No one could. And she shouldn't. The systems are set up to be done automatically . . .as long as you have the technology to handle it. You know," he said looking at Ana, "You're right. We are deep in debt, and I really don't want to add to it. But the computers, and the software programs

they will be able to run, are available right now. At a great price. They will
help eliminate the huge backlog we have in insurance reimbursements. They
will prevent future backlogs; expedite payments; and maybe, just maybe get
us Cash Flow Positive! I fully expect to be able to pay off this loan in less
than a year. It will cost us. I am not going to kid anyone; this isn't free
money. There is an interest rate, but because of the loan's structure, it is
very low."

Ana, despite all that Joseph said, was still not impressed. She could sense
that something wasn't right. She quickly asked why the clinic, which was
admittedly in poor financial condition, was able to qualify for such a good
rate.

Joseph had hoped this aspect wouldn't come up. "It's a 'secured loan,'" he
said, "not just a general obligation loan. The rates on secured loans are
always lower than the rates on general obligation loans." Gus asked him to
explain that. "We are putting up collateral against the loan. Not just our
promise to pay it off."

Gus looked puzzled, but Ana spoke first. "What are we putting up as
collateral?" And gesturing toward her father and herself she asked,
"Shouldn't you have asked us about this first? What are we risking? Our
practice? The building? Our house?"

Joseph looked only at Gus. "No," he said softly. "It isn't that. We are
using stock as collateral. Common stock. And these shares are currently
worth far in excess of the face value of the loan. And the bank that's issuing
the loan happens to know the value of that stock better than anyone."

"Where did that come from?" asked Gus.

"Whose stock? Where did we get that stock?" Ana demanded.

Joseph let out a small sigh. He hadn't wanted to get into this with either
Gustafson, especially Ana. He peeked at her, but then turned back to Gus.
"The stock is mine. I co-signed the loan."

At first, neither one of the doctors said a word. Joseph looked back and
forth at them, waiting for something. "You said you were broke," Ana said
slowly. "You said your ex-wife, and the lawyers, wiped you out!" she hissed.

"No, I didn't." Joseph said immediately, cutting her off. "I said she got
the lion's share of the liquid assets we had when we divorced. And she did!
The part I got . . . well, I had to sell almost everything that could be sold at
the time to pay bills. But I did get to keep some things. A small piece of
property in Brooklyn, and some illiquid investments that she had wanted no
part of." He smiled sheepishly, and added, "One of those illiquid
investments has done quite well over the last two to three years, and is now
worth a good deal more than it was then. I'm using it to get us over this
hurdle."

Ana wasn't convinced, and continued to pepper Joseph with questions.
She wanted to know how much the bank was charging the clinic in interest

for the loan. She wanted to know how much Joseph was charging the clinic for using his stock. How was the clinic going to pay off the loan, in what Joseph had said would be less than a year? What if the clinic couldn't make its payments? What if the value of the stock dropped? Could the bank call the loan?

Joseph was in control. He handled these financial questions as easily as Ana would have handled questions about the 24 hour flu. Gus remained quiet. He sat back in his chair and watched as Ana fired one question after another. And with each question calmly and assuredly answered by Joseph, he grew more relaxed. When Ana finally had no more objections, she threw her hands up in dismay, signed the application, and left the two men sitting there.

"I appreciate what you're doing." Gus said, after a moment. "Frankly, I appreciate all you've done for us since you've been here. You saved the place."

"We're not out of the woods, yet," Joseph cautioned.

"I know, I know. It's just that I think we are on the way to recovery. I don't think we're on the ledge anymore. We may not be on rock solid ground, but we've definitely moved back away from the edge. And we have you to thank for it." Joseph smiled back at him, and almost imperceptibly nodded, acknowledging the compliment. He rose out of the chair and started to leave.

"One more question, if you don't mind?" Gus said. Joseph turned, and looked at him. "This stock we're using as collateral . . . what did you call it?"

"2BIC," Joseph responded, "The number 2, followed by B – I – C. I'm sure you've never heard of it."

"You just told Ana you put up 25,000 shares. And that's worth more than the $50,000 loan?" he said as he cocked his head to one side. "Are you risking your entire stake?"

"Actually, at current market valuation, it's worth . . . " he hesitated a moment, then simply added, " . . . more." Joseph thought for a second about giving Gus a quick tutorial on the Principle of Loan to Value Ratio. But he thought better of it, and closed the conversation by saying, "I have more; but let's hope we don't need more." Joseph started out of the room but stopped himself. "I need you to sign that paper. I already have. It has to go back to New York this afternoon."

Joseph faxed the signed documents back to the bank by 2 PM. The originals were sent via overnight mail shortly thereafter. Confirming phone calls were made to the bankers in New York, who promised to call back no later than noon, Saturday. It was beginning to look like the December 30 paychecks would clear.

Chapter Eight

There were three items on Joseph's agenda for the morning. He would wait, impatiently, for an incoming call from New York. Then there would be an outgoing call he had to make to the sales rep at Seward Supply. Over the past several weeks they had been negotiating the amount that the clinic owed the supplier. They had agreed on a "ballpark" figure. And, finally, there would be a trip to the mall for an electronics shopping spree.

The call from New York came earlier than Joseph had really expected it would. Apparently the bankers wanted to get back home to continue their holiday weekend. The call lasted only minutes. All he wanted to hear was "the loan has been approved, and cash has been transferred." A quick call to his local bank confirmed the wire transfer of funds had been completed.

The call to Seward would take longer. It was hard work and hard negotiating to reach the final figure that Seward felt it was owed. But the end result satisfied both parties and left them both with a new understanding that the relationship would be kept on a more professional level going forward. And just to make them certain that the clinic was sincere, Joseph promised to overnight the check so it would be in their hands on Monday.

The last item on the agenda was a trip to the largest electronics store in the valley. A post-Christmas sale had the place jumping. But Joseph knew exactly what he wanted, and had called ahead to schedule a meeting with the sales manager of the computer department. Details such as delivery dates and service schedules had to be ironed out, but Joseph was in his element as a negotiator. The price of peripheral equipment was bargained until the store manager cried "uncle."

At 4 PM this afternoon the first official practice of the re-born Newcomb Bombers Geetha team was scheduled to take place. And the small secluded pond, down at the end of winding Stassen Lane, had been the practice area for the Newcomb Geetha teams for more than 50 years. And today was no different.

Even though Podalski, Ronnie Rowe and Joseph were the new guys and understandably eager and nervous, the returning veterans were just as excited to get going. By the time Podalski and Joseph arrived 15 minutes early, most of the team was already there. And even though the team's lineup was set, this practice had the feeling of a tryout camp.

No two players were dressed alike. There were different colors on different jerseys, and on sweatshirts, and on jackets, and on sweaters. Players were wearing jeans and sweat pants, and one player was wearing hockey shorts. Most players were wearing gloves but they were as varied as everything else. As the players glided around the small pond trying to loosen up before the practice started, most weren't wearing any headgear. But that would certainly change once the real action started.

The eleven players on the official roster skated around the unofficial coach of the team, Gus Gustafson. The official captain of the team was Moonie. They called everyone into a circle at almost exactly 4 o'clock and began the practice.

Gus did most of the talking, and because of his well-earned reputation as one of the best players to ever "step over the boards," everyone listened. He reminded the players of some of the rules, and then went on to remind them how physical the game had always been. Shortly after that he instructed them all to "take a lap to loosen up . . . and then we'll do some wind sprints." Like any practice Joseph had ever been to, the strenuous part of practice was always greeted with groans.

The players skated swiftly around the pond a few times, each time a little faster than the lap before. Joseph was surprised about how well they all skated, even the larger men. When they had finished a few turns around the pond, they gathered into three groups, and Gus had them race from one end to the other. The distance wasn't much more than 50 yards, but after several sprints most of the players were winded. In the course of the sprints it had become quite clear that Podalski was the fastest skater there. Joseph was not a very close second fastest. Roove, Paulie were next, and Smoke Tully, Jepperson, and Whitey came next. The slowest three were the largest men there: Moonie, Magoo, and B-Ball.

Gus let them take a short breather after the sprints, but then organized a few drills for the team to run. Podalski, Joseph, and B-Ball stood off to the side next to Gus, and watched the others perform certain weaving patterns in two groups of four. Gus made side comments to the three men watching, explaining what the skaters were doing. The verbal signals they yelled out to each other were nothing new to them. They had been part of the Newcomb Geetha team game plan for a very long time. Gus assured the new players that they would soon become familiar with them too.

The signals were coded words that told the titman, center, and both wingers what formation they should shift into. There were signals to instruct the wingers what the titman was going to do. There were colors used, and several other words too. And each signal had a number with it, which determined slight variations. There were even fake signals, which meant absolutely nothing. They were used to trick the other team who would be obviously listening in. There were even hand signals to be used when opposing players had their backs turned!

Gus told the three novices not to worry too much about it; these signals weren't too hard to remember. He had even printed out some diagrams of formations that the Bombers used, and a page listing all the signals.

The practice went on for over an hour until it was almost dark. Lampposts around the small pond began going on, and provided minimum light. The Bombers practiced shifting from one formation to another and back again. They spent 20 minutes going over the "free start" plays they had last used years ago. They had five different plays they used, along with 3 variations. The players didn't take very long to remember them. Gus showed the three new players diagrams he had drawn of the plays. Free starts were a very important part of Geetha, as it was somewhat easier to score from a preplanned play than it was from the ordinary scuffles that went on during the bulk of play.

They had been at it for nearly two hours when some of the players started to complain about it. They were tired, and they were cold. Gus ignored them for a while as he tried to get to utilize all his players. He was obviously pleased that Podalski was so fast, and that Joseph seemed to be very fast and strong too. The practice did not include any full contact or combat, and several times he had to remind the players to only go at "half speed". There was definitely some heavy bumping, pushing and shoving.

When he finally blew the whistle to end practice (to avert an impending full scale rebellion!) the players skated slowly over to the benches, and plopped down. Some jackets were put on to ward off the chill, and some water and beer appeared to ward off thirst. Some good natured teasing began immediately.

"I see you didn't get any faster, now that you're fatter," someone said to Moonie.

"Yeah? I don't think you got any faster either," he lobbed back.

Whitey asked Magoo, "Over the years since we played last . . . have you lost a step . . . or were you just standing still on purpose?" There was laughing and finger pointing all around.

Roove said, "Wait a minute . . . wait a minute!" Everyone quieted down for a moment. Roove put his arm around Smoke's shoulders. "I'm your teammate, right?" Smoke rolled his eyes, knowing something insulting was coming. "And I care about how well you do out there, right?" Smoke nodded, and let out a big sigh. "I think I can suggest a way for you to be as good as you were when we last played." Smoke didn't want to, but had to ask how that could be done. "Well, I think you ought to lose 40 pounds and get 10 years younger."

Smoke immediately called him an obscene word, but Magoo yelled over everyone, "And getting' a little better lookin' sure wouldn't kill ya."

The conversation continued on in the same vein. Standing on the side, Joseph idly asked Moonie why Smoke was called "Smoke." In the course of the next few minutes Moonie explained to Joseph that nicknames were part of the Geetha culture. Most players had them.

"If you're smart, you give yourself one, before someone nails one on you," said Smoke, "Like me!"

Roove chimed in saying that some nicknames aren't too complimentary. "Ain't that right, Magoo?"

"Don't start," the big center replied.

"Some of us are so outstanding that no nickname would be adequate. Right, Gus?" said the winger Tully.

Paulie jumped in, "You didn't get a nickname, Tully, because 'Fat' and 'Ugly' were already taken."

"Even some people who didn't even play get tagged with a nickname," Moonie said. He thought for a second, and then continued, "We got a guy here in the valley that's probably gone to every game that's been played in the last thirty years. He never played in one, but he went to them all. He name is Myron Lomb, but everyone knows him as the 'Lump on the Stump'; 'Lump' for short. He showed up at them all. Gets there early; picks out his spot . . . a tree stump usually. And then he lays out his picnic basket that contains enough food to feed a village. Joseph thought he had heard about this guy before, and B-Ball and Podalski were also familiar with that name.

"Lot of people here in Wackentute get nicknames. You don't have to step over the boards to get one."

"Even your boss got a nickname," someone said.

Joseph turned around to Gus, and said, "'Gus isn't really a nickname for someone named 'Gustafson', is it?" Gus wasn't looking at him, he was looking at Roove.

"I wasn't talkin' about Gus. I meant his daughter," Roove said. Gus scrunched his nose, and shook his head.

"Ana? Ana has a nickname?" Joseph asked him.

Roove smiled, everyone else got quiet. "'Agony Ann.' Agony for short. That's her name. Only I don't think you should use that to her face." The quiet disappeared under a wave of laughter.

"Agony Ann?" Joseph repeated, and then laughed. He tried several times to ask why, but he couldn't stop laughing.

"Are you asking 'why'?" Paulie wanted to know. "Jesus! You shudda seen her play ball! She hurt people!" Gus tried interrupting to defend his daughter, but the team wouldn't listen to him.

"Hell, it wasn't just in sports she inflicted pain." Tully said, "She gave me a needle in the ass a few years ago . . . I think she used a turkey baster!"

"Wait a minute," Paulie said. "How about your nickname? Tell him why your nickname is Moonie".

"Aw, c'mon. Let's not drag that up again."

Several of the players laughed, and Paulie turned and spoke to Joseph, "You thought his name was Moonie? No! His real name is Mooney . . . M-O-O-N-E-Y. Mayor Sean Mooney. But his nickname is Moonie . . . M-O-O-N-I-E." Paulie turned back around to the now embarrassed mayor and said, "Tell him why, Mr Mayor."

Moonie looked at Joseph, sadly, and said, "Man! These guys are merciless." After some further encouragement, the mayor explained that while attending law school at Syracuse University he attended a basketball game one night at the university's famous arena, The Carrier Dome. He went on to explain that it just so happened that that night the Carrier Dome was filled to capacity. "Some 30,000 or so people were there that night," Moonie said. When he hesitated a moment, Tully took up the tale. Tully was a lifelong friend of the mayor's, and had even attended Syracuse at the same time. For approximately 2½ semesters, he said.

"Over 34,000, to be more accurate. And young Sean here, happened to be whacked out of his mind on some wicked demon rum that night." Tully paused here and turned to Moonie to ask him, "And a little ganja too . . . if I remember correctly?" Tully turned back to Joseph to finish the tale. "But he went to the game anyway. Loyal fan that is. And so, late in this close scoring game, when a crucial free throw arched up toward the basket, every eye of the 34,000-plus people in the arena watched it. And as every eye followed that ball up into the air . . . way up behind the glass backboard . . . in the top row . . . dead center behind the basket . . . young Sean dropped trow!"

"Tell him, Moonie," said Paulie, who turned back to Joseph, but pointed at Moonie, "The man here owns the record for 'biggest Moon' in Syracuse University history."

Moonie interrupted immediately. "That's not true!" he protested. "That's not true," he said again. "Well . . . not completely true" he added a moment later. "Some undergraduate mooned a football game back in the late 80's and supposedly got over 44,000 people. That's counting ushers, vendors and both teams." He shook his head, almost regretfully."But you know something? I'm told that record might not be valid. Because that kid dropped out during that semester, so he might have been actually ineligible; not actually in the student body at the moment of the mooning." Moonie looked around to see if anyone was agreeing with him. Then, in a very low voice, he said, "In any case, I got the record for the Law School."

Sunday - December 29

Just because Podalski and Joseph had skated yesterday at practice, it did not deter them from meeting up again this morning for their weekly spin around Lake Custer. And even if they had wanted to, the three young Podalskis wouldn't have let them. They loved their Sunday morning skate with their Dad.

The two skaters weren't the least bit sore from the practice the day before. Yet they knew very well that the practice wasn't as nearly physical as the games promised to be. They discussed the various formations and signals that they had learned yesterday. Podalski talked about the rules and protocols that were second nature to him and the others, but new to Joseph. And Joseph, in turn, broached the subject of Podalski being somewhat smaller than all the other players. "We keep hearing how rough it's going to be. You think you'll be okay?"

Podalski waved that away, "I may not be as big as the other guys, but I'm so much faster than they are. I will trade size for speed anytime."

There was no denying he had the heart to play, Joseph thought. "You're going to have to stay out of their wingers reach. I know you're not supposed to grab, but Gus said some of the lineman in the league are just plain dirty."

"I know. I know," the accountant said, "When I get out there during the game I'll really have to be careful. I could get really tossed around by big guys like Moonie. But when we do the Starts I can really be a big advantage. Those big guys can't stay with me!"

The conversation about Geetha strategy continued between them almost all the way around the lake. Realizing they were coming to the end of their loop, Joseph reflexively asked a business question. "By the way, is there anything left we need to do for Year End? We ready to close the books?" He had asked the question without giving it very much thought. Both of them fell silent. They glided along for another 10 strides, with the only noise being the hissing sound of their skate blades on the ice.

"Hey, it is Year End!" Podalski said with a sly smile. He turned to Joseph.

Joseph smiled back, "Yes, it is. It's Year End. We made it."

Monday - December 30

It was probably the most relaxed Monday morning Joseph could remember having since he had arrived at the clinic back on November 4th. The first thing he did, as usual, was check his overnight emails and voicemails. There were very few. He called Podalski and arranged to meet with him later.

He went into the lab to visit with Figgit for almost an hour. There were necessary and expensive things that needed to be done in that place. When he was finished there, he had a quick chat with Gus to update him on several things that were going on. He stopped by to visit with the always busy Mena.

His final stop was to sit down with Lindsay. He needed to get feedback from her about a number of different things. The primary one was, of course, the status of the backlog of claims.

What she told him pleasantly surprised him. The backlog still existed, but it was smaller than it had ever been. The number of cases yet to be submitted was under 200. And while there were a number of very large claims that would be very hard to clear, she thought that with Sadim's help they just might get through most of them.

The mention of Sadim's name reminded Joseph that he thought he had seen them both at the festival. He almost asked her if she had been there with him. But some nerve fiber somewhere in the back of his brain buzzed, and he kept his mouth shut. He would never know how wise that decision was. Instead, he asked her when she thought Sadim would return. She responded without a moment's hesitation that he might stop by tomorrow. She smiled to herself when she said it. Joseph watched her, and thought that he probably wasn't the only one who thought she had very cute dimples. "Tell him I need to talk with him. It's very important."

"Okay, Boss," she said as he walked off.

His meeting with Podalski started at 2 PM, and lasted two hours. The two men poured over financial statements and reports, adding, and sometimes correcting, the data they held. When they were finished, they double-checked their work. Podalski finally looked up at him and said, "All we can do . . . has been done." He was right.

Tuesday - December 31

Yesterday had been a low volume day at the clinic; today was even lighter. Joseph wandered around the clinic looking for something to do. Other than spending some time with Olney moving some supplies around, he couldn't find anything. Patient flow was so light it was discussed that perhaps they should close early. That idea ran out of gas when Gus said that they could leave, but that he would stay and close up the clinic at the normal time.

The only thing out of the ordinary was when Lindsay called out to Joseph that Sadim was on the phone. Joseph raced back into his office and shut the door. The call lasted longer than Sadim had thought it would. He had thought that when Lindsay told him that Joseph had wanted to talk with him, it would only be to check on the status of the claims. But he soon learned that Joseph had an agenda; and Sadim was a big part of it.

Late that afternoon, staff members began slipping out. The waiting room was empty, and one mom, with a sniffling baby, occupied a treatment room. By 5 PM the building was empty except for Gus, a part-time nurse, and Joseph. He had no special plans for the evening and wasn't in any hurry to leave.

To Joseph, New Year's Eve was never really much of a holiday. For much of his youth he was always involved in or traveling to hockey tournaments over the New Year's holiday. And after he had graduated and gone into business, it had always seemed there was some pressing business deadline that would keep him busy while others tooted horns and drank champagne. While in jail, of course, it was ignored.

Tonight, none of those things was true. But even as he was free to do as he pleased, he opted for the same schedule he had enjoyed for the many previous Saturday nights. He went to the Fireside.

The crowd was perhaps a little lighter than usual when he arrived around nine. Roove, Smoke and Whitey were there; and Dudley was, of course, behind the bar. They all greeted one another, and Smoke said, "We were just talkin' about you." Joseph asked them why. "You put on quite a show, Saturday. Where'd you learn to skate so good?"

Joseph tried to say it modestly, but reminded them, "I played college hockey. Actually I have played hockey since I was five." He looked around at them, and added, "Spent a lot of time on skates up in Michigan. If you wanted to play, you had better learn how to skate."

The conversation went around about how much time each of them had spent on skates as a youth. But as each in turn talked about his career on skates, it became clear Joseph had spent more time playing organized sports, especially hockey. He said he also had played for coaches that were tough taskmasters.

"I played in high school for a guy who had won the conference title just about every year. He won the districts a couple of times, and he won two state titles before I even got there. We won it twice when I was there!" The three listeners were only slightly impressed. Joseph pressed his point. "He used to say, 'There is always a reason for failure, but never an excuse.'"

"Was he a dick?" Roove asked a minute later.

Joseph thought for a moment, and then nodded, "Yes." Everyone smiled. "But he was a great hockey coach." Joseph launched into a story.

"You know what he used to do every year on the first day of tryouts?" He didn't wait for them to answer. "He would line every one of the new kids up on the goal line down at one end of the ice. Then he'd tell them 'I'm gonna time you, one at a time,' and he'd wave this stop watch in his hand. 'You're gonna go from the goal line here all the way down behind the net down there on the other end, and grab the puck we put up on the boards down there....fast as you can. And when you're all done? I'm gonna cut the slowest guys.' Well, I'm telling you, when he yelled 'Go' each one of those kids would go like his pants were on fire . . . roaring down the ice."

"And he cut the slowest kids?" Whitey asked. He silently didn't think that this made him a great coach.

"Hell, no! We were a very small school. We needed every kid who tried out. But he'd watch each kid skate down the ice. Some would slow down as they approached those end boards, and snatch that puck. Some would swerve at the very last second and just brush against the boards, and swipe the puck off the boards. Those guys were wingers, no matter what their time was. The other guys? The ones who just went like hell; in a straight line; not waste any time cutting or swerving; crashed full force into the boards where the puck was? Those guys he made defensemen."

Everyone laughed, totally unsure whether that was true, or he was just kidding around. Joseph didn't give them any time to think about it. "You know how he used to pick his goalies?" They all stared at him. "He would take all the kids who were trying out for goalie down to this bench by the back door of the rink. Then, one by one, he'd take them out the back door into the alley outside for a little chat," he said. "He'd get them outside, and be talking to them for a minute or two . . . and then he would take out a cigarette and light it up." Joseph paused here a moment, and looked at the three listeners' faces. He had them hooked.

He went on, "He'd ask the kid a question, or two, while he was puffing away, and then . . . without warning, he flick the cigarette right at their face!" The faces on all three men looked shocked! Joseph let them stare for minute, and then continued, "If the kid ducked, the coach cut him. If he blocked it with his hand or arm...he put him on the JV team. If he blocked it with his face . . . he was varsity." Whitey and Smoke were wide eyed. Roove was more than a little dubious. Joseph wasn't finished, "Kid who played two years at goaltender when I was a junior and a senior? Made All-State every year. When he first tried out, and went out back for that test? Caught the damn cigarette in midair . . . took a drag, and handed it back to the coach, and nonchalantly asked, 'You drop this?'"

"Oh bullshit!" laughed Whitey, "Now I know you're full of shit!"

Smoke was just laughing and pointing at Joseph. Roove was looking down and shaking his head.

"No, I'm serious," Joseph protested, "Kid had the fastest hands I ever saw. He played two years in the Big Ten; then went to play hockey up in Manitoba somewhere. Wound up in jail, I think. I'm not kidding" But they were having none of what he said.

After they calmed down a little and were refreshing their drinks, Smoke said to no one in particular, "If you want to talk about fast hands . . . and on New Year's Eve, of all nights . . . How about Bilge and O'G?"

"Whoa, that's no lie!" said Whitey. Roove just nodded.

Dudley, who was in the process of replacing Joseph's scotch, froze, looked up and said, "Ah Jeez, let's not bring that up again."

"What happened?" Joseph asked.

"You tell him, Roove. You were here. And unlike Dudley, you were awake for the whole thing." The three men all found that funny. Dudley, still eavesdropping on the conversation, did not and muttered, "I tripped."

Then Roove told the story.

It seems several years ago, in November, Bilge was hanging around the Fireside Inn late one Friday night. Gerry O'Grady – or "O-G" as everyone called him – was in there too. O-G was a handsome guy a few years older than Bilge. He worked for an insurance agency as an agent. And like most people who work in sales, he was a confident guy who had a way with words. Always well-groomed and dressed nicely, he had quite a reputation with the ladies.

He and Bilge got to drinking this night, and talking, and more drinking, and before you knew it they had left together. They were young, somewhat drunk, and owed no one any explanation. A week went by with no further contact between them, but oddly enough, they again met up late the next Friday night at the same location . . . with the same happy ending. O-G called her the following Tuesday, just to say hello. In that conversation he mentioned he would probably be at the Fireside this coming Friday night and would see her, "if she had nothing else to do." That sounded like a "date" to Bilge. To O-G it was simply arranging a fallback plan if the new girl he had just met in Operations at the agency failed to show any interest. But the new girl, Stacy Grammerhill, did show interest, and agreed to go out with O-G the following *Saturday* night. This was fine with O-G. His social schedule was lining up pretty nicely he thought.

This arrangement went on beautifully, as far as O-G was concerned, for the next few weeks. But somewhere along the line O-G must have mentioned to Bilge the New Year's Eve Dinner/Dance held at the Newcomb American Legion Hall. This annual dinner/dance was very popular, and *the* place to be on New Year's Eve for a lot of the locals. Bilge took it that she had a date, and she was thrilled. O-G never remembered it that way at all.

There was never a phone call to nail down the particulars, which Bilge thought odd, but dismissed it as part of O-G's cavalier attitude. The fact that she didn't see him around at the Fireside Inn she wrote off to his being so busy around the holidays. And he was busy . . . by this time he was seeing Stacy Grammerhill three or four times a week. There wasn't any reason he could think of to prolong the relationship with Bilge. So he just never called, and avoided the Fireside Inn. Let it die on the vine, he thought to himself.

By the afternoon of New Year's Eve Bilge was concerned at the prolonged, and total, disappearance of O-G. She had a drink, or two, to steady her nerves. But she knew the affair started at eight, and planned her schedule accordingly. By 7 PM she was dressed and ready to go. But still there was no sign, or signal, from O-G. And under no circumstances on Earth was she about to call him. After 7:30 had come and gone, she started moving from "concern" to "annoyance." By 8 PM, she was pissed.

Nine PM found her back in her jeans and sweatshirt, and highly agitated. She decided to take a swing by the Fireside Inn to have a few drinks and take a look around.

Dudley was tending bar that night and saw her the minute she walked in the door. He had known her for a long time and greeted her warmly. She did not respond. When Bilge walked into the place it was practically empty. On this, the most festive night of the year, most people went to in-home parties or large catered affairs like the one at the American Legion Hall. There were a few people sitting at the bar, and a mixed group was sitting at some tables near the bowling machine and juke box. Bilge looked around and saw Roove and Tully sitting at the end of the bar and joined them. They greeted her when she sat down, but she didn't say anything. The two men shrugged, and then went on discussing some football game that was coming up. The two men were drinking beer, but Bilge was in no mood for beer. She ordered "Jack ... straight up", and Dudley, sensing immediately she was in no mood for casual conversation, poured her drink and moved off. Both men sitting with her could sense her foul mood too, and although cautious not to seem like they were intentionally ignoring her, they tried their best to leave her alone.

Several hours went by as some people came and went from the bar. The football game that had been on the TV when Bilge walked in was now over and had been replaced by some New Year's Eve show from New York City. The two men sitting next to Bilge only looked up at the TV sporadically. Dudley was reading a newspaper behind the bar. At midnight there was a brief cheer and some good wishes tossed around, but everyone went back to their own business quickly.

It was nearly 1:30 AM when O-G walked into the Fireside Inn with Stacy Grammerhill on his arm. He had been drinking, and so had Stacy. Neither one would remember later why they had decided to stop off at the Fireside to have one more drink before heading back to Stacy's place. But they were undoubtedly feeling great, and they walked to the center of the bar and jumped on two adjoining stools. Laughing and talking over each other, they hardly noticed anyone else was there. After getting two drinks from Dudley, O-G surveyed the place. Looking down the bar to where Roove and Tully sat he smiled broadly and was yelling out a New Year's greeting when he spotted Bilge in the dark corner. Roove and Tully smiled and returned the greeting, but saw the expression on O-G's face turn dark. Bilge just stared. O-G turned away from Bilge and focused on Stacy, who was oblivious to the drama. Tully and Roove were puzzled by the reaction, and then noticed the look on Bilge's face. They looked at each other and had the same thought that this was not going to be good.

Before either one could say anything, Bilge slipped off her stool and walked around the bar to where O-G and Stacy were sitting. O-G saw her coming out of the corner of his eye and swung around on his stool to face her. Stacy twisted slightly around to look at this stranger. Bilge started to say something, but O-G interrupted her immediately. "Hey lady, how ya doin? Thought you were goin' to the American Legion thing? That over already?" he said in a loud voice, ignoring the fact she was wearing jeans and a sweatshirt. It was, in hindsight, probably the wrong thing to say.

Bilge started to speak again, intending to explain that it wasn't nice "to stand someone up," especially on New Year's Eve. But O-G interrupted her again saying, "Stacy here, and me, went down to Omar's in South Reddington." It suddenly occurred to him that perhaps the two ladies didn't know each other, so he started to introduce them. "Stacy, do you know . . . ?" Bilge apparently took that in a bad way, and saw that any further discussion on the topic of dating protocol was futile. She let fly with the "old One – Two." Then she quickly added "Three, Four, Five, and Six," free of charge.

Partly because it was unexpected and light-speed quick, and partly because he was a little drunk, O-G never got his hands up. He came off the stool like a landslide. He hit the floor hard in several places like a marionette whose strings have been cut. Bilge considered kicking him, but decided there would be time enough for that later. She turned to find Stacy, but she was gone.

At the first flash of hands Stacy, displaying an incredible sense of self-preservation, hit the ground running. She was out the door nearly before O-G hit the floor. She hitched her way home. She would send her sister back the next day to get her pocketbook and coat.

With her blood up and finding no Stacy to pound, Bilge scanned the room looking to see if anyone else had something to say. Of course everyone was looking down at their drinks, trying very hard to be invisible. Everyone that is, except Roove, who was looking down at O-G on the floor. Standing over O-G, with her back to the bar, Bilge continued to scan the room, from left to right and back again. Holding her fists up near her chin, she was ready for all comers. There were no comers! Nobody was moving. Slowly she turned and looked behind her, and she spotted Dudley . . . looking right back at her. Their eyes locked.

Dudley had frozen with fear at the ferocity of that first flurry of fists. They stared at one another for a very long uncomfortable moment, and then Dudley tried to break the spell by asking slowly, in a very hoarse whisper, "Can I pour you another bourbon, Miss?" It didn't work. For reasons that were known only to Bilge, it infuriated her, and she lunged at him. She stepped up onto the bar rail and reached across the bar for him. But her arms weren't long enough. It didn't matter, because the instant he saw her come at him he fainted and collapsed. The sound of him hitting the floor behind the bar somehow defused the situation, and Bilge began calming down. She slowly glanced around the bar one more time, as if inviting any comments. When none were forthcoming, she went back to her stool in the corner. As she walked past Tully and Roove, both held their breath. When she was back on her stool Roove got up and went around to where O-G was.

O-G was now on his hands and knees wondering what continent he was on. His eyes were blurry and his nose was bleeding. There was something moving around in his mouth that didn't feel normal. He didn't know, nor certainly care at this point, whether she had knocked one of his teeth out, or simply a filling. Roove helped him to a chair and got a wet bar rag to put over his face. Before Roove put it on his face, O-G asked him, "Whaa she hid me wif?"

In the future, Dudley would insist he had tripped.

PART THREE

"The best-laid schemes of mice and men oft go awry."
--- Robert Burns

"There are no good ideas . . . after the third beer."
--- William (Caveman) Cavanaugh

Chapter Nine

Wednesday - January 1

New Year's Day was another Wackentute Valley cold and blustery day. The clinic was closed, but Joseph was there before 8 AM. He had created a New Year "to-do" list last week and began working down it this morning.

There were many things he was able to deal with this morning, despite most other businesses being closed. There was also a list of things he wanted Podalski and Lindsay to do when they came in tomorrow. Private insurance reimbursement had started to get a little better, and he wanted to follow up on that. And, of course, he wanted to talk to Sadim again about the status of the pending Medicaid claims. He also reviewed the status of several matters that he had assigned to outside lawyers.

He reviewed the budget and the payments they were going to make starting tomorrow. The excess funds from the secured loan were burning a hole in his pocket. He even began thinking about giving some of the staff long overdue raises in pay. That was not near the top of the list, however. And, of course, if he had any time left over he could attack the ever present pile of insurance claims that still had to be submitted.

Thursday - January 2

Today, the work day at the clinic began like the work day at thousands of other businesses across the country. There were "Happy New Year" wishes tossed around with wild abandon, with plenty of bright smiles and good cheer. Conversations ran from the football bowl games on TV yesterday to a host of New Years' Resolutions.

And while most of those resolutions would soon be forgotten, revitalized workers once again returned to familiar routines. The staff at the Wackentute Walk-In Clinic was certainly no different. Starting with Joseph Hamilton, who had actually returned to his routine yesterday when he had resolved to be more efficient with his time; to be more congenial to the staff and suppliers; and, finally, to eliminate forever the backlog of Medicaid reimbursement.

Gus had decided that he had to become more involved with the business aspects of the clinic. This was not based on his desire to do it, but rather a resignation that it would be necessary eventually. He knew fully well that Joseph had worked wonders in averting the financial catastrophe; but he also felt certain that he wouldn't have Joseph here forever. Sooner or later, Joseph would have the freedom to return to New York City, and resume his financial career. That career may never return to what it once was, in either prestige or compensation, but whatever it turned out to be the Wackentute Clinic's office manager's job would pale by comparison. His only hope was that Joseph would stay until the clinic was solidly back on its feet again.

Ana had spent New Year's Day doing all those little chores that working people leave for their days off. And while she was busy running errands, her mind was elsewhere. She resolved to find out, "before it was too late" she thought, "just exactly what Joseph Hamilton was up to." The practice at the Wackentute Clinic was hers (and her father's too), and she had to protect it from whatever harm might befall it. It was her responsibility not only for her financial well-being, but also for the sake of the many patients who depended on it being there for them. She resolved to get "more involved."

Mena had spent her holiday with her family. And while she and her husband, cooked and tended to the countless tasks a family gathering demanded, they discussed the pros and cons of her pursuing a dream she had been nurturing for some time. Attaining a Physician's Assistant degree was possible for her if she was willing to take the required courses. It wouldn't be easy as a working mother, but her family seemed willing to pitch in and help. They all said they would, and encouraged her to commit to the task. She had slept on it last night and was still mulling it over this morning.

Both Sadim and Lindsay had a lot to mull over this morning too. Lindsay had determined that the long-delayed plan of becoming a nurse was dead. Once and for all . . . D-E-A-D . . . dead! She had never really wanted to be a nurse, and had only entertained the thought because so many people around her had pushed her in that direction. No, it was not what she wanted, and that was that. On this bright, cold, first business day of the New Year she could only think of one thing she wanted. And *he* had driven off to work this morning at 6:30. He was scheduled to be at far off Holy

Cross Hospital by 8 AM, and that was over 70 miles away. Sadim would be at there the rest of the week, and then had said he would be in Albany all of next week. Since their first date at the King Wenceslas Festival they had talked on the phone daily. Their longest separation had only been four days. And now he was going to be gone for over a week!

And to him, that separation should give him plenty of time to sort out the confusion which had invaded his well-ordered life recently. But the image of the dimpled, amazingly sweet and beautiful face of Lindsay wouldn't leave him alone for a minute. The time away from her would prove not to be the respite he had thought it could be. Her absence only turned out to be a greater distraction than her presence had been. "What is going on?" he whispered to himself as he drove away from Wackentute County.

The clinic was busy with walk-ins and Joseph was busy with outgoing calls. And he was having amazing success at reaching everyone he called. If there was a negative aspect to it all, it had to be that each call took longer to complete than he had expected. One after another, he reached the person he needed to reach. The only exception had been Sadim, and Joseph left a long message on his voice mail.

Hanging up after a long conversation with a lawyer in New York City, Joseph glanced at his watch. When he did, he realized why he felt so hungry; it was nearly 1 o'clock. Deciding to grab a bite to eat before his next call, he wandered off to the pantry.

Some of the staff were getting a late start on lunch too. Mena was sitting with two part-time nurses discussing some upcoming examinations that these two needed for some certification they wanted. Gus was finishing a sandwich, and Ana was preparing a salad. Olney was having trouble getting the microwave to operate.

"I've been thinking." Ana said offhandedly. "I think we ought to meet regularly . . . you, and Dad and me . . . and maybe Podalski too. Maybe even Mena too. Just to go over things. Just so everyone is kept current on everything that's going on around here." She waited a moment, then added; "Don't you think that would be a good idea?" She was talking directly to Joseph.

No one said anything at first, but as Joseph started to respond, Gus spoke up. "You know I've been thinking the very same thing lately. I think that's a very good idea. I think we've . . . Ana and I . . . have let too much of the administrative burden fall on your shoulders." He was talking directly to Joseph. "I really believe that we should be involved in more of it." He stopped, trying to decide whether to ever even broach the subject of Joseph eventually leaving.

Joseph listened to them both, and wondered if they had discussed this between themselves prior to today, and had decided to jointly present it to him. He didn't think so, but the unpleasantness that had surrounded the loan application episode a few days ago might be what prompted this to both of them. It was, after all, their practice, and they had every right to know what was going on. As far as his getting involved in what was happening on the medical side? That probably wasn't that essential but, like chicken soup's effect on a common cold, it couldn't hurt.

Planning a regularly scheduled weekly meeting wasn't as simple as it sounded. After several starts and stops, it was tentatively planned that every Tuesday morning at 7:30 AM, they would gather in Gus's office to review any recent developments and discuss future plans.

Joseph met with Lindsay in his office after lunch. He had anticipated going over the status of the backlog and reviewing any ongoing problems. It turned into something else entirely. "I'm good at this," she suddenly said. They had been talking about the claims that still had not been submitted. It took him by surprise. He didn't say anything because he didn't really understand what she meant. She looked at him earnestly, and said, "I've done a pretty good job at clearing up all these old claims. Haven't I, Boss?" She didn't wait for his answer. "I mean, when we started going after them, there were hundreds. Now there aren't that many. I mean, you helped," she quickly added. "But I think I did most of them. Didn't I?" She looked at him across the desk with the most serious demeanor he could ever remember her having.

"Yes. I would say that you are responsible for most of the backlog getting submitted." He had no idea where this was going. So he said nothing more.

She waited a moment, and then realized he wasn't going to say anything. So, with all the boldness she could muster, she went on, "I want something for that." Then, after a moment's hesitation, she added, "I think I deserve it." Joseph didn't respond again, or even move a muscle; he just looked back across the desk. After a moment of waiting for a response, and not getting one, she went on. "Two things, really." She thought to herself that she was on a roll, and she should just keep going. "I share an apartment with two idiots. They're nice really, but they're idiots. I want to get my own place." It was now-or-never, she thought to herself. "I want . . . I *need* a raise," she corrected herself. "I can't afford my own place on what I get paid now." She had surprised herself that she had gotten the request out without stammering. She plunged on, "It doesn't have to be a lot more. I know we're kinda broke here. But I really need it. I haven't had a raise since I'm here." And then, while she still had enough breath to speak, she added her second request. "And I don't want to work the front desk anymore, either."

Joseph pushed his chair back away from his desk and leaned back. He thought to himself, "No, and no." But he didn't say it out loud. "We are planning on reviewing everyone's compensation," he said quietly. "No one can deny that the entire staff has been more than patient while we've tried to get back on solid ground financially." Don't make a promise you can't keep, he reminded himself. "We are going to try to be fair about it. But I can't say to you . . . or anyone else right now . . . 'when' and 'how much.' I'd be lying to you if I did." He watched her across the desk, and saw a trace of disappointment cross her face. He felt bad about disappointing her. She had been an enormous help in whittling down that backlog. And she had done it while handling most of the responsibilities of the reception desk. "And I can't take you off the reception desk. I have no one to replace you there. I surely can't hire someone new. There's no money right now." She turned her face away from him, and looked at the door. Don't let her get angry, he told himself. "I want you to know how much help you've been. And I want you to know how much I appreciate all you've done. I appreciate it," he assured her. "And Gus and Ana do too. We all know how hard you've worked. You've been invaluable." He hoped he was getting through. She didn't react. "We just need a little more time." He wanted to assure her that he would make it up to her, but that would sound hollow. Looking for something positive, he suddenly asked, "What do you want to do, if not the front desk? I realize that the backlog is way down, and if we're careful we can keep it that way. What do you want to do? Nurse?"

The slight change of subject caught her off guard. She looked at him again, and said, "I could be the bookkeeper. I'm good with numbers." She had thought this through when she had finally realized that she hated working on the reception desk. She explained to Joseph that she thought she could handle most of the bookkeeping that needed to be done. Joseph agreed with her that the bookkeeping and general clerical work needed more attention than it was getting. He thought to himself that he and Phil Podalski had done the lion's share of it up to now, but that needed to be changed. As Podalski's accounting practice grew, he would necessarily spend less time at the clinic, and Joseph was considering about perhaps returning to New York. He didn't share these thoughts with Lindsay, but they added weight to her suggestion.

Friday - January 3

Promises that had been made to various vendors were now coming due. The New Year was here, and people had been told to expect their money. Some checks were written and hand delivered. Some new orders went out.

The phone company had been one of the more neglected vendors that the clinic had. Despite furious phone calls and threatening letters from them, the service had never been shut off. But Joseph and Phil knew they were pressing their luck. With what was left of the secured loan funds the clinic had sent a large check to them. Although they were not entirely paid in full, a grateful representative called to acknowledge receipt of the payment, and accept apologies for past transgressions. In the course of the conversation he offhandedly asked "if there was anything they could do for the clinic?". The call lasted far longer than that man had expected.

Podalski came in for a strategy session after lunch, and initial plans were made for what they hoped would be a framework financial plan and budget for the clinic for the coming year. Although certainly not yet on firm footing, they began to make a plan that would be a guideline for revenues and expenses for the next fiscal year, beginning February 1st.

Podalski had been working on the data, and had been trying to make it as realistic as possible. There were still so many gaps in information that both men realized that this would be a "best guesstimate." But they also both realized that this was a necessary starting point, and although there would undoubtedly be many, many alterations down the road, and they had begun the process.

Very late in the afternoon, Joseph was finishing up a meeting with Podalski when he received a call from Sadim. They exchanged some brief pleasantries, but Sadim seemed to be in a hurry, and got to the point of the call. He had been advised by a friend in the Albany office that a "large check had been issued that afternoon to the Wackentute Clinic."

Joseph called the bank, but no one answered.

Saturday - January 4

The first thing Joseph did upon arriving at the clinic was to call the bank. No one answered the first four times he called. In between calls he checked the clinic's bank balance on-line. There was no indication of a large deposit. Dialing again at 9:04, the vice president picked up and was bombarded with questions from Joseph. Slowly regaining lost composure, the bank officer promised to check around, and call back.

And to his credit he did . . . thirty agonizing minutes later. Unfortunately he had no good news. If the money had been sent, it had not arrived. He assured Joseph that it wasn't unusual for some entities, governmental and private, to dispense money late on a Friday in order to have the money remain in their account — drawing interest — over the weekend. He promised he would watch for it throughout the morning, and would call immediately if it arrived. He was not, however, optimistic.

Practice with the Bombers was held again at 3 PM. And to Joseph, it seemed a little more serious than the previous ones. Players talked and joked less. There seemed to be a more serious attitude toward everything from warming up to attention to detail in the various shifts and maneuvers.

In the previous practice, player mistakes and miscues were ridiculed. Today they were pointed out without humor, and corrected.

The practice began with a review of the rules of the game by Gus. He did it not just because of the three new players, but because none of them had played in eight years. It was a rough contact sport, but there were limits on how far a player could go. Clutching and grabbing would draw penalties, he assured everyone.

He went over the basics quickly. "Remember it's just the titman who can be handling the Geetha at any one time. If you're doing a switch with the titman be sure to have the timing right. Make sure he lets go before you touch it. Two guys on the same team touching it simultaneously, and White will call the foul, and give the other team a free start. If one of our guys is in contact with it . . . HANDS OFF!"

Moonie jumped in at this moment and warned, "Remember this, guys, especially against the Blades, because of their damn whip. It's a killer. You don't want to give them any free starts!"

"Don't worry about the Blades, now. We have a few weeks before we have to deal with them," Gus said. "And pay attention when you're out there. Listen for the signals. Watch out for switches. We have the Reds first; and when Torpedo Red gets loose, someone is going to get hit."

Neither Joseph, Podalski, nor B-ball was sure what that meant, but they would find out. After a 10 minute warm-up exercise, the team went over the diagrammed free start plays and players were assigned to various positions. The team was divided up into two units with Roove, Moonie, Tully and Jeepers forming one side, and Paulie, Magoo, Whitey and Smoke forming the other. The three newcomers stood on the sidelines and watched the action.

First the Roove team did a free start, with Paulie's team defending; and then they switched around and did it the other way. It wasn't very hard for the newcomers to catch on. Paulie's team waited at the imaginary half line as Roove's team began coming at them from 50 yards away. Roove was pushing a very large burlap sack stuffed with rags; which was serving as the practice geetha. The Roove team converged on the defenders, and suddenly scattered in pre-assigned directions. There were some collisions, some stumbling, and finally a lunge by Paulie onto the geetha. Gus blew a whistle, and all the players converged to rehash why the play had not resulted in a breakaway goal.

The tables were then turned as Paulie's unit skated, first down the ice a bit, and then turned and charged Roove's group at center ice. As they did, Gus showed the bystanders the diagram of what Roove had just attempted to do and why it failed.

The collision at mid-ice seemed just as chaotic as the previous one, but suddenly Paulie found an opening and tried to slip through it. Only a last second dive by Tully knocked Paulie's skates out from underneath him and allowed the geetha to slide harmlessly away. Again Gus's whistle sounded, and again the players converged to assess the play.

This went on a few more times as Gus began substituting players in and out of the lineup. B-Ball and Podalski were more familiar with the game than Joseph, having seen it played in their youth, so they substituted in first.

Due to his skating ability....or lack thereof....it was an easy decision as to where B-Ball would play on the team. He was a natural "wing," which was generally where the least able skaters on the team played. A center was normally a better skater than a wing, but always stronger than a wing. The titman was not always as strong as a center, but was invariably the best, or second best, skater on the team. This was where Podalski was best-suited to play. But still, his lack of size and strength were a concern.

But it wasn't long before all three newcomers had gotten in. Gus reminded all of them, newcomers and veterans alike, that this was "practice," and everyone should be going at half speed. "Let's not kill one another out there, okay? We will have plenty of chances for that when we start playing for real."

Joseph would be another story altogether. After a few initial turns at wing, Gus could see that he was a better skater than any other wing or center the Bombers had. He appeared to be strong enough to handle the center position. While he might not be as strong as Moonie or Magoo, he was a far better skater than they were. In fact he appeared to be a better skater than Roove or Paulie. His inexperience at the game would prevent his playing titman anytime soon, thought Gus, but he was potentially an excellent player. Joseph's versatility allowed Gus to keep shifting players around as they practiced free starts for the first half hour.

When they took a five minute break, Gus told them they would start doing shifts and switches next. These involved the players' maneuverings while in play, and did not require contact. They were done at full speed, and occasional mistakes resulted in players taking awkward falls. While falling to the ice is never fun, when it happens because you've made a mistake, it is worse. Crashing to the ice when someone else fouls up is worst of all. And tempers get a little short.

"FUCK!" screamed sprawling Jeepers. When he came to a halt and grabbed his knee, he shouted, "Whose foot was that?"

"You're supposed to turn the other way, Shithead!" answered Paulie, who had tripped also, and had fallen on his arm. He was rubbing it as he glared at his winger, "You're supposed to go to the outside. I go inside. Why the fuck do you think we call it 'crisscross,' Asshole?"

"Okay....okay! Calm down," Gus yelled, trying to regain some control. "Let's do it again." He skated over to where Paulie was regaining his feet, and whispered, "Don't cut it so close. You have plenty of room. If their winger doesn't see it right away, he'll never get you. Even if he does, you'll probably blow right by him." Paulie nodded in agreement.

These words were meant to give everyone a minute to calm down and regain their focus. The practice continued to go over the various shifts and switches the Bombers used. To the veteran players, the movements were second nature before very long. They had learned them and performed them many, many times in the past. To the newcomers it was not so easy.

B-Ball simply wasn't agile enough to do them right. Podalski, however, floated through them with uncanny speed. But the problem remained in Gus's mind about his lack of size. It seemed beyond doubt that Podalski would be manhandled in any one-on-one confrontation on the ice. Joseph was a pleasant surprise to them all. He was a very good skater, and one by one the other Bombers found him to be very strong whenever they tried to move him in the casual contact drills.

In less time than they had all anticipated the players were tired, sore, and done for the day. Gus relented, and called the practice to a halt. As they unlaced their skates and put on warm jackets, Gus strongly recommended they meet again tomorrow. There were groans and objections, but not a single one of them would dispute that they needed more practice. They reluctantly agreed to meet again tomorrow for a short, non-contact drill.

As they finished up, Gus asked Joseph if he had dinner plans. And rather than "grab a quick bite" as Gus suggested, Joseph drove him over to Marie's in Lower Wenwenee. The conversation between the two men seemed slightly awkward to Joseph, and he could not understand why.

The reason was that the two men had their minds on totally different topics. Joseph questioned Gus about the strategy and rules of this new gamer, Geetha. Gus would answer those questions, but invariably steer the conversation back to the clinic. Finally, during their main course, Joseph asked some question about player positioning, and Gus answered, "Has the Medicaid claim backlog been eliminated?"

It dawned on Joseph where Gus's mind was. Joseph paused a minute, and refocused his attention. "For the most part, yes. Lindsay is current in the processing of the new claims . . . both Medicaid and private insurance. The turnaround time on the submission and reimbursement by the private insurers is improving. It's better than it was. Far better, and we have virtually no backlog there. And the backlog in Medicaid claims is down to less than a hundred now. Some of those are going to have to be written off though; we're never going to see that money. But most of them will be filed within a week, or two. Now, having said that, it doesn't mean we've seen the money on the backlog we have submitted. That pile of money is still sitting on someone's desk in Albany being processed." He looked across at Gus, and was surprised again by his interest. "We have someone working from the inside however, trying to expedite the payment." He then added,

"And with some luck, I was sort of hoping that we were going to see some of it today." But then he shook his head, and said, "But it didn't happen. Hopefully Monday." He smiled weakly.

Gus looked at Joseph for a minute without saying anything, and then returned to his Chicken Francaise. "This is excellent." he said looking back at Joseph. Joseph thought about trying to get the topic back to Geetha, but before he could Gus said, "This meeting we're going to have Tuesday morning . . . you, me, Ana and Phil . . . I don't want you to think I'm *checking up* on you." Gus continued, "I just think it's a good idea that I, and Ana, keep up to speed with what's going on at the clinic. Not lose track of the business side again, like I did so terribly before."

The idea that these meetings would be to monitor him hadn't been seriously considered by Joseph. And his immediate reaction was approval. Gus was right. He should stay on top of what was happening. And he should never let it get out of control again. And Ana, as part-owner of the practice, should absolutely be as involved as Gus. "I honestly think it's a great idea. You two should be aware of everything that goes on." He smiled to himself when he thought about how much they would have to absorb to be brought up to speed. "You two have a lot of catching up to do," Joseph added.

"I'm sure there'll be a lot of questions."

"Ask away. The Clinic has gone through quite a bit in the last year," Joseph assured him.

"Oh," Gus said flatly, "You're going to get a lot of questions. I'm sure." He wasn't thinking about himself.

"That's okay. Ask as many as you need. We may not be able to cover all the ground this first time out, but we'll get there. We have time."

"How much time?" Gus asked, before he could stop himself.

Joseph wasn't sure exactly what that question meant. The two men just looked at each other for a moment, and then went back to their meals. He turned his attention to the Shrimp Scampi on his plate. Henry Kryder's offer of a job back in New York City was still open. If things worked out at the clinic the way he had planned, it wouldn't need him in the future. It would, of course, need someone to administer the business side, but not necessarily him. A few minutes of silence passed before Joseph looked up and said, "Who knows? These things have a way of working themselves out."

Sunday - January 5

The "short" practice scheduled for 10 AM was shorter than anticipated. Snow had begun falling after midnight, and it had come down hard. While some Bombers had to dig their way out of their driveways, some others had decided to roll over and go back to sleep. Mayor Mooney had some pressing official duties at town hall, and was also a "no-show."

The new snow was cleared from the skating area with some effort before practice could begin. The six players who did show up practiced some maneuvers at half speed, but there was little enthusiasm. The weather turned even nastier when the snowflakes turned into sleet. It didn't take long for everyone to agree that this practice was over.

Joseph spent the next few hours running some personal errands, and then headed for the Fireside to grab an early dinner and watch some football on TV. The nasty weather outside, and a double header of playoff football on TV, must have kept most people home on this Sunday. The bar was practically deserted. Joseph ate his dinner alone, and then had one drink at the bar before deciding to call it a night. As he started his car, it occurred to him that although he had seen the "Geetha Trophy" in town several times as he drove past it, he had never really inspected it up close. "Why not?" he asked himself.

The weather had turned from the snow overnight to sleet, then to rain, then to a heavy mist by six o'clock. The streets were empty of other pedestrians as he got out of his car across the street from the village green. The diamond-shaped park in the center of the Village of Newcomb was home to the revered Geetha Trophy. It had a few trees scattered about it, and had four brick paths from its corners leading to the center. And there, in the center, was a stone pedestal three foot square and six feet tall. On its top was a three foot high bronze sculpture of a reclining moose. It was curled up, and looked like it was sleeping. It was wet and glistening, with small traces of today's snow and sleet still visible on it. Moving around the pedestal, Joseph saw that on three sides a small sign shouted "STAY OFF." The fourth side had a bronze plaque that read:

GEETHA CHAMPION
FOREVER
NEWCOMB BOMBERS

Mena was right Joseph nodded; it just wouldn't be right if they had to give the trophy to some other town, and then throw that plaque away.

Monday - January 6

Despite the ongoing stormy weather the clinic was hopping when Joseph arrived. Three different delivery trucks were trying to beat the weather and get their deliveries in early. And Olney was having a very hard time trying to make sense of it all. It took Joseph over an hour to take in the deliveries and sort out the confusion. By the time the paperwork had been completed, and the items stacked and stored in some orderly manner, he went looking for a hot cup of coffee.

Ana spotted him heading for the pantry. "Where did you put all that stuff?" she asked.

"That was quite a load." he agreed.

"What was it? Where'd you put it all?" she asked quickly, and then asked three or four more questions right after that. He just shook his head. "How," she then asked slowly, "are we going to pay for all that?"

He could answer her with a long drawn-out explanation. He could tell her about how necessary some of those items were, and how several of them were actually emergency re-supplies. He was going to bring up the Medicaid payment that should be arriving that morning. But he thought that he would cover all that at tomorrow morning's meeting. He thought that his number one priority at that moment was getting himself a cup of coffee. And he thought that she was probably just making small talk as she passed him in the hall, so he simply said, "I have no idea." He meant it as a joke, and kept walking. She didn't take it that way.

Ten minutes later Joseph sat in his office, with his well-earned cup of hot coffee, and stared at his computer terminal. Logged onto the bank account, he looked at the numbers. A wonderfully large credit had been added to the balance overnight. He would have to wait for the paperwork to arrive to ascertain what that money represented....but he was glad to get it!

He called Podalski right away to set up an afternoon meeting. Deciding how to budget the windfall was decidedly less stressful than obtaining it. But creating a budget plan now became an immediate priority. He spent the rest of the morning forecasting expenses.

By the time Podalski showed up at the clinic for the scheduled meeting, Joseph hadn't been out of his office since they had spoken on the telephone several hours earlier. And Joseph had only been on the phone twice, once to call Sadim to see if there were any updates on the balance of the claims due, and once to a lawyer in New York who was counsel to the Kryder Foundation. Joseph had recruited him to work on a similar project.

Tuesday - January 7

The first "board meeting" of the Wackentute Walk-In Clinic started promptly at 7:30 AM. Gus started it off by mentioning some of the problems on the medical side. Podalski and Joseph were really at a loss as to what they should say on these topics. Ana added some color to the topic, and Mena didn't say anything at all.

The conversation somehow got around to personnel requirements and how stretched the staff was. Mena wondered aloud if it was even remotely possible that some additional help be brought on. Joseph said that it was unlikely in the near future, and Podalski started to add that the incremental cost of even part-time help right now was out of the question. Mena didn't like that answer. Neither did Ana.

"We've been putting in 60 hour weeks since I don't know when . . . and you're saying there's no relief in sight?" She seemed more sad than angry. "Something has to be done. You guys have to come up with something." She was slowly turning to anger. "You got money in yesterday. Didn't you? Where is all that cash going?" She was now arriving at "angry."

Podalski was sinking into his chair. Joseph looked around the table, "We are budgeting right now. We are trying to develop a plan that will allow us to bring in some additional people. But that costs money. We are trying to determine if we can afford to raise some long ignored salaries here . . . for some very valuable people. And obviously, that's additional money too." Before he could be interrupted he went on, "We have to upgrade our equipment, and facilities, in several areas . . . before we suffer a major breakdown. A breakdown that will adversely affect everything we're trying to do here." He looked around. Mena looked resigned to accepting what he said, even though she didn't like the sound of it. Gus was nodding. He was on board, thought Joseph. He turned slightly and looked at Ana. The corners of her mouth were turned down, and she was shaking her head.

At this moment Olney stuck his head into the office, and said, "Hey, Boss, the guy from the computer place is here . . . " He then smiled, and added, "With lotta stuff!"

Ana, who had turned around when Olney first interrupted, whirled back around at Joseph. But before she could get a word out Joseph started again. "I can't give you numbers or even a timetable right now. I don't know it myself." He paused a moment, and then continued in a lower voice. "I won't lie to you. I won't try to spin some fairy tale about how everything is going to work out fine. Phil and I finally have some money to work with. We are expecting more, but, until it's in our account at the bank . . . well, you know, we aren't going to count our chickens until they hatch." He glanced around the table, and saw that the only one in apparent agreement with him was Podalski. He went on anyway, "We are working on devising a plan; and we will be able to tell you more when we meet again next Tuesday." He ended the meeting by saying "I have to go," and was gone. Podalski, realizing he was now alone in what could turn into very hostile territory, chased out after him. Gus and Mena just got up and left. Ana sat there, by herself, for a minute, and then muttered, "I don't believe this guy!"

189

Wednesday - January 8

Yesterday had been a whirlwind. The electronics had been delivered and installed. The older computers were returned to their original locations, as tech support people made their way around like army ants, crawling up and over desks and work stations, running wires around, behind, and under those same desks and workstations, teaching Lindsay, Joseph and Podalski how things worked. Everyone on the staff spent some time being tutored on the new systems. Even Figgit Nuuf's lab got involved. A computer for the sole use of the lab was installed and integrated into the overall network. People throughout the building sat wide-eyed as they came to realize what was now available to them.

Today was no different. Again some tech support people from the vendor of the office supply system arrived to help transition the old system into the new. Members of the staff went from wild amazement to complete frustration as the learning process continued through the day.

As Joseph often excused himself to handle another matter or phone call, staff chased down Lindsay with problems. And as she attempted to integrate this new billing system with the old, she had plenty of problems of her own.

The frequency and volume of the shouts between staff members were not lost on the people who came to the clinic. They could easily sense the heightened chaos and frenzy in the building today. There was an edge to the staff today, and the patients sensed it. There were very few complaints about waiting time . . . co-payments . . . or anything else today.

The staff, being more harried than usual, didn't notice that the patients were ever so slightly less demanding today. They were far too busy with their regular chores, on top of learning new procedures and techniques, to realize it. There were intermittent blackouts as power was interrupted in order to safely install new electronics. Rooms became unavailable at random times because technicians were installing equipment; and most importantly, staff members became unavailable at random times as they learned something new. The day became a blur to most of them. Well, not Ana. She watched the goings-on with intense interest, making mental notes every few minutes, and writing down some notes to herself that she wanted to follow up with later. She was trying very hard to not let anything escape her notice.

Thursday - January 9

On Joseph's trips to Italy over the past fifteen years he had been to the Vatican in Rome. On one of those trips he had seen a ceremony at St

Peter's Basilica that elevated several bishops to the rank of Cardinal. It had been filled with all the pomp and circumstance one could expect under those solemn and somber circumstances. The organ music and accompanying chorus, coupled with all the color and pageantry of the Grand Procession by a host of the Church's hierarchy, made a magnificent spectacle.

He was reminded of that drama as he watched the two workers and Olney, as they wheeled the new . . . deluxe . . . color . . . state-of-the-art copy machine into the building this morning. People just stopped what they doing and looked at it as it was slowly rolled, starting from the rear loading dock, down the hallway past the lab and examination rooms to its ultimate destination near the front desk. It lumbered heavily down the hallway, its wheels groaning under the weight of the huge machine A silence came over the usually noisy clinic, to the point at which only the sound of those beleaguered wheels could be heard. Figgit Nuuf and a lab tech stepped out into the hallway after it passed the lab, and stared at it silently. They were not alone, as curious faces peeked out of every doorway that it passed. In Examining Room B there was a 65-year-old man propped up on his knees and elbows, on top of an examining table, wearing only his socks and an ill-fitting hospital gown. He had been anxiously awaiting a prostate exam when the photocopying giant paraded past the door and distracted the normally focused Ana. She stuck her head out the examining room door and watched it as it moved slowly down the hallway away from her. The examinee behind her cleared his throat loudly. Several times.

After what seemed like an eternity it came to a halt at the far wall of the administrative area, just behind the front desk. There the workers removed it from its carton. They stripped the various pieces of packing and cushioning material from its sides and innards. They screwed assorted pieces of plastic shelving to its sides, and attached adhesive decals to locations on the front and top. Wires, connectors, and various electronic umbilical cords were fastened and routed in a dizzying array. User Manuals and various documents concerning warranties, guarantees and other minutiae were stacked on the table next to it. The manufacturer's rep continued tinkering with it, making small adjustments, and finally inserting several different ink cartridges. And then he stepped back. The Admin staff, and a few people in the waiting room, looked on silently. Olney appeared from somewhere with a carton of printer paper and loaded the paper tray under the careful tutelage of the rep. And with a simple nod of his head, the rep instructed Olney to plug it in. Olney complied with a caution usually used in transporting nuclear weapons.

With everyone absolutely speechless, the only sound heard was the low whirring of the machine as it (one of its lights indicated) was "warming up."

The wait for the "READY" light to go on seemed to take forever. And when it did several people mouthed the word "Wow" without realizing it.

The manufacturer's rep provided a quick tutorial to Lindsay, Olney, and Mena, as well as a few demonstrations of the faxing and copying capabilities of this new wonderful machine. And only after taking one more close-up look at it did people begin returning to their jobs.

Friday - January 10

Unlike earlier in the week, the clinic was unusually quiet today. With patient volume low, the people around the building used the spare time to catch up on many overdue projects. This wasn't true for Olney, however. Olney had his hands full with organizing the supplies that seemed to be arriving non-stop. There wasn't nearly enough space on the main floor for it all, and that meant he had to carry much of it down to the basement.

Ana and Gus caught up with some case reviews that they had been anxious to discuss. Mena spent her spare time resolving some staffing problems, as well as organizing supply requests to be submitted to Joseph. The staff in the lab had a backlog of tests to perform and welcomed the brief reprieve from new requests.

Lindsay enjoyed her day more than anyone else. It wasn't the fact that the patient load was lighter today; it was because she expected to see Sadim tonight. He was due back from his extended business trip.

Joseph and Podalski were huddled in Joseph's office all morning. They kept the door closed as a not-too-subtle hint that they did not want to be disturbed. Checking the clinic's bank accounts on-line that morning had revealed that another large inflow of funds from Albany had been credited overnight. This windfall of cash was not all it could have been, but it was substantial. And other than occasional interruptions by Olney, Joseph and Podalski were totally focused on budgeting every nickel of it.

Saturday - January 11

When Sadim walked into the Wackentute Walk-In Clinic this morning he was welcomed with a far warmer greeting than he was used to getting at any of his other official stops. Lindsay just stared at him and beamed. She didn't really care if anyone noticed the look on her face. Joseph, hearing Sadim's voice, came out of his office and hailed him as a conquering hero. Podalski, also in the office this morning, heard the commotion and joined them at once. The medical staff, which had learned through the grapevine how much Sadim had contributed, went out of their way to flash smiles and greetings to the surprised, and somewhat embarrassed, state employee.

Joseph immediately shepherded him, with Podalski, into his office and closed the door. They needed to talk.

That private conversation lasted more than an hour (sixty-seven minutes, according to the very impatient Lindsay who was waiting). And after it was over Podalski was wondering why Joseph had insisted he sit in. While some of that time was spent with them discussing Medicaid procedures, the vast majority of time was spent questioning Sadim on a much wider variety of topics. Podalski said very little during the meeting. Joseph asked the questions, and Sadim answered them. And he was often encouraged by Joseph to elaborate on those answers. And the questions themselves ranged from private to public insurance, and the practices of other health care providers that Sadim knew. But just as many questions concerned Sadim's knowledge of accounting, office management, and skills. When it was over and Sadim had left to have lunch with Lindsay, Joseph asked Podalski what he thought of Sadim.

Practice for the game tomorrow started precisely at 2 o'clock, and it was more intense than the other practices they had had. There was less kidding and joking, and people went about the routines with more purpose than ever before. Mistakes weren't laughed at, and few comments were intended to be funny. It was very apparent that they were taking this very seriously.

Besides the practice being regimented today, it would also last as long as there was enough light to see what they were doing. They had all been on time except Smoke, who had got tied up at his trucking job. He showed up a half hour late, and heard about it from virtually everyone. The players went through the different formations they would use and rehearsed several different kinds of attacks they would use on free starts. Timing and coordination were essential to a successful free start, and had to be practiced over and over again. Gus introduced two new ones to the team that he had devised. They utilized the speed of the newfound winger, Podalski. They also went over signals they would flash to each other during the game. Code words for shifts and switches were tried, and tried again. Timing and coordination were emphasized as the keys to winning the game tomorrow.

When they finally decided to call it quits for the day they retreated to the benches near the edge of the ice. Instead of packing up and going home, they went over the personnel on the other team they would face tomorrow.

"The whole team centers on 'Torpedo Red.' He's the whole thing," Gus started out saying. He was their best player, no matter what position he was playing. Torpedo Red was actually Billy Reddington, who came from the family that the town was named after. Away from the Geetha arena, William Reddington was a pillar of the community, and owner of the

Reddington Funeral Home, as well as Reddington Gardens, the largest cemetery in the valley.

"Oh he's their best titman," Moonie agreed. "But I'd rather see him at titman than anywhere else. He's less dangerous when he's a titman," Moonie said. There was general agreement around the group about that.

"You hafta watch him closely when he moves to center, or wing," Paulie said. "Geez, when he's free to roam around he can cripple you."

"Don't let him get behind you, whatever you do!" warned Gus. "Know where he is at all times when he steps over the boards." Everyone nodded, except the new players. Gus explained to them, "He'll position himself behind you, and then come flying at you. He's big, and strong, and very fast. He'll get up a head of steam, and dive through the air at you like his nickname. A Torpedo! He'll hit you with his head, and it will feel like someone is hitting you with a sledgehammer. It'll hurt like hell if you're expecting it . . . it'll knock you out if you're not!"

The conversation touched on all the other players on the team. "Pastor Pittou," Joseph learned, was a former Jesuit priest who had married a former nun. They ran a multifaceted community center in South Reddington. Despite the humanitarian work he did all week, on game day he could be homicidal. Roove explained that he wore a pad on his left arm during games. Many players wore pads, but not like this one. This pad consisted of foam rubber on the inside and canvas on the outside. In between those layers was a steel tube. When he hit you with this forearm, his patented "forearm smash," it was like getting hit with an aluminum bat!

Their best center-man, other than Torpedo Red, was a player that was called Baboo. Baboo was extremely strong, but only a fair skater. The best things about their other center-men, "Spud" Ataddo and Dennis "The Menace" Reuss, were their nicknames.

Besides Torpedo Red and Pastor Pittou as titman was Gary "Golden Garth" Flinkau. Golden Garth, several Bombers said, was a very poor skater, and could be "slapped cross eyed." And it was generally agreed by all the Bombers that failing to score when Golden Garth was over the boards was a cardinal sin. Some of the wings on the Angels were discussed, but all were dismissed as players. Their two replacement players were named Pasko and G-Man. Paulie and B-ball knew them both, didn't think either one would pose a threat.

No, it was Torpedo Red that had to be neutralized, and Pastor Pittou who had to be watched. All in all, the Bombers considered the Reds an inferior team that they should beat easily. "They want to fight, more than score," someone said.

There was one final bit of business to attend to before they broke up for the day. Gus retrieved a box from the back of his truck. He started to open the box, and said, "Thanks to some very generous . . . anonymous . . .

donors, we have been able to outfit the team again this year!" A few cheers, hoots, and laughs greeted this comment as he pulled some new Bomber jerseys from the box. "I think I got all the names right. And I even think I matched them up with the numbers you were wearing back when we last played." He smiled around to the group, and then said to the three new players, "I got you three jerseys, too." With that he began handing out the sweaters that the Bombers would wear tomorrow. They were kelly green with white lettering. On the front was the letter "B," leaning slightly to the right, and on top of a skate blade. Joseph recognized the logo from the hat that Roove always seemed to be wearing. On the back were the names above a number. After handing out the uniforms to all but one player, he called for quiet. "Now most of you know that most players in the league have a nickname; and they wear that nickname on their team sweater. And these nicknames," he added, "are supposed to be earned, and given to you by teammates or other players"

"Hey, that isn't always true," Paulie interrupted. "Smoke gave himself one. If his nickname was gonna be earned and given by his teammates, the back of his sweater would read 'Shit-For-Brains'."

There was some laughter before Gus raised his hands and reclaimed everyone's attention. "Olney was down here watching practice last weekend, and decided that Phil here needed a nickname right away." Gus didn't explain why Olney felt that way, because it wasn't very complimentary. It seems that Olney felt that because Podalski was so small, he wasn't going to survive very long, so getting him his nickname had to be done sooner rather than later. "So he came up with a nickname that fits his initials and his size too!" Gus handed over a jersey to Podalski, who held it up to read the back. "PeaPod" is what it read.

Phil Podalski was to be known as PeaPod to the Geetha world. Although some people probably wouldn't think that was a very appealing nickname, Podalski loved it. It meant he was an official member of the team. It didn't matter that it wasn't particularly flattering to him. All that did matter was that he was now on the team, and had the uniform, with his new found name on the back, to prove it.

B-Ball's uniform, of course, said "B-BALL." Joseph's jersey simply said "Hamilton," and that was because he hadn't ever played before, nor been here long enough to have a nickname attach itself to him. But that would change.

Sunday - January 12

Joseph skipped the Fireside last night because he "had a game the next day." It was that simple for him; it was that automatic. For as long as he could remember, if he had a game the next day, he went to bed early. He slept well, but woke up early. To burn off some nervous energy he took a slow two mile jog. After breakfast, he went to the lake to watch the early game of the Blades against the Blue Canes.

The Blades – Blue Canes game was determined early, as the Blades dominated from the very beginning. Joseph and several other early arriving Bombers watched as the Blades skated far better than Blue Canes, and seemed to be able to move around at will. Watching a live action game was, of course, far more instructional to Joseph than the practices had been. The game seemed to be as fierce, and as fast, as it had been described.

Late in the game one of the Blades was hit so hard by a Blue Cane that he was thrown over the sideboard into a crowd of people sitting there. The cartwheeling Blade player and two of the fans involved had to be helped to their feet. Joseph had been looking at other action on the ice when it had happened, and didn't see the collision actually take place. But the other Bombers sitting around him all agreed it was the work of "The Dwarf."

When Gus arrived he pointed out several players that he suggested Joseph watch carefully. Those players included Marty Quarf and Cobra Kelly of the Blue Canes, Sandman on the Blades. But of special note, Gus suggested he watch Bill "Caveman" Cavanaugh (who Joseph recognized from that unfortunate meeting prior to The Slide for Life a few weeks ago). And then, of course, there was Superfly. Superfly was the best player in the league, Gus thought. He was very strong, and an excellent skater. He was the primary titman for the Blades, and played with an intensity and fierceness that were probably unequaled in the league. Joseph watched him carefully every time he stepped over the boards. And although he was a novice at the game he could see that Superfly was playing on a different level than those around him.

The Blades moved around with far greater coordination than the Blue Canes. Wing men broke loose and blindsided unsuspecting opponents with regularity. Whenever the Blades were given a free start due to a penalty or a halt, they scored easily. They used a play they called "The Whip."

The center, then the wing men, and then finally the titman would begin skating, one behind the other, very fast toward the center line. As they neared the center line they would join hands, and then when they reached the center line the lead skater, the center, would stop . . . pivot . . . and use centrifugal force to swing his three teammates around him at high speed. The last man in the line, the titman, would now be on top of the geetha and hurtling into the opponents' end at such high speed that even if a defender got in his way he would be knocked aside. Once clear of defenders, the Blade's titman would steer the geetha to the pezzle unimpeded. Joseph had to admire the tactic. It was so simple, yet so effective.

Late in the game Joseph noticed across the pond that the Angels were arriving. The players were wearing jerseys of various shades of red. Some were well worn, and some looked brand new. The front of the jersey had a set of moose antlers, topped by a halo, on the chest.

On his side of the ice the Bombers were mostly there and lacing up their skates. They eventually gathered beyond the pond area, out on the larger lake to begin warming up. It felt good, to Joseph, to be in uniform again, getting ready to play a game. It had been too long.

The jerseys were alike, of course, but the rest of the attire for the Bombers varied widely. Some were in jeans, while others wore sweat pants. Paulie and B-Ball were coordinated in matching green football pants. They were wearing matching headgear too. It was always left to the discretion of the individual player as to what pads they wore and protection to use (Jardine Vault included). Most players wore a hockey or lacrosse helmet, some with a face shield, and some not. These two had opted for football helmets. They were quite a sight.

The Blades — Blue Canes game finally ended with the lopsided score of 10 to 3, which included 6 whips. Joseph had watched it carefully, and had to admit it was a maneuver that had been executed brilliantly by the Blades. It was simple, and incredibly effective. He was impressed.

At the conclusion of the game the Blades went through an elaborate, rehearsed victory dance that congratulated themselves, and then retired to their bench. Some local volunteer firemen sprayed the ice with water, which quickly froze, to give it a renewed smooth surface.

Shortly thereafter, the Angels brought out their geetha. It was a letdown. It turned out to be nothing more than a folded, lumped—up pile of industrial carpeting which had been soaked with water and allowed to freeze. It was heavy and more square than round. Teammates had warned Joseph that the Angels were a motley crew, and the shabbiness of their geetha was to be expected.

When the game started, the Bombers' first line had Moonie at center, and Tully and Jeepers on the wings. Roove was the titman. They were faced by the Angels' titman, Golden Garth. They had Torpedo Red at center, flanked by Weegie and Gateman at the wings.

Their lineup surprised Gus, who thought out loud that they must be looking for some matchup advantage. He wondered why they had Torpedo Red at center. But if they did that, why not start Pastor Pittou at titman. Whatever they had planned did not work. Roove soon caught Garth leaning the wrong way, and deked him into falling down. There was a race to the Angels pezzle, which Roove won. Behind the play Torpedo Red hit an unsuspecting Tully with a bone-crunching hit, leaving Tully at half speed for the rest of the day.

While immediate restitution seemed like the normal response, Gus moved among the players on the bench telling them to "get the game in the bag before we hit them back." Reluctantly, most players agreed.

Paulie lined up at titman for the second line of the Bombers, and held off the Angels' second line with Torpedo Red now at titman. They battled to a draw over the next four minutes. When a halt was called, the Bombers sent out their third line to defend against an Angels' free start. Gus felt this line was a good balance of the skating skill of PeaPod and Joseph with the strength and savvy of Roove and Magoo.

The Angels attempted a whip of their own, but it was poorly done, and resulted in their titman losing his balance and falling off the geetha. In a mad dash to regain control, the Angels' center, Menace, failed to see Joseph coming at him from the side, and was knocked sprawling. He went down hard, and had trouble getting up. With a temporary man advantage the Bombers gained control of the geetha and scored, making it 2 − 0.

Joseph stayed out on the ice as a center for Roove at titman. They lined up against the Angels' Pastor Pittou at titman with Baboo at center. Joseph was immediately thrown around by Baboo, who was incredibly strong. But Joseph was the far better skater and soon was easily out-maneuvering him. He would hand fight the strong man, but avoided Baboo's attempts to clutch and grab. He would lead him as far away from where the two titmen were battling and then release and charge the unsuspecting Pastor Pittou. This freedom allowed him to switch with Roove at titman, and come at Pastor Pittou from his blind side. After doing this three times he could hear the Angels titman groan when he got hit. Roove and Joseph were taking turns pounding on him, and he didn't like it.

With Joseph back on the geetha, he glanced around to see where Roove was. Spotting him as he approached, he maneuvered the geetha around to his right in order to give Roove a clear shot as he, again, approached Pastor Pittou from behind. Joseph tried to give nothing away as Roove gained speed as he approached. Maybe he glanced in that direction, but only for a split second. No matter how long it was, it was enough. Enough for Pastor Pittou to swing his left arm around like a club, and he hit Joseph on the side of the head, just above his left ear.

If Joseph had chosen to wear a hockey or lacrosse helmet he still would have been stunned. If he had joined Paulie and B-Ball in wearing a football helmet, it still would have hurt. But Joseph had decided to go lighter. He wore an abbreviated bicycle helmet that didn't cover his ears. Despite a warning from Gus that he should use more protection, he had opted for the lighter choice. That, in retrospect, was a major miscalculation. After today's game he would seriously reconsider that decision. But at this precise moment, Joseph was wondering where all those stars had come from. He was wondering where the buzzing was coming from. And he was wondering why the day had gotten so bright, so suddenly.

What happened in the next few minutes had to be relayed to Joseph a little while later. He had trouble remembering. His knees buckled, and he fell to the ice. Pastor Pittou took sole control of the geetha and steered it deftly around his lumbering center Baboo, who had a very easy block on Roove, and scored the Angels' first goal.

When Joseph finally got back to the bench, Gus was waiting. He began talking to him, but Joseph didn't hear him. He had not lost consciousness, but was still dazed. He knew people were around him, but his head felt "light" and sounds were muffled. He could feel the cold, but still felt slightly numb. Gus was right in front of his face talking, but Joseph couldn't seem to focus on what he was saying. Suddenly, he saw Ana's face come into view above and behind Gus's shoulder. She, oddly enough, looked totally different to him.

She was beautiful. Her skin looked so soft, and was slightly red from the cold. The hood of her jacket was up and surrounded her face. A tuft of her blond hair peeked out between her hood and forehead. It was a golden white color he had never noticed before. Her eyebrows were neatly trimmed. There were two little lines at the corners of her eyes he had never seen before either. And her eyes . . . her eyes were an icy blue that were incredibly beautiful. Why hadn't he ever seen them before? The only makeup she wore was a very pale pink lipstick . . . or maybe it was only the cold making her lips that color? He gazed at her as if she were a total stranger . . . a beautiful total stranger. He noticed features on her face that he had never seen before. Her teeth were so white . . . her mouth was open . . . she was saying something. He tried to listen. Her voice sounded so soft, so sweet. He tried very hard to focus on what she was saying. He tried to read her lips. She seemed to be singing it. It finally came through.

"I warned you, asshole."

The rest of the first half remained a very sloppy game. Perhaps it was due to the "rust" of the players after not having played in several years. And no doubt some of the blame was the general lack of ability by some of the Angels who seemed more interested in smacking people than playing. The Angels scored a tying goal a few minutes later when Torpedo Red and Baboo both hit Roove at the same time. That foul escaped the attention of White who was distracted by a near fistfight between two wings. The play in the last six minutes of the half deteriorated into a very nasty affair. But there was no more scoring, and the half ended with the game tied, 2 -2.

Joseph had spent the rest of the first half, and some of the halftime, warming up in someone's car parked nearby while drinking a hot chocolate. He recovered slowly, and then rejoined his teammates on the sidelines shortly before the start of the second half. He didn't enjoy being told by his teammates that "the Angels were laughing about how hard Pastor Pittou cracked you." He craved revenge. His old competitive fire was back and burning fiercely.

With Joseph insisting he was ready to go, Gus and Roove began making a plan. The conversation centered around getting mismatches on the matchups between lines. Gus had some ideas in mind, and Roove, Moonie, and Paulie began discussing how to make it work. Joseph listened.

When the second half started, the lineup the Angels sent out was different than any one they had used before. It caught the Bombers off guard. They had expected Pastor as titman, but they had also expected Torpedo Red at center, or, at least, Baboo. What they got was Spud at center, and Weegie and Auclair at the wings. These were not their best players. The Bombers had sent out Roove at titman, and a line of Moonie flanked by Whitey and Jeepers. The Bombers were clearly at a big size advantage with this match—up, and immediately began pushing the Angels around.

On the sidelines, the rest of the Bombers began talking about a plan to work against the next Angel lineup. Theorizing that the Angels would send out their bigger players, they drew up a plan that would counteract that size. They didn't have long to make this plan because Roove got the best of Pastor Pittou quickly and drove the geetha deep into the Angels' end. The Bomber wings were having little trouble maneuvering the Angels' wings out of the way. And, with very little trouble, Moonie manhandled Spud so decisively that Spud finally was thrown to the ice. At that point Moonie turned to the retreating geetha, and came after the Pastor from behind. Pastor Pittou must have sensed impending disaster from the noise of the crowd, and started to turn his attention away from the opposing Bomber titman. Roove needed only the smallest distraction from him, and wrestled control of the geetha away. It was only thirty unimpeded yards to the Angel pezzle, and the Bombers were up 3-2.

The next Angel line sent out, to attempt to re-tie the game, contained their strongest players. Torpedo Red was their titman, with Baboo at center, and Menace and Pasko at wings. Each one of them was strong, but only Torpedo Red was a very good skater. The Bombers countered with three strong players, Paulie, Magoo and Joseph, and then added PeaPod. The plan was to get PeaPod free with the geetha, because no one the Angels had on the ice could skate with him.

The plan, in theory, was a good idea. But getting PeaPod possession of the geetha, without having him wrestle with one of the Angels, proved to be very difficult. For the first sixty seconds of action, PeaPod was thrown around like a rag doll by any Angel that happened to get a hand on him. And with him constantly being thrown out of action, it allowed the four remaining Angels to outman the three Bombers despite their general inferiority in skating.

In spite of being outnumbered, the Bombers found themselves, and the geetha, edging down deeply into the Angels' end of the ice. Joseph, after a number of switches with his line mates, was suddenly going head-to-head with Torpedo Red. And surprisingly, most of all to Torpedo Red, Joseph was getting the best of it. Although Torpedo Red was probably as strong and as good a skater as Joseph, he seemed to be more interested in mixing it up than in outmaneuvering his opponent. Making clumsy lunges and wild swings at Joseph, he was easily avoided. After being held off by this "new guy," a frustrated Torpedo Red grabbed Joseph, and with the geetha in tow, crashed into a cluster of the other players. And they collided like tenpins, careening into one another; they all lost their balance, and fell to the ice.

The crowd went silent as the players fell. The pileup resulted in mayhem as players on both teams scrambled to get back up on their feet. Baboo, of all people, was the first to recover and came out of the chaos with sole possession of the geetha, while most of the other players were still sprawled on the ice.

He started off, with a big head start, down the ice toward the Bomber pezzle at the other end. Players looked up from various prone positions to see him heading off with the geetha. Of all the Bombers on the ice, only PeaPod was now on his feet, but now at least 50 feet behind Baboo. PeaPod said a very determined, "Oh man!", and took off after him. Although possibly the fastest skater in the league, he had a lot of ground to make up. He skated furiously, as the once silent fans recovered, and began to roar in support of the two players racing away from the rest. Baboo lumbered on, and peeking up he saw his path to the pezzle was clear. And although no one would ever say his mind was a major thoroughfare, one thought did cross it at this point. He couldn't remember the last time he had scored a goal in a geetha game. And the thought that he was about to do that very thing made him dizzy.

PeaPod's short legs couldn't take long strides; but he certainly could take quick ones. He caught up with the hunched-over Baboo as they crossed the half-line. PeaPod didn't have a plan to stop the much larger and stronger Baboo, and he knew he didn't have the time to devise one either. With one last quick stride he dove into the air, reaching with his left hand for the geetha and his right hand for Baboo. He grabbed the geetha as he landed on Baboo's bent over back and instantly wrapped his right arm around the big man's throat. In desperation to hold on, he gripped tightly. This momentarily surprised Baboo, but didn't stop the behemoth as he continued on his path to the Bomber's pezzle and Geetha glory. The noise from the crowd was now electrifying.

What happened next has become part of Geetha lore.

Baboo's exertion at skating this hard, this long, pushing the geetha, and carrying another player on his back necessitated heavy, heavy breathing. And although PeaPod didn't realize it at the time, his death grip around Baboo's throat was preventing any air from reaching Baboo's lungs. The excitement and exertion of pushing the geetha the length of the ice, without benefit of breathing, was beginning to take its toll on the lumbering center. His face was now crimson; his eyes were beginning to bulge and water. His mouth was wide open, and reality was starting to dim. In fact, despite how loud the crowd was roaring at this point, neither Baboo nor PeaPod could hear it.

PeaPod could sense that the Angel's center was perhaps slowing down, but unless he did something more the big man was going to score. Still holding the geetha with his left hand, PeaPod squeezed his right arm as tightly as he could around Baboo's neck and began sliding off Baboo's back to the left. Baboo, with his two hands pushing the geetha, resisted this sagging of P–Pod's weight to his left by trying to lean his body to the right. The pressure on his windpipe tightened.

After a few more strides, PeaPod had nearly slid off Baboo's back when his bent left leg touched down on the ice. At that instant he pushed off on it as hard as he was able, launching himself into the air, twisting violently. Baboo, just about to lose consciousness, didn't resist. Both players sailed up into the air; PeaPod's front to Baboo's back, rotating almost in slow motion . . . in a very weird sort of pas de deux. PeaPod, completely disoriented, loosened his grip; Baboo, also somewhat disoriented BUT now able to inhale, sucked in air. Then they hit.

The dual pirouette had nearly rotated a complete 360 degrees, when they crash-landed back onto the ice. Baboo's head hit the ice hard, but was partially protected by the hockey helmet he wore. PeaPod's hockey helmet had no face guard, and because it didn't, his nose met the back of Baboo's helmet in a clear mismatch. In a jumble of arms, legs, screams, and moans they slid entwined along the ice toward the sideboards. Baboo was struggling mightily to free himself from the equally struggling PeaPod when he hit, headfirst into the unforgiving 2X4 sideboard. PeaPod, repeating his unfortunate collision of just a moment ago, again crashed into the back of Baboo's helmet. This concluded the playing of Geetha for both men this day.

Joseph, who had gotten up and had been chasing the two, was several strides behind them when they pirouetted up off the geetha. He avoided them as they sailed off to the right, and he grabbed control of the slowing, now unattended, geetha. Pushing hard on its right side he steered it away from the pezzle and slowly began making a wide left turn. With no Angel to contest the move he began to turn it back up the ice. In the last few seconds of the turn, as he neared the sideboards, a small alarm bell went off in his head.

This "inner alarm bell" is not something everyone has. Or perhaps everyone is born with it, but it requires cultivation. Was it hot wired into his genetic code? Or perhaps all the competitive sports he had played in his youth had helped to hone it in him. But his "inner alarm" was working today. Without knowing why . . . without questioning the instinct for a second, he fell flat onto the geetha. Lying prostrate on it, his head and shoulders were suddenly two feet lower than they were nanoseconds ago.

The Torpedo had lined him up. Skating furiously behind what he thought was this unsuspecting new player named Hamilton (according to the name on the back of his sweater), and just out of his sight only 10 feet away, Torpedo Red took two more powerful strides. Closing his eyes he dove headlong at Joseph's back left shoulder. When a moment passed . . . uneventfully . . . Torpedo Red opened his eyes just in time to see the sideboard flash by beneath him as he sailed out of bounds. The bone crushing blindside hit on Hamilton was not to be.

He looked up, expecting something bad. What he saw was Byram Lomb's face, and that would be what he remembered seeing later. Little else. Byram Lomb was just under six feet tall, and just over 350 pounds. This rapt Geetha fan had just watched the action unfold at the other end of the ice. When Baboo had broken free moments ago, Lomb nearly rose to his feet in excitement. The pursuit by PeaPod had been breathtaking. When PeaPod had caught up with Baboo and had struggled with him, Lomb had almost cheered. And only after Baboo and PeaPod had released their grip on the geetha and spiraled away, and Hamilton had taken control of it, had Byram turned his attention away from the action to retrieve his lunch. As he was lifting his sandwich to his mouth, he looked back up and saw Torpedo Red's approach. (His internal alarm system was nowhere nearly as honed as Hamilton's.)

Defensively he raised his hands to cover his face, while every other muscle in his body stiffened to such a degree that it resembled rigor mortis. This could certainly be considered a normal reaction considering the circumstances, and about whom we're talking. Unfortunately those defensively raised hands still held a Berry-flavored drink in the left, and the meatball sub in the right. The face of Byram Lomb . . . the hands . . . the Berry beverage . . . the meatball sub . . . Torpedo Red's marble hard head . . . all met simultaneously. The sound was a combination of "splish," "squish," and "thunk." The colorful explosion of the food, the drink, and the blood from Byram's nose hit virtually everything within 10 feet.

Sitting next to him at that moment was his wife, MerriLuAnn. She, hit in the forehead by something, simply fainted. Myram, stiff as a board, rotated back off the stump he had been sitting on and landed on the top of his head, his feet straight up in the air. Probably because of his Rigor Mortis reaction to Torpedo Red's approach, he remained inverted for a moment, and then continued the rotation until he was face down in the snow. Torpedo Red ricocheted away from the collision and landed a few feet away. He wouldn't move again until EMT's put him on the stretcher.

Joseph got back up on his skates and, virtually unopposed, skated the length of the ice, avoiding the two defenders, who were being manhandled by his two remaining blockers, and scored easily. This put the Bombers on top 4 to 2. With Baboo and more importantly, Torpedo Red, now sidelined for the day, the Bombers were clearly the far better team.

Later, with only minutes to go in the game and the Bombers now safely leading by a score of 5 to 2, Joseph knew he didn't have much time. He managed to get back on the ice matched up against Pastor Pittou again and was soon locked up with him near the sideboard, one on one. Very aware of the Pastor's potent left "club," Joseph constantly moved away from it by sliding to his own left, away from the Pastor's club. Pittou, with every intention of smacking this newcomer again, followed him around the geetha until they found themselves stuck against the sideboard. Knowing White could call a halt at any moment, Joseph had to act fast. He leaned over the geetha, just inches from Pastor Pittou's face, and said something.

The startled Pittou responded, "What?"

"I SAID 'WHERE THE FUCK IS *NORTH* REDDINGTON?'" screamed Joseph. The Pastor was stunned. Or confused. Or both! Joseph seized the moment and leapt over the top of the geetha, landing at the pastor's left. And as soon as he did he clamped his own hands down on the Pastor's left hand, pinning it to the geetha. He wanted no more to do with that "club" today. With both of them pushing on the same side of the geetha now, it began gaining speed as it slid directly across the ice.

Pastor Pittou struggled to get his left hand . . . his *weapon* . . . free, but Joseph held it firmly down. And with the Pastor preoccupied trying to free his "club," he failed to notice as Joseph twisted slightly around to his right and grabbed Pastor Pittou by the seat of his pants and yanked his butt up into the air. The move caught the Pastor totally by surprise. With his buttocks being held in the air, his skates 10 inches above the ice, and his pants twisted tightly, and painfully, around his groin, he knew instantly he was in a very vulnerable position.

And adding to his concern was the fact that the geetha was now traveling at a very high rate of speed. To relieve the pressure and pain in his groin he shifted all his weight forward onto his hands, which were still on the geetha. When he did, Joseph noticed the weight shifting and without a moment's hesitation threw the pastor forward using his own strength and the Pastor's momentum. The pastor soared over the top of the geetha, somersaulted in mid-air, and hit the ice spread-eagled, flat on his back, and continued to slide along. He was momentarily stunned, while his momentum sent him skidding feet first at high speed along the ice, with Joseph furiously pushing the geetha just two feet behind him.

With his legs spread wide apart the Pastor hit the sideboard exacerbating the split no man his age should do. The pain shot through his body like an electric charge; from his groin through his torso, through his neck, to the top of his head it flashed. It arrived at the top of his head the same instant that the still-trailing geetha did. This hundred-plus-pounds of frozen carpet, still being pushed by Hamilton, drove him still harder into the sideboard and spread his legs even further apart. Hands clutching at the fire storm in his groin, he sat up bolt upright and stared at the crowd on the other side of the sideboard, who was looking right back at him . . . and screamed.

Joseph surveyed the scene from a few feet away, admiring his work, and then he collected the geetha and skated unimpeded down the ice for an easy score.

Chapter Ten

Monday - January 13

Two things surprised Joseph on Monday. First of all was how sore he was from yesterday's game. He awoke with a headache that was probably more the result of the post-game victory celebration at the Fireside than the result of Pastor Pittou's club. But his whole body felt like a black-and-blue mark. He didn't remember getting hit this much, but he had the aches and pains to prove that he had. He reminded himself that the game had been played at high speed, with tough strong men.

The second thing that surprised him was how many people he ran into this morning that commented on the game. The counterman as well as a few customers at the coffee shop where he picked up his breakfast started it off. And everyone on staff at the clinic had something to say to him about the game. Patients coming into the clinic, as well as deliverymen and vendors there to do business, seemed to want to rehash the game with him. He was asked several times about his run-in with Pastor Pittou, and was quick to point out who had come out on top in the end. He was certainly the focal point of everyone's attention there, until Podalski came in at 10:30.

The fact he was wearing sunglasses did not conceal the two pronounced black eyes he had. Fussed over by the entire medical staff, and gawked at by everyone who saw him, he immediately became the center of attention. Everyone wanted him to take off the sunglasses and recount his epic struggle with the Angels' mammoth center at the crucial point of yesterday's game. He was assured by one and all that that episode would never be forgotten by any who saw it. Embarrassed by it all, yet secretly pleased by the notoriety of his exploits yesterday with Baboo, he finally retreated to the seclusion of Joseph's office.

"You okay?" Joseph asked as they settled into their chairs.

"Oh yeah! Gus checked me out yesterday. Looks a lot worse than it really is." Joseph noticed that he was leaving his sunglasses on. Podalski

206

continued, "Probably broke my nose. Oh man, I should have worn a face guard. Damn sure I'll wear one next week."

"You're going to play next week?"

"Sure, why not?"

Joseph didn't respond, but thought to himself that Podalski was one tough little accountant. The two men returned to the task of mapping out the future financial road map for the clinic.

Olney interrupted them twice to announce that deliveries of supplies had arrived. As Joseph was away tending to the details of the delivery, Podalski continued on his own. At 1 PM they decided to break for lunch.

The pantry was full when they arrived, and the talk was all about the game. Podalski was peppered with questions and praise. He tried to act nonchalant but was thrilled inside. The questions got around, after a while, to how bad he had hurt himself. He gallantly waved the concern away, saying that it was "part of the game," and it "looked worse than it was."

It was Figgit who startled everyone by saying that Podalski was better off than most of the other people who had gotten hurt yesterday. Someone asked why. "He saw it coming," Figgit answered.

One of the deliverymen who was there enjoying his lunch asked, "What does that have to do with it?"

Figgit straightened up and said, "One of the prime factors in the severity of pain from trauma is a function of its anticipation." No one said anything. Figgit looked at the deliveryman, and said, "If I ask you to place your hand on this table . . . so I can strike it with . . . " he looked around, and apparently seeing nothing that suited his purpose, he arbitrarily selected a phantom hammer . . . "with this hammer." He raised the imaginary hammer up above his head, and then brought it down violently. "It would hurt you very much." He paused for a moment, and then asked, "Would it not?"

The truck driver, who had no idea what he was involved in, cautiously answered, "Yes."

"But if we go about eating . . . and finishing our lunches . . . and 20 minutes from now you are finishing up your delivery . . . . And you happen to rest your hand on a nearby wall . . . and I come up behind you . . . and pound that hand with the hammer . . . wouldn't that hurt worse?"

The driver had no answer. No one did. But the driver did have a question. "Am I gonna have to keep my eye on you for the rest of the day?" he wanted to know.

"I am only trying to make a point," Figgit answered. "A painful incident, that is *un*anticipated, has a pain quotient that is a multiple of two, perhaps three . . . the data is incomplete" he said as an aside, "than that of one that is anticipated. And the nature of the actual event is not a factor in the multiple, I might add. Whether it is something as trivial as a toe stub . . . to something more painful, like a directed strike to the testicles . . . "

"WHOA! . . . WHOA! . . . WHOA!" Mena yelled. "That's it! Don't we all have some work to do?" The room emptied as quickly as a well-rehearsed fire drill. Partially finished sandwiches and drinks were dropped into the garbage can on the way out the door.

Moments later, only Figgit, Joseph and Podalski were still in the room. Podalski caught Figgit's eye and asked, "You said 'The data is incomplete'?" He waited a moment before going on. "There's data? About . . . " Podalski paused for a moment, trying to find the right words, "About guys getting hit in the . . . in the groin?"

Figgit nodded. "Yes, but it's part of a larger study. But that study itself is incomplete. There's so much conjecture due to the lack of formal studies."

"Can't imagine how hard it must be to recruit volunteers for . . . " Podalski said, as if wondering out loud, " . . . for those studies!"

Joseph and Podalski returned to their financial planning a few minutes later. They stayed at it for the entire afternoon; the only interruptions were silent grins as they thought back on the lunchroom conversation.

Tuesday - January 14

The regularly scheduled staff meeting was a series of fits and starts. It started later than usual because Gus had got stuck on a conference call with some doctors at the county hospital. He no sooner got off the phone when Ana was called away to take an emergency phone call. There were a series of calls that started a few minutes later, and by then the clinic's doors were open, and patients were streaming in. The final blow was a call for Joseph. When he heard who was calling, he simply got up and left, stating "I have to take this call." The staff meeting was over, and Ana was not pleased. She worried out loud, to anyone on the staff who'd listen, that things were getting out of hand, again.

Joseph didn't hear a word she said. He was, by now, in his office on a conference call with "people in New York." The call lasted, according to Joseph, twice as long as it should have. He reminded himself that when bankers and lawyers are involved, everything takes longer . . . and costs more.

The 11 AM appointment with the personnel recruiter started right on time. One by one, people from around the clinic came in and joined the recruiter and Joseph in his office discussing what they needed. Mena, Figgit, and even Lindsay, had their turn discussing possible additions; what qualifications and skills would be required; and, as always, what it would cost. And each, in turn, had to be assured that the discussion was about "additions", not "replacements." Joseph, incidentally, made a mental note to have this discussion with Gus and Ana regarding taking on a doctor that could lighten the workload for those two. But, he figured, that could wait until next Tuesday's staff meeting.

The meeting with the recruiter lasted several hours as specifics were discussed and parameters set. When it was finally over it was much too late for lunch, so Joseph satisfied himself with a bottle of water and a candy bar from the deli across the street.

When he walked back in from the deli, Lindsay told him he had missed a call from "a Mr Montoya from New York." She handed him a slip of paper with the phone number on it. Intrigued, he called back right away.

An unenthusiastic Montoya picked up the phone by answering, "Montoya."

"This is Hamilton. You just called?"

"Oh, yes. Mr. Kryder asked that I give you a call to help you make a grant request to the Foundation." He went on to explain that Kryder had impressed upon him that this request be "expedited"

"How …. *expedited?*"

"Mr. Kryder told me that I could expect your full cooperation, and given that the paperwork, etc., etc., etc., is done properly, we could forward a partial, preliminary, emergency portion of the grant . . . as soon as tomorrow."

Wednesday - January 15

The several hours that Joseph spent with Montoya and some of his staff yesterday afternoon, and night, had been painful, although it would prove very rewarding. He left the office several hours after everyone else at the clinic had gone home. And as tedious as dealing with Montoya was, and as nitpicking as some of his staff were, it was worth it. And an added benefit had been that because he was so busy with them he had been able to honestly plead "too busy" to Ana the several times she walked into his office.

The grant request was a paperwork marathon. But they had made a good start, and the first hurdle was cleared. He expected "a preliminary transfer of funds" today. He sat at his desk this morning expecting a windfall. He wasn't disappointed.

Using his computer to check the clinic's account at the bank several times since he had arrived that morning, he was stunned at 10:26 AM when the cash account at the bank suddenly showed a large credit. He called Podalski, and would have told Gus and Ana next, but the delivery of new lab equipment arrived just then. The rest of his day was spent checking the paperwork, and moving equipment around. He hadn't seen her, but at one point in the afternoon Ana came looking for him. She found him as he was trying to move a large, heavy, delicate machine to a new location. He and Olney were wrestling it across the floor as Figgit provided useless guidance. As Joseph's tone of voice indicated that he was nearing his boiling point, she thought better of interrupting him and went back to her patients. But not before she noticed all the new equipment that was piled up on the tables, as well as on the floor of the lab.

Thursday - January 16

Joseph beat the two phone company installers to the clinic this morning by three minutes. They, too, must have believed in getting an early start to the day. After establishing with Joseph that they were "on site" at 8 AM, they spent the next 30 minutes having coffee in the pantry.

That was all right with him. He wanted to follow up with Figgit to be certain that the new equipment was functioning properly. He was also able to fit in two calls to New York. One was to Henry Kryder, to whom now Joseph felt a debt of gratitude. The call lasted too long, but Joseph was not about to cut it short. Henry touched on the subject of Joseph returning to New York again, and Joseph diplomatically put up a mild resistance to the idea. But he didn't outright reject it. The second call was to Bernie and Barry for an update on the situation at 2BIC. It was all good.

"Where is all this stuff coming from? Dad, he's out of control! How much did we borrow? Isn't that all spent by now?" Ana had these and many more comments and questions for her father. She had glanced into the lab again this morning and was dazzled at all the new things that were in there. With cartons, and boxes, and packing materials strewn about it appeared that more had been delivered than there actually was. But as she returned from the lab she came upon the two telephone installers piling up the boxes and cartons that contained the new phone system they were about to install. It was a very impressive pile, and it was too much for her to accept. She had questions, and she wanted answers. She abandoned hope of confronting Hamilton, so she cornered her father.

"Have you seen what's coming through the door? Do we have any idea how much this stuff is costing us?"

He couldn't debate the point; it was a considerable amount of merchandise. Everywhere one looked there were cartons and boxes: some opened, some closed, and some empty. It would have looked like Christmas morning, but there was no wrapping paper. There was, however, bubble wrap strewn on the floor in almost every room. And, of course, there was the squad of installers scurrying around. He also noticed at this point that these installers were still bringing more cartons into the clinic. When a third installer showed up 20 minutes later, and the three of them began running wires, installing jacks, and replacing old phones with state-of-the-art base units, it left Ana shaking her head.

Friday - January 17

The transfer of funds from Albany covering Medicaid Reimbursements for last year's 4th quarter was made sometime during the night. It was there on Joseph's computer screen when he checked the bank balances this morning.

The money, of course, was important. It assured the ongoing work of the clinic for the immediate future. But it also provided some longer term financial stability. And, finally, it gave Joseph and Podalski a realistic view of the clinic's full year's revenue stream. They now had a full year of actual data. And although the numbers would obviously vary from year to year, they could now model financial plans, project expenses, and anticipate revenue with a modest degree of certainty. It would be better if they had the numbers for the past three, or even five, years; but this was a solid start.

He was ecstatic, and his cheerfulness knew no bounds. Everyone on staff could sense it the minute he entered a room. He spent the rest of the day contacting people he had been unable to deal with over the past three days. He called many people to catch up on the status of various projects. He even spent some time helping Olney moving supplies from one location to another, including several trips to the basement. Which was where he was the one time Ana dropped by his office for a chat. She was not pleased with his apparent disappearance.

Saturday - January 18

Between the 4th quarter Medicaid money from the state and the grant from OCS, Joseph found himself with a very unique, yet pleasant, dilemma. How best to spend it! Cautious not to spend like the proverbial "sailor on shore leave," he reviewed the many options he had.

Podalski, who had not been at the clinic since Monday, arrived early with some ideas of his own. He had been in contact with Joseph throughout the week, but had recently been busy building his own private accounting practice. His association with the clinic had given him some exposure to a few small businesses in the area, and the new fiscal posture of the clinic had shown him in a better light. Not only had he begun signing up a few new accounting clients, but he also was picking up some business as a tax preparer as that season approached.

The two men worked very hard allocating funds and forecasting revenue streams. The proposed financial plan was starting to take shape as realistic projections could now be made. Working on separate aspects of the plan, they occasionally would "fit their pieces together," and to their delight, it all seemed to mesh. They were almost giddy. Unfortunately they lost track of time.

"Oh, I 'm glad I caught you both," Ana said, sticking her head in the door. "I want to ask you two a few questions about some of the things we're getting in here." It certainly, in hindsight, seemed like a reasonable request to Ana, all things considered.

Both men, startled by the unannounced voice, looked at their watches. "Oh damn!" said Podalski, "We're going to be late. Look at the time!"

"Go ahead. Run," said Joseph, "I'll clean this up." Both men were on their feet. "Tell them I'm right behind you," Joseph said as Podalski grabbed some papers, shoved them in folder, and headed for the door. Joseph began piling the rest of the papers into three different stacks on the end of his desk. Neither one of them acknowledged Ana's presence. She was mildly annoyed. And even more so when Podalski brushed past her, without a word, and disappeared through the back door. She turned her attention to Joseph.

"Excuse me," she said with than a touch of sarcasm. "We need to have a little talk."

"Bad time for me. Give me a rain check, OK?" he said, not looking at her as continued tidying up the desk.

"We *really* need to talk. There's a lot of goings-on here that need to be explained."

"Great. Why don't we go through it all at Tuesday's staff meeting? We'll have all morning." Joseph looked at his watch again, shook his head, and said, "Look, I'm really late for practice. I have to go." With his coat draped over his shoulders, he hurried past her down the hall.

"Wait a minute," she said to his retreating back, "I need some answers." He might have heard her, but he showed no reaction, and an instant later he was out the door, and gone. "That son of a . . . " she whispered to herself.

The weather was very cold, and the sky was low and gray. The forecast for tomorrow was for even more miserable weather. It was going to be a test of the players' wills. When Joseph arrived for practice he was twenty minutes late. Roove unconvincingly tried to tell him that there was a tradition that anyone late for practice had to buy the entire team drinks that night at the Fireside. "Nice try," was all Joseph said.

He also noticed that Podalski was standing on the sidelines. While Tully had fully recovered from his encounter last week with Torpedo Red, Gus

212

explained that he had expressly forbidden PeaPod to play this week. PeaPod had argued that he was fit to play, but his words fell on deaf ears. Gus wouldn't budge.

The practice went well, with the players all hustling about and executing various maneuvers with very good precision. Trying to stay warm in this weather had a lot to do with it. Shifts went well, and a few new wrinkles on their free start plays were added. After 45 minutes, it was generally agreed that they had had enough.

When they returned to the bench area and began unlacing their skates, Gus began the player review of the Blue Canes. It was immediately apparent that the singular focus for the Bombers would be Marty "The Dwarf" Quarf. He was not only their captain, but was their best player, by far. Joseph had watched him briefly last week against the Blades, and had been impressed. He stood out among his teammates, and held his own against the various Blade players he had battled. The Blue Canes had been outmanned by the Blades, but none of the fault lay with The Dwarf.

One thing puzzled him, however. "Why do you call him "The Dwarf?"" he asked no one in particular. He had incorrectly assumed that the nickname referred to his lack of height, and after watching him last week he realized that that was not the case.

It was explained to Joseph that the nickname was a little misleading. The Dwarf was as tall, or taller, than Joseph's six feet three inches. He was probably one of the tallest players in the league. The nickname, it turned out, was based on the remarkable shortness of the Dwarf's legs. But his torso more than compensated for them. He was enormous from the hips up. "He's just as tall sitting down as he is standing up," Roove said offhand.

"And he's a brute," Magoo added quickly.

"Dwarf's a fuckin' beast," said the Bombers' wingman Tully. He was recalling a game played years ago when The Dwarf had lifted him off the ground and threw him over the boards. Several other Bombers had their own unpleasant memories of run-ins with The Dwarf. And it just wasn't his ferocity that made him stand out; he was very strong, and an excellent skater. And he was absolutely fearless.

The problem the Blue Canes had was that the talent level dropped off a cliff after The Dwarf. Other titmen they had were "Blue Demon" Freeman, "Style" Traskota, and "Savior" Jones. Their centers were large and strong, but very immobile. Their names were "Big Man" Baggott and "Okie."

Joseph heard the wings mentioned – "Nickles", Giggans, and "Fluke." The Blue Canes also had two replacement players, "Hardly" and "Mo." None of the Blue Cane mentioned seemed to generate any respect from the Bomber players. Gus emphasized again, and again, and again that The Dwarf had to be neutralized. "He scored three times against the Blades last week," he said. "Including one time when Superfly was on the ice with him." Joseph noticed that that seemed to be significant to the other players. "I watched the whole game." Gus went on. "He hasn't lost anything since we last played."

Several Bombers began telling stories of run-ins with The Dwarf in past games. Paulie remembered Dwarf grabbing him by the arm once, and spinning him around so fast he nearly broke it. It sounded painful. Magoo and Moonie agreed that he was probably the strongest guy in the league. "He's not sneaky, like Torpedo Red," said Roove, "But he'll cripple you if you don't see him coming!" Players all agreed that keeping tabs on his whereabouts on the ice was a sound idea. The Bombers' centers promised to constantly update their teammates about where he was during the game.

"Oh shit ... I almost forgot," Roove said suddenly. "We got a new name for one of our players." Several Bombers asked him what he meant. "I was talking with some of the Blue Canes during the week, who watched our game against the Angels, and it seems that they now have a name for our rookie here, Hamilton."

Joseph was pretty sure it wasn't going to be too nice, but like several others, he asked Roove what it was. Reluctantly he said, "Go ahead, and tell me what it is."

Roove paused for a moment, letting a little drama build up. "'Hoist,'" he said with a laugh. "After hiking Pastor Pittou's ass up into the air . . . and producing that world class "wedgie" last week . . . someone on the Blue Canes said 'from now on, that guy is gonna be known as 'Hoist' Hamilton.'"

The Bombers had a good laugh about the new name, and then began heading off for home. Gus caught Joseph's eye. "Hoist! That's a good one. It suits you."

Joseph knew there was nothing he could do to change it, so he smiled and shrugged, "And how about you? You never got a nickname?"

"Well, I was called 'Goals' for a short time ....but it never really stuck." Gus admitted that it was probably a little too complimentary to be any good. "Most names tend to have a little bite in them."

"Like 'Agony Ann'?" Joseph asked.

"Exactly," Gus had to admit. "A word of caution, by the way." Gus looked at Joseph sternly, and said, "I would like to remind you that using that nickname in her presence might prove costly."

"Point taken." Joseph nodded. And he thought to himself that that piece of advice hadn't really been necessary.

Joseph decided to change the topic, and asked Gus if he had watched the Blades' free starts last week. Gus thought for a minute, and then said, "It's a killer. They did that whip seven times, and scored on six." He paused for a moment to let it sink in, and then added, "If they execute it correctly, it's unstoppable."

"How did the Blue Canes stop it that seventh time?" Moonie asked.

"They didn't. The two Blade wingers in the middle of the whip didn't grab each other's hands tightly enough, and the whip came apart midway through the swing. Cobra was on the geetha, but he didn't have enough speed working for him to elude the Canes waiting for him. Big Man crushed him."

Sunday - January 19

Today the players would fight the elements as much as each other. The morning was dark with very heavy gray clouds spreading across the valley. And gusts of wind caused it to feel even colder than it actually was. Geetha players around the valley prepared for their games by layering on weatherproof clothing designed to protect them. Giving up a little flexibility was considered a good trade-off for a lot more warmth.

When Joseph arrived at Lake Custer an hour before game time, he was not surprised by how cold it was there. What amazed him was how many people had shown up to watch! The sides of the ravine around the pond were teeming with spectators. The foul weather hadn't held the crowd back in the slightest.

After quickly putting on his skates he took a lap around the lake to loosen up. He was grateful to Gus for suggesting he wear woolen gloves underneath his hockey gloves. All in all, he felt fairly comfortable.

As he skated around the lake he saw some familiar faces. Although Byram Lomb seemed to be missing, MerriLuAnn was there. He also noticed PeaPod sitting on a blanket with his whole family. At first he didn't recognize him because PeaPod had a hooded jacket on and a scarf covering his nose and mouth. But those two black eyes were an unmistakable giveaway. When Joseph waved to them, the children waved frantically back. And although Joseph didn't see them, Lindsay and Sadim sat next to each other in two beach chairs up near the top of the incline.

Seeing PeaPod's face, he was reminded of his own injury from last week. Although it was relatively minor compared to PeaPod's, he decided to take another lap, trying to work out a knot in the muscle of his right thigh. It had been hit hard sometime during last week's game, and it had been stiff all week. He thought that he was lucky that that was his only physical problem. He was very glad that there were no lingering problems from the whack on the head he had taken last week. The game was as violent and bruising as he had been told it would be. And considering some of the injuries the other team had suffered, he thought the Bombers were lucky to have only lost PeaPod for this week's game. He remembered that the injuries to Torpedo Red and Pastor Pittou had been more serious. As the name "Pastor Pittou" crossed his mind, he smirked.

215

The Braxtburg Town Blue Canes were congregating near their bench when they began taking off their jackets. Joseph now got a good look at their uniform sweaters. They were silver in color, with blue lettering. The front of their shirt displayed two crossed dark blue canes, with their curved handles facing out. In the uppermost section of the crossed canes was the capital letter "B." In the left hand section was a "B," and in the right section was a "C." On the back of the sweater was a name, on top of a number.

The players all wore blue lacrosse helmets with blue hockey gloves. None of the uniforms, or equipment looked used. Jeepers saw Joseph staring across the ice. "Like to call themselves the best dressed team in the league," he said.

As they began warming up, Joseph began sneaking peeks across the ice to try to identify some of the players he had heard about yesterday. He spotted their large center, Big Man Baggot, right away. He was easily identifiable because of his size. Style Traskota was also noticeable because he seemed much more at ease on his skates than most of the others. The Blue Demon (Joseph could see that name on the back of his uniform) began doing sprints down at one end of the lake. But as he looked the entire team over, one player began to stand out. The other skaters milling around seemed to defer to him and pat him on the back whenever he wandered near them. Had his legs been proportionate to the rest of his body, he would have stood head and shoulders above all his teammates. But his legs were short. But they were the only undersized thing about him.

Even under his multilayered, bulky uniform it was easy to see he was barrel-chested and brawny. He had an enormous head. His arms reached down well past his waist. He moved around easily, and it was apparent he was very comfortable on his skates. Joseph knew that this was Marty Quarf, AKA the Dwarf.

A few minutes before the start of the game, Joseph was standing next to Roove down near the end of the pond. They were catching their breath after doing a few sprints. They were waiting for the Blue Canes to bring out their geetha.

"Hope you break your leg, 26 . . . you sonuvabitch!" said a husky voice in the crowd close behind them. He was obviously talking to Roove, who wore number 26.

"George! You ought to be ashamed of yourself! That is so inappropriate," said a much sweeter voice, an instant later.

Joseph, who had played competitive sports most of his life, knew to ignore the comments coming from the crowd, but this comment seemed particularly venomous. Joseph started to turn around to see who was talking, but Roove stopped him immediately. "Don't turn around! Don't turn around." he repeated. "Ignore it," he added.

"Don't you want to see who said it?" Joseph asked in a whisper.

"I know who said it. I know that voice."

"Who is it?"

Before Roove could answer, the "sweeter voice" could be heard again. "How can you say something like that?"

Roove whispered to Joseph, "The Mayor from Lower Wenweenie . . . that's Mayor Neidermeyer."

The "harsh voice," now in a much milder tone, apparently talking to the "sweet voice" said, "Twenty-six is Hagedorn, dear." And then he added, "*Roove Hagedorn*." A few seconds of silence went by.

Then Joseph and Roove heard the not-too-sweet-anymore-voice say, "I hope they snap your fucking neck, Hagedorn." Joseph and Roove decided this would be a good time to skate back to their bench.

Only a few of the Blue Canes escorted their geetha to center ice. And they did not seem to exhibit much enthusiasm for it. This surprised Joseph, who had expected much more fanfare. When they pulled the cover off it, they simply skated away, back to their own bench. Their geetha was, at first glance, simply a truck tire. It was a very big truck tire perhaps, but just a truck tire.

Upon closer examination it was a Michelin X-ONE XTA, Model 445/50R225. It was black, and a company sales brochure would have told you that it weighed 187.5 lbs. It had a radius of 40 inches, and was 17.1 inches high when lying flat on its side. There was a metal rim still inside it adding to its weight. The noise from the crowd, however, indicated that, although they didn't know the specifics, they were impressed, and warmly approved that selection.

The game began with Roove as titman, and Moonie centering for Tully and Jeepers. The Blue Canes countered with Dwarf at titman, with Big Man centering for Nickels and Hardly. It was no surprise that Dwarf was too strong for Roove. The Bombers had expected that, and had planned for it during yesterday's practice. Every time Dwarf began to overpower Roove, the Bomber titman would steer the geetha off in another direction. The more nimble Roove could outmaneuver the stronger Blue Cane by not opposing the direction the Dwarf pushed, but rather by jumping from side to side, never allowing it to travel in a straight line. The path the geetha took during their confrontation zigzaged all over the ice.

Several times the Bombers switched positions, allowing Roove a few breathers. They were, as a team, much more coordinated than the Blue Canes, who relied heavily on the Dwarf. After nearly five minutes of uninterrupted play, an exhausted Dwarf called a time-out.

The Blue Demon now stepped over the boards for the Blue Canes with Okie at center, and Giggans and Fluke on the wings. The Bombers countered with Paulie at titman, and Joseph (wearing his newly acquired lacrosse helmet, with protective face guard) centering between Whitey and Smoke.

Paulie wasted no time overpowering the Blue Demon. And the Blue Demon wasted no time calling out for one of his teammates to switch with him. The Blue Cane center named Okie, who had his hands full trying to contain Joseph, foolishly turned his attention away from Joseph for a moment. Feeling the Blue Cane relax his grip and start to slip away, Joseph moved in closely and drove an elbow into the opposing center's solar plexus. In a split second it seemed to Okie that every molecule of air in his body rushed out. There was the "thud" of impact followed by the long breathy "hoooo" of escaping air.

Released by the incapacitated Okie, Joseph turned toward the Blue Demon and lined him up. As he flew toward the Blue Cane from his blind side, Paulie coyly watched him approach, and released his hold on the geetha just before Joseph arrived. Pulling his hands off the tire and holding them up for the Blue Demon to see, he smiled at his momentarily confused opponent.

But then reality set in for the Blue Demon and he flinched, but it was much too late. Hit by Joseph's shoulder, he was sent sprawling in a head long dive. He had to be grateful that he landed quite smoothly, and slid for over thirty feet before hitting the sideboard. As he congratulated himself on coming out of that relatively unscathed, the Bombers took the geetha down the ice on a four man to two advantage and scored easily.

The rest of the first half went no better for the Blue Canes. Their only threat on the ice was the Dwarf, and he was effectively neutralized by the more nimble Bombers. The rest of the Braxtburg Town Blue Canes could not match up with their counterparts on the Bombers. They had no titman capable of handling either Paulie or the newcomer, Hamilton.

With one minute left to go in the first half, the Bombers were winning 3 – 0. And that included a beautiful goal by the Bombers off a free start. An intricate weave by the linemen had led to Joseph cutting back against the flow, and allowing him to skate untouched the length of the ice to score. It had been diagrammed and practiced yesterday, and had worked to perfection today. The Bombers were feeling very good about themselves. That ended when the Blue Canes were awarded the second free start of the day.

Dwarf, Okie, BigMan and Nickles lined up for the Blue Canes. Opposing them, the Bombers sent out Moonie, Magoo, B-Ball and Paulie. Unlike the finesse or choreographed plays the Bombers had used, the Blue Canes came up the ice in a "T" formation. That simply meant the three linemen were side by side by side, and the titman (Dwarf) was five feet behind the center of the line.

The Bombers attempted to take on the bull rush charge, and did fairly well withstanding it. But at the collision B-ball lost his balance and inadvertently slid into the feet of Paulie, knocking him off balance too. Dwarf had veered off at just this moment, and got safely behind the Bomber defenders. Dwarf easily outraced the nearest pursuers and scored the Blue Canes' first goal.

When the second half started, the mismatches resumed. Despite the continued strong play of the Dwarf, the Blue Canes were wanting everywhere else. The Bomber lead soon grew to 4 − 1. Shortly afterward both teams had a free start opportunity, but neither team scored.

Just over eight minutes into the second half, the Bombers called a timeout to rearrange their lineup. When the game resumed a minute later the opposing forces had Roove matched up against Lyle "Style" Traskota at titman. They started out struggling, but Roove was soon getting the best of it. Style, who reasoned he had to do something to stem the tide, began reaching across the geetha and tugging on Roove's face mask. When White seemed to be oblivious to the repeated blatant fouls, Roove decided to solve the dilemma himself.

Style continued grabbing and pulling on Roove's face mask several more times. But Roove just stared blankly across the geetha back at Style, without saying a word. He allowed this to go on for another 30 seconds, when he suddenly jerked his head and stared off and above Style's right shoulder. With a burst of frenzied enthusiasm, he yelled, "GET HIM, HOIST!"

Whatever success Style had enjoyed as a Geetha player had not been attained through above average strength or skating finesse. It had come from a keen sense of self-preservation, and lightning-like reflexes. He resorted to those traits instinctively now. The concept of "Hoist" approaching from his rear was processed with computer like speed, and Style twisted immediately around to his right, fully expecting the Bombers' new weapon of groin destruction to pounce on him. He had pulled his right arm off the geetha and held it out in front of him, planning to ward off the attack from his rear.

But there was no Hoist descending on him. Hoist Hamilton, at this moment, happened to be on the Bombers' bench. As a matter of fact, there weren't any Bombers descending on Style at that moment at all. He realized in an instant he had been tricked. "Damn," he thought to himself as he whirled around once again to face Roove.

Roove hadn't thought Style would fall for the distraction so easily, and was pleasantly surprised when he did. He took advantage of Style's lack of focus to pull his own right hand off the geetha, and put it as far back behind him as he could. When Style began to turn back around to face him, Roove swung his arm around with all the force he could muster. And just as the Blue Cane titman was fully turned back around to face him, the palm of Roove's open right hand hit the earhole on Style's helmet.

Style said nothing. He just smiled ever so faintly, blinked twice, and collapsed. He was helped to the sidelines by two of his teammates shortly thereafter while the Bombers celebrated, the score now being 5 – 1 in their favor.

The Blue Canes were well aware of the mismatches in their lineup. Dwarf was playing virtually every shift at titman or center, and to his credit he was playing extremely well. They devised the strategy to go for a halt at every opportunity. This strategy offered two benefits for them. It allowed frequent breaks for the tiring, overused Dwarf. And it also allowed for them to use free starts, which they felt was their best chance to score.

Over the next several minutes White called four halts. And while that was an unusually frequent number of times, no one scored. The Bombers did not score because their execution was sloppy, and they wound up tripping over each other as they tried complex movements on their attempts. That was due equally to the fact that they had not practiced these moves often enough; and that by this time in the game, they were all fatigued.

The Blue Canes, on the other hand, tried nothing fancy. They simply put their biggest players out there, with Dwarf pushing the geetha, and charged right into their opponents, attempting to blow past them. They, too, were tiring, and got nothing done.

When White called another halt, it was the Blue Canes' turn for the free start. The Blue Canes sent out their players, and the lineup surprised the Bombers. The Dwarf was out there, of course. But also out there were three other Blue Cane titmen: Blue Demon, Savior, and a mostly revitalized Style. These four were easily their fastest, and best, skaters. The Bombers had already sent out Moonie, Magoo, B-Ball and Paulie, because they had been expecting the Blue Canes to try to power their way through the Bombers again.

"Listen up," The Dwarf told his teammates as they huddled near their Start Spot. "I'm going to be titman. You three guys line up right in front of me." The three Blue Canes stared at their leader, and nodded. "I want Demon on the left, Style in the middle, and Savior over on the right. Stay close to each other." The three players began arranging themselves in a line. "When we take off, I need you to skate as fast as you can . . . right at them." The three were nodding. "Go right at them. They're going to think we're going to do some fancy maneuver . . . because we got our skaters out here, but we're not!" He was shaking his head. They were leaning forward, looking right at him, shaking their heads right along with him. "When we get right up to them . . . I'll yell . . . " he suddenly paused. "What's a good signal word?"

"How about Apache?" suggested Style after a minute.

"No, that's an old one. Let's use "Operation Tornado." I bet they never heard that one before," offered Blue Demon.

Savior chimed in with a suggestion of "Nitlicky." "I just made that word up. They've never heard that before. It'll confuse them."

"How do you spell that?" Blue Demon asked.

The debate over which signal to use could have gone on, but White called down from the center line for them to get moving. "Wait a minute," Dwarf finally said, "I'll just yell "BLUE!", and when I do I want Style to cut to his right, and hit the guy on their right end. Full blast! They'll never expect it. They're going think we're going to do some fancy swerve, or something. Demon . . . you swerve right too, and smack the guy in the center of their line. They're going to be shuffling their feet, and won't be set. Just blast him. And Savior, when those two guys cut right, you wait a split second, and then cut left behind them and smack . . . full blast . . . into their guy on the left. You see what I'm saying?" he asked them. They nodded. "Those cuts will open up a hole just between their center and the guy on the left. And I'll go through that hole so fast they'll never have a chance." Sounded simple, and it was. Dwarf fully expected the Bombers to see the speed that the Blue Canes had sent out, and to think that they were going to use a plan involving speed and elusiveness around one of the flanks. "Now remember, you got to skate as fast as you can down there. I'm going to be right behind you. Stay close together," was his last instruction as they took their positions in front of the geetha, and heard the Dwarf say, "Let's go!"

Whatever shortcomings they may have had as players, or as a team, speed wasn't one of them. In only a few strides they were going down the ice very fast. The Dwarf, although a superior skater and incredibly strong, had trouble staying close behind as he pushed the bulky, heavy geetha. The Blue Cane phalanx roared up the ice, and as the crowd noticed the speeding attack, the noise level rose.

The Bombers waited impatiently at the center line when the Blue Canes were huddling. Gus shouted from the bench for them to be careful, when he first noticed the speed players they had sent out. This was not what they had expected, and the Bombers did not have their faster skaters out there to face the swift Blue Canes. They saw that they did not match up well with this lineup. They were momentarily confused, but it was too late to do anything about it as the Blue Canes broke their huddle and started up the ice at them.

At first the Bombers spread out in a wide four man line. As the Blue Canes came up the ice tightly bunched, the Bombers' defensive formation drew closer together. As the Blue Canes drew nearer, still tightly bunched, the Bombers got even closer together. The close proximity of the defenders was exactly what the Blue Canes wanted. The Bombers were certain that the approaching Blue Canes would dart one way or another at the last minute. Paulie, who was the outside man on the left of their formation, decided that because the Blue Canes were so tightly bunched as they approached at full speed, he should slip back behind the line of his teammates, at the last second, to become a second line of defense.

Dwarf screamed, "BLUE!", and Style instantly cut to his right, aiming at B-Ball on the right of the Bomber line. Blue Demon did his part too. He crashed full speed into Magoo in the center. Savior, with superb agility, waited a half second for his line mates to cross in front, and then piled into Moonie on the left. It was choreographed, and executed, beautifully.

But all three Bombers had a half second to brace themselves. These flying irresistible forces of speeding Blue Canes hit the immovable objects of big, strong, braced Bombers. Unfortunately the outcome did not have the chance to be decided. Because before that outcome could be decided, and before the "hole" had a chance to appear, or not appear, the Dwarf and the hurtling geetha hit the mass of bodies from behind. In hindsight, he was a bit too close.

And the fact that it hit that mass of bodies below their knees made a very big difference. Bodies flew off in different directions like corn in a popper with the top left off; only faster. And when Dwarf saw that there wasn't going to be a hole, only a frightful collision, he abandoned ship, so to speak. He would have escaped the calamity totally unscathed had he not tripped over someone's leg as he tried to avoid the pileup.

Paulie, who was standing several feet away, wasn't involved in the mayhem at all. In fact when the geetha veered away from the scene of the carnage, he chased after it. It had been slowed down only slightly as it had somehow been re-directed toward the side of the pond. Paulie raced after the now unescorted geetha, and had nearly caught up with it as it approached the sideboard. When it hit the sideboard he was only a few feet behind it. Its reaction to the sideboard was not what he had anticipated.

It unexpectedly came back at him like it had been shot from a cannon. He instinctively bent over quickly and tried to catch it with his hands. But it went through his hands like a teenager through his first paycheck. Next up for the geetha were the toes of Paulie's skates, and those, also, the geetha discarded instantly with great force. This caused Paulie to begin a rapid forward flip. And he simply did not possess the gymnastic skill to complete the maneuver. He wasn't even close. It turned out to be far short of the required 360 degrees. And, not surprisingly, he did not 'nail the landing." His skates were only the first of the many parts of Paulie that hit the ice in the next split second.

The geetha, after rebounding violently off the near side and discarding Paulie, was now rocketing across the ice in the opposite direction. The seven other players involved in the collision a moment ago were still collecting themselves at center ice. Only The Dwarf was back on his feet, and assessing the situation. Wisely seeing how futile it would be attempting to control the hurtling hunk of rubber The Dwarf quickly plotted an intercepting course. And after figuring correctly and skating furiously, he positioned himself alongside the speeding Michelin, and jumped on top of it.

Now, once again, in sole possession of the geetha, Marty the Dwarf Quarf was feeling very good about himself. Lying on top of the geetha as it sped across the pond at high speed, he began to prepare for the unavoidable collision with the fast approaching sideboard on the other side. Unafraid, he slid his body back on the geetha, a position that would allow it, and not his head, to make the contact with that ominous sideboard. He had that right. And he braced himself for the inevitable crash. Correct again.

But The Dwarf also had two things wrong. He forgot, or maybe he did not know, the Laws of Physics. And although he had indeed slid his body back on the geetha, he had inadvertently left the fingertips of his right hand curled over its front edge.

A geetha of moose carcass would have hit that sideboard, absorbed the blow, and rebounded slightly away. A geetha like last week's folded, frozen carpet would have hit that sideboard and crumpled like a tin fender. In both cases, Marty would probably have still hung onto the geetha. But a geetha that is a truck tire? Well, that geetha would have to obey the laws of vulcanized rubber and elasticity. And in so doing, it would collide into the sideboard, compress a bit, then freeze for a nanosecond . . . and then rebound violently off the sideboard at even greater speed. (Paulie knew this now.) When the geetha hit the sideboard Marty would be subject to a different Law of Physics. Sir Isaac Newton's First Law of Motion states that "A body in motion tends to stay in motion.' Marty obeyed that law.

He "stayed in motion," continuing at high speed . . . up and over the sideboard. Seeing a player go airborne always held a special thrill for the fans of Wackentute Geetha . . . and the Dwarf did not disappoint. And the fingertips on his right hand, crushed for an agonizing moment between the sideboard and the tire, acted as the pivot point as his body rotated up into the air.

Jeannie and Tom Snitz were long time fans of Geetha, and the Braxtburg Town Blue Canes, and as such had arrived early for the game. They had secured a good spot for their picnic blanket about fifteen feet up from the sideboards near the midline of the pond. There they now sat, sitting side by side, enjoying the action. But at this particular moment, they weren't paying as much attention to the game as perhaps they should have. Jeannie was looking down at the cup of hot chocolate she was pouring for Tom. Tom was looking off to his left at the girl in the extraordinarily tight beige ski pants. Neither saw Marty coming at them. They both remembered hearing a muted "Oh shit!" an instant before impact.

The seven players still on the ice decided independently to allow the geetha to "calm down a little" before taking up the chase. And despite their somewhat battered bodies they were able to track it down as it ran out of steam. The remaining Bombers, including a very shaky Paulie, not only outnumbered but clearly outmuscled the remaining Blue Canes, and scored another goal. The Bombers had a commanding 6 to 1 lead.

With Marty Quarf's day as a Geetha player now finished, the Blue Canes were severely undermanned. The match-ups between the lines were very uneven, and the Bombers took complete advantage of them.

At center Moonie was starting to overpower a weakening Big Man. And Okie was no match for the Bombers' Magoo. Their wings were no match for the Bomber wings either. But the real mismatch was at titman. The combination of Hamilton's strength and skating ability, along with the Blue Canes understanding of why he was called "Hoist," proved to be too much for the opposing titmen.

Late in the game, after the Bombers had scored again, making it 7 to 1, Gus was using B-Ball and Joseph as much as he could. With the game safely in hand, he wanted them to get as much game experience as possible before next week's game against the dreaded Blades. He was using Hoist exclusively as a titman to replace Paulie, who would flinch until Tuesday from his run-in with the rebounding geetha earlier.

Hoist was the titman, with Magoo taking a shift at center and Tully and B-Ball at the wings. They were facing a lineup of Savior, Okie, Fluke, and Hardly for the Blue Canes. Savior was being outplayed by Hoist, while Magoo and Okie were comparably slow and evenly matched. Fluke and Tully were also evenly matched. The real mismatch was at the other wing. Hardly, although not a very good skater, was better at it than B-Ball. But B-Ball was far stronger than the lanky Blue Cane. Hardly was getting beaten up pretty good, and also nearing exhaustion, when he heard a signal called and thought he was supposed to switch with his line mate, Fluke. Grateful for the reprieve, he broke away from the less nimble B-Ball. He skated in the direction of Fluke. But Fluke hadn't heard any signal for a switch, and continued on in his battle with Tully. Sensing that the switch was not with Fluke, Hardly looked around trying to determine where he was supposed to be going. He glanced around and quickly saw all three of his teammates were fully engaged with their counterparts, and not looking to switch. This confusion caused him to break one of the cardinal rules of Geetha. Simply put, it said, "Don't EVER stand still on the ice."

In his confusion he looked left, and then right, and back again, as he tried to figure out where he was supposed to be. He didn't look behind him. Mistake. While this was going on, B-Ball knew exactly where he was supposed to be and was trying furiously to get there. Hardly had broken away from him, and he was trying to catch up. At first, he slipped a bit, but then charged after his opponent with all the skating skill he possessed. After several strides he was going as fast as he was able. It didn't matter because Hardly was, at this point, standing still.

The ensuing collision resulted in Hardly doing what figure skating fans would concede was a nearly impossible transition from a standing position . . . to a Double Lutz . . . to a Camel Spin . . . to a Choctaw Turn . . . to a Besti Squat . . . and finally to a prostrate position. During these wild gyrations he would lose his helmet, one glove, and his Jardine Vault and consciousness, in no particular order.

The game ended with the Bombers winning by a score of 7 to 1.

The Blades won 9 - 0, over the very shorthanded Angels, in the second game. They scored on 5 free starts, which included three intentionally set up by them. The game's outcome was really never in doubt. They just wanted to be sure to win the game, and win it by at least four goals. They were very aware that the Bombers had won their first game over the Reds by four goals (6 - 2), and their second game by six goals (7 - 1). Their goal differential was 10 goals. The Blades, on the other hand, had won their first game by seven goals (10 – 3). As soon as the Blades were comfortably ahead in this second game by four goals (making their goal differential now 11 goals) they began to play conservatively. The object was to go into the championship game next Sunday against the Bombers with a better goal differential. If that game ended in a tie . . . there was no overtime in Geetha games . . . then the team with the highest point differential would be declared the winner of the Geetha Trophy.

Most of the Bombers stayed around to watch the game. It was an impressive display of Geetha by the Blades, but the Bombers were most impressed by how efficient the Blades executed their free starts. The whip they employed was deadly. The Blades knew they were being scouted, and as a result played very conservatively once the outcome was no longer in doubt. In fact they tried to disguise their lineups and shifts most of the second half. They did not use their whip on free starts after going up 5 - 0.

Monday - January 20

Once again, Joseph was amazed at how sore he was when he woke up this morning. Yesterday's game, as he remembered it, seemed to be a fairly easy win. He didn't remember getting hit especially hard by anyone, and other than two occasions when he slipped, he didn't get knocked down at all. In spite of his recollections, he was sore all over.

And he was amazed again at how many people commented to him this morning about yesterday's game. It seemed that everyone he ran into had been at the game. When he arrived at the clinic the first person he saw was

Mena, who asked, "Is Paulie all right? Will he play next week?" After assuring her that he thought Paulie would recover in time and be ready for the Blades, he retreated to the peace and quiet of his office.

Podalski arrived, unexpectedly, shortly after 9 AM. He had rearranged some meetings he had previously set up, and decided instead to spend the morning at the clinic. Joseph was glad because they had a great deal of unfinished work left over from Saturday's meeting which had ended abruptly.

The pair worked through the morning, going long stretches without a word being spoken. But while Joseph was totally focused, Podalski would occasionally become distracted and ask some question about something in yesterday's game. It was obvious he was feeling bad about having had to sit it out.

"I stayed and watched the beginning of the Blades game. They looked really tough. That whip of theirs is deadly." he said out of nowhere.

Joseph looked up, and nodded. "It looks pretty good. I don't know how to defend it."

"I was thinking about it yesterday. Maybe if we . . . " his voice trailed off. He waited a minute, and then started again, "I drew up some diagrams . . . " then he stopped, and shook his head. "I don't think we can stop it." Then he added, "Even if we can get Moonie and B-Ball in front of it. It's just too fast."

"I think maybe we ought to give it some thought this week. You, me, everyone . . . and I know Gus has been looking at it very carefully. We ought to be able to figure some way of derailing it." He smiled across the desk at the forlorn accountant with the two enormous black eyes, who had never before looked so sad to Joseph. "Let's get back to work," Joseph suggested.

Podalski left after lunch, and Joseph continued working on the financial plan. A quiet afternoon turned into a quiet night as Joseph organized data and put pieces in place. It was after midnight when he was finally content that he had enough in place to be able to present, at the very least, a preliminary plan at the staff meeting tomorrow morning.

Tuesday - January 21

Ana came to the meeting determined to get some answers. After listening to a litany of complaints by his daughter, Gus too wanted to know how the recent improvements had come about. When they had settled into their chairs and had run through some items on the medical agenda, Gus turned to Joseph and asked to update them on the business side.

"First, the good news," Joseph said brightly. He had the undivided attention of the others in the room. "I believe we are close to being able to add some part-time staff. And I don't just mean admin. I'm talking about professional people." No one said a word. He turned to Mena, and said, "With your help and guidance in the selection process, I think it's possible we may be able to add an RN for up to 20 hours a week. Maybe more. That should reduce your work load by a considerable amount." He smiled across the table to her.

"Are you kidding?" was all she was able to say.

Before she could say another word he added, "Your six day work week is over." After letting that sink in for a moment he turned around to Figgit, and started to say something.

Figgit interrupted, "I don't want any more help. I want a new . . . " Joseph didn't hear what he had said. He started to ask Figgit to repeat it, but Figgit was already pleading his case. He began talking, uncharacteristically, very fast. He said that the item was just recently introduced, and was an absolute necessity. He added that it could be purchased for less than $20,000. He tried to continue, but by now Ana was shouting.

"HOLD IT! HOLD IT! HOLD IT!" Everyone turned and looked at her. "Hold on just a minute, please" she said softly. The staff settled back into their seats. Ana looked directly at Joseph, "Let's get back to this new nurse business. Did you find someone . . . who is *qualified* . . . who will volunteer for those 20 hours a week?"

"There's an employment agency in Port Newhampton that specializes in medical personnel. We've talked to them, and they feel they can set us up with someone who can help us out."

"We're going to pay them?" she asked, and then added, "With what?"

"I think we can fit this into our budget. We can try," he added.

"And my Sellers 5600? Can we fit that in the budget?" Figgit asked.

"Wait a minute, Figgit," Ana said, holding up her hand. "Where is all this coming from? Are we going to take out another loan?" She turned around and looked at her father. "Did you approve any of this?" Gus looked back at his daughter, then across the table at Joseph. Joseph began arranging some papers in front of him.

"Before we start paying other people money, why don't we see if we can pay our own people a little bit more?" Gus wanted to know.

"We are going to," Joseph immediately said. "If the records we have are correct, there haven't been any salary increases in well over a year. Maybe two? What I think we can do is increase the salaries by five percent now and then perhaps look at it again later this year. It will all depend on how our cash flow looks." He looked around the table; everyone stared silently back. "We can't guarantee anything now. Let's not make promises we can't keep. But our esteemed accountant here," Joseph smiled, "Mr Phillip Podalski, seems to think . . . ."

"Where in hell is all this money going to come from," Ana barked across the table?

"Do we have the money for this?" Gus asked, after a very awkward moment of silence.

There was a crash outside the room. Someone yelled "SPILL!" Several voices could be heard yelling orders. Olney dashed by the open door. Then he reappeared in it a moment later. "Doctor Gus....you better come on out here!"

The meeting broke up as first Gus went out to deal with the emergency, and then Ana followed him a minute later. "This isn't finished. We still have to talk!" she said as she flew out the door following her father.

The bleeding little boy, who had been rushed in by his mother, was followed shortly thereafter by the older man with the asthma attack. In no particular order following them was a badly bruised laborer, a woman in labor, a vomiting infant, etc., etc., etc.

Although the clinic wasn't a hospital emergency room per se, for many people it was the nearest medical facility available. And in a medical emergency, for most people, there was no essential difference between a medical clinic and an emergency room.

The reaction to a medical emergency is usually very different for the person having it, and the person who is treating it. The clamor and drama of the event always seems quite dire for the recipient; and but for the people treating the situation, although it is serious, it is often not too far from routine. By the time things calmed down at the clinic today it was mid-afternoon.

After taking a break for a cup of tea, Ana wandered back to the administrative area looking to restart the morning's conversation. When she found it somewhat empty she asked Lindsay if she knew the whereabouts of the two men. "Podalski?" she answered, "He left at noon. Said he'd be back tomorrow morning." And when Ana asked about Joseph, Lindsay told her that he and Figgit had left to look at some "stuff" that Figgit wanted to buy.

Wednesday - January 22

As usual, Ana arrived for work at the clinic a little before 8 AM. She began her workday as she normally did, with a cup of tea and a review of some cases on her desk. But this morning she also kept an eye out for Joseph, or even Podalski, because she wanted to follow up on the those grandiose plans, as she referred to them to her father, that had been suggested yesterday. By the time she was seeing her third patient of the day, she was painfully aware that she had seen neither Joseph nor Podalski at the clinic yet this morning.

When she spotted Figgit walking past an examining room she chased after him. "Hold on a minute, Figgit, I want to ask you something." He stopped in his tracks, and turned around warily. "Where were you yesterday afternoon?"

"Mr. Hamilton and I went to inspect some . . . " he hesitated, and then added, "some equipment that is available.... and I think we should buy."

"Really? What 'equipment'" she wanted to know. Then, before Figgit could answer, she changed the question to, "How much is this 'equipment' going to cost?"

At this moment they were interrupted by a workman who walked out of the Record Room at the end of the corridor. Ana turned to him, and asked him, "Who are you?"

"Arnie," he said.

"Why were you in our Record Room?" She was concerned that a total stranger had been in close proximity of the patients' charts. They were extremely confidential.

"That's where the elevator is."

"That elevator doesn't work. Why were you in our Record Room?" she asked again.

"Cuz that's where the elevator is," he repeated, and then added, "I fix elevators. Excuse me; I gotta go to the john." He walked away. He didn't seem the least impressed that he was being challenged by a person in a white lab coat, with a stethoscope draped around her neck.

Ana watched him as he walked to the end of the hall and went into the restroom. When he had gone, she noticed that Figgit had also wandered away. She thought for a moment about going after Figgit, but decided to investigate this "Arnie" first.

She walked to the Record Room, and noticed immediately that a large shelving unit had been pulled away from the wall. Olney was sitting on the floor next to it. "Arnie told me to stay here while he went to take a . . ." he stopped. "He had to go to the bathroom," He corrected himself. "He wanted me to stay here and not let anyone fall into the elevator shaft while he was gone."

Ana edged closer to the open elevator door and looked down. There was a work light hanging off a rail in the shaft lighting the entire area. Ana could see a tool box on the floor, and several tools on the roof of the elevator car one floor below.

"Don't fall down the shaft!" said a voice suddenly behind her. It was Arnie.

"Why are you here? Who called you?" she asked him.

"Your office guy. Hamilton. Called me in for an estimate."

"And if I may ask.... what is your estimate? What will it cost to make this thing work again?"

"Hard to say right now. Still gotta pull apart the motor and see what's what. But it doan look so good. Ya probably gonna have to junk the whole block. New one? Rebuilt?" He shrugged his shoulders and paused as if he was working a number up in his head. He went on, "Think you're gonna have to recondition the tracks, cables too, probably. I dunno, I'm guessin' under 30 grand, but I gotta do a lot more lookin' around. May not be worth it. You may need a whole new unit." He let that sink in for a moment, and then added, "Then yur talkin' 50 plus. Could be 75 thou if we gotta do the whole thing over." She unwillingly made a face as if she had just tasted sour milk. He started to turn away, but then looked back at her and asked, "Tell me something. This Hamilton guy who called me? Is that the same 'Hoist Hamilton' of the Bombers?"

Ana didn't believe the man had just asked her that, and could feel the blood rushing from her head. She just stared at him and said nothing. After a moment she turned around and left. She was going to find her father. This was now more than she could understand. It was beginning to frighten her. In the hallway she ran into Figgit again. "Wait!" she commanded as she raised her hand to stop him. "This equipment, you and Hamilton want to buy....the stuff you looked at yesterday.....just tell me one thing." She took a deep breath, "How much money are we talking about?"

"Mr Hamilton's negotiating with them," he said, not answering her question. But then she made a face at him, and he said, "They are asking $32,000."

The blood drained from her face; she tried to breathe normally, but couldn't. She put her hand on the wall to steady herself. Figgit saw her reaction, and beat a hasty retreat back to his lab. Before he had reached the refuge of his lab, Ana had already tracked down her father. They *really* needed to talk, she assured him.

Several hundred miles away, in New York City, some bankers and lawyers, and an army of assistants, were putting the finishing touches on an Initial Public Stock Offering.

Thursday - January 23

When Joseph did not appear at the clinic yesterday, Ana's imagination took off. Her imagination was creating horrible scenarios that would explain the absence, and one was more horrifying than the next. She pestered her father, starting before they even had breakfast, about "cornering this rat." She tried to convince him that they should call the bank and freeze their accounts before any unauthorized withdrawals could be made. Gus didn't think that that was necessary, but agreed to give the bank a call if that would make her feel any better. She was frantic, and that was even before Joseph failed to show up again at the clinic this morning.

"Lindsay?" asked Ana as she and Gus approached the front desk. "Do you know where Mr. Hamilton is this morning?"

"Yeah, I think so," Lindsay answered without looking up. "The Boss said he and Podalski had a to go down to the bank. Said they'd be back by 11."

"Why?" Ana said in a flash. "Why'd they have to go to the bank?"

"Didn't say." she replied, again without raising her eyes from the computer screen she was looking at. "But I think Sadim's with them," she added, as an afterthought.

"Who's 'Sadim'?" Ana wanted to know.

Lindsay, a bit annoyed at the question, wanted to say her boyfriend, but chose to remind them that he was the representative from the state that handled the Medicaid reimbursement. She did remind them both that they had met him a few weeks ago. Gus now remembered, but Ana didn't.

When 11 AM came and went, without Hamilton showing his face at the clinic, Ana started, once again, to panic. "Where is he, Dad? He should have been back by now."

"Calm down. Maybe he checked in with Lindsay. Ask her again." her father answered. He didn't show it, but he would have had to admit that it wasn't like Joseph to be away from the clinic this long, and be out of touch.

"I think we ought to call the bank and freeze the accounts," Ana said for the fifth time today. "Something is going on, and it's not right." Her mind was racing. Suddenly she asked her father if he had Hamilton's parole officer's name and number. "He ought to be notified!"

"About what?" Gus asked her.

"Dad, he has a guy in here fixing the elevator. That is going to cost us $50,000." That wasn't exactly true; certainly not yet. But she excused herself because she was trying to make a point. She went on, "He and Figgit are in the process of buying 30 some odd thousand dollars' worth of *used* equipment . . . from God-knows-who!" She wasn't finished. "He wants to give everyone around here a raise . . . he wants to hire I-don't-know-how-many-part-timers." She took a breath, and went on, "And we're going to do this with money we've borrowed?" She could not understand why her father was not as worried as she was.

"We also have received reimbursements from the state. Large reimbursements! Don't forget that." He smiled at her. "We have to calm down," he said, meaning *she* had to calm down. "What we need to do is sit down with him and go through this."

"Fine! That's a great idea." she nodded in agreement. "Okay, where is he?" She waited a minute to let the question hang in the air. "He is GONE!

VANISHED! He was supposed to be here by 11, and it's almost 12. Where is he?"

Gus couldn't answer her question, but he hoped Lindsay could. He walked out to the front desk, and asked her when Joseph and Podalski would be back. She told them she wasn't exactly sure. She didn't say that Sadim had called her, and said he would see her tonight. But he had also relayed a message to her from Joseph that Joseph had had to go to New York City right away, and would be back sometime Friday. She relayed that part of the message.

"Oh my God!" whispered Ana, "He's on the run!"

Damn, thought Gus.

Friday - January 24

"Okay, we think he's in New York," Ana said calmly. She and Gus were sitting in Gus's office. "What we don't know is why or how long he's going to be there. Or even if he's coming back!"

"He said he'd be back today," her father corrected her.

"I'll believe that when I see him walk through the door."

"Let's not panic just because he took a day off," Gus answered her. "He hasn't taken a day off since he got here."

"We should call his parole officer. He's not supposed to just come and go as he pleases." She was nodding to herself. "Do you have the number?"

"Take it easy." Gus was starting to lose his "calm." "I'm sure he's allowed some leeway. After all, all he did was leave the valley. He's still in the state."

"We don't know that. All we know is that he *said* he was going to New York," Ana corrected her father. "He could be anywhere by now." She paused for a moment, and then added, "He could be on his way to who-knows-where by now." Then she hastily added, "With our money!"

Lindsay stuck her head in the door and told them that Joseph was on the main phone line. Before Ana, who jumped at the phone, could reach it, Gus clicked on the speakerphone. The connection was poor, and Hamilton's voice could barely be heard. He said something about being sorry for this sudden unscheduled trip, but it couldn't be helped.

"Where are you?" Ana was nearly yelling.

"In Albany," he told them.

"I thought you told Lindsay you were going to New York."

"I was in New York. I'm in Albany now."

Before Ana could hurl another dagger, Gus cut in. "When are you going to be back?" he asked, and then added, "We have a big game Sunday." He was desperately trying to keep the conversation light.

"Oh, I'll be back in time for practice on Saturday. Don't worry."

"Why . . . " Gus started to say, but he didn't know how to phrase it.

Ana jumped in. "Why did you take off for New York? What's going on?"

"What?" was all they heard Joseph say. "I think I lost you." they heard him say a moment later. Then the line went dead.

"Look, we have to find out what he's doing," she said after a moment's silence. "What's he doing in New York? He's throwing money around like crazy. Where's it coming from? We should do an inventory of our narcotics cabinet." She was working herself into a lather.

"Okay, I'll sit down and talk with him as soon as he gets back."

"No, WE will."

Saturday - January 25

Ana began looking for Hamilton as soon as she arrived at the clinic this morning. Who she found, to her dismay, was the elevator guy, Arnie, again back in the Record Room down in the elevator shaft. In response to her questioning, he assured her that "Hoist" had told him to come back and start doing the preliminary work to fix it. She was incensed that he hadn't cleared this with her, or her father.

A bustle of activity in the lab caught her attention. Upon investigating she was told by Figgit that the negotiations for the new equipment must have gone well, because Joseph had called him to get ready for its arrival. And Figgit was extremely excited because it would include a "bone density table."

Ana spent the rest of the morning just waiting for Hamilton to show his face, but that didn't happen. When she ran out of patience, she had Lindsay call Podalski at home. His wife told Lindsay that he was "in Albany this morning," but assured her he would be back by later today. Gus tried to calm his daughter down, but in truth he had concerns too. The morning at the clinic seemed to never end. Although there wasn't an especially heavy patient load, the tension overhanging everyone made for a very long morning. Every time a door opened Ana came rushing toward it in hopes of seeing Hamilton walk in. By the time the clinic closed for the day, everyone was ready to bolt out the door. Even Gus was eager to go. And it wasn't just because he was looking forward to the practice of the Bombers that was scheduled for 2 PM. The only one who lingered at the clinic was Ana, who still held out hope that Hamilton would show his face.

Practice did start promptly at 2. And everyone but PeaPod and Hoist was there on time. Warm-up exercises had begun when those two popped out from the parking lot, and they soon joined the team on ice. PeaPod, in his newly acquired motorcycle helmet with plexiglass face shield, drew comments from everyone at practice except Gus. He was trying very hard to keep his focus on geetha, and not on the storm raging back at the clinic.

In the next ten minutes the Bombers were practicing new shifts, and also a new formation for free starts. Gus, trying to best to utilize PeaPod's speed in the game plan, introduced several scripted shifts that would allow him to break loose. Roove, Paulie and Hoist were taking turns as titman, and it was apparent to one and all that the depth the Bombers had at this position would be a great advantage.

The practice went well for over an hour, until they began to practice defending against the Blades' dreaded whip. Gus, as well as several others, suggested various schemes to defeat it. But, in all honesty, no one seemed to think that they had solved their dilemma. The problem was obvious, even to the less experienced players. The whip came at them fast, and the defenders had virtually no time to defend it. Not only was the speed a factor, but also its direction couldn't be determined until the last moment when it rotated around the left . . . or right? Bombers moved in and out of the lineup, as they tried to recreate the Blades weapon and defend against it. A contributing factor in failing to neutralize it was the fact that the Blades was the only team in the league to do it correctly. One group after another tried to replicate the execution of the Blades, while other team members tried to stop it. Several times Joseph stood off to the side and watched it. He asked himself several times "There has to be a flaw. Where is it?"

The player review after the tired Bombers called an end to the practice went as the previous ones had. All the Blades were well known to the Bombers. The Blades had no replacement players. The wings were discussed, and preferred match-ups were noted. The Blades' wings were fairly good, and would be stronger than the last two opponents had been.

The conversation got more animated when the topic turned to centers. It was agreed by all that Caveman was very strong, and a fairly good skater for a man his size. And although slightly faster and more agile, only to a very slight degree was Sandman not quite his equal. The real reason they stood apart from other centers in the league was their innate nastiness. Both players led the league in "meanness'! It was asserted by someone that both players had metal inserts in the knuckles of their gloves. Their third center was not as worrisome to the Bombers as the first two. His name was Kip. When his name was mentioned, Joseph heard Paulie say, "I want a piece of that fat bastard." Kip was described as being shorter, but heavier than Caveman and Sandman. He was not as good as a skater either. But he was a very dirty player. Everyone was warned about him.

Finally they got around to the Blades' titmen. The names Gheza and Cobra came up immediately, but were almost as quickly disregarded. The main man for the Blades was Superfly. He was acknowledged as an extremely good skater, and as strong as anyone in the league. He could play equally well within or far outside the rules. He was savvy, shifty, and rarely, if ever, made a mistake. He or Cobra would pilot the geetha during the whip, and both were expert at it.

This brought the conversation back around to the whip. Again players offered suggestions and various observations about it. But no one could offer a sure fire way to defeat it. Everyone agreed that allowing the Blades as few free starts as possible would be a good strategy. No one, however, suggested how that could be done. On this somewhat dreary note the practice ended and people began to go home.

As Joseph unlaced his skates, Gus sat down next to him. "We have to talk," was all he said.

Joseph misunderstood, and shook his head, "Don't know what to tell you. I seen them do it 5 . . . 10 times in their two games. I don't know how to stop it." Gus smiled, and told him he wasn't referring to the whip, but that he wanted to talk about the clinic. He wanted to get a grip on what was going on. "Sure!" said a somewhat surprised Joseph. "Right now? Here?" he asked. Gus assured him that wasn't what he meant, and they mutually agreed to meet for dinner that night. Neither would remember which one suggested that Ana join them. Podalski was sitting nearby as they spoke, and eavesdropped on the conversation. He didn't say anything, but he smiled.

Joseph waited at a corner table in Marie's for the late-arriving Gustafsons. When they arrived, and made eye contact, he waved. Only Joseph smiled. Once settled at the table, there was no small talk. Gus studied the menu while Joseph suggested a wine. Ana just sat there, stone-faced. It was very uncomfortable.

Joseph tried to keep the conversation going, and Gus too contributed. But by the time the entrees were done it was painfully obvious that the situation was strained. Why put this off any longer? Joseph thought to himself. "Okay," he started, "what seems to be the problem?"

Ana sat straight up in her chair. Gus grabbed the floor. "Joseph," he said," Can you fill us in on what is going on?" He looked pained. "I mean, we've discussed recently the possibility of the clinic taking on some part-time help." He cocked an eyebrow at Joseph. "Can we afford it?"

"Not just the clerical help," Ana jumped in. "You talked about adding physicians. And RN's! And on a regular basis."

Joseph looked at Gus, then at Ana. Before he could say anything, Gus asked, "And raises! For our own people. God knows Mena deserves more money for all she does; but can we swing it? I hope you haven't raised her hopes unnecessarily."

"And Lindsay," Ana interrupted. "You told her she would get a raise too. And you told her that she wouldn't have to work the front desk anymore. We're going to hire someone new to do that?"

"I told her we would work on both those things. I was very explicit. I gave her no timetable. She knows that." Joseph was trying to set the record straight. Then he thought that this was a good time to bring up a related topic. "We're also going to have to start paying Phil Podalski more money. God knows he's earned it."

"Okay, we are going to give everyone raises, as well as hire new staff. Part-time AND full time?" Ana cocked her head as if asking if she had got that right. Joseph just looked back at her. "And we are going do all that while we are on some kind of wild spending spree?" Joseph just looked at Ana. Gus watched Joseph. "What have we been buying lately? A new phone system? A copier that does everything but walk your dog? How much was that? $10,000?" She was guessing. "Figgit has so much new stuff coming in; he can't fit it all in the lab. He has cartons stacked in the hallway. Did we buy all this with that loan you slid under the door?" Joseph flinched. "How much did we borrow? I remember the application saying $50,000." She only paused for a second, and then pounded on, "Well, by any estimate, we've spent a lot more than $50,000 lately. Did you take out another loan? Oh, by the way, the *new elevator* may cost more than all those things combined!"

Joseph let her run out of breath, and asked, "Would you like more wine?" She was exasperated, and couldn't respond. He turned to Gus. "Anything you want to add? Or ask? I want us all on the same page."

Gus felt his daughter had asked some very valid questions. He wanted them answered. Joseph added some wine to his glass, and then looked at the two doctors seated with him. "Where do I start?" He smiled. "The Medicaid reimbursements backlog that had built up over the past eighteen months has almost been eliminated. Yes, we are nearly current. And that is due to the extraordinary efforts of Lindsay, and to a slightly lesser degree, Sadim."

Joseph went on to explain that with the tutoring and mentoring of Sadim and the new electronic submission system, the backlog had been successfully entered, processed, and reimbursed over the past several weeks. And under the present circumstances, with Lindsay focusing on accounts receivable and accounts payable, the clinic was now able to monitor its cash flow more precisely. What now remained outstanding were a few isolated cases that the clinic would probably have to "write off." While unfortunate that those revenues would be lost, the bright side was that they were small, and would have a slightly positive tax consequence for the clinic. "They are definitely not a total loss," Joseph told them.

He gave the two doctors a moment to digest that news, and then continued, "As for the loan, it is still outstanding, but the clinic could retire it at any time now. It's been left outstanding for a purpose."

"Why?" Ana mouthed the word.

He explained that he had used that loan to carry them through the year end; it was, at the time, very necessary. But subsequent to that, the clinic had started getting the Medicaid reimbursements and could have paid it off with them. "I decided not to." Joseph said flatly. Ana and Gus both sat back in their seats. Joseph went on to explain he wanted that item on the balance sheet to illustrate how precarious their financial situation was. It was an important component in keeping the IRS at bay while the situation was resolving itself. "We have come to a meeting of the minds with our friends at the IRS. I think that is safely behind us." Then he smiled and said, "Never underestimate the value of a good tax attorney."

Ana reached for her wine glass, and saw it was empty. Joseph poured half his glass into hers. Gus took a long drink of water. "We, Podalski and I, have been able to start forecasting the clinic's financial plan going forward. We have a better idea of what our revenue and expenses are going to be. Thanks again, in part, to the work Lindsay has done. But it's also because we now have a much better picture of what they were in the past. Carl Sufton has been very generous with his time with Podalski, and has been able to fill in a lot of blanks. We are still fine tuning some seasonal adjustments that are still hazy, but we're getting there."

He knew he was opening a can of worms when he went on to say, "We have also gotten a leg up on our expenses due to the first part of a three-part grant from the Kryder Foundation."

"What's the Kryder Foundation?" both Gustafsons asked simultaneously.

"Not What . . . Who . . . Henry Kryder was my boss; the CEO and Founder of OCS Financial, back in New York. He is an extremely wealthy man, and apparently a grateful one too; whose family foundation saw fit to give us a grant for the work the clinic does for some of the less fortunate here in the Wackentute Valley. More is coming, but they heard our distress call and rushed an immediate partial grant to us about two weeks ago. It allowed us to acquire certain luxuries, like a phone system that is dependable; and a copier . . . that we leased, not bought . . . that can function for more than a few days at a time and not break down."

"And will it pay for the elevator too?"

"No, unfortunately." he said, but then brightened and told them, "Arnie's going to give us a good deal on the price. He's apparently a big fan of the Bomber Geetha team! Has been all his life." Neither doctor returned Joseph's smile. Joseph continued, "But that's going to have to be done anyway. We need to get that working." Both the doctors wanted to know why. "We need to be able to take in supplies, etc., etc., etc., and be able to store them in the only space in the building that isn't needed for patient care. That's the basement. There's an awful lot of room down there going to waste. When we move all our excess equipment and supplies to the basement it will free up a lot of space on the main floor for patient care. And that includes expanding the waiting room, which you have to agree is beyond 'cramped.' A functioning elevator will allow freer and faster access for all concerned. We can also install a two story filing system for patient records; which will not only greatly expand capacity, but will free up a great deal of floor space on the main floor."

"The subsequent Kryder Foundation grants will pay for that?" Gus asked.

"No. No, they won't. They are going to underwrite the additional doctors and nurses. The funding for the elevator/floor space program has got another source." They expected him to go on, but he didn't.

After a pregnant pause, Ana asked, "Who's going to pay for that?"

"We've lined up some other grant money for that."

"Who?" Gus wanted to know. Who was going to give them money for an elevator?

It wasn't something Joseph wanted to discuss now, but he knew that it would come up eventually. "Another foundation." he simply said. In an attempt to divert the conversation he started to tell them about the new filing shelves that would hold the patient records. The shelves would be on the racks that would span two floors, and could rotate around, providing an enormous increase in capacity, yet reducing the space it currently occupied on the main floor. He was stopped short by an insistent Gus.

"Who's paying for it? What foundation?"

After a moment's pause, Joseph said, "The Geetha Foundation."

"What . . . ?" She stopped, and then corrected herself, "Who is this Geetha Foundation?" Ana asked in a very controlled, calm voice.

"Me." Joseph said. "I just funded it this week."

"You?" asked Gus, just as calmly as Ana had sounded a moment ago, but there was more than a trace of disbelief in his voice. Then he added, "Funded it with what? How much is this Geetha Foundation grant going to be?"

Joseph looked back across the table at both of them before answering. "Final budgeting isn't complete," he said, "But, all told, we estimate it will come in at between 80 to 100 thousand. Elevator repair, construction, and installation of the new filing system." Gus nearly asked if he meant 80 to 100 thousand *dollars*. Of course, he means dollars, Gus chided himself.

"Where are you getting that money?" Ana asked very slowly. She was more frightened than confused. She realized she had no idea what was going on.

"I'm rich." Joseph said.

It was all too much for the Gustafsons to comprehend. It hadn't been easy even for Joseph to stay abreast of developments as they unfolded, and he was far closer to it than these doctors were. After suggesting they sit back for minute and order some coffee and desert, Joseph started to tell them what had happened.

Ana interrupted again, and reminded Joseph that he had said he was "broke." "I never said that," he corrected her. "I said that my divorce settlement had left me with very few liquid assets. My ex-wife had gotten most of them, and the lawyers working on my defense took what was left." Both Gustafsons looked at him and said nothing. He really didn't want to elaborate, but felt he had no choice. "She was looking for a clean break, and a quick getaway. She wanted cash, and anything else she could quickly turn into cash. She took the beach house because we had a very small mortgage left on it, and she could sell it easily. She wanted the liquid securities we owned and, of course, her jewelry. I got to keep less liquid securities; some art; and a parcel of real estate we owned in Brooklyn. The condo in the city? The cars? They were all leased. I walked away from those. The few pieces of art were sold over time. At a loss! When all was said and done, the cash was unevenly divided. But I was in no position to negotiate at the time."

The coffee was delivered to the table, and the three people there all but ignored it. Joseph picked up the story by going back in time to a year before the divorce, and the "mess in Southampton" surfaced.

He had promised a friend back then that he would sit down and talk with two young engineers who had a start-up company that was trying to develop an idea they had. The meeting was arranged, and they told Joseph they were looking for help. He barely understood what they were talking about, but let them say their piece. They said they needed to quit their present jobs to work full-time on their idea. They also needed work space for the project. And they needed some sort of income for living expenses. By the end of the meeting Joseph was candid, and told them that what they needed was venture capital; i.e., "seed money." And that, unfortunately, was not something that OCS did. He wished them the best of luck, and sent them on their way.

Not too long after that nonproductive meeting, OCS, led by Joseph, was putting the finishing touches on one of the largest financial deals in the city's history. A man with enormous holdings in real estate in and around New York City was nearing his 70th birthday, and had decided to cash it all in. He was selling nearly 30 different parcels of real estate, including everything from vacant lots to a forty story office building in Manhattan.

And there wasn't one buyer for the whole lot, but seventeen different entities purchasing different parts of the liquidation. The complexity of the deal with so many parties involved was enormous. And although there had been glitches all along the way through the myriad negotiations, the deal was coming to a head. And at the very last minute the seller advised OCS that there were two other pieces of land that needed to be included. Or there would be no deal at all!

There was a week to go before the scheduled closing date when he had made this surprising demand. Finding additional buyers in the time available appeared to be impossible. Neither property could be remotely described as "desirable." One was a two-story office building in a commercial area of Queens, and the other was a four-story residential property in a somewhat shabby section of Brooklyn. The building had an empty storefront on the first floor and three two-bedroom apartments above (one of those was also empty). This last minute bombshell resulted in chaos on the executive floor at OCS.

With the scheduled closing looming, Joseph, somehow, came up with a solution. He proposed that the Queens property be donated to a charity the seller knew well. And the Brooklyn property? Joseph bought it himself. At the time he bought it he thought he would just turn around and sell it once the smoke had cleared. His bonus for orchestrating this enormous deal would more than offset any loss he took on the Brooklyn property.

But the two engineers he had spoken with two weeks ago had somehow left an impression. Once the huge real estate transaction was in the rear view mirror, Joseph began to rethink their dilemma. It was, absolutely, not something OCS would care to invest in, but perhaps he could get involved.

He ultimately proposed to the two men that they move into the empty apartment in his building. Additionally he proposed that they set up their workshop in the empty store-front on the first floor. He also suggested that they could quit their current full-time jobs and do some part-time tech support work for OCS, which would provide them with some walking-around-money. The rent for their apartment and the storefront space could be paid in stock in their nascent company. It wasn't worth very much at that time, but by doing it this way the two engineers would have very little out of pocket expenses. After some minor haggling over terms the deal was struck.

"That's where 2BIC came from?" Gus said. Joseph smiled, and nodded.

"For the past five years they have been working on developing a voice activated response system that had quite a few possible commercial applications. Electronic voice recognition . . . voice activated . . . remote controls! The possibilities seem endless. In your car, for instance, once your voice is programmed into it, nothing but your voice can turn it on! Can't steal it if you can't turn it on. Same goes for your TV. Your computer. It's useless to anyone else. And it's smart too. 'Turn on the radio.' It does. 'Turn off the defroster.' It does. And your TV/DVD/stereo system? You just tell it what you want it to do . . . and it does it. No more fumbling with three remotes and twenty two different buttons. They've been at it for years, and nine months ago, they made a major breakthrough."

"And you've been collecting their stock for all that time?" asked Ana. Once again, Joseph nodded and smiled. Both Ana and Gus were thinking about the exact same question. They wanted to know how much stock he had.

"The 2BIC Corporation issued," he paused, and rephrased it, "They had an IPO . . . an Initial Public Offering of their common stock last Thursday." He wasn't really sure that either doctor knew what that meant. He continued with a statement that they both could more easily understand. "They sold 30% of their company to the public. That was 9 million shares at $8.50 each." Joseph could see the both of them trying to quickly do the math in their head. He saved them the trouble. "That works out to 76 million dollars."

"And that means the 25,000 shares you put up as collateral for our $50,000 loan is worth ...." Gus whispered.

Again Joseph did the math for them, "At $8.50 a share that works out to $212,500. And the bank that lent us the money is an afffiliate of the firm that underwrote the IPO. They knew exactly how much the collateral was worth. They were very comfortable lending us the $50,000."

Gus shook his head in amazement for a minute, and then stopped still. He stared at Joseph, "And didn't you say you had more stock?"

Joseph had reluctantly sold some of the stock he owned in the offering on Thursday, but only a small percentage. He, of course, wouldn't tell them, but he had a great deal more. For the past five years they had been paying their rent with stock they had initially, and optimistically, valued at five cents a share. And for the first three years of the arrangement it was, in fact, absolutely worthless. Two years ago they had made a breakthrough that had been very encouraging. And since then they had made small, but steady advances. As of last Thursday the IPO had made Bernie and Barry very wealthy. And the value of the 2BIC Corporation stock that Joseph still held was worth, at current market prices, in excess of 18 million dollars.

"I told you. I'm rich."

Sunday - January 26

Finally, it was game day. The day was sunny, and, of course, very cold! Joseph was up early with an excess of nervous energy. When he was done with breakfast he went for a short jog. This was a routine he had had when he played hockey in college. Once back in his apartment he laid out his uniform and equipment. Slowly he dressed, and, although early, he left for the game.

When he arrived at the pond he was surprised to see so many people already there. It was just after 11 AM and the parking lot was nearly full. He went down to the pond, and saw several players milling around their respective benches. The Blades were the "home team," and had the near side bench. Joseph walked around the pond and went to the Bombers bench.

Tully, Smoke, Magoo, and Jeepers were already there. Nervous mumbled greetings were passed around, and Joseph put on his skates. It was early, but he decided to skate a little to release some nervous energy. He took off his shoes, and laced on his skates, and stepped over the boards. In only a few strides on the ice he felt the nervousness slipping away. He was at home.

He glanced over at the Blade bench and saw some familiar faces and their now familiar uniform. The Blades dressed all in black. Their jerseys, their pants, their gloves and helmets were all black. On the front of their jerseys was an upward-pointing knife that had a gold handle and a white blade. Across the top of the knife the word "Blades" was printed in white block letters. Caveman was there, talking with a group of other Blades. They were talking and laughing too loud, he thought to himself. His years of competitive sports had given him the insight to know that they were as nervous as he was. Then he noticed Bilge standing just outside the circle of players, staring at him.

A few minutes later he saw Superfly arrive. The other Blades lined up to say hello to him. He greeted each man with indifference, almost like a king acknowledging a fawning court. He slowly took off his long black leather overcoat and revealed his supposedly "hand tailored" Blade uniform. (That was the rumor.) Joseph thought he looked big, and even slightly menacing. He definitely cut an imposing figure. He stood off to the side from the rest of the team, and gazed around the pond. Standing erect, with head held high and one hand on his hip, he looked as if he was posing for a statue. He fidgeted with his helmet (a custom-designed polo helmet with a tinted shield that covered his entire face), and occasionally waved to someone in the crowd.

The players on both sides, and even the crowd, stopped whatever they were doing when the SANDUCCI & SONS – FINE MEATS & POULTRY truck began backing down the slope behind the Blades' bench toward the pond. People who had set up picnic blankets in the path of the truck scattered to get out of the way. People pointed and conversations stopped as the truck, beeping its reverse gear warning, approached the edge of the pond. The driver, who was receiving guidance from ten different people, stopped the truck just a few feet shy of the pond's edge. The mechanical tailgate platform on the rear of the truck was raised to the level of the rear door. With much fanfare the rear door on the truck was opened.

One of the Blade's players (it was Rickey Gheza) went into the truck. A moment later he pushed out, with great effort, a covered pallet onto the mechanical platform. The platform was lowered and the pallet was shoved, again with great effort by several Blades, onto the ice. This covered pallet was then guided to center ice by the Blades. Superfly skated leisurely, directly behind it. The dramatic effect of its arrival was noticeable on the Bombers' side too. Since the truck had backed down the slope every Bomber had stopped skating and warming up, and then watched as the covered geetha was ushered to center ice. They, and almost everyone in the crowd, were mesmerized. The Blades who had brought it out skated back a few feet and joined the rest of the Blade team standing there. They shuffled around into a straight line. Caveman and Sandman stood in front of them, nearer to the covered pallet. Superfly slowly approached the front of the Blade formation, and finally stopped right at the pallet's edge. People in the crowd moved around to get a better view of whatever it was at center ice. Superfly began skating again, slowly, very slowly, twice around the covered pallet; never taking his eyes off the Bombers. He stopped between it and his team. He looked around. He looked at his teammates, and nodded. He scanned the entire crowd. Then he looked directly at the Bombers' bench and pulled the tarp off the pallet.

There was a gasp!

There was a geetha. No, not just a geetha . . . but a GEETHA! It was a MOOSE! A curled up...ice-encrusted, reclining moose! There wasn't a single person at Corrigan Pond that didn't doubt their eyes at what they were seeing at center ice. Many people were astounded. Many were amazed. Some people began cheering. It's been said that some people even started crying.
"Is that what I think it is?"
"Holy shit!"
"That can't be! That just can't be."
The Bombers, for the most part, were stunned. A real geetha hadn't been used since before most people there had been born. There was total silence near the Bombers' bench. After a minute or so, Gus's voice was heard. "Get me out there. Someone skate me out there!"
It was Hoist, probably because he was not a native to Wackentute and not caught up in the significance of it all, who offered an arm to Gus. Gus, in regular shoes, leaned on him as they made their way out to center ice. "What is that?" he said to the Superfly. Superfly said nothing. He did not want to break the spell. Gus turned to the referee. "What the hell is going on here?" He asked the referee. The referee was speechless. "Is that real?" asked Gus, peering at the thing on the pallet.

The referee, as stunned as everyone else, said, "This is the first time I'm seeing it too." He turned around and looked at Superfly.

"Yes, it is," said Superfly finally. "We found it Wednesday. What's better than having a genuine geetha for the final championship game?" He paused a moment, then said snidely, "Aren't we lucky?"

Gus continued to stare down at the geetha, and then looked up and said, "There hasn't been a moose in Wackentute Valley for thirty years. Where'd you find it?" He was suspicious.

The Blades had gathered around the geetha by now, and Caveman answered, "Maybe he's been wanderin' up in the backwoods, up in the hills . . . where there ain't no people . . . like a Jedi." That was followed by silence. Some Blades were nodding. All the Bombers there were puzzled.

"Like a Jedi?" asked the referee.

"Yeah," Caveman assured him, "Wanderin' around . . . stayin' outta sight . . . probably shy . . . not let anyone get near him . . . you know . . . just like a Jedi."

Gus looked at the referee, who was just as confused. Hoist broke the stunned silence, "What are you talking about? Do mean the Jedi from the Star Wars movies?"

"No . . . shit man . . . Jedi! . . . those big hairy fuckers that wander around on snowy mountains and the North Pole," said Caveman, who was now getting somewhat exasperated by the failure of these people to understand.

"Yeti? . . . you mean Yeti? Y – E – T – I?" asked Hoist.

"Shit, I don't know how you spell it . . . the big fuckers . . . eight feet tall . . . everyone knows they're out there, but no one ever caught one. Maybe this fuckin' thing's like that." Caveman thought his explanation was sound. He didn't understand what the problem was.

Hoist asked what he thought was an honest question. "Are you confusing 'Yeti' with 'Jedi'?"

"I think Hoist is making fun of you, Caveman. I think you ought to kick his ass," said Superfly, interrupting.

"I'm gonna kick your ass," Caveman said.

Superfly smiled slyly at the Bomber titman before he could say a word. "You shouldn't have said that, smartass." He then turned to his teammates and shouted, "Blades! Back to the bench!" And in a flash they had all skated away, leaving Gus, Hoist and the Referee, White, standing there.

A little less than two weeks ago, a moose had fallen out of the sky and landed in Caveman's lap. That's exactly the way he had described it to Superfly. Caveman had been sitting at the end of the bar in The Cozy Cockfight an hour before closing one night, when he heard a slightly drunk customer talking to the bartender about "a fuckin' moose." A moose? He leaned in closer and got the details.

It seems this customer was from "up north" somewhere, and a month ago a young moose had wandered onto his small farm and taken up residence in his barn. It apparently stayed around because the farmer's kids kept feeding it. Now it wouldn't leave no matter what the guy tried. Caveman, who had been drinking since mid-afternoon and was oblivious of that old piece of country wisdom that stated "there are no good ideas . . . after the third beer," had an inspiration. He took the guy's name and number, and said he might be able to solve his problem. He even promised that the guy would make some money on it. He called Sandman the next day. Shortly after they spoke, he called Superfly. A plan was hatched and put in motion.

On the Wednesday evening before the Bombers game, Sandman made his last delivery of the day and then headed for The Cozy Cockfight. Parking around the back, he emptied the remaining contents from the back of the brand new Sanducci & Son Fine Meats & Poultry refrigerated truck into the cooler in the storeroom in the back of the bar. Completely emptied of meat products, Sandman and Caveman drove the truck 90 miles north toward a small farm near the Canadian border.

Once in the general area they promptly got lost. A phone call to the farmer got them directions to the front gate of the farm where they met the farmer. Standing on the running board of the truck, he directed them to a cluster of small buildings a hundred yards from the house. The truck approached a square pen 50 feet long on each side, with a small building and a barn forming two sides, and high fences in front and back. The truck stopped, and the men got out and followed the farmer to the front fence. Looking over the five foot high top rail, the three men peered into the darkness, and as promised, near the fence at the rear of the pen stood a moose. Over four feet high at the shoulder, Caveman thought that it probably weighed at least 200 lbs. The men stared at it for a few minutes, agreeing wordlessly that this was exactly what they had bargained for. The farmer, who was impatient, broke the silence to remind them what they had come here to do. It was "as promised" and he wanted the $150 they had agreed upon. Caveman and Sandman couldn't disagree; it was a moose all right! Caveman handed over the money, and Sandman went back to his truck and retrieved a rifle. The farmer, who took frequent nervous glances back at his house, asked Sandman if he had ever shot a moose before.

"No" he answered quickly. He looked over at Caveman. Caveman shook his head. "Shot a deer once," continued Sandman, "Hit it in the ass. I had to follow that goddamn thing for two miles before I caught up with it and killed it. Had to shoot it three times." The farmer shook his head in the darkness. He thought these two guys were clowns, but he didn't care. He'd soon be rid of them. He was making some money, and getting rid of the moose. That's all he cared about.

"Make this a one-shot kill, okay," he said. He didn't want to wake his kids or alert his wife about what was going on. And he certainly didn't want the State Police coming around. This wasn't hunting season, and nobody here had a license anyway. He wanted this over and done with, and to get this moose and these guys, on their way, and off his farm, as soon as possible.

Sandman loaded the rifle and laid the barrel on the top rail of the fence. Shifting his stance slightly he took aim. Caveman and the farmer tensed. Moments passed. Then Sandman put the rifle up and said, "Shoot him in the heart, right?" The other two men nodded, although neither was really sure. "Moose heart the same place a deer heart is?" Sandman asked, "A little above and behind the shoulder?" Caveman didn't have a clue.

The farmer thought that that was right, but was starting to worry that this was going to turn out badly. He didn't want to give the $150 back and he was already out the $20 he had spent on the load of vegetables he had bought to use as a lure to get the moose into the pen. The moose was eating everything on the farm he could find, besides what the farmer's kids were giving him. He was breaking down fences. He was shitting all over the place. Hell, he was scaring their chickens! He wanted it gone. "Head shot, man. Hell, shoot it in the head. That'll kill it. One shot. Boom. All done." He said suddenly.

"Not too messy, though. Too messy and we can't use it, remember." whispered Caveman. "Hit it in the eye," he suggested. "Then we can glue it shut, and no one will be able to tell."

"'Hit it in the eye'?" Sandman said turning to Caveman. "Are you fuckin' jerkin' my chain? Who ya think I am? Fuckin' Annie Oakley?"

The farmer tried to get everyone settled down. "Look, you ain't shooting a cannon there. What is it? A 3-0-8? At this range it'll do the job, and not blow his head off. Probably go right through. Neat and clean." He had no idea, but wanted this finished.

The guy sounded like he knew what he was talking about, so it made sense to Sandman. He raised the rifle again, and aimed. The moose, perhaps sensing the danger, began to move. It turned and faced the three of them. Sandman, looking down the rifle's sight, saw right into the moose's eyes. And he thought the moose was looking right back at him. He couldn't move. Caveman and the farmer, not noticing the Sandman's reluctance, tensed again. Seconds ticked by. Then Sandman exhaled loudly and lowered the rifle. Caveman wanting this over sagged with disappointment. The farmer was reaching the end of his patience. The moose, apparently losing interest, turned away. Sandman seized the moment . . . the rifle came up . . . he aimed . . . and fired. The recoil stunned Sandman. The sound made Caveman and the farmer jump. The moose took a half step, stiffened, and fell. The Blades had their geetha.

After Gus and Hoist made their way back to the Bomber bench they were bombarded by the same question from every player. Was it really a geetha? After assuring them all it certainly appeared to be, Gus tried to get them all to regain their focus. Only Hoist seemed unaffected by the Blades' stunning move. With the game only minutes from starting the Bomber players only focus seemed to be the geetha at center ice. The game plan was fading fast.

The first half started with Hoist against Superfly. And Hoist realized immediately that Superfly was as strong and fast as people had told him he would be. He was also quick and nimble. Hoist began to wonder if he was going to be able to handle him. "One shift at a time," he recited to himself, remembering the mantra he had always used when playing against quality teams. He would work hard . . . as hard as he could . . . and let what happens, happen! What he didn't know was that Superfly was having the same thoughts. Superfly was fast coming to the conclusion that Hoist was as good as any titman he could remember. He was strong and quick, and was going to be a challenge.

Both players, after a minute or so went by, redoubled their efforts. Neither one seemed to be gaining an advantage as the contest became a test of brute strength. After three minutes into the contest their muscles began to quiver and their breathing came in short bursts. Sliding slightly first to the left, and then back to the right; a little bit forward . . . then a little bit back . . . neither man was able to gain control of the hairy, curled-up geetha. "The first shift is the trendsetter," Hoist remembered coaches telling him throughout his hockey career. He found some hidden reserve of strength somewhere, and suddenly pushed the geetha, with Superfly trying to resist the move, slowly toward the Blades' end of the ice. The movement was not even ten feet, but it was a definite move in the right direction for the Bombers. Superfly sensed it too and spit more than said, "Poosick."

The word had sputtered out from the contorted face of Superfly, but Joseph heard it clearly. Joseph wondered if he had tried to say something and his Jardine Vault had jumbled it; or had he just grunted? Whatever it was, it caught him off guard and he lost his focus and momentary advantage. But the move had made Superfly lose a small piece of his confidence and he instantly decided to play for a halt.

When two titmen would pin the geetha to the sideboard, or otherwise create a stalemate, White would call a "halt." That would award a free start to one, or the other team, who would take alternate turns. The Blades, being the home team, had the free start after the first halt. Superfly, of course, knew this and played for the "halt" by steering the geetha toward the sideboard and pinning it there with Hoist on the other side. When White blew his whistle for the halt, Hoist was barely able to muster the strength to skate back to his bench. When he reached the sideboard it was an effort for him to step over it. He took two steps to reach the bench and collapsed onto it. He asked no one in particular how much time was left in the game, thinking it had to be nearly over.

Superfly was incredibly tired too, but he wasn't going to miss his turn at the whip. The whip was the Blades' pride and joy. It was a scoring opportunity, and Superfly didn't like to share those with anybody. His line mates, Caveman, Dougle and Rowinski, were tired too after the unusually long first shift, and were replaced for the free start by Sandman at center and McKie and Smitty on the wings. But there was also a strategic move here too. While Caveman, Dougle and Rowinski were stronger for the most part than the other three, the latter group was, by far, better skaters. And as such, were better suited for the whip.

The four Blades gathered down at their start spot, and spoke quietly with each other. Superfly, peeking up at the Bombers' lineup as they formed at the center line, noticed that Hoist was not out there. That, he considered, was a small moral victory after the brutal confrontation they had just had.

White blew his whistle to resume play, and the Blades began skating toward center ice, where the Bombers awaited them. Skating slowly, they weaved left and right, trying to mask their attack plan. Everyone, of course, knew that they would employ the whip. What was unknown was whether it would come from the right, or the left. They increased their speed as the approached the center line. Suddenly they formed a straight line, one behind the other. The Bombers really weren't surprised, knowing it was coming. As the Blades neared the center line they were skating very fast with Superfly, pushing the geetha, trying very hard to keep up with his speeding teammates. Sandman, the one in front, suddenly reached behind him and joined hands with the second man in line, Dougle. Dougle, in turn, reached behind him to join hands with Rowinski. Rowinski, without looking, simply put his hand back knowing that Superfly would be there. And he was.

At this precise moment Sandman knew he was at the center line, and therefore began his pivot. Digging his skates in for leverage he began to swing his body around in a tight pirouette. Centrifugal force brought Dougle flying around Sandman at very high speed. And, in turn, Rowinski came around the formation at a dizzying speed. The grasp of every man in the chain was essential, of course, for its success. But the last man, Superfly, was not held by that third man. It was Superfly who held the wrist of the third man. Because the release of the titman in the whip had to be at exactly the right moment, it was necessary for the titman to decide when that exact moment was. And Superfly trusted only himself to make that decision. Superfly grabbed the wrist of Rowinski firmly and tucked knees up onto the geetha. He was riding on top of the geetha, using the force and momentum of his three teammates up front to propel him. It was poetry in motion. The Blades had perfected this maneuver over the years, and were far and away the best team at doing it. And this time was no exception; they carried it off flawlessly.

Although the four defending Bombers knew what was coming, they did not know whether the Blades would spin to the left or right until the last second. That left only two defenders on each side to stop the titman. And the titman came around that corner at such a high velocity that only by being directly in its path would the defender be able to deflect it away from their pezzle.

Paulie, of the Bombers, was the closest defender when Superfly came around the turn, and despite lunging, he barely touched him as he went by in a blur. Once clear of the defenders line, Superfly put his skates back on the ice and steered the geetha into the Bombers pezzle with ease. The Blades were winning, 1 – 0.

Superfly, triumphant, raised his weary arms to the sky, and skated to the Blades' bench amid the cheers of his team mates and Blade fans. "The first of many," he said to anyone who'd listen. "The first of many."

The triumphant Blades left their line out there for the next face-off, only putting in Cobra at titman for the exhausted Superfly. The Bombers countered with Roove at titman, with Magoo centering, and Smoke and Whitey at the wings. Only thirty seconds into the play, Roove was able to pin the geetha in a corner and create a halt. The Bombers had their first chance at a free start.

The same lineups stayed out on the ice, as the Bombers planned to try to neutralize the linemen of the Blades, and try to get Roove isolated on Cobra. (They unfortunately did not have the whip in their arsenal of plays.) He was stronger to begin with, and with momentum behind him they felt he would easily overpower the Blade. They were right, and it should have worked. But in the ensuing charge by the Bombers someone lost his footing, someone slipped, someone fell into a slightly off balance Roove, and the geetha slid away.

When the game continued, the ensuing struggle looked like it would be a standoff by the two lines. The only clear advantage was between the two titmen. Roove continually pushed the geetha deeper into the Blades end. Unable to create another halt, the Blades called for a switch, and a tiring Smoke lost track of his opponent, McKie.

McKie wasn't the strongest or fastest skater on the ice, but he was an experienced player. Realizing he was free of a blocker for an instant, he turned immediately toward the geetha with the intention of double-teaming the Bombers' titman.

Roove never saw him coming, and was hit from behind by the onrushing wingman, and sent sprawling. Cobra, suddenly free of the stronger Roove, began skating furiously up the ice. No one on the Bombers could catch him, and he scored easily.

The Blades were up 2 – 0, and just as importantly had allowed Superfly, and his line mates, several minutes of rest on the bench. But when Superfly and Caveman returned to the ice they didn't have their two usual wingmen with them.. Hoist, Moonie, Tully and Jeepers went out after them.

As the two sides began battling each other, Paulie and B-Ball were on the sidelines still comparing notes on being defeated by the whip. Paulie was the first to notice that instead of Dougle and Rowinski, the Blades were using Kip and Pops at wing. He let B-Ball know, and the two men glared out at the pair of Blades.

"Is Paint out there too?" B-Ball growled. Their eyes darted from one Blade to another trying to see the identity of the other Blades under the helmets.

"No, that's Superfly and Caveman," said the resigned Paulie. "Don't worry," he added, "We'll get our chance. We'll get our chance."

From the start of this shift the action had drifted back into the Bombers' end. But as the battle entered its fourth minute, it was starting to edge in the other direction. Kip and Pops were getting tired. The struggle between Caveman and Moonie was epic. But they were also starting to wear down equally.

The wings of both teams had drifted away from the centers and the titmen as the struggle went on. Hoist tried to steer the geetha behind the Blade center who was preoccupied fighting with Moonie. Hoist was using an old tried-and-true strategy that made the Blade center the only one of the four with his back to the geetha. After finally achieving the position he wanted, he called out a switch for he and Moonie. But the crafty Superfly had seen it coming, and when Hoist released the geetha to blindside Caveman, Superfly pushed the geetha into the feet of the departing Bomber titman. Hoist went down like a tree. Moonie attempted to reach the fast-departing, unencumbered Superfly but Caveman held him off. Superfly scored the third goal of the game for the Blades. The following celebration and chatter from the joyous Blades' bench could be heard all over the pond.

"Three nothing. Three fuckin' nuthin'!!"

"We gonna kill 'em"

"Gonna bring that trophy home today, man. Gonna bring it home!"

The Blades were, by now, starting to feel very good about themselves, and beginning to think the game was well in hand. Superfly decided to take another breather with his first line, and sent out Cobra, Sandman, McKie and Smitty.

Hoist was furious with himself. He insisted on going out again on the next shift. And after glancing toward the Blades' bench, he took Paulie, B-Ball, and PeaPod out with him. His mind was working very fast. He told B-Ball to occupy Sandman, and "don't let him go." He instructed Paulie to "dance" with McKie for 15 seconds than lose him, and take out Smitty.

"PeaPod? You are going to have to hold on with Smitty until Paulie arrives." PeaPod nodded that he understood. "Then when Paulie takes out Smitty, you head for the geetha. I will take out Cobra, and leave it sitting there all alone for you!" Everyone nodded, and then moved to the center line for the next start.

These sorts of things always look good in the planning stage. And, truth be told, it was a good plan. Hoist, despite Cobra's shiftiness, was steering the geetha as far away from the other players as he could. Right from the start B-ball began manhandling Sandman, and Sandman wasn't used to that. The surprised and resentful Blade center didn't try too hard to escape, but rather fought back at B-ball, trying to give as good as he got. He was getting a beating, and he didn't like it.

The trouble was at the two other spots. PeaPod was taking a pounding from the much heavier and stronger Smitty, while waiting for Paulie to arrive and relieve him. But Paulie was having a terrible time trying to break away from McKie, who was clutching and grabbing with wild abandon. After what seemed like a very long time to poor PeaPod, Paulie finally broke loose and descended on Smitty.

Once Smitty saw that he was about to be double-teamed, he turned his full attention to the Bomber who posed the bigger threat, Paulie. A freed up PeaPod wheeled around and skated as fast as he could toward the two battling titmen. McKie viewed all this from twenty feet away, and had no illusions about chasing down PeaPod.

Hoist and Cobra saw PeaPod coming at high speed. Hoist turned back to Cobra and smiled. He said something about precious parts of Cobra's body were about to be crushed. Cobra's obvious instinct was to defend himself, but how could he do that and maintain control of the geetha? The question was still swirling around his head when Hoist came over the top of the geetha, and landed on him. They both fell to the ice. PeaPod arrived a second later, got behind the geetha, and went unimpeded down the ice for the Bombers first score.

An exhausted Joseph, an exultant PeaPod, and their two line mates joined the other Bombers at their bench celebrating their goal. With nearly six minutes left in the first half the Bombers had started their comeback.

The starting lineup for the Blades came out for the next start. The Bombers sent out their starting lineup too, but Roove was subbing for the very tired Hoist at titman. The sides played to a stand-off. The centers and wingmen were very evenly matched. Each team tried a switch or two, trying to confuse its opponents and create an opportunity, but the two lines stayed at each other's throats.

And in over four minutes of running time, Roove played the much-heralded Blade titman, Superfly, to a standstill. Using every Geetha tool he possessed, Superfly could not get the best of Roove.

As they played on, Superfly saw White raise both arms indicating they were in the last minute of the half. In a burst of inspiration he stopped pushing the geetha, and allowed Roove to push it, unopposed, to the sideboard. And there Superfly pinned it.

Roove was sorely disappointed he had fallen into that trap. There was less than a minute to go in the half, and the Blades would now have another chance with their whip. In an attempt to stop it the Bombers sent out their strongest players, Moonie, Magoo, and B-Ball, to man the front line. They selected PeaPod to play "the chaser," the position twenty yards behind their line.

It didn't matter. The Blades executed their whip with precision and power. Propelled by a whip of Sandman, Smitty and McKie, Superfly was launched through the defense untouched, and even went past the fleet PeaPod before he had a chance to react. The Blades' score made it 4 – 1, and they had their 3 point lead back again.

The Blades cheered the play. The Bombers watched in silence. The only one who said a word was Hoist. Gus, standing next to him, heard him say to himself, "That's not a whip . . . It's a chain!"

The remaining seconds of the half were played out with Paulie battling Cobra. Paulie pushed the geetha into the Blades' end, but there wasn't enough time left to mount a serious scoring threat. The half ended with the Blades leading 4 to 1.

The Bombers' sideline was quiet during halftime. There were idle conversations and some false bravado among the mostly depressed players. Hoist checked the free start rules with Gus. Getting the answers he needed, he went off and sat with PeaPod by themselves.

Paulie was talking to Gus. "I ain't shittin' yer. It was movin around. I felt it." Gus thought he must be mistaken. "Could it be having ...." Paulie searched his brain for the right words. "You know, Gus, sometimes people jerk around after they're dead."

"Postmortem tremors?" Gus suggested. Paulie nodded. "Well, I'm not a veterinarian, but I suppose it's possible. It's not totally uncommon for people. But for humans, it usually happens shortly after death, if at all." He thought about it for a moment, and then added, "But this moose died nearly a week ago, according to Caveman. That's too long, I think."

Paulie ended the discussion by saying, "I'm tellin' you; it moved."

"You know what's more amazin' than that?" asked Roove standing behind them. "I didn't see no exit wound! You'd think a head shot would go right on through."

Before a startled Gus could ask Roove what he meant, Hoist asked the three of them to join PeaPod, Moonie and him for a short strategy session. He wanted to talk to all them about the whip.

Back across the pond, on the Blades' sideline, the players were relaxing in the last few minutes of halftime. Tony "Sandman" Sanducci was trying to relax, but he was worried about the second half. In the first half he had paired up against the center of the second line of the Bombers, which meant he was facing Magoo. Sandman and Magoo were fairly evenly matched. Although Magoo was perhaps a little stronger, Sandman was the better skater. But on Sandman's last two shifts on the ice in the first half he hadn't faced Magoo. Magoo had been replaced by B-Ball. Sandman had struggled against B-ball. Now he was the better skater by more than a little, but B-ball was short, squat and far stronger. Sandman was having trouble controlling him. In fact, B-ball had tossed him around fairly easily! Avoiding contact with the opposing center was not an option for him, but he knew he couldn't match up with him. If the Bombers stayed with that lineup, it could spell disaster. He wondered if they would, or would he get lucky by them switching back to Magoo?

Ricky Gheza was the third line titman for the Blades, and as such, didn't get very much ice time. He was a fairly good skater, tall and a bit on the thin side, but with long arms and legs. Physically he was on a par with most players; it was the mental part of the game that escaped him. Verbal signals and remembering formations were a just a bit out of his reach. But he was okay with that. He knew perfectly well that Superfly would take all the minutes he wanted, and Cobra would also try to play as long as he could. That didn't leave very much playing time for him. But frankly, that was just another thing in the very long list of things in life that didn't bother him.

Gheza, who was one of the few players in the game without a nickname, was tapping his toes together to the tune of "Yellow Submarine" as he passed away the time during halftime. He was looking around noticing for the first time today the size of the crowd. It was the largest he thought he had ever seen at a Geetha game. As his eyes passed over the pond in front of him he saw the referee standing at center ice with the geetha at his feet, and a thought occurred to him (a somewhat uncommon occurrence).

What are we gonna do with the geetha?" he said to the player sitting quietly next to him.

"What?" asked Sandman, somewhat annoyed at the verbal intrusion.

"What do we do with the geetha after the game? We gonna bring it back to the victory party?" he asked.

"I don't think Caveman wants the fuckin' thing back at the bar. Just stink the place up," Sandman said. The victory party had already been planned to be held immediately after the game at Caveman's smaller bar in Port Newhampton – The Cannon Factory. But the plain truth was that putting a week old moose carcass in that place wouldn't have really detracted from its ambience even a little bit. How it maintained its license from the Board of Health to stay open was a tribute both to "creative" negotiations with

Health Inspectors, and to the fact that the entire building was so encrusted with dirt that it couldn't fall down. Using the restrooms at the Cannon Factory was an act of valor. Sandman wasn't looking for conversation, and wanted Gheza to shut up, but Gheza persisted.

"I think we oughta take it back . . . kinda like it's a trophy, or somethin'." Gheza said as he twisted around and looked up behind the bench. "Your truck is gone . . . how we gonna get it back to the party?" he said, still looking all around the slope up behind the bench.

"We don't need that goddamn thing as a trophy. We gonna get the real trophy from Newcomb right afta the game. We don't need that piece a shit." He twisted his head around to where his truck had been just to check what he already knew. "Yeah, I know my truck is gone. My father took it. He's gotta go pick up a whole shitload of stuff at the wholesalers." Exhaling, he reverted back to the first topic. "Look, man, Caveman don't want it back at the bar. Forget it." Sandman was thinking of getting up and walking away. He had a lot on his mind facing him in the second half. He started to rise.

"It's already got a 'whole shitload' of shit in it," answered Gheza.

A puzzled Sandman stopped and looked at Gheza. "What are you talkin' about? My truck? The back was empty . . . except for the geetha. I emptied it out myself when I went and got the fuckin' geetha."

Gheza shook his head no. "Geetha shit the truck, man," Gheza said nonchalantly. "Your dad gonna clean it out?"

"No, my Dad's not . . . what?" Sandman said, "What are you talkin' about?"

Gheza knew shit when he saw it. "Thing shit the truck. Shit all over the floor back there. I know; I was back there." Sandman started shaking his head in disbelief, but Gheza continued, "I pushed that damn thing out on the pallet when you got here. Remember? I was back there. Were you?" Gheza was insistent. Sandman hadn't been in the back of the truck since he put the geetha in there on Wednesday night. He had looked in the back this morning when he got the truck, but had only glanced. When he had got to the pond this morning he had stayed behind the wheel of the truck to back it down to the edge of the pond. He hadn't trusted anyone else to drive the truck. If he had scratched, or dented, or damaged the truck in any way his father would kill him. He had used the refrigerated truck to store the geetha since he had "obtained" it Wednesday night. Using every deceitful bone in his body, he had kept the carcass in the back of the truck and out of the sight of his father. He had cleaned out the back of the truck to avoid any chance of contaminating any food products. Now his father had taken the truck to the wholesalers to pick up a huge order of meat they needed for next week's deliveries. The state inspector would undoubtedly be there. And Gheza was saying that the geetha "had shit the truck"!

"Fuckin' thing is dead. Dead geethas don't shit!" Sandman yelled angrily at Gheza.

Dougle, a wing-man, was standing there listening. "Sounds like the title of a movie. 'Dead Geethas Don't Shit.'" He thought it was funny.

"Sound funny to you? This ain't fuckin' funny, asshole." All Sandman could think about was his father's face when the state inspector looked inside the truck and saw the moose shit. Sandman was having a very bad day. Just then the referee blew his whistle, and motioned both teams to send out the players for the beginning of the second half.

Superfly led Caveman, Dougle and Rowinski out to center ice. This was, in his mind, the best combination that the Blades had. He watched as Hoist, Moonie, Tully and Jeepers came out from the Bombers' bench to join them at center ice to begin the second half. Superfly, caught up in the excitement of a 4 to 1 lead with only a half left to play for all the marbles, turned quickly to his teammates, took his Vault from his mouth and blurted out before the Bombers got close, "One more goal . . . that's all we need . . . They'll quit if we *daggle* just one more goal!" The Blades nodded knowingly.

"Daggle?" Rowinski asked Dougle quietly as they skated a few feet away. Dougle just shrugged. The two teams lined up. After a moment's hesitation the referee blew his whistle to start the last 20 minutes in Wackentute Valley Geetha League history.

The struggle between Superfly and Hoist was as intense as any Geetha match had ever been. A minute into the second half, the geetha was pinned against the sideboards. And both teams, with their best lines on the ice, and still fresh from the halftime break, deployed for a Bomber free start.

The strategy they used might have been different, but the result for the Bombers in their second attempt was exactly like their first attempt. The three linemen raced up the ice in front of Hoist, veering slightly to their left. At the last moment Hoist had planned to cut to his right. He either tripped, or just cut too sharply and fell. In any case the attempt went for naught.

When the game restarted, the titmen resumed their epic battle. Superfly, with his confidence rebounding because of the failed Bomber free start, used every trick his much longer experience had taught him to put this game on ice. He used every ounce of energy, strength and guile he possessed. But Hoist held him off.

The geetha moved slowly in one direction for a moment or two. But then back it came the other way. Neither man could gain a clear advantage. The men circled the geetha as it slid forward and back, from side to side. But never did it move any appreciable distance from where it had started. Both men were becoming exhausted, but neither would surrender to the other. After several minutes of nonstop exertion, the geetha slid slowly toward the Blade bench. Hoist could hear the labored breathing of Superfly, and suddenly thought that Superfly might be playing for a stoppage. The Blades would get the next free start. When the two men, still struggling furiously, pushed and shoved the geetha into the sideboard, Superfly held it against the boards, content to have that stoppage. The whistle blew. The two men looked at each other. Superfly smiled smugly. He was exhausted after the lengthy battle, but he considered it a victory. He grabbed Cobra as he stepped over the boards, and whispered in his ear. "Ice it!" was all he had the breath to say.

Joseph was spent, as tired as he had ever been, but he wasn't coming off the ice. Not now! Gathering what strength he had left, he skated to the far side Bomber bench and collected the three players who would join him as they defended the Blades' free start, and their notorious whip.

"We've talked about this. We all know what we have to do." He looked directly at PeaPod. "Remember, it's up to us. You or me. You have to hit him at the right time. Not too soon . . . and sure as hell not too late!" The Bombers - Hoist, PeaPod, Roove and Paulie — skated out to the half line and watched as the Blades formed up at their start spot deep in their territory. The Bombers spread out into a standard "box" formation with Hoist and PeaPod lined up on the half line 20 feet apart. Roove and Paulie lined up 20 feet behind them. "Play off me . . . don't move too much . . . just move as much as I do," he instructed his teammates. Joseph could see PeaPod's still-blackened eyes peering out from behind the face screen of his helmet. "And when the second man grabs hands . . . when they cross that line . . . you've got to be going . . . going HARD!" PeaPod nodded. They had gone over it several times at halftime. Joseph reassured himself that PeaPod understood what had to be done. But he also wished that the whip the Blades would do would be one going to his left. That would place the responsibility of breaking the . . . the CHAIN . . . before it snapped on himself, not PeaPod.

The Blades gathered down at the start spot and talked among themselves. Gesturing and glancing up the ice at the Bombers, they finally gave each other high fives and fist bumps, and then started slowly skating toward the Bombers. As they started to skate they did not notice that the Bombers were slowly backing away from the half line, and had made sure the referee knew they were doing it.

Superfly, on the sidelines, saw them backing up too, and wondered why. He also noticed that Hoist was still on the ice. He was suspicious, but felt in a few moments that his team would score off their whip, making the score 5 to 1, and that would all but ice the game.

Sandman led the way toward the half line, skating slowly at first then picking up speed. Smitty and McKie, the two burly wingmen, weaved back and forth behind him. And behind them, Cobra pushed the geetha hard in an effort to stay up with the other three. They gathered speed as they approached the Bomber formation, which they failed to notice was well behind the center line. As they slowly increased their speed they still had not tipped off which way they were going to snap their whip.

Sandman was now moving very fast when he suddenly twisted his torso around and reached back with his left hand for McKie, who was to be the second link. They were coming around our right side thought Joseph. He shouted out the word "Go!" for PeaPod, but PeaPod had seen it already, and was moving.

McKie, while grabbing Sandman's hand, twisted himself around searching for Smitty's hand. Joseph, Roove and Paulie began moving slowly to the right in anticipation of the geetha coming around that end. PeaPod was hurtling at his target.

The Blades didn't notice them move. They were too busy lining themselves up by grasping each other's hands, and gaining speed. Sandman turned his head toward the Bombers to judge where to make his pivot. He knew it ought to be as close to the defenders (whom he assumed would be at the centerline, not 15 yards beyond it) as possible. And when the whip snapped, it would leave no time or space for them to intercept the now rocketing titman and geetha. He approached the defender on the left and gauged the distance. That would be the defender that would have to contain the geetha as it rocketed around their left wing.

Sandman suddenly swerved hard to the right and started the rotation. His eyes were on that left defender, but his peripheral vision caught sight of something on the right. McKie felt Sandman's grip tighten on his own as the Blade center started the rotation. He also felt Smitty's grip as he began the violent turn. He watched the defender out in front of him slightly to the left. He was suddenly puzzled when something else appeared directly in front of him. It hadn't been there an instant before! It took only a split second for him to recognize what it was. It was his skates!

For an instant he wondered why his skates would be chest high out in front of him. Why, he wondered, was he was flying through the air? This wasn't good, he instantly determined. Realization led to panic. He released his grip on both Sandman and Smitty. The fact that the other two didn't make a simultaneous release resulted in his aerial course becoming frighteningly erratic. He had no idea how this had occurred. He was sailing through the air at very high speed totally out of control . . . and he knew he was going to hit something very hard very soon. Smitty, on the other hand, had seen . . . something? . . . hit McKie's legs from behind, and send him airborne. He came to the conclusion in a flash that it would be best to save himself. McKie's hand was released easily but the trailing Cobra was still holding on. Smitty yanked it as hard as he could, and released the unsuspecting Cobra.

Throughout the crowd you could hear a collective "gasp" as the Blade titman was now on his own. Perched on top of the speeding geetha, and looking for the clear path to the pezzle, he suddenly realized he was no longer connected to the whip. There was no 'clear path" in front of him. There was no clear anything in front of him.

And everyone heard him as he moaned a deep, prolonged "whoooooa". He felt himself sailing along on top of the speeding and wildly spinning geetha. He was going very fast, but because of the spinning he did not know in what direction. Perhaps pilots in plummeting jet planes would appreciate the thought process Cobra went through at this time.

"Get out . . . you're out of control . . . save yourself!" he thought to himself, and he pushed himself up into the air, off the geetha. Somehow managing to land on his skates an agonizingly long one second later, he knew he was traveling fast. He fought to regain his balance and sense of direction because he knew he probably only had seconds before disaster struck. His awareness of where he was came quickly. With his skates miraculously squarely underneath him, and his arms outstretched for balance, his eyes focused on the scene now directly in front of him. It was the end of the Blades' bench, only ten feet away! He was heading out of bounds! He barely had time to leap into the air, before his feet would crash into the sideboards.

When Superfly had led his teammates off the ice a few minutes ago it was not only the Blade's titman who had been exhausted. Caveman had had just finished an epic struggle against the equally tired center for the Bombers, Moonie. Caveman collapsed on the end of the bench and slumped over, totally spent. It was not only the effort he had just put out that that caused his weariness, but also the fact that he had at least another 15 minutes more to go, and he wasn't sure he had enough left in him. As he sat there breathing heavily, Bilge suddenly appeared standing over him. Usually Superfly did not allow any "civilians" access to the Blade players during a game. The bench area was clearly off limits to non-players. But no one, not even Superfly, could tell Bilge what she could or could not do.

"Whatcha lettin' him push you around for?" she asked. Caveman didn't want to hear this, but he had to save all his fight for the ice. He sat silently. "You oughta be smackin' that fat bastard all over the place." She wasn't finished. "Geez, Bill, you can't let 'em do that," she complained. Caveman wanted to explain that he wasn't "letting" him do it. Moonie was as strong as a plow horse. But Caveman just wasn't up for an argument right now. He started to look up at her to ask her to back off, but suddenly stopped.

She was looking down at him, willing to let him explain his shortcomings, when she saw him look past her, and out toward the ice. And his eyes got very wide. Her peripheral vision saw something coming at them from the ice on the right.

Psychologists tell us that when humans are suddenly confronted with an unexpected threatening situation they will usually react in one of two ways. "Flight or fight" is the way that they describe those two alternate reactions. And they say that the more normal reaction of the two, i.e. more than 95% of the time, the reaction will be "flight". Most people will instinctively flinch, or retreat, from a sudden unexpected threat. But Bilge wasn't "most people." The fast approaching, airborne, out-of-control Cobra sailed over the sideboard and was coming right at Bilge. And Bilge, as if she had been getting ready for this very thing for the past two months, put her right foot back ten inches for leverage, planted it firmly, and shot a thunderous right hand into the chest of the incoming Cobra. She stopped him in mid-flight, cracking two ribs and knocking him cold.

"Christ Almighty, Babe. I think ya killed him," Caveman finally said as he, and several other people looked down at Cobra lying very still on the ground where he landed.

The rest of the Blades from that line were not much better off. Sandman, who had been in the middle of the pivot when McKie had let go, went down hard. The centrifugal force of the pivot man could only be controlled by the drag of the trailing wingmen's weight. When they released their grip, Sandman was victim of forces he couldn't hope to understand. Moving with a speed his skating skill didn't recognize, he lost his balance and was suddenly parallel to the ice. Gravity took over and deposited Sandman awkwardly, forcefully, back onto the ice.

Smitty, the third man in the chain, didn't fare any better. When he was released by McKie, and he in turn had broken free of Cobra, he had fallen hard onto his back as he slid toward the sideboards. His arrival at the sideboard was neither slow nor graceful. The "silver lining" of the collision was that, at least, he didn't crash in headfirst. He hit the sideboard on his right side (and couldn't raise his right arm over his head for the next several days). Oddly enough, in retrospect, he was grateful to get off that easily. It was McKie, of all four line mates, who suffered the longest term injury. It was McKie that PeaPod had submarined.

As the Blade line mates joined hands and gained speed, they approached what they thought was the center line. PeaPod began inching forward, whispering to himself, "Oh man . . . Oh man . . . Oh man." As they crossed the actual center line and started to whip to their left, PeaPod skated hard at their backs, repeating "Oh man!" to himself out loud. And as their line began to circle around, PeaPod, who was now moving at maximum speed and shouting, "OH MAN!", dropped into a very low crouch and hit McKie in the back of his knees.

McKie never heard him shouting and, more importantly, never saw him coming in the instant before his skates went off in different directions. The feet inside those skates, naturally, went with them. The ankles above those feet followed them. The two legs followed suit, and also went in those same different directions. The divergence ended there. The pain was instantaneous, and McKie knew immediately that life would never be the same. Perhaps it was a blessing that when McKie hit the ice, it was headfirst. The momentary unconsciousness was a temporary reprieve from the "fire down below".

Hoist dodged bodies as they flew by him. After a moment, he realized he stood at center ice with no Blade anywhere nearby! He saw Sandman lying on the ice, apparently stunned. Both McKie and Smitty were lying near the sideboards, and Cobra was . . . was missing! He did see the geetha sliding slowly on the ice nearby, after apparently rebounding off the sideboards. He skated to it quickly and guided it, unopposed, down to the Blade pezzle for an easy goal. After knocking off the pezzle, he turned around and again took stock of the players on the ice. Paulie and Roove were chasing him down the ice, cheering wildly. And then he saw PeaPod sitting on the ice, pumping his fists in the air and yelling his head off. It was now 4 to 2. The Bombers were in the game.

The Blades, on the sideline, stared out in stunned silence. They didn't seem to know what had just happened to them. Sandman began picking himself up off the ice very slowly. He had taken a very nasty fall and was hurting all over. Smitty was getting up just as slowly. He too had fallen hard, and he had also crashed into the sideboard. Blade players from the bench stepped over the sideboard to help McKie get to his feet. He wasn't able to move under his own power, and was helped onto the bench. Out of the sight of the Bombers, Cobra was being revived on the bench. He was groggy and was having trouble breathing. And he was whispering to anyone who'd listen that he was done for the day. Superfly stared out at the celebrating Bombers congregating near their bench on the other side of the pond. A minute ago the Blades were about to "ice" the game by going up 5 to 1. And with just over 15 minutes to go in the game, the Blades were just about certain the Trophy was theirs. But now it was 4 to 2, and several of their players were probably out for the day. And most importantly, the Blades' most feared weapon, their edge – The Whip – had been defeated. More than defeated, it had been annihilated!

"Gheza," shouted Superfly, "You're in at titman." Superfly was still tired from the opening five minute duel with Hoist. Gheza, with Paint, Kip, and Pops would have to go out and do a shift while the first string rested up a bit more. Superfly called out to these four seldom used players as they started out onto the ice., and instructed them to just go out and hold off the Bombers for as long as they could. "We're still up by two goals, and there's only 15 minutes to go. Just hold them, damnit . . . hold them! . . .

Nissalwix!" The four looked at each other, and then at Caveman for some sort of clarification. Caveman shrugged his shoulders.

The Bombers across the ice were still celebrating their surprising reversal of fortune when White told them to send out a line. Hoist needed a rest, and Gus knew it. Gus told Roove to take the titman position, with a line of Smoke, Magoo and Whitey.

"No! Wait a minute!" shouted Paulie. He was looking across the ice, and saw the new Blade line skating to center. "That's Paint going out there, B-ball. And that fat one is Kip. Yeah, it's Kip. And the other fat bastard is Pops! All three of them are out there. We gotta go out there. C'mon, B-ball. Those are the fuckin' guys we want. This is our chance. Maybe the last chance we get." B-ball was stepping over the sideboard before Paulie finished talking. He never said a word.

"Wait a minute. Don't do anything stupid," warned Hoist, who was too tired to stop them. He worried that a foul committed now could ruin whatever chance they had. He turned to Gus, trying to understand why they had gone out so fast.

Gus, still standing next to him, said, "It's an old grudge. Those guys were at Paulie's wedding when the brawl broke out. They're the ones that smacked Dee Dee." And then he added, "Besides, this late in the game I think White is just going to let us play. I can't see him calling any fouls now, short of Capital Murder." When Hoist heard Gus say that they had "smacked Dee Dee" he turned to him, "Why did they hit the bride," he asked?

"Well," Gus explained, "I think it's because she was biting Kip at the time, and Paint was just trying to get her to unlock her jaws." Gus turned his focus back to the game. "Stay on him, Roove. That's Gheza," Gus called out to him. "He's sneaky quick. Stay on him."

When the game commenced, the stronger Roove began pushing Gheza and the geetha down into the Blades end. The linemen paired up and started a loud and fearsome hand fight amongst themselves. Gheza took advantage of the distraction they caused every few minutes by reaching across the geetha and grabbing Roove's face mask. Roove tried to ignore the infraction, knowing that with only one hand on the geetha Roove could easily outmuscle Gheza. After a few minutes had gone by, Roove was getting the better of it, although Gheza was whacking the hell out of his head. Gheza knew he was losing ground and decided something more drastic had to be done. Glancing around quickly, he noted the location of the various linemen doing battle, and also where White was. Seeing White turn slightly to watch two lineman battle for a moment, Gheza seized the opportunity and leapt across at Roove. Illegally removing *both* hands from the geetha he grabbed at Roove's throat. The quickness of the move caught Roove by surprise. Reacting too slowly, he lost his balance and slipped and fell, leaving Gheza in sole possession of the geetha. Gheza, momentarily facing his own goal, turned slightly and began pushing the geetha laterally across the ice. Behind him Roove had struggled to his feet and started to chase him. And behind Gheza on his right, Magoo and Kip and Paulie and Pops had stopped fighting each other and had begun pursuing him too. Off to his left near the half line, B-ball and Paint had seen his escape and began skating parallel to him across the ice, ignoring each other.

Many in the crowd rose to their feet in excitement. The Blade bench (except for Cobra and McKie) began cheering wildly about this turn of events. The Bomber bench looked on in disbelief at the missed call by White and the desperate state of affairs they were now in. A goal by the Blades now would be a disaster.

It was at this moment that Gheza straightened up, released the geetha, and recoiled in horror with a scream. Everyone on the ice heard him. Everyone at the game heard him. Different people would remember different things about this game in years to come. But they would all remember that scream.

Gheza skated off to the right, looking back in horror at the geetha. Roove was the first one to arrive at the now-unescorted geetha. He slowed it to a stop, turned it toward the Blades' goal, and began moving slowly while looking out for the other players as they closed in on him. Pops had gone further across the ice than the geetha and was now cautiously circling back from the right at it. Kip, also moving cautiously and unencumbered by Magoo, who had initially stumbled, was coming at Roove from the left. Roove watched as the two Blades slowly closed the distance between them and attempted to box him in. He did not know where his blockers were, and was afraid to turn his head to look for them with these Blades closing in.

Ever so wary of Roove faking one way or another, the two Blades closed to within ten feet of the geetha with their eyes like laser beams on their target. Magoo, who was trying to make up for his stumble, was skating faster than his ability allowed, and although trying to collide with Kip, he missed and sailed past. The blur of Magoo going past, missing by inches, distracted Kip for an instant . . . and he never saw B-ball until too late. B-ball, skating faster than he ever had before had Kip in his crosshairs. With arms outstretched, he reached out at Kip, and with his stubby, fat, incredibly strong fingers grabbed handfuls of Kip's thigh muscles and lifted him up off the ice. The scream of Kip probably would have been more memorable than even that of Gheza, had any air escaped his lungs. But it was a silent scream.

Magoo, having missed Kip, saw Pops right in front of him and crashed full speed into the nearly stationary wingman. Pops never even had the chance to flinch. The unexpected arrival of the speeding behemoth Magoo lifted the burly Pops off the ice. He landed on his hands and broke three fingers.

While all this was going on, Paulie had circled around the right of the geetha and had come across behind Roove. He spotted the slow-moving Paint coming up behind the Bomber titman, intending to hit him from the rear. And because the slow moving Paint was so intensely focused on hitting the unsuspecting Roove from behind, he never saw Paulie coming from his right. Paulie bent over at the waist and drove into Paint from the side, at the hip. Paint would limp for weeks.

Roove saw the two Blade wingmen in front of him wiped out by his blockers. He heard Paint's groan behind him, and he could see Gheza skating off, warily, away from him. He had a clear path to the Blade pezzle, and he took it. It was a triumphant moment for Roove as he leisurely skated down the ice and scored the goal that made it 4 – 3. And if it weren't for the twitching movements of the geetha he was pushing, the moment would have been perfect.

The Blade bench was howling at Gheza as he came back to it. Everyone was yelling at the same time. They all wanted to know why he had relinquished possession of the geetha.

"Just gave it away, man. What's the matter with you?"

"How can you just skate away from it?"

"You gave it to them!"

"Are you fuckin' crazy, you sonuvabitch?"

Superfly grabbed him when he got close, and looked right into his eyes. "Are you . . . " he said, too angry to finish his thought. Pulling him closer so that only inches separated their noses, he screamed, "WOGGIN MOTH?"

Gheza had no idea what the question was, but he had an answer. He looked right back at Superfly and said, "It moved, man .... *it moved!* Goddamn thing scared the shit out of me. That thing moved!" he repeated. "I thought you said it was dead. It's a geetha, man, it supposed to be dead!" He was in dead earnest.

Superfly listened to him, and then turned to Sandman and Caveman standing a few feet away. Suddenly calm, he said to them, "It's dead, right? That IS a 'carcass', isn't it?"

Caveman turned and looked at Sandman. Sandman, feeling his day descending into the fires of hell on so many levels, answered quietly and feebly back, "I shot it in the head, man. It's gotta be dead." He paused a moment, hoping Caveman would back him up. Caveman said nothing.

Gheza wanted nothing more to do with the geetha. He didn't tell anyone, but when he had started skating with the geetha he was looking around for Bombers. Then he felt it move. When he looked down at it, it was looking up at him. "Don't send me back out there ...I ain't going. I quit." He wasn't fooling around. He sat down on the bench, and began unlacing his skates. It wasn't easy because his hands were shaking so much.

On the jubilant Bomber side the players were still congratulating one another, but questioning why Gheza had done what he did. Roove thought he had the answer, and pulled Gus aside. "Hey, Doc," asked Roove. He thought he should use "doc", instead of "Gus" because he figured it was a professional question. "Can that thing still be moving? Even though it's dead?"

"What?" Gus asked. "It's moving? Are you sure?" He said nothing about his halftime talk with Paulie.

"Felt like it was." Roove said, but then second-guessed himself and added, "Ah hell. Maybe not. Maybe I just got caught up in the excitement. It was pretty wild out there just now." Hoist came over when he saw them whispering.

"What's going on? You okay?" he asked Roove, thinking he might be hurt. Roove waved him off, and moved away. "What have we got left? About ten minutes, I guess? I think we might be able to pull this off!" he smiled at Gus.

The Bombers sent out their top line of Hoist, Moonie, Tully and Jeepers. The Blades responded with Superfly (who was their only true titman still available) with Caveman, Dougle and Rowinski. Before going out to the center start, Sandman grabbed Superfly and whispered to him, "You wanna take this?"; he gestured to the partially hidden object in his right hand. Superfly looked down and saw, unmistakably, a blackjack.

"Are you nuts? What for?" he asked, confused as to what Sandman was thinking.

"Smack Hoist with it. Or that fuckin' moose, if it moves," answered Sandman, who was feeling very antagonistic by now. Superfly ignored him, and skated out to center ice.

The first thing Superfly did when he approached White was ask how much time was left. White told him that only 10 minutes and a few seconds remained in the game. Although Superfly was worn out, he felt he could hold on for 10 more minutes. "Ten more minutes" he told himself. "Ten more minutes and the trophy is ours forever," he calmly said to the Blades around him. Caveman, Dougle and Rowinski barely heard him.

Hoist, Moonie, Tully and Jeepers came out to face them. Before White could restart the game, Superfly skated back toward his linemen again. Raising his eyebrow and nodding knowingly at them, he leaned in and whispered to them. "Twallat kig" he assured them, and then winked.

When White blew the whistle to begin, both teams started as if they were fully rested. Their intensity and strength felt at the same level they were when the game first started. But as the seconds, then minutes, ticked by, Moonie and Caveman realized their stamina was fading quickly. The two wings from each team again matched up evenly, and were canceling each other out. Switches were out of the question. The stalemate of the linesmen left everything in the hands of the two titmen. And Superfly finally had to admit to himself that he was starting to fade. He thought that Hoist must be just as tired, and tried to rally.

But every time he would twist and change directions, Hoist would counter the move. After what seemed like an eternity, Superfly caught sight of the sidelines and realized he had been maneuvered down into his own end. Glancing around quickly he saw that the Blade pezzle was only 50 yards away, and the geetha was being pushed toward it. He reluctantly realized that Hoist Hamilton was winning. He hoped for a moment that maybe time would run out, but that was just desperation. He tried to rally, but each time he renewed his effort Hoist countered and moved the geetha closer to the Blade pezzle.

The crowd noise was a constant roar now as the players struggled. Growing ever more desperate, Superfly began grunting, and shoving, and swinging wildly at the Bomber titman. And although he frequently connected, it seemed to have little effect on his opponent. Finally, he mounted one huge effort and swung his right arm at the side of Hoist's head. The Bomber saw it coming and backed out of reach. The momentum of the missed swing twisted Superfly around, and caused him to fall flat onto the geetha. That effort, and the resultant fall, caused him to lay motionless for a moment on top of the geetha. Regaining his composure he opened his eyes. Only inches away was the geetha's face, its eyes staring into his ... and then, with its huge pink tongue, it licked his face shield.

" GUPPUS!!!!"

There probably wasn't a single person at the game who didn't hear distinctly what Superfly said. There also wasn't a single person at the game who could tell you what "Guppus" meant. Leaping off the geetha as if it were on fire, he stumbled and fell to the ice. Hoist Hamilton took sole control of the geetha, and zoomed to the Blade's pezzle only 30 yards away. With one minute and 58 seconds to go, the score was tied 4 to 4!

The Bomber bench was ecstatic. Unbelievably, they had tied the score. A win . . . and permanent possession of the Geetha Trophy was within their grasp. A quick strategy session was held between Gus, Moonie, Roove, and Hoist and it was decided they should put the best skaters out there for the final two minutes. Because of the score differential rule they knew they would lose the trophy if the game ended in a tie. They knew they needed to score once more.

When he returned to the team bench everyone was asking Superfly what had happened. Everyone but Gheza, who had a very good idea what had happened. Questions poured in at Superfly, but he ignored them all. Caveman shouted everyone down, and joined with Superfly, Sandman,

Dougle and Rowinski in a small huddle. "Man, we can't panic!" Dougle said to the small group. "Yeah, we're tied, but there's less than 2 minutes left. Remember if it ends in a tie, we win! We're way ahead on point differential, remember? We just got to hold on for two fuckin' minutes."

"Geez, we can do that," said Rowinski. "I can stand in a fuckin' fire for two minutes to win this thing. Damn!" The enthusiastic wingman looked around at everyone, hoping to encourage them all.

Caveman said nothing. He was too tired. Sandman offered nothing. All he could think of was his father, the state inspector and the back of his fouled truck.

Superfly suddenly blurted out. "We lose if that *yillet* gets up and leaves before this game is over." Surprisingly, they all knew what he meant. Everyone stared at him anyway. No one said anything. Superfly looked around the circle of faces, as he wiped saliva off the face shield of his helmet, "If it recovers . . . *from being dead*," he stopped and stared at Sandman, "and runs off before the game is over . . . we have to forfeit. We lose!" He took a deep breath and stared at his teammates. "When White blows that whistle, grab your guy . . . don't let him loose! Just hold on for two minutes." Superfly, now staring again at Sandman, said "Gimme the hammer." Sandman handed him the blackjack.

"Whaddya gonna do with that?" someone asked him.

"I am going to smack the shit out of that geetha if it moves." He nodded. "And Hoist too . . . for good measure."

White was at center ice, and looking very oddly at the geetha after bringing it back to the center line. He was asking himself if he had really felt it twitching as he returned it back up ice. The arrival of the two teams and their joint question about time remaining got him to refocus on the game. He advised them how much, or rather how little, time was left.

Despite their exhaustion Caveman, Rowinski, and Dougle were out there for the Blades. Superfly was, of course, titman. The Bombers, who were not nearly as tired as the Blades, with the possible exception of Hoist, put out who they thought were their best skaters. The Bomber linemen were Roove, Paulie and PeaPod, and Hoist was the titman. Again their strategy was to get some distance between the wings and the titmen, and then have PeaPod break away. Hoist would push Superfly off the geetha, and allow the swiftly approaching PeaPod to grab the geetha and go!

When the whistle blew, all eight players on the ice flew into action. With renewed energy they went full tilt in trying to out muscle, or out maneuver, their opponent. The Blades all knew the game was very close to ending. They wouldn't have to hold on for long. The Bombers knew their window of opportunity to win this was going to be opened only briefly. The battle was joined, and the seconds began ticking by.

White, too, was fully charged up. In the last few minutes of the game . . . of perhaps the last game of Geetha EVER . . . he would have to be sure that nothing the least bit controversial happened.

Hoist jostled with Superfly, and felt he was gaining an advantage. But he kept glancing left and right anticipating PeaPod's arrival. PeaPod was nowhere to be seen! He was matched up with Rowinski on this shift, and the instant the action had started, the exhausted Rowinski had grabbed PeaPod and thrown him to the ice. He then fell on top of him. PeaPod wasn't going anywhere.

Superfly felt himself being edged into his own end. He knew immediately he was too tired to resist the stronger titman any longer. He thought that there couldn't be very much time left, but he could not take the chance. Without drawing anyone's attention to what he was doing, he slipped Sandman's blackjack into his right hand and swung at Hamilton. Hoist saw the swing coming, but not the blackjack, and dodged it. Superfly tried again, and the effort, as well as Hamilton's dodging it again, jostled the geetha they were handling. Now, not only were the eight players and referee moving out on the ice . . . the geetha was definitely starting to stir!

Superfly and Hoist felt it immediately. They looked at it; then they looked at each other as if looking for confirmation of what they felt! Could this be true? Thoughts raced through Hoist's mind about what Roove had insinuated earlier. Could this thing be flinching? Could there be "postmortem tremors" a few days after it had supposedly died? Superfly wasn't asking himself any questions at this point. He took advantage of the distraction the twitching geetha was causing his opponent, and swung again. His aim was better this time, but not perfect. He hit Hoist a glancing blow off the top of his helmet. The Bomber titman slipped and fell. But the momentum of the swing also caused Superfly to twist around, lose his balance, and fall. The geetha slid slowly away. None of the other players were close enough to take possession. It wouldn't have mattered if they were. A huge gasp went up from the crowd, and all nine skaters on the ice froze when the geetha raised its head!

Superfly was the nearest player to the resurrected beast, and to his credit, the first to react. And he knew instantly what he had to do. He could not let it get up. Jumping to his feet, he took several quick, long strides toward the geetha and then dove through the air. He landed right where he wanted to: right on top of the slowly awakening but still woefully drowsy geetha.

The jolt of the leap and landing caused Superfly's helmet to fly off. That, of course, he ignored. It certainly didn't matter to him now. The only thing that mattered to him now was keeping that geetha pinned to the ice for what could only be a minute or so longer. If he could do that, he knew, victory and glory would be his. However, the geetha wasn't in on the plan, and immediately tried to struggle to its feet. Attempting to raise its head again, it could feel the frantic Blade titman trying to hold it down. And besides that, it now felt it was being pushed along the ice.

Hoist Hamilton had regained his feet and was behind the struggling geetha, with the Blade titman on top, pushing it down the ice. Superfly was unaware of the lateral motion as he tried to prevent the vertical. When the geetha suddenly began raising his head, despite all Superfly's efforts to keep it down, Superfly altered his plan. He realized his strength, even if he wasn't tired from a full game of Geetha, was no match for a moose, so he quickly shifted his body so his torso was on top of the moose's head. His full body weight should be enough to hold it down, or so he thought. After a momentary stalemate the moose began raising his head again. And when he got it up, despite the flopping up and down of Superfly on it, he suddenly straightened his two front legs so that he was now in a sitting position. Having this heavy flopping weight on his head was not the only concern in the moose's mind. He noticed he was sliding along the ice quite rapidly now, and could feel that the pushing was coming from behind.

Now no one really knows how a moose's mind works, but it seems likely, in hindsight, that he considered solving the "flopping problem" first. Suddenly he ducked his head, and the flopping weight flipped over in front of him. For a moment he was relieved to be rid of it.

Hoist, at this time was trying to push as hard as he could because he did not know how much time was left in the game. When he saw Superfly flip over the top of the geetha, he had an unobstructed view of the Blade pezzle, now only 100 yards away. But his main concern was that he could not let the moose stand up. If the moose got up, he knew he wouldn't be able to control him enough to knock off the pezzle. Hoist leaned down hard on the rump of the sitting moose, while pushing the animal forward as hard as he could. As they traveled down the ice, the sitting moose would try to raise his rump, and Hoist would use all his weight and leverage to force it back down on the ice.

The suddenness of the moose ducking his head had caught Superfly by surprise. Totally off balance, he involuntarily cartwheeled over the top of the moose's head and landed flat on his back, directly in the path of the sliding beast. Momentarily stunned, he made no effort to avoid the oncoming animal. In an instant, the moose's forelegs got tangled up with the arms and legs of the prone Blade titman as it slid over him. In one of the more unfortunate events of the day, the titman slid under the moose as his rump was rising. When Hoist subsequently forced that rump back down, the moose sat squarely on Superfly's face. And in all honesty, despite his prior focus on winning this game, all Superfly could think about now was getting this moose's ass off his face.

With an even greater motivation to free himself than ever before, Superfly struggled like a man possessed. In the space of only these few seconds many ugly thoughts were going through Superfly's mind.

Hoist's mind, on the other hand, was focused totally on the outcome of the game. He had kept the moose's rump down on the ice (or actually on Superfly's face) in order to keep control of it. The poor beast struggled to stand up but as tangled as his legs were with the struggling Blade beneath it, it could not find the leverage to do so. The crowd was now in an uproar. It watched as the Bomber titman steered the frenzied beast, with a struggling Superfly underneath it, at the Blades' pezzle. White and the other players on the ice stood transfixed as the two titmen and geetha sped away. Both benches watched in silence . . . in awestruck anticipation as the trio approached the Blades' pezzle.

The crowd knew there was only a little time left. According to the rules, White would raise both arms into the air when there was one minute left to go in the game as a signal to the teams and crowd. He had already done so. And when they were only thirty seconds left to go, he would lower one of his arms. He had already done that too. With ten seconds to go he would drop the other arm, and the crowd would count down the last seconds. The crowd was now counting.

Hoist, still pushing furiously on the sitting geetha, was fast approaching the pezzle as he heard the crowd roaring, "FIVE . . . FOUR . . . " He released his grip on the moose's rump only feet from the pezzle. The moose slid into it, with the still struggling Superfly underneath. "THREE . . . TWO . . . " and sent the pezzle skidding off to the side, making the score Bombers 5 .... Blades 4!

Now free from the pressure on its rump, and seeing the sideboard fast approaching, the moose stood up. But without any traction, it could neither slow down nor change its direction. Its only option was to jump into the air to avoid sliding into the wooden sideboard barrier, much like Cobra had done earlier. Launching itself into the air to clear the barrier, the moose surveyed the area ahead that would, in the next instant, be its landing zone.

And right in the center of that "zone" was a large man wearing a red parka, who at that moment was pouring soup from a thermos into a cup. He glanced up at that moment and saw the descending moose. With his eyes suddenly wide open, and his mouth showing a slight smile, and oddly enough, displaying neither flight nor fight, he sat in resigned anticipation.

It was a far more destructive collision for the outweighed and stationary Byram Lomb than it would be for the sailing moose. The moose, after pausing for a moment to refocus from the collision, got to its feet and ambled away.

It was recovered shortly thereafter, and brought to the Wackentute County Petting Zoo. The head wound it had received from the glancing blow of Sandman's bullet, which had caused it to be in a coma for a few days, was treated successfully. It would live a very long and contented life there at the Petting Zoo, being continuously fed by staff and visitors alike. The staff members, however, were never able to explain its lifelong fear of people wearing red parkas. Byram Lomb too suffered from the aftereffects of that unfortunate occurrence. For the rest of his life the sight, or even aroma, of pea soup made him twitch.

And Superfly was perhaps the most unfortunate victim of all. After he and the geetha had hit the pezzle, they parted ways. The geetha had stood up and leapt into the air on its way to that unscheduled rendezvous with Lomb. But that departure suddenly allowed Superfly to see the light of day again. He was also able to spit out his now somewhat fouled Jardine Vault and suck in some fresh air, which his lungs had been deprived of for the past 30 seconds or so. But the fresh air he was sucking in was suddenly knocked out of him as he unexpectedly, at that moment, hit the sideboard very hard.

Moments later Caveman and several EMT's attempted to revive the temporarily dazed, and bruised Blade titman. They bombarded him with questions and concern about his wellbeing.

"Can you feel your toes?"

"Can you squeeze my fingers?"

"How many fingers am I holding up?"

"What's *that* on your face?"

Superfly had only one response for all the questions; and that was a question itself. "Norky?" he asked dreamily.

These last few minutes would give Superfly nightmares for years. He was never able to erase from his subconscious mind the visual that the moose had just implanted on him.

The Bombers' 5 to 4 victory celebration erupted at the pond, and then later wound noisily, with car horns blaring, in a cavalcade all the way back to the victory party at the Fireside Inn. The team, the families of the team, and the fans of the team made up only part of the victory party.

The bar was jammed with people from all over Newcomb. Hell, there were people there from all over the Wackentute Valley. People who had once played for the Bombers in years gone by were there. Folks who had rooted and supported the Bombers for most of their lives joined in the fun. PeaPod's three sons raced around and through the crowd recreating some of the plays they remembered seeing today. Mena and her husband (he had somehow managed to fit into his old Blue Cane sweater) were there. Lindsay and Sadim, holding hands, joined the celebration. Hoist was introduced to Roove's girlfriend. Olney moved through the crowd wearing Gus's old Bomber's sweater. Arnie was even there, and he kept calling Ana "Doc." But, remarkably, she didn't even seem to mind!

There were people there wearing South Reddington Angels sweaters, and others with the Blue Canes' sweater on. And there were several other team sweaters there that Hoist didn't recognize at all. Some of these people were celebrating the Bombers' win, and probably just as many were celebrating the Blades loss! Several came over to Hoist and introduced themselves. That included Torpedo Red in a neck brace. Pastor Pittou was there telling every Bomber he spoke to that they had "truly done God's work" today when they defeated the Blades. He was very tentative, however, when he approached Hoist.

The noise from the blaring jukebox, the yelling and singing and laughter of the deliriously happy crowd combined to make the noise level nearly painful. But it wasn't.

Joseph, Gus, and Ana had found a table in the dining room section, far enough away from the mayhem in the bar so they could, at least, hear themselves talking. They weren't talking much, but rather they were drinking in the jubilation that surrounded them.

"I can't believe we won it." Gus said several times.

"What a finish!" Ana said," shaking her head in disbelief.

"You know," Joseph finally said, "Life is a lot like Geetha."

Gus turned slightly towards him, and smiled. Ana half smiled, and asked him, "How? What are you talking about?"

"In Life, just like Geetha, you push . . . and get pushed back. You struggle to find your way, to use your talents to achieve some goal . . . and all the while there are forces working against you, and they have to be overcome. You get knocked down. But you realize you have to get back up again." Gus raised his eyebrows, and nodded in agreement. Joseph continued, "And sometimes you have to knock something, or someone, down." Ana started to say something, but Joseph interrupted her, and continued, "But in the end, it all comes down to this . . . hit the pezzle with a dead moose, and it's all good."

He raised his glass of scotch, and took a sip. It was all good.

Coming in 2015…..

Fort Dubious

Chapter One - Prelude

Since the dawn of time it seems that royalty has found it difficult keeping their throne "in the family", so to speak. The principals - those royal (sometimes ruling) families around the world, and Europe in particular - are a rather close knit sort of group, often due to arranged marriages between and within families for political reasons. And, sadly, these unions of limited gene pools all too frequently result in offspring who have sometimes been found wanting in certain areas. Not the least of which is their decision making abilities. This has had many unfortunate results. Remember that these people have been responsible for the welfare of their subjects, and make crucial decisions concerning economics, law, foreign relations, religion, etc. for the populace. This lack of sound judgment frequently manifests itself after some monarch has expired.

Kings, or queens for that matter, have never thought it necessary to leave a will. And somewhere back in the fog of unrecorded history the concept of Primogeniture took root. This simply meant that the eldest son would a inherit the estate –be it a farm or a kingdom- of his deceased father. "The King is dead …. Long live the King!" Old is out – New is in. Sounds simple, no? This practice of Primogeniture provided a simplified process at a time of great grief and stress for all concerned. Unfortunately this process did not always sit well with second sons, or third sons, or the fourth, or the fifth, etc. Daughters often thought it heinous. Brothers, sisters, uncles, nephews and aunts; just to name a few, also found it wanting. Spouses, generals, popes…..ah, the list goes on. Sad to say, a satisfactory solution to this problem has escaped European Royalty to this day. (On a brighter note there are far fewer Royals in Europe (as well as elsewhere) concerned with this enigma in this day and age.

In the year of 1714 AD this process was, unfortunately, in full bloom. Queen Anne, from the Scottish House of Stuart, Queen of Great Britain, died on August 1st. Her husband, George of Denmark and Norway, Duke of Cumberland, had predeceased her, and they had no surviving children. Despite a prearranged plan of succession, put in place by the Act of Settlement (passed by parliament in 1701) that had decreed that the crown would pass to George I of the House of Hanover, there were objections from the House of Stuart. Loud ones!

The House of Stuart was still very upset about how the last Stuart king, James, had been forced off the throne by the Hanover forces of William of Orange in 1688. They wanted their kingdom back. The people from the House of Hanover demurred. The squabble between the two houses ran intermittently from that initial ouster in 1688 almost until the middle of the next century. In August of 1745, Charles Edward Stuart (Bonnie Prince Charlie), the last legitimate Stuart heir to the British crown, sailed from exile in France to Scotland with a small army to press his claim. They were known to history as The Jacobites. Rallying many Highland Scottish clans around him, as well as an assorted batch of English Episcopalians and Irishmen, he marched south from Scotland toward England. The English forces were slow to respond, and the rebels, The Jacobites, scored a few small, but impressive victories. At Prestonpans (east of Edinburgh) they won their most impressive victory that September. However, in April of 1746, the rebels ran into the House of Hanover forces of lowland Scots and English regulars, commanded by the son of King George II, Prince William ("Sweet William" or "Stinking Billy" depending on which side you were on) at the Battle of Culloden. The battle was a rather one-sided affair with the Stuarts coming in a distant second. Bonnie Prince Charlie narrowly escaped with his life, and little else, and scurried back into exile in France. Thoughts of restoring the Stuarts to the throne were permanently shelved by Bonnie Prince Charlie, and replaced by one love affair after another (including one with his married first cousin!). Oh, those Royals!

The House of Hanover, in an effort to put this Stuart claim to rest once and for all, came down rather heavily on the Scots after their victory at Culloden. The treatment of the disloyal Highland Clans was brutal and unrelenting. The harshness ranged from heavy taxation to the confiscation of the private property of suspected Stuart loyalists. Many were arrested, jailed, deported, or even executed. Soldiers roamed the countryside for years afterwards attempting to extinguish the Stuart flame forever. They even went so far as to ban the wearing of the Scots' beloved tartans. The Scots did not take to this too kindly.

Two and a half years after the Battle of Culloden, British troops were still in the highlands. And in the isolated, desolate lake district of northern Scotland, a twenty man detachment of the Royal West Essex Dragoons, were patrolling, village to village, trying to ferret out any remaining "traitors" in the area. Despite being Dragoons, they were on foot. All their mounts, except their commanding officer's mount and the horse pulling his baggage cart, had been reassigned to a more favored unit. The men were not pleased. Trudging the highways and byways of this inhospitable hilly country in the winter had worn their boots, and their patriotic fervor, to the nub.

This evening found them waiting out the daily blustery rain storm in their makeshift quarters. The barn they currently called 'home' had a roof that leaked, and its walls only partially protected them from the gusting wind outside. Their evening meal, which they had confiscated from a nearby farmer, hadn't been enough to go around, and they were all still hungry. Their commanding officer was Colonel Oliver Highcross, a mean spirited, inept tyrant whom all the men hated. He had achieved his high rank in much the same way many men of this era had achieved theirs. Rich and powerful forebears gave it to him. In this case that referred to his father, the Duke of Nunch, and former Admiral in His Majesty's Navy. The famous, and oft decorated, Admiral had obtained the commission for his obnoxious son, and then had him sent off to the far north of Scotland. Out of sight - out of mind.

As usual, Col. Highcross left the Sergeant-Major in charge of the troop when he had earlier ridden ahead to the next village. Sergeant-Major Bottoms, who had eaten his full before allowing his men to join in, assigned Corporal Westport to take charge of the troop, and then bedded down in the driest corner of the barn. Cpl. Westport and the soldiers made the best of what was left for dinner. All but Private Wilbur Smith, that is. He was "Blinking Willie" to his comrades, due to his constant nervous twitch, and he was the lowest in rank, with the least seniority, and the last in line for any consideration in the company. He had been assigned to accompany Col. Highcross as his personal guard in this hostile country. As he jogged alongside the mounted colonel they made their way to the next village. They made an odd pair.

Pvt. Smith was taller than Col. Highcross, by about a foot. The colonel weighed more, by about 80 lbs. The colonel had very small round eyes, placed very close to the sides of his arching nose. His small mouth was unusually far from that nose, and his chin was non-existent. All these smallish features were at the center of his large round face. These facial traits were in sharp contrast to his impressive military bearing; and his attire was tailored and immaculate despite the travel in the rough terrain. He carried extra uniforms in his large baggage cart.

274

The private's face and body were alike. Both were long and narrow. His incessant blinking caught and held any onlooker's attention so thoroughly that most were unable to describe any other physical features he had. His uniform was filthy and didn't fit him, and hadn't since the day it had been issued to him. And the private slouched as if he was a foot taller than he actually was.

The colonel had decided to spend his evening, after his long day in the saddle, in the local tavern. He almost always did. He had discovered early in his deployment to Scotland something the locals called "the water of life". We know it as Scotch. Pvt. Smith was assigned to accompany him to the tavern, as far as the door, and stand guard against any local ruffians.

Upon entering the tavern Col. Highcross took stock of his surroundings. The only two people in the room were a barmaid and a barman. The combination of the overcast sky, and the small windows in front provided very little light. The fireplace along the side wall was empty, and thus provided neither heat nor light. Three candles provided what little light there was. One was just inside the front door; the second was on the bar which was positioned along the back wall. And a third candle was on one of the small tables in the room. Before closing the door behind him, the Colonel turned and had a brief conversation with Pvt. Smith. Neither the barman, nor the waitress standing nearby heard exactly what was said. The waitress, however, thought she heard one of them say "Stinkin' Willy".

The colonel closed the door behind him, and sat down on a bench at the only table with a candle. He only glanced for a moment at the barman, but then gave the barmaid a long measured look. She was, perhaps, past her prime, and a tad overweight, and there was no smile on her face. Because it was her job, she reluctantly approached the officer. She didn't like the English in general, and she especially hated the ones in uniform. She had lost a husband and a brother in the recent war; but of the two, she only mourned her brother. The squat English officer greeted her with a smiling face. She saw it as a lecherous grin. "Good evening, Mrs." he said, barely above a whisper. She was unable to muster a reciprocating smile. He took a long look at her, head to foot and again smiling, said to her, "I want something to eat." And a moment later, "And drink. What have you got?"

The barman, and owner of the tavern, stood 5 feet 4inches tall, and weighted 120 lbs soaking wet. But despite his diminutive size he ruled his roost. Knowing full well the animosity that his barmaid harbored for the English military he thought it best to intervene. "I'll take care of the gentleman, Kenna," he said to her, and quickly positioned himself between the two. He then turned immediately to the British officer. "I have some very good stew, Sir. Just made it up this mornin'." He smiled and lied. He went on to add that the ale he had in stock was the very best, and the local whiskey was even better. The officer was hungry, but his attention stayed on the barmaid as she sashayed out of the room into the back kitchen. Disappointed to be deprived of her company he told the barman to bring the stew, and added that he better be 'damn quick about it'.

In no time at all the barman returned with a plate of the five day old stew made up of some local vegetables and vegetation, with some parts of various animals. He had added a splash of whiskey, and spit in it for good luck. He was no fan of the occupying British Army either, but a customer was a customer. He added a chunk of stale bread and a tankard of ale, and placed it all in front of the Colonel.

"That woman? You called her 'Kenna'. She's your wife?" the Colonel asked.

"Oh no, Sir. Her name's Kenna MacBride." He said, "She works here for me, I own this place. I'm Tom Kilgore. The poor dear is a widow twice over." He added. "I pay her what I can to help feed the little ones at home."

Colonel Highcross was going to ask how her husbands had died, but then realized he didn't care, so he asked, "Where'd she go?"

"Just to get a breath of air, Sir. She's been workin' the entire day for me. I'm sure she'll be back in a moment." He answered without the foggiest notion of where she was.

"Good." said the officer. "Tell her to come and sit with me. I don't like to dine alone."

The barman went back into the kitchen to retrieve her for the Colonel, but Kenna wasn't there. "Damn!" he thought to himself. "Now where's she off to?" Kilgore returned to the front and sadly told the officer she had gone off to take care of one of her children, but would be back in no time.

Annoyed slightly, Colonel Highcross told him to send her out the minute she returned. "And take this ale back. It's piss. Bring me some whiskey."

When she burst in the back door 10 minutes later she was out of breath, and flushed from running. She tried catching her breath as her boss started to pepper her with instructions. "Get out there right away. And be nice, damn it. And push him on the whiskey. Get him to buy you some of it. I think we . . . ."

"Shut up and listen!" she hissed at him just louder than a whisper. She leaned in close to him; her breast heaving with heavy breathing, and perspiration glistening on her face. "Do you not know who that bastard is?" she asked in disbelief. He looked at her in silence, and then shook his head. "That's Prince William, you ninny. 'Stinking Billy' himself!" Her eyes were bulging out of her head.

He started to disagree with her, "Nah, it can't be. I don't think that's the Prince...."

But she cut him off. "It is, I tell ya." She said. "I heard him saying 'Stinking Willy'." She paused, and then corrected herself, "Stinkin' Billy."

The owner was skeptical, to say the least. "You heard what? I think it's supposed to be 'Stinkin' Billy'. Not 'Willy'. Isn't it?" And do ye think a soldier would call the Prince by that name, anyway? Do ye? And he's only got one guard out front? Don't you think that the Prince would have…."

She cut him off again. "It's him. I know it. I saw him once. That's a general out there. And that general is Prince William himself." She was certain, and she wasn't going to debate the point. She whirled around, wiped her face and breast with a rag, and went out into the dining room. She was right that the man in front was an English officer. And she had seen Prince William, in the flesh, several years ago in Edinburgh. But she hadn't been very close to him. And, truth be told, this fellow out front was certainly no 'prince' (on any level). And he was not even a general. The uniforms were similar, but the differences were just too subtle for her eye. But in her mind she was sure, and that set the wheels in motion for the calamities that followed.

Owen Dundoon stood very still, trying hard to stay out of the misting rain. He was under the only patch of roof still above the abandoned stable, but the gusting wind kept him wet. He peered out the partially open front doors, and watched the sleeping guard on the covered front porch of Kilgore's tavern across the street. The guard had a blanket tightly wrapped around him; his long musket, with the bayonet attached, leaned against the building at his side.

Owen heard the commotion behind him from probably fifty yards away as it approached the rear of the stable. Heavy footsteps, grunting and cursing preceded Dick's MacCoot's entry through the long gone back door of the stable. "Jaysus, Mary and St Joseph! Could you make any more noise than that? You could wake the dead!" Owen growled at the rain soaked, panting Dick.

"Holy Mother of God!" was all Dick could say, at first. He repeated it several times. A moment later, with some wind restored, he looked at Owen, who hadn't taken his eyes off what he had been looking at, and said, "Where's the riot? Norman came racing up the lane like a madman, told me to get my gun, and get here as fast as blazes." He paused, and tried to see what Owen was focused on. Then he added, "What in hell is goin' on?"

"Thank Christ you didn't wake that damn guard. He must be half dead. Or maybe half deaf? I don't know which!" He turned slowly to Dick. He towered over him. Owen was over six foot tall, and was thick everywhere. Behind his back he was described by friends and foe alike 'as big and strong as an ox, and only a wee bit smarter'. He was nearly bald on top of his large head, and his arms and hands were huge. He tended the livestock on the estate of a wealthy landowner in the area, and had, at one time or another, been bitten, kicked, scratched, or otherwise assaulted by every one of them. He didn't particularly like animals.

Dick, on the other hand, was smaller and not nearly as strong. But he considered himself very much smarter. That was open to debate. He spent his days avoiding work of any kind, and usually was very successful at it. He spent most days fast asleep, and wandered through the neighborhoods at night looking for anything not nailed down. Both had been recruits in the failed Jacobite Rebellion; but neither had seen any fighting. Disappearing from the ranks when danger was in the air seemed to be a skill both possessed in abundance.

"Ya know who's sitting in Kilgore's at this very moment?" Owen asked Dick. Dick shook his head. With a gleam in his eye, and a broad grin, Owen said while nodding slowly, "Stinking Billy!"

"Whaa?" was Dick's first response. Owen smiled, knowing he had stunned his friend. "Ya daft!" Dick said, "Prince William? Prince William, son of King George? Have ya been drinkin', yer big fool? What in the name of God would he be doing up here? And without an army around him for protection!" Owen explained to him, in a soft voice so as not to alarm the single guard across the street that Kenna had come to him in a mad dash not twenty minutes ago, to tell him that the Prince was, indeed, in Kilgore's at that very moment.

The fact that Kenna said she was sure it was the Prince was all the certainty that Owen needed. Owen was madly in love with Kenna MacBride. In his eyes she was the perfect woman, and despite her rough demeanor and girth he wanted very much to be her third husband. When she had come charging down the lane that short time ago to his stable, and grabbed him by his shirtfront, and issued him her instructions he never uttered a word. Instead, he flew into action.

Dick wasn't so sure. Owen kept saying that Kenna was certain. Dick processed the information again, this time more slowly. He came to the conclusion that it was possible ..... remotely possible ..... that Prince William ..... son of King George II of Great Britain ..... "Stinking Billy" ..... might ..... possibly may ...... a very remote chance ..... be across the street in Thomas Kilgore's Tavern. "So what?" he was finally able to say.

"'So what?' 'So what' yer say? Here's our chance. Here's our chance on a silver platter, lad!"

"'Our chance for what? Whaddya talkin' about?" Dick was confused. He always felt uncomfortable when Owen came up with ideas.

"To kill him, of course! Why'd ya think I told Norman to getcha and ta bring yer gun?"

Dick was shocked. A million thoughts raced through his overburdened brain. The only thought he was able to communicate was, "Just mine?"

"Jaysus, Mary, and St Joseph! No, yer fool. Norman's getting' his too. And both of mine! I told him to bring some knives too, just to finish the job if we have to." Owen was bursting with pride that he had, without a moment's hesitation, hatched this entire plan. It was actually Kenna's plan, but Owen left that fact out. Dick would have been only slightly more confident had he known that, but he didn't. Dick's lack of confidence was not based solely on the source of the plan, however. As he thought it all over it occurred to him that he had never shot a man before. In fact, he had never shot **at** a man before!

The two men stood in silence for the next ten minutes. Owen peered out through the doors and watched the sleeping guard, and for any sign of movement at the doorway of the tavern. He began to worry that their young friend Norman wasn't going to get back in time with the three extra guns before Stinking Billy left. He hoped that Kenna would be able to stall him until Norman arrived.

He didn't have to worry. At that moment Kenna was sitting on the English colonel's lap, encouraging him to finish his fifth cup of whiskey. Kenna (with Tom Kilgore's encouragement) was running up the man's bill by drinking water, and charging for whiskey. She was also thinking that in about one hour this "son of a bitch" would be dead in the street. The officer, oblivious to this planned scenario, was enjoying himself immensely with a lady on his lap, and getting progressively drunker. They were both feeling very good.

Dick was not so gleeful. His less-than-admirable track record of petty pilfering, laziness, and general antisocial behavior was about to take a major step upward with the assassination of Prince William. He had come up with at least fifty reasons why they shouldn't do it, but Owen wouldn't listen. "Jaysus, Mary, and St Joseph! Are yer forgettin' what this bastard's done? Are yer fergettin' what he done to Kenna? Made her a widow! Killed Timmy MacBride."

"I never liked Timmy, you know." Dick said quietly, to no one in particular. And then turning, and looking right at Owen said, "Besides, Timmy was probably shot by one of our men. He was shot in the back. Remember?" Another possibility occurred to Dick, and he added softly again, "Or he might have been running away when he got shot."

Owen didn't want to argue the point. He switched gears. "How about Niall then? Her brutha. You knew him, and everyone who knew him, liked him. He was a good soul." Owen didn't think Dick could argue that point. He was right; Dick didn't want to argue that point. Dick wanted to go home.

Just then Norman McMulvey came crashing through the rear of the stable carrying two rifles, a blunderbuss pistol, and a scythe. Tucked into his belt were two long knives. "Mother of God! You're a regiment!" said Dick. Norman was only slightly smaller in size than Owen, and still in his teens. The two older men were heroes to him for opposite reasons. He admired Owen for having a steady job. And as a bonus that job was tending to animals. That, to Norman, was an ideal job. On the other hand he admired Dick because he had no job. He lived, apparently to Norman, a life of perfect leisure. This apparent contradiction went a long way in explaining how Norman's mind worked. Or didn't.

"Quiet!" ordered Owen. The three men silently went about divvying up the guns and knives. The scythe was left leaning up against the wall. All three men had flintlock muskets that Owen and Dick had stolen from a battlefield several years before. Finally curiosity got the best of Dick. "Why did you bring the scythe?"

The still panting Norman said, "I could only find two knives."

"I think that one without the handle is a bayonet." Dick corrected.

Norman looked back at Dick, and said defensively, "Owen wasn't very specific, you know."

"Quiet!" Owen said again. "Now listen; we may not have much time." The other two men looked at him. "When Stinking Billy comes out the door, we'll be ready for him. But we'll wait till he moves away from the door. Kenna said she'll wait till he's out, and then shut it and lock it behind him. We don't want him dodging back in there for cover. Once the door closes ..... we'll race out from here .... screaming like bloody witches from Hell ..... halfway across the street ..... we'll halt, stand, and fire .... all three of us! Then you two drop your rifles and charge him with the knives to finish him off ..... if we haven't done the job already. While you two are charging the rest of the way across the street I'll pull my pistol, and fire again. Four shots. Two knives. That oughta do the job."

Dick saw a flaw immediately. He had no desire to do the up close work that a stabbing would require, so he suggested, "I'm a good shot. Why don't I do that second shot, and you take the other knife."

Owen disagreed, "Who the hell told you that you're a good shot? You're a terrible shot. Besides, the pistol is mine. I ought to shoot it."

Dick took a new tack. "I don't feel so good about running in front of you while you're firing off that blunderbuss." He shook his head, "You just might get me in the back, like poor Niall."

"It wasn't Niall that got hit in the back. It was Timmy. Niall got hit by a cannon ball. Stop yer fussin'." chided Owen. ""If it'll make you feel any better I'll shoot the pistol first, and save the musket for last." That did not, contrary to Owen's opinion, make Dick feel any better. Norman chimed in saying that he ought to fire the pistol because he was the fastest runner. The two older men looked at each other in confusion. The conversation continued to meander from one topic to another as Dick looked for an honorable, or at least viable, way to avoid involvement.

After what seemed like an hour's worth of bickering back and forth, Dick asked what they should do with the guard. There was a minute's silence before Owen wondered, "Good Christ! What if he shoots back?"

"Who," asked Norman?

"The farkin' guard, yer twit. He's got a musket!" This wrinkle caused another long animated disagreement between the three conspirators. They took turns proposing that the guard would be so flummoxed by their screams and shots that he'd be no factor at all. And each took a turn suggesting that this guard might be an experienced hardened British soldier fully capable of shooting the three of them dead in seconds. Dick was sure the latter was true. They weren't finished discussing the possibilities, and certainly nowhere near a solution to their dilemma when a flurry of motion at the front of the tavern caused them to freeze. The door had swung open.

Only moments before, in the tavern, the owner had suggested to the now very drunk colonel that they should settle accounts. The colonel, who was accustomed to running roughshod over the locals he dealt with on a daily basis, dismissed the idea out of hand. He wanted to prolong the evening's festivities with the now wildly attractive Mrs. MacBride, and thought perhaps, if anything, he would leave a few shillings or maybe even a half a crown ("if Mrs. MacBride is nice to me!"). This angered the barman who had tallied up the inflated tab to nearly two crowns. He came around the bar, after picking up his 'Billy stick', as he called it, a short club wrapped in leather he kept back there for occasions such as these. He was not going to be denied.

The Colonel didn't see him approaching, but Mrs. MacBride, who had started for the door, had and she was not about to let a dispute over the bill derail her plan for the evening. In a flash she threw her arms around the colonel's neck, and put her face only inches from his. In the softest voice she could muster she told the colonel he had to pay the bill, "Cause I'm in the mood, right now." She let the last word ease ever so slowly out of her mouth. The colonel staggered to his feet, nearly dropping the barmaid to the floor. He fumbled quickly through a pocket of his coat, and spilled several coins onto the table, some fell to the floor. He had no idea what the amount was; he didn't care. The Colonel, who had unbuttoned his pants after his second plate of stew, did not re-button them. He somehow got his coat back on, and buckled his sword belt around his lower chest.

Kenna MacBride and Colonel Oliver Highcross made their way to the front door. He wobbled; she walked. He leaned; she bore his weight. She quietly opened the front door to the early evening light, and cooed to the officer, "Sssssshhhh. Don't wake your guard. We only need us two for what we're gonna do!" The drunken officer giggled. The guard stirred. Kenna froze. She watched as the guard shifted his position on the stool slightly, but then resumed his nap. She motioned to the officer to be quiet, and led him out onto the porch. Glancing across the street she spied the three faces in the stable doorway.

Kenna was staring at them. They thought she was nodding. The officer was staggering. The guard was still asleep. Owen gripped the two others by the arm, and said "Wait for her to get inside." And he had no sooner said it when she suddenly whirled around, nearly knocking the officer off his unsteady feet; she jumped back inside the door and slammed it shut.

That startled Tom Kilgore, who was oblivious to the unfolding plan, and was on his knees collecting and counting the coins the Colonel had dropped. When he heard the door slam, he looked up and said, "Huh?", and then immediately returned to his coin retrieval.

Outside, the Colonel attempted to regain his balance. The guard stirred. And Norman, Dick and Owen all emerged from the stable and raced across the street toward the tavern hollering like mad men.

Colonel Highcross, who had initially turned around confused by Kenna's sudden departure, whirled back around again to the noise in the street. The startled guard jumped to his feet, sending his stool spinning away, and stumbled slightly when his feet got tangled in his discarded blanket. His musket, left leaning against the wall, got jostled by the stool and fell over. When the weapon hit the ground it discharged. Pvt Smith had loaded and cocked his weapon before settling down to his nap ('in case I need it in a hurry' he had rationalized) and left it leaning against the building. Inside the tavern Kenna was hoping that the shot she heard was from one of her compatriots, and that the ball had found its mark. Kilgore, who was once again crawling around on his hands and knees searching for the Colonel's coins, rose to a kneeling position confused about the commotion.

The three assassins racing across the street halted immediately at the sound of Smith's discharging weapon. Each one turned to the other to see if there was any damage done, and if they were all still in unison. Their shoulder to shoulder formation reaffirmed their resolve, and the three men raised their muskets and pulled the triggers.

Dick, who was standing in the middle, was the only one to fire a shot. To each of the five men involved, it sounded like a cannon. Dick, inexperienced with firearms and a tad nervous, may have used a little too much powder when he loaded it. The flash nearly blinded him, and the recoil almost threw him to the ground. The ball hissed between the two Englishmen, and through the front window of Kilgore's Tavern.

When that second shot was immediately followed by the exploding window of his tavern Kilgore was, at first, bewildered. "Someone's shot my winda?' Kilgore asked no one in particular. Then in a much louder voice yelled, "What in hell is going on out there?" Kenna, who was standing with her ear to the front door, didn't answer him.

Owen, on the left, knew exactly why his gun didn't fire. In the excitement of the charge across the street, he had forgotten to cock back the hammer. He now corrected his mistake, and again began taking aim.

Norman, on the right end of the line, was baffled when his hadn't fired. He took the weapon from his shoulder and looked down at it, inadvertently pointing it right at Dick. Dick would have screamed at him for doing that, but having the muzzle of the musket 3 inches from his nose took his breath away. He took a step backward, away from the muzzle, and inadvertently bumped into Owen just as he pulled the trigger. The shot was well off the human target, but dead center on the other front window.

For Dick the unexpected blast and flash of the musket firing inches behind his head, after just having Norman's musket inches from his nose took their toll. They took the wind out of his sails, and the resolve out of his knees. Dick dropped to a kneeling position.

Up on the porch the two British soldiers were in a state of panic. When the screaming first began neither man had any idea what was going on. The guard had been in a deep sleep only seconds ago, but was now wide awake after his musket had fallen and fired. The consumed alcohol had the colonel two steps behind the Private in understanding the situation. Dick's musket shot became, in a manner of speaking, a serious wake-up call to them both. And they had both very clearly heard that ball sail between them and crash through the window on the wall behind them. They both turned toward the now missing glass and realized it hadn't missed them by very much. Pvt. Smith, now clearly in fear for his life, bent over to retrieve his weapon. The Colonel, now aware he was a target, contorted his body in an attempt to make himself smaller. This action caused his still unbuttoned pants to slip from his hips and drop to his ankles. He looked out into the street, and saw the other two assassins preparing to fire. And with Pvt. Smith bent over, Col. Highcross correctly assessed he was to be the only, and therefore likely, target. His instantaneous assessment of the situation called for allowing his pants to remain down, but he felt Smith needed to be raised right now! Grabbing Pvt. Smith by the shoulders he yanked him back into to an upright position, and slid in behind him. The Colonel correctly guessed that the slender Private did not provide total coverage for him, but 'something was better than nothing'. For the colonel the transition from drunken stupor to sobriety was progressing quite quickly.

The discharge of Owen's musket (although by the reaction of the other window it was wide by 10 feet) gave the two British soldiers increased motivation to improve their situation. As the colonel peeked from around the private's shoulder at the assailants, Pvt. Smith once again tried to reach his fallen musket. Jerking himself free of the officer's grip, he bent over. The officer, fully exposed to the attackers now that Smith was doubled over, began to scream. There were so few other options he thought he had. Pvt. Smith heard him, and thought the colonel might have been shot.

That's the scene that Norman saw as he once more lifted his musket to his shoulder and took aim at the porch. The soldier, bent over at the waist, was standing directly in front of the screaming officer whose pants were down around his ankles. That just doesn't look right, thought Norman, and again he hesitated. But he dismissed it an instant later, and tried to refocus his aim on the officer.

Moments after the shot had shattered the first window; Tom Kilgore got up off the floor and made his way cautiously to his broken window. Disbelief and dismay was what he was feeling. It would be expensive, and take a long time to replace the broken window because there wasn't a glazier within miles. As he peeked out the now 'open' window he took in the scene. In the dim evening light he saw three men with guns out in the street. In this fading light and haze of gun powder smoke, he couldn't make out who they were, but they looked somewhat familiar. Right outside the window were the two English soldiers on his porch, jostling around. "What in hell's goin' on out ....." he started to say. Before he could finish his question another musket fired, and his other window now exploded into the room, in many, many pieces. He whirled around to see his other window in a thousand pieces on the floor. That ended the curiosity phase of Kilgore's involvement in the episode. More spitting out the words than speaking them, he roared, "MOTHER OF CHRIST! ....WHO'S SHOOTIN' MY FOKKIN' WINDAS?"

Out in the street, Owen had dropped his musket and was now struggling mightily to free his pistol, which was apparently stuck in his belt. He did not know at this moment that the private was fighting furiously to free himself from his commander's grip. Owen was under the impression that the guard was probably now taking aim at them, or more importantly, *him*. Finally pulling the blunderbuss free, he got his bearings and realized that as he had struggled to free his gun he had somehow turned around and was now facing down the street. He whirled around to get his bearings. And at that moment, Norman fired his shot.

Only a moment before, Kilgore, fit to be tied at the annihilation of his precious windows, strode toward the front door currently being held shut by Kenna. In his hand was his Billy stick, and he had every intention of going outside and bashing a few heads. "Get out of my way!" he roared at

Kenna, intent on bringing havoc to the transgressors outside. Kenna knew him, and she knew that tone of voice. She got out of his way. He flung open the door and stepped out onto the porch. Here he had a fateful momentary hesitation. It was initially caused by the indecision about who he was going to hit first with his Billy stick. That was instantly followed by his recollection of the age old adage concerning the rash stupidity of "bringing a club to a gunfight." Although too smoky in the fading light to recognize the people in the street, he could clearly see the huge pistol, held by the man on the right, pointing in his direction, and alas, the muzzle of that weapon seemed only a few yards away.

Norman had his sights set right on the screaming Colonel. But the sudden opening of the door just to the right of the Colonel, and the emergence of the raging barman completely unraveled him. Involuntarily, he shifted his aim a few inches to the right, closed his eyes, and fired.

This sudden jerking movement by Norman's gun muzzle caught Kilgore's eye, making him glance in that direction. He distinctly saw the flash of powder and heard the musket fire. He would remember, for the rest of his life, the puff of smoke at the muzzle's mouth and the musket ball flying out of it. And the smiling face of the Devil himself (he swore to this) on that musket ball as it came straight at him in slow motion. Had Kilgore been 5 foot 7 that ball would have gone directly between his eyebrows. But at 5 foot 4 he was merely left with a slight scratch on the top of his bald head, and a pair of pants he could never wear again. The musket ball, after tickling the top of Kilgore's skull, continued on through the open door and hit a cask of ale resting on the bar; adding it to the victims list of the Kilgore Tavern.

Kenna, just inside the doorway, grabbed the now unconscious barman by the collar and pulled him back into the tavern. Again, she slammed the door shut.

Norman watched as the bottom of Kilgore's feet receded back into the bar. He felt torn between the elation of a nearly perfect shot, and the dismay that it had been the wrong target. Dick was still struggling to regain his feet. Owen was trying to steady his outstretched arm, which held the heavy pistol. He knew only too well that this was his last chance at getting Prince William.

Up on the porch, Pvt. Smith took advantage of the momentary lull when he saw the colonel's sword in front of his chest. A handy sword is better than a missing musket he correctly assessed, and snatched it from its scabbard. He turned to the assailants in the street, and raised the sword above his head. He would have charged them had he not jammed the blade into the overhead of the porch, where it stuck fast.

Now, without even his sword, the colonel knew he was totally defenseless. He looked out into the street. The man on the extreme right had a huge pistol in his hand, and was aiming it. The man in the center was on one knee, and probably reloading. And the man on the left had a musket in one hand and a knife in the other. Assessing his situation, along with the exertion of manhandling Smith, the adrenaline rush, the long expulsion of breath by screaming, the food poisoning effects of the stew, and, of course, the alcohol he had consumed, finally took their toll. Col. Oliver Highcross passed out.

Pvt. Smith continued to struggle with pulling the sword out of the overhead, without success. Both Owen and Norman stood mesmerized as Smith, gripping the handle of the upraised sword with both hands, danced with his feet in midair as he attempted to yank it free.

At this exact moment the half-dressed but fully armed rest of the troop raced around a corner into the street, not 50 yards away. They had heard the very first shot, and although most of them would have preferred not running to the rescue of the colonel, Sergeant-Major Bottoms had insisted. What they saw as they turned into the street were the armed assailants in the street; and they also saw Pvt. Smith, with the sword held high over his head, his feet dancing in the air, and the prostrate colonel on the porch.

As the first ten of the twenty men turned the corner, Owen saw them out of the corner of his eye; he calmly stepped around his two comrades, raised his pistol at them and fired. The blunderbuss, a notoriously inaccurate weapon at this distance, sent its load of lead buckshot out in a wide pattern, and hit a great many things; windows, walls, etc. None of those things were human, however.

But the flash and noise of the pistol shot, as well as the accompanying ricochets and breaking glass, caused the first two ranks of hard charging soldiers to halt dead in their tracks. This resulted in the men in the next few ranks crashing headlong into their mates up front. This human pileup brought the pursuit to a temporary halt. And that confusion allowed Owen, Norman, and the suddenly coordinated and fleet of foot Dick to retreat back into the stable they had come from, and continue on through the back door (without slowing down to pick up the scythe), and on into the woods beyond. In a very impressive display of stamina none of the men stopped running for thirty minutes.

ABOUT THE AUTHOR

Michael McInerney has been an author, brother, father, husband, marathoner, paratrooper, trader, and veteran. He chooses to live near the beach, but dislikes sand. Go figure.

He can be contacted at: michaeljpmcinerney@gmail.com